Praise for

THE BRILLIANT DISASTER

"Rasenberger goes deeper into the Bay of Pigs catastrophe than ever before and delivers the fullest story yet. . . . Thanks to Rasenberger's skillful writing, *The Brilliant Disaster* reads more like a thriller than a history book, making it accessible to any reader with even the faintest interest in the topic."

—*The Daily Beast*

"A balanced, engrossing account of the U.S.-backed invasion of Fidel Castro's Cuba . . . Rasenberger succeeds admirably in offering a nuanced view of the entire botched operation. . . . Graceful, dramatic writing makes this well-worn story new again."

—*Kirkus Reviews* (starred review)

"Rather than come down on one side or the other, Jim Rasenberger's new book lets the facts speak for themselves. . . . Its context is richly detailed, its tempo novelistic. Forthright and accessible, it delineates a convoluted chain of events leading to humiliation and tragedy."

—*The Miami Herald*

"An enthralling and illuminating history of the bloody mess that unfolded on the beaches of Cuba's Bay of Pigs."

—*The Dallas Morning News*

"This gripping investigation relives the events as they unfolded on a day-to-day and hour-by-hour basis. Especially absorbing is the harrowing story of 1,113 prisoners of the Cuban government (others had already been executed) and the effort to win their release. . . . [An] important and engrossing work."

—*Library Journal* (starred review)

"This is great history, the anecdotal type chock-full of details about larger-than-life historical figures brought down to human size."

—*The Buffalo News*

"Jim Rasenberger delivers a well-organized and reported history of the Bay of Pigs as well as a concise evaluation of its consequences. Drawing on recently declassified government documents as well as first-person accounts of the invasion, he presents a sober, comprehensive account sharpened by the fifty-year-old lens of retrospection."

—*Pittsburgh Post-Gazette*

"A vivid and fleet-footed account."

—*Washingtonian* magazine

"Rasenberger provides an outstanding chronological day-by-day, nearly minute-by-minute, account of the operation that was first planned during the Eisenhower administration and inherited by JFK. . . . In the end, Rasenberger makes the case for the large impact that the Bay of Pigs had on historic events that followed, including the Cuban Missile Crisis, the building of the Berlin Wall, the involvement in Vietnam, and the election of President Nixon and Watergate, among others."

—*Idaho Statesman*

"A brilliant book . . . Students of history too young to remember the events of that April in 1961 will appreciate the thoroughness. For those who lived through that chilling time, it is a page-turner. The details, many of them unknown until now, become as exciting as the story itself. The body of work is exhaustive but the writing seems effortless."

—*Charleston News Alternative*

"This is an excellent book. . . . Rasenberger has crafted a masterpiece, well written, fast moving, and easy to read."

—*InCity Times* (Worcester)

"A brilliant analysis . . . Rasenberger has an excellent eye for the interesting detail and the memorable quote."

—*Citrus County Chronicle*

"Fifty years after the Bay of Pigs disaster, Jim Rasenberger does a terrific job of documenting the faults of all parties engaged in the operation. . . . Unlike some Bay of Pigs accounts, this retelling, much to the author's credit, spreads the blame around."

—*Studies in Intelligence*

"A gripping narrative . . . Rasenberger provides interesting details about the aftermath, including the Christmas-time release of the captured fighters several years later, his attorney father's role in that episode, and sums up how the Bay of Pigs continued to reverberate from the Cuban Missile Crisis to Watergate."

—*Publishers Weekly*

"What I love about Jim Rasenberger's richly detailed, startlingly revisionist account of the Bay of Pigs invasion is his sheer storytelling ability, the wonderful, steady march of plot and counterplot, of heroes and foils. His tale is chock-full of larger-than-life characters—from JFK to Castro, mafia bosses, and the steely-eyed, hypersmart men of the New Frontier. *The Brilliant Disaster* is what history ought to be: sharply drawn and with a constant eye on the big picture."

—S. C. Gwynne, author of *Empire of the Summer Moon*

"If you like *Mad Men*, spy novels, and lucid writing, you'll love *The Brilliant Disaster*. If you're new to any of these, consider Jim Rasenberger your guide to one of the most fascinating and dramatic episodes of the Cold War, post-Korea and pre-Vietnam. He has written an amazing account that speeds along, one dramatic cloak-and-dagger scene after another, all judiciously reported. The people in his book come to life, vividly—you hear them, see them, and understand them, although you may not agree with them. This is highly entertaining and engrossing history."

—Doug Stanton, author of *Horse Soldiers*

ALSO BY JIM RASENBERGER

America, 1908

The Dawn of Flight, the Race to the Pole, the Invention of the Model T, and the Making of a Modern Nation

High Steel

The Daring Men Who Built the World's Greatest Skyline

THE BRILLIANT DISASTER

JFK, Castro, and America's Doomed Invasion of Cuba's Bay of Pigs

JIM RASENBERGER

SCRIBNER

New York London Toronto Sydney New Delhi

SCRIBNER
A Division of Simon & Schuster, Inc.
1230 Avenue of the Americas
New York, NY 10020

First Scribner trade paperback edition April 2012

Manufactured in the United States of America

3 5 7 9 10 8 6 4

Library of Congress Control Number: 2011004178

ISBN 978-1-4165-9653-0
ISBN 978-1-4391-0047-9 (ebook)

Insert photograph credits: 1, 2, 8, 15, 24, Associated Press; 3, Getty Images (*New York Daily News* Archive); 4, Museo del Che Guevara; 5, by Alberto Korda; 6, 7, 25, CIA; 9, National Park Service; 10, 18, public domain; 11, Getty Images (Alfred Eisenstaedt); 12, Getty Images (Joseph Scherschel); 13, 26, John F. Kennedy Library; 14, Getty Images (Gilberto Ante); 16, 19, 20, 22, Cuban Heritage Collection, University of Miami Libraries, Coral Gables, FL; 17, Getty Images (Edward A. Hausner); 21, Navsource.org; 23, Getty Images (Miguel Vinas); 27, author.

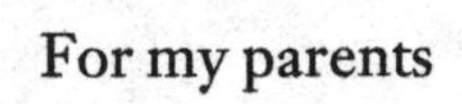

For my parents

CONTENTS

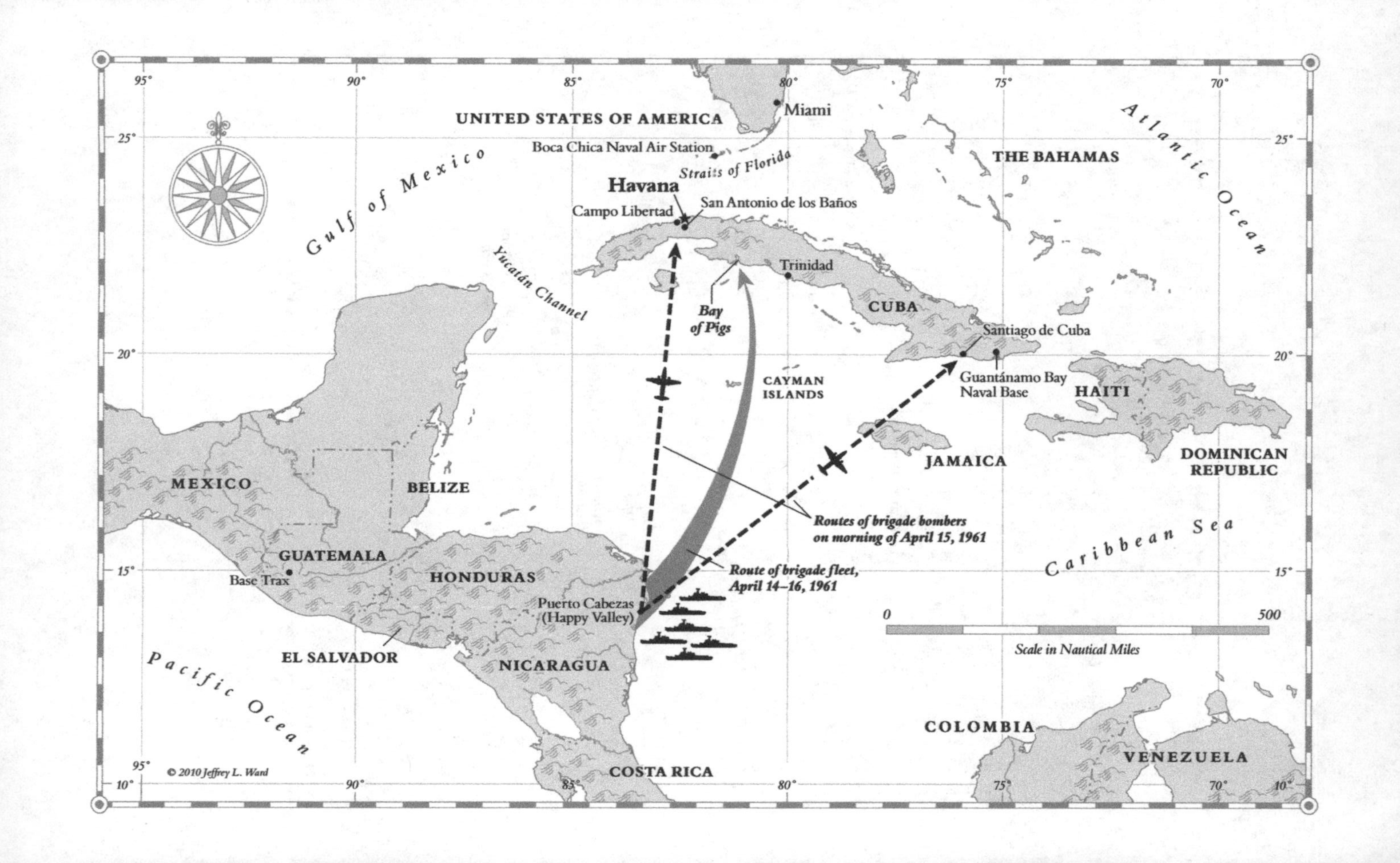
UNITED STATES OF AMERICA
Miami
Boca Chica Naval Air Station
Straits of Florida
Havana
Campo Libertad
San Antonio de los Baños
Gulf of Mexico
Atlantic Ocean
THE BAHAMAS
Yucatán Channel
Trinidad
Bay of Pigs
CUBA
Santiago de Cuba
Guantánamo Bay Naval Base
CAYMAN ISLANDS
HAITI
DOMINICAN REPUBLIC
JAMAICA
MEXICO
BELIZE
GUATEMALA
Base Trax
HONDURAS
Puerto Cabezas (Happy Valley)
EL SALVADOR
NICARAGUA
COSTA RICA
Routes of brigade bombers on morning of April 15, 1961
Route of brigade fleet, April 14–16, 1961
Caribbean Sea
Pacific Ocean
0
500
Scale in Nautical Miles
COLOMBIA
VENEZUELA
95°
90°
85°
80°
75°
70°
25°
20°
15°
10°
© 2010 Jeffrey L. Ward

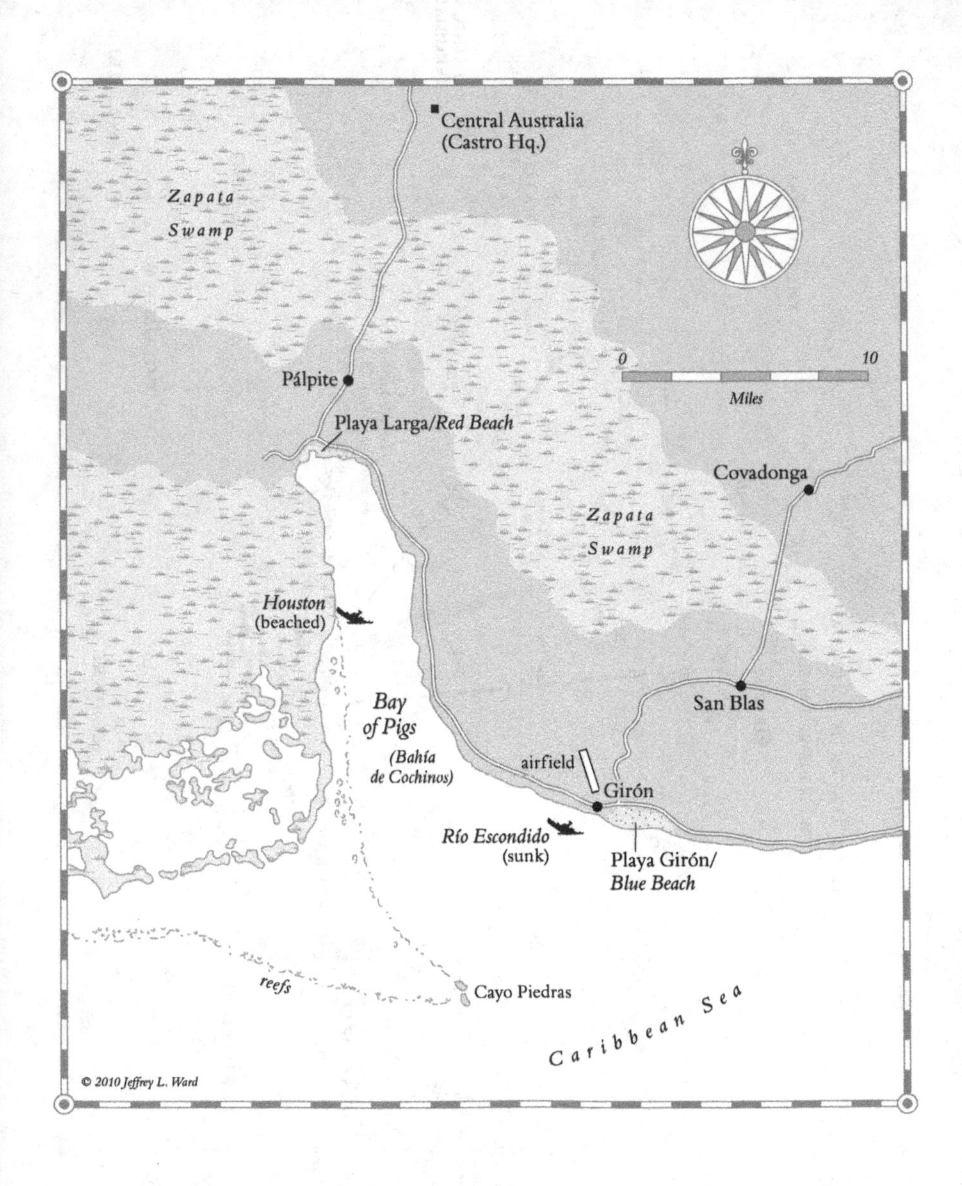
Central Australia
(Castro Hq.)
Zapata
Swamp
0
10
Miles
Pálpite
Playa Larga/Red Beach
Covadonga
Zapata
Swamp
Houston
(beached)
Bay
of Pigs
(Bahía
de Cochinos)
San Blas
airfield
Girón
Río Escondido
(sunk)
Playa Girón/
Blue Beach
reefs
Cayo Piedras
Caribbean Sea
© 2010 Jeffrey L. Ward

INTRODUCTION

"The Bay of Pigs Thing"

BACK IN THE first half of the twentieth century, America was a good and determined nation led by competent men and defended by an indomitable military—that, anyway, was a plausible view for Americans to hold fifty years ago. The First World War, then the Second World War, asserted and confirmed America's place of might and right in the world. Even in the decade after the Second World War, as a new conflict in Korea suggested there were limits to what the United States might accomplish abroad, it would have been a cynical American who doubted he or she lived in a powerful nation engaged in worthy exploits.

And then came the Bay of Pigs.

In the early hours of April 17, 1961, some fourteen hundred men, most of them Cuban exiles, attempted to invade their homeland and overthrow Fidel Castro. The invasion at the Bahía de Cochinos—the Bay of Pigs—quickly unraveled. Three days after landing, the exile force was routed and sent fleeing to the sea or the swamps, where the survivors were soon captured by Castro's army. Despite the Kennedy administration's initial insistence that the United States had nothing to do with the invasion, the world immediately understood that the entire operation had been organized and funded by the U.S. government. The invaders had been trained by CIA officers and supplied with American equipment, and the plan had been approved by the Joint Chiefs of Staff and the president of the United States. In short, the Bay of Pigs had been a U.S. operation, and its failure—"a perfect failure," historian Theodore Draper called it—was a distinctly American embarrassment. Bad enough the government had been caught bullying and prevaricating; much worse, the United States had allowed itself to be humiliated by a nation of 7 million inhabitants (compared to the United States' 180 million) and smaller than the state of Pennsylvania. The greatest American defeat since the War of 1812, one American general called it. Others were less generous. Everyone agreed on this: it was a mistake Americans would never repeat and a lesson they would never forget.

They were wrong on both counts.

Mention the Bay of Pigs to a college-educated adult American under the age of, say, fifty and you are likely to be met by tentative nods of recognition. The incident still rings discordant bells somewhere in the back of our national memory—something to do with Cuba, with Kennedy, with disaster. That phantasmagorical phrase alone—Bay of Pigs—is hard to forget, evoking images of bobbing swine in a bloodred sea (or at least it did in my mind when I first heard it). But what exactly happened at the Bay of Pigs? Many of us are no longer certain, including some of us who probably ought to be. At about the time I began thinking about this book, Dana Perino, the White House press secretary for President George W. Bush, good-naturedly confessed on a radio program that she confused "the Bay of Pigs thing" (April 1961) with the Cuban Missile Crisis (October 1962). Given that Ms. Perino was born a decade after these events, her uncertainty was understandable. But coming from the woman representing the president who launched the invasion of Iraq in 2003—an exercise that repeated some of the very same mistakes made in Cuba in 1961—it also was unsettling. Presumably, somebody in the Bush White House considered the history of the Bay of Pigs before sending Colin Powell to the Security Council of the United Nations (an episode, as we shall see, bearing striking similarities to Adlai Stevenson's appearance before that same body in April 1961) or ordering a minimal force to conquer a supposedly welcoming foreign land.

Then again, if history teaches us any lesson, it is that we do not learn the lessons of history very well. Almost as soon as the mistakes of the Bay of Pigs were cataloged and analyzed by various investigative bodies, America began committing them again, not only in Cuba, but elsewhere in Latin America, in Southeast Asia, in the Middle East, in Africa. By one count, the United States has forcibly intervened, covertly or overtly, in no fewer than twenty-four foreign countries since 1961, not including our more recent twenty-first-century entanglements in Iraq and

Afghanistan. Some of these have arguably produced long-term benefits for the United States. Most clearly have not.

The surfeit of interventions gives rise to a fair question: considering all that has occurred since 1961, why should the Bay of Pigs still demand our attention? Next to Vietnam and Iraq, among others, the Bay of Pigs may seem a bump in the road fading mercifully in the rearview mirror. The entire event lasted a mere five days and cost the United States roughly $46 million, less than the average budget of a Hollywood movie these days. One hundred and fourteen men were killed on the American side, and only a handful of these casualties were U.S. citizens. Add to this the fact that America was embarrassed by the Bay of Pigs and the tale has everything to recommend it for oblivion.

Even if we would forget the Bay of Pigs, though, it will not forget us. There among the mangrove swamps and the coral-jeweled waters, some part of the American story ended and a new one began. Like a well-crafted prologue, the Bay of Pigs sounded the themes, foreshadowed the conflicts, and laid the groundwork for the decades to follow. And what followed was, in no small measure, a consequence of the events in Cuba in 1961. It would be facile to credit the 1960s to a single failed invasion—many currents combined to produce that tsunami—but the Bay of Pigs dragged America into the new decade and stalked it for years to come. Three of the major American cataclysms of the '60s and early '70s—John Kennedy's assassination, the Vietnam War, and Watergate—were related by concatenation to the Bay of Pigs. No fewer than four presidents were touched by it, from Dwight Eisenhower, who first approved the "Program of Covert Action" against Castro, to Richard Nixon and the six infamous justice-obstructing words he uttered in 1972: "the whole Bay of Pigs thing."

MY TELLING OF the Bay of Pigs thing will certainly not be the first. On the contrary, thousands of pages of official reports, journalism, memoir, and scholarship have been devoted to the invasion, including at least two exceptional books: Haynes Johnson's emotionally charged account published in 1964 and Peter Wyden's deeply reported account from 1979. This book owes a debt to both of those, and to many others, as well as to thousands of pages of once-classified documents that have become available over the past fifteen years, thanks in part to the efforts of the National Security Archives, an organization affiliated with George

Washington University that seeks to declassify and publish government files. These newer sources, including a CIA inspector general's report, written shortly after the invasion and hidden away in a vault for decades, and a once-secret CIA history compiled in the 1970s, add depth and clarity to our understanding of the event and of the men who planned it and took part in it.

If what follows is not quite a story never told, it may be, even for those well acquainted with the event—especially those, perhaps—a different story than the one readers thought they knew. Because the Bay of Pigs was so cataclysmic and personally anguishing to so many involved, and because it raised questions about core American values, its postmortems have tended to be of the finger-pointing, ax-grinding, high-dudgeon variety. This includes personal memoirs and reminiscences, but also serious and measured works such as Johnson's and Wyden's, both of which were colored by the circumstances under which they were written. Johnson's book, published just a few years after the invasion, was authored with heavy input from leaders of the Cuban exile brigade and is raw with their pain and resentment. Wyden's book was written in the late 1970s, following Watergate and an inflammatory Senate investigation into CIA-sponsored assassinations (the so-called Church Committee), when national outrage for government subterfuge was at a high point and esteem for the CIA hit new lows. The book announces its bias on the very first page, when Wyden describes the CIA as "acting out of control" during the Bay of Pigs. Many other books, articles, and interviews have added to the riot of perspective: those by Kennedy partisans who damn the CIA; those by CIA participants who damn Kennedy; those by Cuban exiles who damn both, and Castro, too; and those by Cuban nationals who hail the events of 1961 as a great defeat of American imperialism and a defining episode in the hagiography of Fidel Castro.

With the possible exception of Castro, no one came out of the Cuban venture smelling sweet, but over time the CIA came to assume the rankest odor of all. Starting with the publication of two important memoirs by senior Kennedy aides in the fall of 1965—Arthur M. Schlesinger's *A Thousand Days* and Theodore Sorensen's *Kennedy*—a steady stream of books championed the view that John Kennedy was a victim in the Bay of Pigs, and especially a victim of the CIA's arrogance and malfeasance. Several recently published books that treat the Bay of Pigs suggest this view has won out and is now conventional wisdom. One recent bestseller, David Talbot's *Brothers: The Hidden History of the Kennedy Years*

(2007), describes a defiant CIA driven by "cynical calculation" while engaged in an effort to "sandbag" President Kennedy with the Bay of Pigs. Another, Tim Weiner's history of the CIA, *Legacy of Ashes* (2007), portrays an agency that managed to combine duplicity with dereliction, somehow running circles around Kennedy and his advisers even as it tripped over its own two feet.

The more complicated truth about the Bay of Pigs is that it was not ginned up by a nefarious band of agents in the bowels of the CIA, but rather produced by two administrations, encouraged by countless informed legislators, and approved by numerous men of high rank and intelligence, even brilliance, who either did know, or should have known, what they were agreeing to. As for why they did this—"How could I have been so stupid?" is how Kennedy phrased the question—the answer is that all of them, from the presidents to the Central Intelligence Agency, from the Pentagon to the State Department, were operating under conditions that made the venture almost impossible to resist. At a time when Americans were nearly hysterical about the spread of communism, they simply could not abide Castro. He had to go. And the CIA, in 1960, was the tool Eisenhower, then Kennedy, intended to use to speed him on his way.

Unsettling as it may be to conjure a "rogue elephant," as the CIA was often described after the Bay of Pigs, making and executing lethal and boneheaded foreign policy on its own, more troubling may be the possibility that the Bay of Pigs—or any number of subsequent disasters abroad—was driven by irrational forces and fears in the broad American public, and that its pursuit and failure reflected not one man's or one group's moral or intellectual failings, but the limits of a democratic government's ability to respond sensibly to frightening circumstances. By the time the Bay of Pigs occurred, it almost was rational—a logical conclusion arrived at from a set of premises that were, in 1961, practically beyond question. Clearly the CIA chose the wrong way to go about unseating Castro, but really, is there any good way to overthrow the government of a sovereign nation?

My goal in these pages is not to defend the CIA, or anyone else, but to treat the participants with more empathy than prejudice, the better to understand their motives. As a litany of misdeeds, the Bay of Pigs is dark comedy; only when we consider it in the full context of its time does it reveal itself, instead, as Greek tragedy. Not all participants in the affair behaved well, but of the many extraordinary facts about the Bay of Pigs, the most surprising may be that it was the work of mostly decent and intelligent people trying their best to perform what they considered to be the necessary emergency procedure of excising Fidel Castro. With a few notable exceptions—Senator William Fulbright was one—it never occurred to any of them that America could tolerate Fidel Castro's reign. Certainly it never occurred to them that Castro's reign would outlast the administrations of ten U.S. presidents.

IN SOME WAYS, this is a tale from the distant past. Other than the frozen state of relations between the United States and Cuba, virtually unchanged since 1961, we live in a world that is very different from the one that produced the Bay of Pigs. The Cold War is over; the War on Terror has taken its place as our national bête noire. Fidel Castro, in retrospect, seems a benign threat next to the likes of Osama bin Laden. But America is still driven by the same conflicting motives and urgencies that landed the country at the Bay of Pigs fifty years ago. On the one hand, we are a people convinced of our own righteousness, power, and genius—a conviction that compels us to cure what ails the world. On the other hand, we are stalked by deep insecurities: our way of life is in constant jeopardy; our enemies are implacable and closing in. This paradox of American psychology was apparent well before the Bay of Pigs—Fidel Castro pointed it out to Richard Nixon in 1959, as we will see in this book's first chapter—but compounding it after 1961 were new concerns about the limits of American power, not to mention the limits of American competence and morality. The days of the "splendid little war," as Ambassador John Hays famously called the United States' military venture in Cuba in 1898 (during the Spanish-American War), are long gone now. Instead, we get complicated, tormented affairs that never seem to end. In this respect, at least, the Kennedy administration earned this book's otherwise oxymoronic title, and without irony: their disaster was brilliantly brief. It could have been far worse, as a number of very smart people noted afterward. What does it tell us that some of those same smart people—"the best and the brightest," author David Halberstam indelibly tagged them—later engineered America's descent into Vietnam? Irony never strays far from this tale.

We are still trying to come up with the solution to the conundrum that gave rise to the Bay of Pigs: how to use American power to make the world to our liking, but do so in a manner that holds true to the values we espouse. One piece of evidence that we have not quite figured this out can be found, coincidentally, on the eastern tip of Cuba, where the United States still holds prisoners from the War on Terror at Guantánamo. What to do about this and similar matters remains the problem of our current president, Barack Obama, born in August 1961, a few months after the Bay of Pigs.

As it happens, my own life began just after the Bay of Pigs and was soon touched by it, albeit obliquely. In December 1962—when I was a few months old—my father was briefly but significantly involved in the episode's dramatic finale. A young and politically involved lawyer at the time (he'd done advance work for John Kennedy), he was recruited to join Robert Kennedy's pre-Christmas effort to bring home more than a thousand men who had been taken prisoner by Fidel Castro during the Bay of Pigs. For an intense few weeks leading up to Christmas 1962, my father and several other private attorneys, as well as men from the attorney general's office such as Louis Oberdorfer and Nicholas Katzenbach, virtually lived at the Justice Department as they worked to secure the prisoners' release. My father's role was small, and came only near the end. I mention him here to point out that I grew up more attuned than most to the Bay of Pigs fiasco, and yet I can't say my understanding of it was at all clear. I suspect that to most people around my age, the Bay of Pigs is an incident of the dim, dark past, like a childhood memory of something not meant for children's eyes. Meanwhile, for older Americans—those of my father's generation—it's a memory that is fading.

Not so in Cuba, as I learned when I visited the island in the spring of 2010, on the invasion's forty-ninth anniversary. To Cubans, the Bay of Pigs episode is known simply as "Girón," after the beach where the invasion began and ended, and the Cuban victory there is one of the founding mythologies of modern Cuba. Schoolchildren learn of it when they are young and are never allowed to forget. Every April, billboards throughout Havana herald it anew, and Playa Girón becomes a kind of mecca for invasion tourists and government officials. Passing a giant billboard that announces Girón as the site of the PRIMERA DERROTA DEL IMPERIALISMO YANQUI EN AMERICA LATINA (First Defeat of Yankee Imperialism in Latin America), busloads of schoolchildren and military personnel arrive at the small seaside hamlet. They visit the battle museum, poke into the shops, and walk down to the palm-shaded beach where the "mercenaries" first landed. Local laborers slap a fresh coat of white paint onto the base of the telephone poles and line the main road into town with palm fronds, sprucing up for the dignitaries who will arrive from Havana on April 19 and stand on a platform in front of the Hotel Playa Girón to declare the victory all over again.

Meanwhile, at the western end of the beach where the invasion occurred, two military sentries stand atop an old shack that has been turned into a military post. Day and night, they look out to sea with high-powered optical equipment, searching, waiting, as if expecting, any moment, an invasion force to arrive all over again.

PROLOGUE

"Balls Were in the Air"

Saturday, April 15, 1961

Washington, D.C., 3:28 A.M.

THE NEWS IN the first dark hours of the first day was mostly good. Or so it appeared in the early editions of the morning papers, already composed and printed long before the sun began to rise on the morning of April 15, 1961. Soon the papers would be sliding into mailboxes or sailing across front lawns, carrying headlines that told of an America prosperous and resurgent. The economy was bouncing back from a recession that had weighed upon the last months of the Eisenhower administration. Industrial production, housing starts, the stock market, incomes—all were rising. "Let's get America moving again," John Kennedy had exhorted in one of his catchier campaign slogans. Now he was president, and he was making good on his words.

Kennedy had been in office for only three months as of mid-April, but many Wall Streeters already gave him credit for the lift in the economy. "By one of those curious turns peculiar to public opinion, the New Frontier idea, after being viewed with considerable skepticism last summer, seems suddenly to have caught hold," a stock analyst named Bradbury K. Thurlow had mused in the *New York Times* the previous week. Americans seemed to agree. John Kennedy's approval rating was 73 percent in the latest Gallup poll. His personal pollster, Lou Harris, charted him at an astonishing 92 percent.

Though Mr. Thurlow did not say so in his editorial, Kennedy's popularity owed less to his new policies—not so different, really, from his predecessor's—than to the new style of leadership he brought to the White House. Chiefly, this style was defined by vigor and action. The elderly President Eisenhower had run a "passive, do-nothing" administration, according to one New Frontiersman; Kennedy's was going to be an "active, do-something" administration. "The air had been stale and oppressive," wrote another Kennedy aide, Arthur M. Schlesinger Jr.; "now fresh winds were blowing."

The new president was young, cool, handsome, and rich. He was surrounded by a staff of even younger acolytes who put aside soaring careers at America's top universities and corporations to serve him. He had a fetching and devoted wife in Jacqueline; an adorable three-year-old daughter, Caroline; and a new baby son. The previous afternoon, Friday, April 14, one of the first warm and sunny days of spring, as flowers bloomed in the Rose Garden, tourists gazing through the White House fence had been treated to the sight of Jacqueline playing tennis on the White House court. Little Caroline was observed frolicking nearby. An Ohio woman told a reporter she'd seen the president himself out on the lawn "swinging golf balls."

"He wasn't swinging golf balls," her husband corrected her. "He was swinging a golf club."

"I don't know what he was swinging," replied the woman, "but balls were in the air."

Balls were indeed in the air that spring, and the president was juggling them, by most accounts, deftly. Since coming into office in January, he'd showered Congress with new bills and messages, delivered scores of speeches, and stood for weekly live televised press conferences. His advisers and cabinet officers were a breed of men, wrote Arthur Schlesinger, who "carried a thrust of action and purpose wherever they went." The deadline for everything, said Arthur Goldberg, Kennedy's secretary of labor, "is the day before yesterday." The president himself read fast, more than a thousand words a minute, according to press accounts, and he read *everything*. "I never heard of a president who wanted to know so much," said Charles Bohlen, a veteran American diplomat.

In addition to being ambitious, impatient, and voracious, Kennedy and his fellow New Frontiersmen were aggressive and tough. They possessed—that word again—*balls*, as in grit, aggression, testicular fortitude. More specifically, in the context of 1961, it meant that these were men, unlike some of their more appeasement-oriented fellow Democrats (read former presidential candidate Adlai Stevenson), who could be trusted to stand up to the enemy. And the enemy, in 1961, meant Communists.

Communists were the dark cloud Americans saw when they gazed behind the silver lining: the mushroom-shaped thunderhead looming over the backyard barbecue. Such was the strangeness of life in the spring of 1961. Never had Americans known such plenty; never had they known such dread. They lived in a newfound land of freshly sprung suburbs, of high-finned, chrome-trimmed automobiles, of push-button washing machines and electric stoves and aerodynamically shaped furniture. In the morning, they breakfasted in brightly colored, appliance-accessorized kitchens; evenings, they relaxed in Naugahyde recliners and bathed in the contemporary luminescence of pole lamps and television sets. They enjoyed more leisure time and more disposable income than any generation in history. They were the first generation of Americans to worry less about the necessities of life and more about "lifestyle," a word that debuted in *Webster's Third New International Dictionary* that year.

But the pleasures of Americans' new lifestyle were curtailed by other commonly used words and phrases of 1961, such as "missile gap," "annihilation," and "Soviet-Sino conspiracy." Hardly a day passed without newspapers reminding them that the Soviets were pressing for control of West Berlin, that Laos and Vietnam were falling into the clutches of the Chinese, that Reds were on the march across the globe, including, incredibly, on the island of Cuba, ninety miles off the cost of Florida—a mere "eight jet minutes" away, as Kennedy had so often pointed out in campaign speeches. And now the Communists had a foothold in outer space, too. Three days earlier—April 12, 1961—a cosmonaut named Yuri Gagarin had become the first man to orbit Earth in a spacecraft. Another win in the Soviets' column; another chance for Nikita Khrushchev to gloat: "Let the capitalist countries try to catch up with our country!"

This was exactly the kind of challenge the New Frontier was prepared to meet. One of the headlines in the *New York Times* that Saturday morning confirmed Kennedy's determination: MAN-ON-MOON AIM CUT YEAR BY U.S. Just three days after congratulating Khrushchev for the "technical achievement" of Yuri Gagarin's flight (the word choice seemed to imply that grander achievements lay beyond the Soviets' grasp), President Kennedy was ordering NASA to speed up plans to put a man on the moon. "What can we do?" Kennedy demanded of his staff. "Are we working twenty-four hours a day? Can we go around the moon before them?"

John Kennedy had put down a marker for prodigious achievement many months earlier while campaigning for the presidency. In speeches, he referred to Franklin D. Roosevelt's much-heralded first hundred days in office and proposed to move even faster with the New Frontier than Roosevelt had with the New Deal. "[A] President's first 90 days," he told an audience back in September, "are his most important."

For the moment, at 3:28 that Saturday morning, the windows of the White House were dark, the midnight oil doused. The sky over Washington was moonless and cloud-patched. In a few hours, John F. Kennedy would rise from bed and begin his eighty-fifth day as president.

Puerto Cabezas, 2:28 A.M. (3:28 EST)

AS JOHN KENNEDY enjoyed his last good night of sleep for days to come, the operation to overthrow Fidel Castro was launched eighteen hundred miles southwest of Washington, D.C., at a place called Happy Valley. This was the code name the Central Intelligence Agency had assigned to Puerto Cabezas, Nicaragua, a hardscrabble, dirt-road coastal village wedged between the Caribbean Sea and the Central American jungle. The time was just before 2:30 A.M. in Nicaragua, but Happy Valley was loud and ablaze.

Under the glow of floodlights, eight B-26 Douglas Invaders lined the end of the landing strip. The planes were Second World War relics that had been acquired from a U.S. Air Force "boneyard" near Tucson, Arizona, then repaired, refurbished, and repainted to resemble the B-26s in Fidel Castro's air force, right down to the FAR (Fuerza Aérea Revolucionaria) markings on their fuselages and tails. The markings were a ruse, meant to sow confusion when the planes attacked Castro's air force, his *real* air force, later in the morning.

The planes' engines rasped and roared as ground crews made final checks and preparations for flight. In the distance, beyond the bubble of artificial light, the dark shapes of twelve-man army tents hunkered under the jungle canopy. Sturdier structures rose closer to the edge of the runway: an airport control tower; a mess hall; a chapel; a command center surrounded by barbed wire. One structure advertised itself with a sign over the door: BAR. Inside, men not otherwise occupied slaked their thirsts and passed empty hours drinking beer, courtesy of the CIA.

No amount of beer could dull the discomforts the men had been enduring at Happy Valley these past few weeks. In addition to being oppressively hot and damp, this corner of the Central American tropics was infested with scorpions, spiders, and venomous snakes. The shower was a horizontal pipe that ran over a wooden platform and emitted a tepid trickle. The latrine was a lime-coated trench covered by a wooden plank. A trip to either shower or latrine could be hair-raising, since scorpions tended to lurk in both. One man had already been airlifted back to Florida with a scorpion bite on his backside, a development that had done nothing to encourage personal hygiene or digestive regularity at Happy Valley.

Puerto Cabezas may have lacked domestic amenities, but as a launchpad for an invasion of Cuba it was well equipped. To begin, there was the 6,200-foot-long concrete landing strip, installed by Americans during the Second World War to defend the Panama Canal. The location of the strip, about 550 miles south of Havana, put it far enough from the target to avoid raising obvious suspicions, but within range (if only just) of a B-26 outfitted with auxiliary fuel tanks. Moreover, the 1,500-foot wooden pier reaching out into the Caribbean from the center of town was perfectly suited to accommodate a small armada of ships—just the sort of armada that had departed from Puerto Cabezas ten hours earlier.

Over the previous three days, infantrymen of the Cuban Expeditionary Force—Brigade 2506, as the men called themselves—had flown in aboard C-54 cargo planes from their training camps on the far side of Central America, in Guatemala. Arriving in groups of fifty or so, they had filed to the railway cattle cars that transported them to town, then marched down the long pier to their appointed ships. They made a motley procession, these men of the brigade. Some were barely beyond boyhood, others well advanced into middle age. Some marched with the carriage of trained professional soldiers, others stumbled to keep up. Most of the soldiers were dark-haired and spoke Spanish, but moving among them were men with Nordic features, squinty eyes, twangy American accents, and all-American swagger. The brigade soldiers wore crisp new uniforms but the half dozen ships they boarded were vintage freight vessels so tarnished by rust they quickly turned the men's uniforms the color of dried blood.

Just before the ships pulled away, as the brigademen stood at the railings of their ships waving the colored scarves of their battalions, a spooky apparition had suddenly appeared in the dusk. Luis Somoza, dictator of Nicaragua and ally of the United States, stood on the pier, surrounded by gunmen. Wearing a white suit and a layer of white cosmetic powder on his face, he came to wish them bon voyage. "Bring me a couple hairs from Castro's beard," Somoza called out. Then the dictator had vanished, and the ships of the Cuban Expeditionary Force vanished, too, steaming into the evening.

NOW IT WAS a new day, and the first B-26, captained by a handsome and taciturn thirty-eight-year-old former Cubana Airlines pilot named Gustavo Ponzoa, was starting down the runway. Other than the bombing raid a few hours hence, the next few moments would be the most critical of Ponzoa's flight. His plane was loaded thousands of pounds beyond its 35,000-pound limit. In addition to two 500-pound bombs and ten 250-pound fragmentation bombs, it carried eight wing-mounted rockets and eight nose-mounted .50-caliber machine guns. Auxiliary fuel tanks added many hundreds more pounds. These tanks would extend the range of the plane and give it more breathing room over Cuba. But first the plane had to get airborne.

The B-26 accelerated slowly, reluctantly lifting just at the end of the runway and nearly brushing the trees below. The moment the plane was up, Ponzoa extinguished the wing lights. Then another plane followed. And another, gathering speed, rising, and quickly melting into the darkness.

The men left behind at Happy Valley stood near the runway in the dark and counted the departing planes of the so-called Cuban Liberation Air Force; the total came to eight. The brigade's B-26 fleet was sixteen planes, so just half the planes had taken off. "Is that all?" one of the American pilots, Albert C. Persons, asked out loud when the last plane was gone. *Is that all?* It's a question that would haunt the participants of the invasion, Cubans and Americans alike, for years to come. For the men who were there that night in Happy Valley, it was the first inkling that something was not right with the operation to which they'd committed months of their lives and would, in some cases, soon sacrifice their lives entirely.

Washington, D.C., 4:00 A.M.

ACROSS THE MALL from the White House, the cherry trees were in blossom along the edge of the Tidal Basin, their buds shivering in a cool breeze. Nearby, at the base of the Lincoln Memorial, rose a plain two-story wooden building, one of several remaining "tempos" that had been thrown up on the Mall during the Second World War and now served as offices for the Central Intelligence Agency. Known among CIA officers as Quarters Eye, the building appeared as quiet and dark as everything around it. Only deep inside, behind the blackened windows, beyond the locked doors controlled by keypad codes, was there evidence of action.

In the Hollywood version, men would be sprinting down corridors, grabbing telephones, and barking orders. Reality was more static: a room festooned with laminated maps of Cuba; bleary-eyed men nursing cups of coffee; the ambient clack of a teletype machine. It was a tableau short on motion, perhaps, but roiling with tension nonetheless. The men inside Quarters Eye had been working toward this moment for months, twelve to sixteen hours a day. They had been spending nights here, resting on makeshift cots when exhaustion overcame them. They had run gauntlets, jumped through hoops, and worried themselves sick between bursts of hope. Now, for a few hours, there was little to do but sit back and wait for the attack to begin.

PART I

HONEYMOON

April 15–October 26, 1959

1

"Viva Castro!"

April 1959

Washington, D.C., April 1959

WHEN, REALLY, did it begin? Was it the day in 1956 Fidel Castro landed on the coast of Cuba with a small band of followers to begin his quixotic campaign against the dictator Fulgencio Batista? Was it in the early-morning hours of January 1, 1959, when Batista, dressed in his New Year's Eve tuxedo, piled cash and family members into an airplane and fled to the Dominican Republic, leaving the country in Castro's hands? Was it, rather, fourteen months later, March 17, 1960, the day President Eisenhower approved the CIA's "Program of Covert Action" to unseat Castro?

Or did the trouble between Cuba and the United States reach much deeper into the past, to Teddy Roosevelt's triumph at San Juan Hill, to the U.S. victory in the Spanish-American War and the succeeding decades of American intervention in Cuban affairs?

In fact, all of these episodes, and many more, were stations on the way to the U.S.-backed invasion of Cuba. Easier than narrowing the origins of the conflict is identifying the moment when it might have been avoided: when some measure of amity between Cuba and America still seemed possible; when Fidel Castro still appeared to many Americans to be the sort of man they could live with, accommodate, and even, perhaps, admire.

Such a moment arrived two years before the first bombs fell on Cuba—two years, in fact, *to the day*. Dwight Eisenhower was beginning his seventh year as president. Richard Nixon was vice president and the presumptive Republican nominee for the 1960 presidential election. John Kennedy was the junior senator from Massachusetts, still mulling a run at the Democratic presidential nomination. And Fidel Castro, three and a half months after conquering Cuba, was celebrating his triumph with a visit to America. His entry into U.S. airspace was a kind of invasion in its own right—a charm offensive. He came bearing a hundred cases of rum, countless boxes of Cuban cigars, and a warm *abrazo* for every man, woman, and child he met.

Castro landed on the evening of April 15, 1959, at Washington, D.C.'s National Airport. The time was two minutes after nine and Castro, typically, was two hours behind schedule, but this did nothing to dampen the enthusiasm of the fifteen hundred admirers awaiting him near the tarmac. "Viva Castro!" the crowd erupted as the door of the Cubana Airlines turboprop swung open and the man himself stepped out. "Viva Castro!"

He looked every bit the legendary guerrilla as he stood atop the airplane ramp, bathed in camera lights and the roar of the crowd. He was a large man, more than six feet tall, clad in rumpled green fatigues and high black boots, the uniform he and his cadre had worn through the battles of the Sierra. He carried an army kit on one shoulder, and an empty canvas pistol holster dangled from his belt. And the beard, of course: that famous beard Castro and his fellow *barbudos* had cultivated while fighting Batista's troops in the wilds of Cuba. *Barbudos* translated as "bearded ones" but sounded like "barbarians," a suitable cognate for the "bearded monster," as one U.S. senator had already taken to calling Castro.

"Viva Castro!"

As the shouts rang up from the tarmac, Castro descended, followed by an avalanche of ministers, businessmen, bodyguards, and others whose roles were more difficult to define. The State Department had been trying to get a fix on Castro's entourage for weeks, but the mercurial Cubans kept coming back with new numbers—thirty-five, then seventy, multiplying, at last, to ninety-four. For the State Department, the changing number was just another sign of the chaos that seemed to percolate around Castro wherever he went, as if he were making it up on the spot, dreaming it as it happened—*it* being the revolution, the new Cuba, this maddening creation called Fidel.

Castro was making his first appearance in the United States since riding into Havana at the start of the year, but the thirty-two-year-old rebel leader was no stranger to America. Newspapers and magazines had been tracking his exploits for years. The general outlines of his biography were familiar: the privileged but combative boyhood as the illegitimate son of a wealthy landowner in eastern Cuba; the student years at Havana University, where he earned both a law degree (hence the honorific "Doctor" often attached to his name) and, more important, a devoted following in the bloody *gangsterismo* political scene of 1940s Havana. There had been a short-lived marriage in 1948, when he took a break from school and politics to travel with his new bride to America for an extended honeymoon. Given what came later, the most remarkable fact about this sojourn was how comfortably Castro had fit into the belly of the imperialist beast, studying English in New York City and enjoying the fruits of capitalism (including a new Lincoln) as much as any other red-blooded young man in postwar New York. Nonetheless, he had returned to Cuba after three months and resumed his life as a revolutionary.

It was in the summer of 1953 that Castro had first come to the attention of the American press. On July 26 of that year he led an attack on an army barracks in Santiago de Cuba. The attack failed miserably but made Castro a hero in Cuba. Castro was sentenced to fifteen years in prison. Batista, in a gesture of goodwill unbecoming of a ruthless dictator, released him after just two. Castro went into exile in Mexico City, befriended a young Argentinean doctor named Ernesto "Che" Guevara, and raised funds to support a new attack on Cuba. In December 1956, in the company of Guevara, his brother Raúl Castro, and seventy-nine other men, Castro sailed across the Gulf of Mexico and through the Yucatán Strait to mount another quixotic attack on Batista's forces. Nearly all the rebels were killed within days of landing, including Fidel Castro, according to Batista's government. And so the world believed until Herbert Matthews, a writer for the *New York Times*, managed to track Castro down in the Sierra Maestra, where he found the rebel leader hiding among the peasants like a modern-day Robin Hood, not only alive but apparently prospering and gathering forces. Matthews's articles from the Sierra Maestra made Castro into a worldwide legend, and the legend only grew as Castro continued to survive and pile up victories. When, at last, Batista fled Havana on New Year's Day, many Americans were as thrilled as the exultant Cuban masses. An evil man had been deposed; a new man, young and idealistic and charismatic, had won the hearts and minds of much of the world.

And now here he was in the flesh, stepping onto the tarmac into a crowd of U.S. officials.

"Viva Castro!"

Before Castro could shake hands with Roy Rubottom, the State Department official there to greet him, a hundred or so fans suddenly rushed through a ring of police. Castro received the swarm of adulation with handshakes and hugs, then wended his way to a thicket of microphones. Generally, microphones inspired him to long and rambling orations. Not tonight. His voice was hoarse and soft, and surprisingly high-pitched for so large a man.

"I have come here to speak to the people of the United States," he began in halting English. "I hope the people of the United States will understand better the people of Cuba, and I hope to understand better the people of the United States."

He turned for the limousine parked on the tarmac, then strode right past it to a large crowd shouting from the other side of a chain-link fence. His security detail, including local police officers and forty agents from the State Department's Division of Physical Security, scrambled to keep up. The State Department had already fielded numerous threats against Castro and had every reason to worry an assassin might try to gun him down. But the greatest danger to Castro, evidently, was going to be Castro himself. "He must be crazy," one of the guards observed as Castro flung himself at the crowd.

CRAZY WAS A common assessment of Fidel Castro in certain quarters of the American government. Few Americans were sorry to see Batista go, and the United States had quickly recognized the new regime. But some officials, such as Roy Rubottom, the assistant secretary of state Castro left standing on the tarmac, were already expressing grave doubts about the new prime minister. Both CIA intelligence and firsthand reports from Cuba suggested that Castro was erratic, tyrannical, and bloodthirsty. Since arriving in Havana at the start of the year to take the reins of government, Castro had either ordered or allowed the executions of more than five hundred Batista supporters. Between executions, he'd delivered stupendous diatribes, some lasting as long as three or four hours and many of them laced with anti-American sentiments. American conservatives such as Senator Barry Goldwater were particularly alarmed by the tone of the new Cuban leader, but even the liberal and outspokenly pro-Castro New York congressman Adam Clayton Powell had returned from a March visit to Cuba with alarming tales of a man who slept a couple of hours a night, kept himself awake with high doses of Benzedrine, fell frequently into incoherence when talking, and had, in general, "gone haywire."

The Fidel Castro who arrived in the United States in April 1959 may have been sleep-deprived and criminally indifferent to his own safety, but he was not noticeably incoherent or haywire. On the contrary, he struck most of those who met him during his eleven-day visit to America as reasonable and amiable, even charming.

Among those who would not get a chance to experience Castro's charms firsthand was Dwight Eisenhower. The president had excused himself from meeting the Cuban revolutionary by decamping to Augusta, Georgia, to play golf. Eisenhower was not kindly disposed to revolutionaries in the first place; moreover, he was irritated by the circumstances that brought Castro to Washington. Generally, a foreign head of state would not think to visit America without an official invitation from the State Department. Castro had come, instead, by invitation of the American Society of Newspaper Editors (ASNE) to deliver the keynote address at the organization's annual meeting on April 17. In Castro's defense (and ASNE's), he had accepted the invitation before he officially became Cuba's prime minister. Still, it was an unseemly breach of protocol for him to show up like this, and Eisenhower was not pleased.

As it happened, Castro's arrival in the United States came on a very difficult day for Eisenhower. That morning, the president had learned in a phone call that his longtime secretary of state, John Foster Dulles, was resigning, effective immediately. For eight years, Dulles had been the ballast, if not the rudder, of Eisenhower's anti-Communist foreign policy. Now he was in Walter Reed Army Hospital with terminal abdominal cancer. That John Foster Dulles should end his career on the very day Fidel Castro landed in America is one of those coincidences that would seem, like so many others of the next two years, to have been plotted by a roomful of cackling Soviet scriptwriters bunked up in a commune near the Kremlin.

THE MORNING AFTER his arrival, Castro awoke in a bedroom in the Cuban embassy on Sixteenth Street and began to practice his English. An aide ran out to buy him a comb and toothbrush. Castro was usually indifferent to personal hygiene, but he was eager to make a good impression on the Americans. He even managed to arrive on time for a luncheon later in the day with Acting Secretary of State Christian Herter. The men chatted cordially, then exchanged toasts. Castro bounced out of the lunch beaming. Herter, cane in hand, emerged sober but impressed. After the lunch, Herter informed President Eisenhower that he found Castro to be "a child in many ways, quite immature regarding problems of government." A few days later, though, a State Department memorandum described the Cuban prime minister as "a man on his best behavior."

This was, as far as it went, an accurate appraisal. Before coming to America, Castro had wired a New York City public relations firm to advise him. In addition to urging Castro to smile a lot, the publicists suggested, less astutely, that he shave his beard to adopt a clean-cut appearance. Castro wisely ignored the latter tip. The beard was part of his mystique. People *loved* the beard. Indeed, popular novelty items in America that spring were fake Castro beards woven from treated dog or fox hair. "When we finish our job," Castro told one interlocutor, "we will cut off our whiskers."

The most sensible advice the public relations executives gave Castro seems to have been this: *tell them what they want to hear*. And what they wanted to hear in the spring of 1959—"they" being government officials, the American press, and the public—was that Fidel Castro was not a Communist.

"What is your connection with communism, if any?" asked Senator Alexander Wiley of Wisconsin when the Cuban visited the U.S. Capitol on Friday morning.

"None," Castro replied, then went on to repeat variations of the answer for the next hour and a half. Afterward, senators and congressmen pronounced themselves cautiously satisfied. "I feel reassured about a number of matters I've been concerned about in Cuba," said Senator Russell Long of Louisiana. Representative James Fulton, a Republican from Pennsylvania, pronounced Castro an "*amigo nuevo.*" Even Senator George Smathers of Florida, a persistent critic of Castro, came away impressed. He remained convinced that Castro's government was "peppered" with Communists, but the prime minister, Smathers acknowledged, appeared to be a "good man."

Everywhere the question was the same: *Are you a Communist, Dr. Castro?* Have you ever been a Communist, or do you sympathize with Communists? Everywhere Castro gave the same answer: *No, he was not a Communist*. Never had been. Never would be.

* * *

CASTRO'S TRUE IDEOLOGY in April 1959 is, even now, difficult to pin down. Certainly there were Communists around him and close to him, men who had fought alongside him in the Sierra Maestra and now served in his government and army. His brother Raúl and his chief adviser, Ernesto "Che" Guevara, both had strong ties to the Communist Party. Most informed American observers, though, concluded that Castro was telling the truth when he said he was not a Communist. He had never been in the Communist Party, and while he welcomed Communists into his revolution, he welcomed Cubans of other political stripes, too. As for his relationships with Communists in other countries, he had none. His first known contact with any Soviet official, in fact, came during his visit to Washington that April, when he exchanged pleasantries with the Soviet ambassador during a reception at the Cuban embassy.

A more interesting question than *when* Fidel Castro became a Communist is *why* Americans were so intent on divining his ideological affiliation. Twenty-first-century Americans may find the obsession with Castro and communism slightly bizarre, if not hysterical. Americans who lived through the darkest days of the Cold War, though, will recall the issue as absolutely essential, even downright *existential*. The spread of communism was the defining geopolitical concern of the age—the organizing principle on which nearly every act and policy of U.S. foreign relations depended.

There was, in fact, plenty to fear. State-sponsored communism had risen with startling swiftness after the close of the Second World War. Russia and China were in Communist hands and apparently conspiring to spread their creed to every hill and dale on the globe. And there was no shortage of places ripe for cultivation. As European powers pulled out of former colonies, struggling new nations in Africa, Asia, and the Middle East saw in communism an ideology that offered a way out of imperialist shackles. President Eisenhower famously described the spread of communism from nation to nation as a domino effect. A more apt analogy might be germ theory. As each new country succumbed to communism, it would presumably infect its neighbor, which in turn would infect *its* neighbor, and so on, until the contagion was forcibly checked—or until Communists ruled the world. Communists were not modest about their viral creed. Sooner or later, Khrushchev had infamously warned the West, "We shall bury you."

Schoolyard taunts were typical of the Soviet premier, but Americans could not easily dismiss them. They had lived through the Second World War and watched Adolph Hitler actively seek world domination. They had every reason to believe that Khrushchev and Mao Tse-tung were seeking it, too—and plenty of evidence the Communists had the tools to succeed. The same year China went Red, 1949, the Soviet Union had exploded an atomic bomb, wiping away in a single detonation America's monopoly on the most destructive force ever unleashed by humans. Eight years after that, in 1957, the Soviets had leaped ahead in space technology with Sputnik, the first satellite ever launched into orbit. Sputnik was a stunning blow to American morale, but more important than the satellite itself was the rocket the Soviets had used to launch it. If they could make a rocket with enough thrust to carry a 184-pound aluminum sphere to the edge of Earth's atmosphere, it stood to reason that they could produce rockets capable of delivering nuclear-tipped intercontinental ballistic missiles to the heart of the United States.

Not only did the Soviets lead in missile thrust, they were ahead in missile numbers, too. Or so it was feared. According to conventional wisdom at the time, they owned a significant advantage in intercontinental missiles, as high as three-to-one. The "missile gap" would later be exposed as a canard, but not before it induced many worrisome headlines and sleepless nights. *Newsweek* put it this way at the start of 1959: "If the intercontinental ballistic missile and the thermonuclear warhead are the ultimate weapons which man has devised for destruction, then the forces of Premier Nikita Khrushchev are unquestionably ahead." In a blaring rhetorical headline *U.S. News & World Report* asked, HOW READY IS U.S. FOR WAR? The answer, the magazine informed its readers, was: *Not very.*

Beyond very real and definable anxieties regarding nuclear obliteration, a vaguer insecurity seemed to grip many Americans of the 1950s. This was reflected in edgy bestsellers such as *The Man in the Gray Flannel Suit* and *The Ugly American*, in which American might, for all its obvious fecundity and influence, was portrayed as a tenuous and at some level hollow proposition. Richard Nixon's so-called kitchen debate with Nikita Khrushchev in the summer of 1959, in which the two men squabbled about the respective merits of their nation's kitchen appliances, would be hailed as a victory for Nixon's debating skills and a rousing defense of American prosperity and industry, but in the end Nixon's argument was strikingly vapid. This was America's great claim? That it had better dishwashers?

Of course, the larger question was: why, if Americans were so sure of the superiority of their economic system over communism, were they not more confident in its ultimate triumph? "Yours is a great country," Castro would tell Nixon when they met during his visit to Washington that April. "Your people, therefore, should be proud and confident and happy. But everyplace I go you seem afraid." Another bestseller in America that spring supported his observation. Titled *What We Must Know about Communism*, the book was a scarifying survey of the Communists' growing reach and ambition. "We have written this book because we had to," the authors Harry and Bonaro Overstreet declared in the book's introduction. "There comes a point when the world's peril turns into every individual's responsibility."

What all of the fear meant, reasonable or not, was that the specter of a Communist country ninety miles from America was intolerable. The beautiful island nation that America had liberated from Spain and supported economically for decades simply could not be a vassal and beachhead of the international Communist conspiracy. And so the question had to be asked: *Dr. Castro, are you a Communist?*—and Dr. Castro gave the right answer: *No, I am not a Communist.*

AS IF TO drive home Americans' fears of nuclear-armed Communists, the afternoon of Castro's second full day in Washington, April 17, happened to coincide with a peculiar national rite of mid-twentieth-century America known as Operation Alert. The sixth annual drill organized by the Office of Civil and Defense Mobilization, Operation Alert, 1959, was meant to prepare Americans for nuclear attack. The drill postulated a bombardment by a fleet of enemy aircraft (presumably of Soviet origin) that had been spotted flying over northern Canada, heading for the United States. For a few hours that spring day, Americans were supposed to imagine they were under nuclear attack.

The first sign of the mock attack came at 11:30 A.M. in the East—10:30 in Chicago, 8:30 on the West Coast—when television and radio programming was replaced by urgent warnings broadcast on dedicated frequencies. At 12:30 P.M. Central Time, air raid sirens sounded a second warning in Chicago. Moments later, an imaginary ten-megaton hydrogen bomb landed at Sixty-third Street and Kedzie Avenue. According to the drill's specifications, 229,625 Chicagoans died instantly in the blast zone and another 622,284 were severely injured. Hundreds more make-believe bombs rained over the nation that afternoon. In New York City, where participation in Operation Alert was compulsory, lunchtime traffic came to a halt. Times Square cleared out and became a "sunlit wasteland," according to the *New York Times*, as New Yorkers sought shelter in subway stations and stores, restaurants and bars. "People ate and drank and looked at the empty streets from behind plate glass," the *Times* reported. IT WAS SO QUIET, wisecracked a *New York Daily News* headline, YOU COULD HEAR A BOMB DROP.

Washington, D.C., too, was targeted in Operation Alert, but no one there seemed to pay the drill any mind. As the capital went up in imaginary flames outside, Fidel Castro stood at a podium inside the ballroom of the Statler-Hilton Hotel, delivering his keynote address to the American Society of Newspaper Editors. "I have said very clearly that we are not Communists," he told the audience in full-throated English. "Our revolution is a humanistic one." Castro gave the editors a litany of reassurances bound to ring pleasantly in American ears. Though he would legally expropriate some privately owned lands, he did not intend to confiscate American property as part of his agrarian reform program, he informed them. Free elections were on the way. As for a free press, not to worry—he cherished it as "the first enemy of dictatorship." The editors had greeted Castro with tepid claps, but now, as he finished, they applauded enthusiastically.

CASTRO WENT ON to enjoy a few more hectic days in Washington. Grinning cheerfully and grappling gamely, if not always successfully, with the English language, he entertained rowdy guests at the Cuban embassy and dashed around town in a siren-blaring motorcade. Everywhere he went he attracted excitement and admiring glances. "He has such kind eyes," one woman observed of him. "Doesn't he remind you of a younger Jimmy Stewart?" asked another. He stopped at a school playground to play peekaboo with small children. He signed autographs and lurched irrepressibly toward any friendly mob and its potentially homicidal embrace. On Saturday evening he gave his already agitated security detail the slip and went out for a midnight snack of Chinese food. "Go get me a tent," an exasperated agent of the State Department's security force was overheard muttering under his breath. "I got everything else for this circus."

On a drizzly April 19, following visits to Mount Vernon and the Lincoln and Jefferson memorials, Castro returned to Capitol Hill to meet Richard Nixon. The vice president escorted Castro through the Capitol, quiet on this Sunday afternoon, to his office. For two and a half hours, Castro and Nixon spoke. The meeting was private, but six days later Nixon sent a classified memorandum about it to the president and several other members of the administration. This memorandum remains the best record of the meeting and a curious, possibly seminal, document in the history of the Bay of Pigs.

According to Nixon's memo, Castro arrived at the Capitol "somewhat nervous and tense," concerned he had performed poorly on *Meet the Press* earlier in the day. After reassuring his guest he'd done just fine, Nixon lost no time in lecturing Castro about the value of free elections, habeas corpus, and other fine points of democracy. "I frankly doubt that I made too much impression upon him but he did listen and appeared to be somewhat receptive," wrote Nixon. The conversation turned, inevitably, to communism. Nixon had a long record as a Communist-buster, going back to his attacks on Alger Hiss in the 1940s, and was just the man to shake the red off a young rebel. As Nixon harangued Castro about the dangers of communism, Castro grew irritated—"This man has spent the whole time scolding me," he later told an aide—but remained polite, if not quite solicitous.

The Nixon-Castro meeting is intriguing not only for what transpired but also for Nixon's depiction of it later. In his 1962 book *Six Crises*, Nixon would describe his encounter with Castro as the turning point in his view of the Cuban leader. Quoting the memo he sent to Eisenhower, Nixon wrote that he "stated flatly that I was convinced Castro was 'either incredibly naïve about Communism or under Communist discipline' and that we would have to treat him and deal with him accordingly—under no further illusions. . . ." Nixon claimed that he at once became the administration's chief advocate for overturning Castro.

Actually, Nixon's original memorandum, which became public only twenty years after he wrote it, belies his own description of the document. Although Nixon did state in his memo that Castro was either "naïve" or "under Communist discipline," he also added that "my guess is the former" and that, overall, his impression was "somewhat mixed." Not exactly warm praise, but hardly a decisive call to arms. Richard

Nixon apparently shared the ambivalence held by most of official Washington toward Fidel Castro in April 1959. The only thing he knew for sure was that Castro possessed "those indefinable qualities which make him a leader of men" and that "we have no choice but at least to try to orient him in the right direction."

New York, April 1959

ON MONDAY, APRIL 20, Castro boarded a private rail car at Washington's Union Station and entrained up the eastern seaboard to Princeton, New Jersey, where he stopped to address a seminar of mostly adoring Princeton University students. The following morning, Castro's caravan sped down Route 206 to the Lawrenceville School, one of the nation's oldest and most prestigious boarding academies. Wearing a long, dark trench coat over his fatigues and clenching a cigar between his teeth, Castro entered the school's stone chapel to address six hundred boys in jackets and ties. The political philosophy of Fidel Castro was probably not on the curriculum most of the boys' parents envisioned when they sent their sons to Lawrenceville; nor was this ivy-clad chapel a natural habitat for the rebel of the Sierra Maestra. But the boys greeted Castro with "thunderous applause," according to the school newspaper, and Castro, for his part, said nothing to offend. "I feel something sad of not knowing well the English to express my emotion," he told the boys apologetically. "I cannot speak long here for two reasons. One, because the train is waiting and I have a large program and here in the United States somebody have taught me to be punctual. Second, because my English this morning didn't woke up very clear."

It was in New York City that Fidel Castro took his circus to the zoo. The chaos began the moment he stepped out onto the concourse level of Pennsylvania Station on the afternoon of April 21. Twenty thousand screaming well-wishers packed the train station and spilled for blocks onto Seventh Avenue. A scrum of police tried to usher Castro quickly through the crowd, but he was not to be denied. "I must see the people!" he called out, breaking through the security perimeter to clutch hands and return embraces. It took half an hour to maneuver him through the crowd to his hotel, the Statler, directly across Seventh Avenue.

The next four days passed in a whirl of press conferences and lectures, of meetings and interviews, Castro beaming through most of it like a man on his second honeymoon. He visited Columbia University, toured

City Hall, rode to the top of the Empire State Building, and shook hands with Jackie Robinson. Wherever he went he was besieged by photographers and reporters. *Life* even caught him in his hotel one morning, tousled from sleep and wearing striped pajamas.

There were private moments, too. One of these occurred behind closed doors at the Statler, where Castro was interviewed by a CIA agent. The interview had been arranged by Castro's minister of finance, Rufo López-Fresquet, a politically moderate economist who hoped to prove that his boss was no Communist. "We shall bestow on him the fictitious name of 'Mr. Frank Bender,'" López-Fresquet later wrote of the CIA agent who came to visit Castro. The name was a giveaway. Frank Bender was the alias of a German-born CIA veteran named Gerry Droller. One American official had described Droller to López-Fresquet as "the highest authority of American intelligence on the Communists in Latin America." This rather overstated the case. Droller did work on the Latin America desk of the CIA, but an "authority" he was not. For one thing, he spoke no Spanish. His own colleagues at the CIA tended to dismiss him as a know-it-all who blew a lot of smoke—literally. He had a passion for cigars that rivaled Castro's.

Maybe it was the cigars that got to Droller's head. In any case, he came out of the three-hour meeting in a state of near intoxication. "Castro is not only not a Communist," he exclaimed to López-Fresquet, "but he is a strong anti-Communist fighter."

A year later, Gerry Droller, alias Frank Bender, would be working with a task force at the CIA to remove Fidel Castro from power and, if possible, eliminate him from the face of the Earth.

AMONG THE IRONIES attending Castro's 1959 trip to America were the great lengths to which U.S. federal security agents and local police went to keep him alive. No visitor to America had ever received such lavish protection. Few had ever disdained it so cavalierly. What had been true in Washington was doubly so in New York. From the moment Castro arrived late Tuesday morning, he was surrounded by concentric rings of federal agents, plainclothesmen, and uniformed police officers, all of whom he treated with a mix of bemusement and benign neglect. "The hell of it is you never know when, where or how he's going," a police officer told the *New York Post*. "He just decides every once in a while to go for a walk and talk to people."

The police stepped up their already extraordinary measures as the week progressed and threats on Castro's life proliferated. The most picturesque of the reported plots against him had five brothers traveling from Chicago in a black and white 1957 Chevrolet with Florida license plates. 5 HUNTED IN CASTRO DEATH PLOT, the *Post* blared on its front page on Thursday, April 23. The brothers were presumably seeking vengeance on behalf of organized crime. Plenty of people wanted Castro dead for political reasons, but for the mob it was strictly business: one of Castro's first acts as Cuba's leader had been to shut down the mob-run Havana casinos.

The five brothers were soon tracked to Philadelphia, where it turned out they were engaged not in a Castro death plot but in honest labor. No sooner was this threat resolved, however, than a new one surfaced: now two men were speeding east from Detroit in a "dirty gray" Cadillac with Michigan plates. As Port Authority police kept a close watch on incoming lanes of bridges and tunnels, enterprising journalists tracked down Meyer Lansky in Florida. The infamous mobster and former dean of the Havana mob was living in financial ruin, thanks largely to Castro. Lansky refused to speak to reporters, but his wife took the phone. "It's a lie," she said of a mob plot. "It's so ridiculous there is no answer." Another mobster with Havana ties, Joe "Doc" Stracher, was reached in Las Vegas. "What plot? I've got nothing to discuss," said Stracher. "Forget about it."

The drama came to a head on Friday, April 24. Castro was scheduled to give a speech in Central Park that evening, by far his largest venue yet. Police urged him to call it off in the interest of self-preservation and public safety, but Castro refused. Before the speech, Castro relaxed with an impromptu visit to the Bronx Zoo. As he and his entourage sauntered around the zoo, passing astonished mothers and gaping children, Castro seemed to enjoy himself immensely. He fed potatoes and carrots to the elephants. He offered sugar to a gorilla. He ate a hot dog and rode on a miniature electric railroad. And then, to the dismay of everyone present—especially those charged with keeping him alive—he leaped over a protective railing and reached his fingers through the cage to pat a Bengal tiger on the cheek. "This is like prison," said Castro, sympathizing with the tiger. "I have been to prison, too."

CASTRO WAS STILL at the zoo when crowds began to gather in Central Park. By four-thirty, the area in front of the band shell was thronged.

At six, police began to muster. The NYPD brought in nearly a thousand officers, including dozens on horseback. Lookouts were posted on Central Park West rooftops to watch for snipers. Powerful searchlights scanned the trees and "flickered over the scene like heat lightning," according to the *New York Times*, "turning the leaves pale violet and brilliant green and the trunks of the trees a luminous white."

Castro arrived at eight-thirty behind a motorcycle escort, stepping onto the band shell stage to cheers and shouts of "*Viva Castro!*" He addressed the crowd in Spanish for two hours under a fair night sky. Occasionally, a roving searchlight flashed over him and he shaded his eyes with a hand. He spoke of Cuba's aspirations and praised the United States for its understanding. Whatever hard feelings he'd had for his neighbor to the north seemed to have softened. As he had put it in English in a speech earlier that day to the National Press Club, he would return to Cuba with a "stronger faith" in the bond of friendship.

He was still speaking when a scuffle broke out behind the band shell. Two policemen had come upon a young man lurking on the slope back there. When they searched his belongings they found a bomb manufactured from a footlong section of a vacuum cleaner handle, filled with a mixture of sulfur and zinc. The young man told the police that he had come to the park "looking for excitement." Castro, unaware of the commotion behind him, went on talking for another fifteen minutes.

He left the city the next morning, just as he had arrived, by train and surrounded by thousands of people. "Thank God that's over," exhaled a cop as the train pulled away. The police were happy to see him go, but few could deny the visit had been a success. "He made it quite clear that neither he nor anyone of importance in his Government so far as he knew was Communist," concluded an editorial in the *New York Times*. "By the same token it seems obvious that Americans feel better about Castro than they did before."

Within months, the U.S. government, having just spent millions of dollars and employed thousands of men to protect Fidel Castro from harm, would be taking the first steps to remove him from power by whatever means necessary.

2

"Point of No Return"

Summer–Autumn 1959

Washington, D.C., July 1959

"DO YOU HAVE information respecting Communist infiltration in the Castro government?"

"Yes, sir."

"Is the Castro government infiltrated by Communists?"

"Yes, sir."

It was the middle of July, a warm and humid day in the swelter of a Washington summer. Major Pedro Díaz Lanz, the thirty-two-year-old former commander of Fidel Castro's air force, sat before a microphone in a U.S. Senate conference room, politely answering questions in halting English. Major Díaz Lanz had commenced his long journey to Washington in late June, fleeing Cuba in a small sailboat and washing up in Miami a few days later. Immediately summoned to Capitol Hill to appear before the Senate's subcommittee on internal security, he first testified in closed hearings, then, on July 14, in an open hearing. He told the senators hair-raising tales of Communist infiltration at the highest ranks of the Cuban military. Officials in the Castro regime were now affectionately calling one another "Comrade." The word "God" had been stricken from the Cuban constitution. Just three months had passed since Castro's visit to America, but already the senators' worst fears were apparently being realized inside Cuba.

The trouble had begun almost the moment Castro returned home from his trip to North America. On May 17, Cuba launched a sweeping program of agrarian reform that limited most landholders to fewer than a thousand acres and curtailed ownership by foreigners. None of the new measures were especially radical or surprising: Castro had been talking about such reform for years. Moreover, most Latin American experts, including some in the U.S. government, agreed that some type of land redistribution was necessary in Cuba if democracy was to take root. Still, many Americans greeted Castro's move as an ominous step on the road to socialism. Particularly anxious were American owners of sugar mills and cattle ranches in Cuba, some of these as large as half a million acres. Castro's government promised compensation in the form of long-term bonds, but landholders worried—correctly, it turned out—that Castro would expropriate their property without compensation. Then Díaz Lanz arrived in Washington to confirm the worst.

"Since Castro took over in Cuba are changes being made in the insignia on military equipment in Cuba?" asked J. G. Sourwine, counsel for the Senate subcommittee.

"Yes," responded the major.

"What changes?"

"A red star put on vehicles."

"A red star painted on military vehicles?"

"Yes."

"Do you know what those red stars mean?"

"It is a Communist insignia, sir."

A few days after Major Díaz Lanz's appearance in Washington, his charges were seemingly validated by a shake-up in Cuba's government. The country's figurehead president, Manuel Urrutia, had gone on Cuban television apparently intending to blast Díaz Lanz for his treasonous testimony. But before the interview was done, Urrutia was committing an impeachable offense of his own, admitting that Communists were, in fact, doing "irreparable harm" inside Cuba. Castro immediately began taking steps to throw Urrutia out of office. "I am not Communist, and neither is the revolutionary movement," Castro insisted. "But we do not have to say we are anti-Communists, just to curry favor with foreign governments." Castro replaced Urrutia with Osvaldo Dorticós, a known Communist sympathizer.

ONE OF THE puzzles of Fidel Castro's behavior during 1959 is why, after winning himself a store of American goodwill that spring, he seemed so determined to squander it that summer. Did he suffer a sudden change of heart? Had more radical members of his inner circle, notably Che Guevara and Raúl Castro, chided him for being too friendly to his American hosts and pushed him leftward upon his return to Cuba? Had he simply been bluffing when he said he wanted good relations with the United States and forswore communism?

Fidel himself favored the last version, at least in hindsight. He claimed that he had been a "convinced Marxist-Leninist" for a decade or so before his visit to the United States, and implied that he strategically made nice in April to gain time to lay the groundwork for his programs without U.S. interference—in other words, that it was all part of a premeditated master plan. The American ambassador to Cuba at the time, Philip Bonsal, for one, did not buy that. "Castro has delighted his followers by picturing himself as the crafty deceiver of people who deserve to be deceived," Bonsal later wrote. He tended to rewrite history to make himself appear more in command of his destiny than he really was. "He is not a thinker or a planner; such plotting as he does is in the narrow field of personalities," observed Bonsal. "He is rather the vehicle of a mysterious force that drives him on to his goal of personal power."

Despite his own retrospective claims, the truth appears to be that Fidel Castro was still in his protean pre-Communist phase when he came to America and was telling the truth when he denied Communist ties. His feelings for America were still inchoate, too. On the one hand, he seems to have genuinely wanted Americans to like him and took pleasure in their adulation. On the other hand, he harbored volumes of ill will toward the behemoth to the north.

Castro's conflicted feelings about the United States reflected those of his compatriots. While the two countries had a long and, in some respects, mutually beneficial history, the relationship was fraught with paternalistic expectations on the part of the Americans and simmering grievances on the part of the Cubans. These dated back to the Platt Amendment, a 1903 act of Congress guaranteeing the United States certain powers and rights over Cuba as a condition for withdrawing American troops after the Spanish-American War of 1898. The Platt Amendment had been rescinded in 1934, but few Cubans forgot it. Nor could they forget the continued presence of Guantánamo Bay Naval Base, an American holding at the eastern end of Cuba, another legacy of the Spanish-American War. The fact that Americans had for years controlled the country's economy added to an impression of U.S.

hegemony. Eighty percent of Cuban utilities, including the telephone company and the electric company, were owned by Americans prior to Castro, so every rate hike or service outage was a Yankee affront. Forty percent of the sugar industry was American-owned, and the United States accounted for the lion's share of the sugar market. This meant that Cuba lived by what the United States was willing to pay for sugar. No matter that the United States paid better than the international market price; the dependency rankled Cuban pride.

Adding insult to injury, some Americans treated Cuba as if it existed to satisfy their lowest cravings. Sweet rum drinks, teenage prostitutes, live sex shows, and gambling at the mob-run casinos in Havana were all on the menu in the 1950s for visiting Americans (who included, on at least one occasion, a young U.S. senator named John F. Kennedy). Cubans had admittedly benefited from American tourist dollars, but the Cuban who gained the most was Fulgencio Batista. This went to the real sin of America from the Cubans' point of view: its historical tendency to back and enrich corrupt dictators such as Batista or, before him, Gerardo Machado and Ramón Grau. Such men had made life miserable for average Cubans with their reigns of graft and terror. Batista himself had pocketed as much as $300 million at the same time that tens of thousands of his countrymen starved. Ruthless and shameless, Batista was America's man in Havana, and his sins became, in some measure, America's.

As Castro voiced his fellow Cubans' resentment toward the United States, he also came increasingly to appreciate its value to him. Those deep veins of rancor, properly mined, could yield political gold. The more successfully he could paint America as the enemy of Cuba, the easier to explain away the fact that the Cuban economy was failing, or that his government was unstable, or that he had more aptitude for making anti-American speeches than he did for actual governance. The American government, for its own reasons—fear of communism mainly, but also petulance and domestic politics—played right into his script, taking the part of Goliath against his David. The more vocally he accused America of acting the part of a bullying imperialist, the more America behaved like a bullying imperialist. In return, the more the Eisenhower administration fretted that Castro was leading Cuba into communism, the closer to communism he crept.

Might the Eisenhower administration have short-circuited the vicious cycle? Or did Eisenhower, in fact, accelerate it? The question of

"Who Lost Cuba?" was to be debated ad nauseam in the press over the next several years, with conservatives such as William F. Buckley Jr. of the *National Review* blaming liberals who had been taken in by Castro's deceptions (notably Herbert Matthews of the *New York Times*) as liberals chastised the Eisenhower administration for driving Castro into the arms of the Soviets.

Rufo López-Fresquet, the politically moderate finance minister who had traveled to America with Castro in April, took up the question in his memoir *My Fourteen Months with Castro*, written after he turned against Castro in 1960. In the long run, wrote López-Fresquet, productive relations between the U.S. government and Fidel Castro were never in the cards: "Nothing the U.S. could have done, not the highest degree of cooperation, understanding, or sympathy, could have caused Castro to remain a friend." Nonetheless, López-Fresquet pointed to several opportunities missed early in Castro's regime by the Eisenhower administration to court moderate elements of Cuban society—those Cubans who were happy to see Batista gone but not happy to see Cuba falling into Communist hands. "The policy of the U.S. should have been directed toward denying Castro the chance to present Americans as enemies of social, political, and economic progress in Cuba," wrote López-Fresquet. Referring back to Castro's 1959 visit to the United States, he singled out the "diplomatic discourtesy" Eisenhower had shown by refusing to meet Castro; a mere matter of protocol, perhaps, but one that alienated some of the same Cuban moderates the United States should have been courting. And it would have been useful if the United States had also taken the opportunity of Castro's visit to offer economic aid to Cuba, despite the fact that Castro conspicuously failed to ask for it. "If this had been done, Castro could not have later claimed that the U.S. did not wish to help the revolution."

In general, U.S. actions either pushed moderates to the left or left them out in the cold. The United States insisted Cuba immediately pay up, in cash, for example, for any American-owned lands expropriated in land reform measures, a demand both unrealistic and niggling, according to López-Fresquet, since everyone knew Cuba did not have the assets to do this. Worse was letting Major Díaz Lanz testify in front of Congress. This reeked of old-fashioned American high-handedness—"a direct interference in the domestic affairs of Cuba by an organ of the United States government" is how the American ambassador, Philip Bonsal, later characterized the Cuban perspective.

* * *

AS ANGER AND suspicion volleyed across the Florida Straits that summer, it fell to Ambassador Bonsal to play monkey in the middle. A dapper fifty-six-year-old Foreign Service veteran, Bonsal was in many ways a perfect fit for the assignment. Cuba was practically in his blood. His father, Stephen Bonsal, a newspaper correspondent for the *New York Herald*, had reported from the island during the Spanish-American War. Philip had grown up hearing stories of Cuban revolutionaries at the dinner table. Later, as a young man, Bonsal lived in Cuba for a time, first working in business for an American corporation, then returning on his first assignment for the State Department. He knew the island's history, and he understood how that history weighed on its relationship with the United States.

Bonsal also possessed the even-keeled, elastic temperament necessary for negotiating with Fidel Castro's government. While reasonably skeptical of Castro's intentions, he was willing to engage revolutionary ideals in a way that his conservative predecessor, Earl Smith, had never done. On the rainy February night he'd arrived in Havana to assume his assignment, Bonsal told a bearded emissary of Castro's regime that he admired the revolutionaries' bravery in overthrowing Batista. The comment was widely and favorably reported in the Cuban press. A few weeks later, when Bonsal sat down with Castro in person to discuss U.S.-Cuban relations, the good feelings appeared to be mutual. "I was encouraged to believe that we could establish a working relationship that would be advantageous to both our countries," he later wrote of the meeting.

Operating from his office in the six-story U.S. embassy near the Havana waterfront that summer, Bonsal pressed American concerns on Castro, at the same time reminding his colleagues in the State Department that while there were indeed Communists within the Castro government, there also remained many fervent anti-Communists. "I strongly recommend that for the present we continue policy of friendliness toward Castro and GOC [Government of Cuba]," he cabled to the State Department on July 7. "In many respects," he added on August 2, "it is the most hopeful regime Cuba has ever had."

If Castro was aware of Bonsal's efforts to defend him, he was in no hurry to express his gratitude. He let the summer pass without granting the American ambassador a single face-to-face meeting. Interestingly, one of Bonsal's more helpful contacts in Castro's government was Foreign Minister Raúl Roa. By the time the Bay of Pigs invasion occurred two years later, Roa would have evolved into an attack dog for Castro, but in this earlier incarnation Roa was an anti-Communist moderate who hoped to span the gulf between the United States and Cuba almost as fervently as Bonsal did. On the evening of September 3, 1959, Roa finally prevailed on Castro to meet Bonsal. Dining at Roa's Havana apartment, the three spoke for six hours, until 2:00 A.M. The Castro who showed up that evening was much the same man who had visited the United States in the spring—friendly, reasonable, almost contrite. Bonsal went back to the American embassy buoyed by renewed hopes for relations between the countries. "Castro's first reaction to my statement was that I was unduly pessimistic about [the] state [of] our relations," Bonsal cabled his State Department bosses the following morning. "Castro regrets some of his own statements against US government. . . . He stated that he likes and admires Americans, especially tourists for whom he is planning great things."

Havana, October 1959

CASTRO MAY NOT have meant everything he said to Bonsal over dinner, but he was plenty serious about attracting American tourists to Cuba. Six weeks after his dinner with Bonsal, he hosted his first major tourism convention, having convinced the American Society of Travel Agents (ASTA) to hold its annual meeting in Havana. He would show them the wonders of Cuba, and they, in turn, would generate dollars for the Cuban economy. Two thousand travel agents descended upon Havana that October. Ideally, the convention would be an occasion to find common ground between Cuban and American interests—to remind Americans of the charms of Cuba and to remind Cubans of the beneficence of Americans. But that is not how it turned out.

The crisis began on October 19, the opening day of the convention. That morning, at the starkly modern twenty-five-story Havana Hilton, Castro welcomed the travel agents to Cuba. He spoke enchantingly of his ambitious plans to open new beaches, build new roads and hotels, to make the Pearl of the Antilles "the best and most important tourist center in the world." Ambassador Bonsal, present in the audience at the Hilton, later recalled that Castro "appeared in the sunniest of moods, exuding cordiality toward his American guests and most eager to stimulate tourist traffic from the United States."

In retrospect, it seems likely that Castro was already stoked for an eruption by two developments that had occurred in the days preceding the convention. The first of these was his discovery, in mid-October, that the U.S. State Department had been interfering with his attempt to buy military jets from Great Britain. The Eisenhower administration had asked Britain to halt the sale, and Britain had complied. The press got hold of the story after a State Department official leaked it. When Castro found out, he was indignant.

The second development did not make the newspapers. This concerned a visit to Havana that October by a forty-six-year-old Russian who went by the name of Alexander Alexeyev. Though Alexeyev presented himself in public as a reporter for the Soviet news agency Tass, he was, in fact, a KGB officer representing the Soviet government on a "special mission" to Cuba. With his arrival in Havana in early October, and his late-night meeting with Castro in the wee hours of October 16, came the first significant contact between the government of Fidel Castro and the government of Nikita Khrushchev. Castro, already feeling vengeful toward America, was emboldened by the interest the Soviets took in him and his little country.

Castro's demeanor changed from hospitable to hostile on the afternoon of October 19. The proximate mood-changer was apparently a letter from Huber Matos, a high-ranking and much-heralded soldier who had fought with him in the revolution. Matos now served Castro as the military governor of Camaguey, a province in central Cuba. For weeks, Matos had been complaining privately about the growing presence of Communists in Cuba, especially in the army, which was under the command of Raúl Castro. In his letter, Matos told Castro that he was resigning his post so as not to become an "obstacle" to the revolution. Then, bravely, rashly, he admonished Castro for allowing Communists to flourish. "Now, Fidel, you are destroying your own work," wrote Matos. "You are burying the revolution."

In fact, by these words, Matos effectively buried himself. Two days later, on the morning of October 21, he was sitting with his wife in their home in Camaguey when a knock came at the door. The man on the other side was Camilo Cienfuegos, an old friend and fellow hero of the revolution. Chief of the Revolutionary Army, Cienfuegos had come to arrest him. Matos was flown to Havana at once to stand trial for treason.* News of his arrest spread alarm among both American officials and moderate Cubans. Castro may have had personal reasons for arresting Matos—he never took kindly to having his judgment questioned—but he was also, for the first time, explicitly equating anticommunism with treason.

Later that same Wednesday, in the evening, Fidel Castro was chatting with a group of travel agents on the lawn behind the Hotel Nacional, with clear views of the sea and the Havana skyline, when a World War II–era B-25 bomber suddenly appeared over the water, flying in low from the north. As Castro and the agents watched, the plane's bomb chute opened and out poured a blizzard of leaflets, fluttering down over the streets of Havana. People ran to grab the leaflets. A strongly worded condemnation of Fidel Castro and his brother Raúl, the leaflets were signed by Pedro Díaz Lanz—the same Pedro Díaz Lanz, formerly of the Cuban Air Force, who had testified before the Senate subcommittee in July, the same one who was now piloting the B-25 over Havana.

For half an hour, the B-25 passed over Havana before Díaz Lanz was finally driven off by antiaircraft fire. By the time the plane left, two Cubans were dead and dozens injured. The casualties were probably inflicted by shells of Castro's own batteries, but Castro insisted they were caused by "bombings" from the plane. Díaz Lanz's air drop was not just an act of propaganda. It was, charged Castro, an act of war.

Castro was outraged—or at least pretended to be. First came an impassioned four-hour televised speech on the night of October 22, lasting until 3:00 A.M. the next morning. A mass rally followed on October 26. After dramatically descending in a helicopter over a crowd of several hundred thousand people, Castro, gripping a rifle in one hand, mounted a platform in front of the Presidential Palace and launched into the most anti-American speech he had ever delivered. He compared the leaflet drop to Pearl Harbor—not the last time he would use the comparison—and insinuated that the United States was behind it, if not explicitly then at least complicitly. After all, the United States had knowingly permitted the plane to take off from its shores. "We give them a naval base here in our country and they give us war criminal bases with which to bom-

* Matos would serve twenty years in prison. Cienfuegos would meet his own hard fate several days after arresting Matos, when his plane vanished over the sea under mysterious and, some believe, suspicious circumstances. His remains were never found.

bard us." As Castro spoke, Cubans armed with placards and machetes marched on the U.S. embassy and the Havana Hilton, where travel agents were beating a hasty exit from the suddenly combustible city. Safe to say that none would be signing up clients for getaway packages to Cuba anytime soon.

The U.S. government—and Philip Bonsal, from inside the besieged embassy—tried to assure Castro that America had nothing to do with Díaz Lanz's flight. There were two hundred airfields in the state of Florida alone; how could the United States be responsible for every private plane that took off from these? Castro responded with his own rhetorical question: How could a nation that expected to protect itself from incoming Soviet missiles lack the wherewithal to patrol planes leaving its own shores?

By this point, discourse had dissolved into absurdity. Neither party was genuinely interested in understanding the other. Even Bonsal, for months the keeper of the common ground, knew the chance for reconciliation was lost. "Castro's performance of October 26," Bonsal later wrote, "spelled the end of my hope for rational relations between Cuba and the United States." Those late October days were, as the historian Theodore Draper would put it, the "real point of no return."

The realization was dismaying. And yet among the lessons of that October was the kernel of a solution to the problem of Fidel Castro. Not a pretty solution, to be sure, but a means, a method, that would allow America to return reason to Cuba and free that island from the clutches of Communists. As Major Díaz Lanz had demonstrated with his swashbuckling leaflet drop, there were Cuban exiles from Castro's regime, many residing in Florida, who despised communism, who pined for their old country, and who were ready and willing to risk their necks to oust Fidel. Some, like Díaz Lanz, had even been trained in the military as soldiers and pilots. It was so obvious, really. They were an army in waiting.

PART II

A PROGRAM OF COVERT ACTION

November 3, 1959–January 19, 1961

3

"It's a Secret"

November 1959–March 1960

Langley, Virginia, November 3, 1959

ON THE BRIGHT, crisp morning of November 3, 1959, President Eisenhower set out by limousine from the White House to the Virginia suburbs of the capital. His first stop after crossing the Potomac River was a boilerplate ribbon cutting to mark the opening of a new spur of the George Washington Memorial Parkway. Eisenhower made a few cursory remarks, cut the ribbon, and dipped back into his limousine. The motorcade then continued along the very stretch of empty parkway Eisenhower had just officially opened to traffic. The hills of Fairfax County blazed with the last patches of autumn color. Through the trees along the parkway the president could glimpse the blue green surface of the Potomac River where it swept fast and wide between the suburbs of Maryland and Virginia. Eisenhower was enjoying the culmination of one of his better years in office. His health, after a series of maladies in years past, had been robust. The American economy was healthy, too, and the president's popularity was higher in Gallup polls than it had been in years. But if Eisenhower had reason to feel content that autumn morning at the end of 1959, he nonetheless could hear the fly buzzing near the ointment. Its name was Fidel.

Castro had been in power ten months now, but Eisenhower was still not sure what to make of him. At a press conference on Wednesday morning, October 28, two days after Castro's inflammatory speech at the mass rally in Havana, Eisenhower had responded to a reporter's question about the Cuban leader—*"What do you suppose, sir, is eat-*

ing him?"—with bafflement, if not a touch of obtuseness. "[H]ere is a country that you would believe, on the basis of our history, would be one of our real friends," the president told the press corps, apparently unaware that anti-American sentiments had been simmering in Cuba for decades. "The whole history—first of our intervention in 1898, our making and helping set up Cuban independence . . . the trade concessions we have made and the very close relationships that have existed most of the time with them—would seem to make it a puzzling matter to figure out just exactly why the Cubans and the Cuban government would be so unhappy."

If Eisenhower did not understand the attitude of the Cubans regarding America, he was starting to clarify his own intentions regarding Fidel Castro. His patience had worn thin. Eisenhower was not a rash man, but he was not a waffler, either. He had been making weighty decisions for the better part of his adult life—decisions, as in his planning for the D-Day invasion of France in 1944, on which the very fate of Western civilization hung—and once he'd set his mind, he tended not to look back. Within days of Castro's eruption in Havana, and just ten months after Castro's victory over Batista, Eisenhower started to make decisions that would lead to the secret American operation to remove the Cuban leader from power.

The first of these decisions had come on October 31, when the president provisionally approved a draft of a new State Department policy on Cuba. "The Current Basic United States Policy Toward Cuba," as it was titled, marked a clear reorientation of the administration's approach to Castro. Drawn up by Roy Rubottom, the assistant secretary of state who had welcomed Castro at National Airport back in April, the new policy defined the United States' objective to "encourage and coalesce opposition to the Castro regime's present form" while avoiding "giving the impression of direct pressure or intervention." The general idea, Rubottom later explained, was "to support elements in Cuba opposed to the Castro Government while making Castro's downfall seem to be the result of his own mistakes." Articulating the policy was the job of the State Department. Putting it into practice, though, would be a job for the Central Intelligence Agency.

THE PRESIDENT'S MOTORCADE turned off at an interchange near Langley, Virginia, just ten miles from the White House but still largely rural in 1959. After following a curving lane and passing through a security checkpoint, the motorcade entered a wide clearing high on a bluff above the Potomac. The trees gave way to an enormous rutted construction site, acres of upturned dirt and earth-moving equipment. At the center of the site were the foundations of what was evidently going to be a very impressive building. Already rising from the nine-acre hole at the center of the site was a forest of concrete columns and beams, the framework of the building's first two floors. By the time the building was complete, six more floors would rise above these.

A crowd of five thousand, including legislators, local government officials, and journalists, were already gathered near the structure as the president arrived. Mixed into the crowd, indistinguishable from the other middle-age bureaucrats, were the top-ranking officers of the Central Intelligence Agency. Most of these men had driven out to Langley with their families that morning, their well-coiffed wives smiling under made-up faces, their scrubbed children happy to be released from school for the day. There was Charles Cabell, deputy director of the CIA, with his wife and two children. Robert Armory, deputy director for intelligence, had arrived with his wife and son. The deputy director for plans, Richard Bissell, came with his wife and two of their four children. Allen Dulles, director of the CIA, was there, too, of course, accompanied by his wife, Clover. All had come to lay the cornerstone for the new headquarters of the Central Intelligence Agency.

Even lacking the president's attendance, this would have made for an extraordinary gathering. The CIA was generally a clandestine outfit, where employees kept their jobs secret from neighbors, where budgets and expenses were sealed from Congress, where switchboard operators still answered phones by reciting the CIA's number rather than divulging the agency's name (so that, as one CIA official put it, "people will not know they are calling the CIA if they do not know they are calling the CIA"). Yet here was that same agency now publicly sharing the details of its new headquarters, opening its doors to the Washington press corps, providing facts and figures to anyone with a press badge.

The data were impressive. Upon completion, the building would contain a million square feet of office space, a thousand-seat cafeteria, a five-hundred-seat auditorium, and enough parking for three thousand automobiles. Even if this was just the tip of the CIA's iceberg—some reporters speculated that as many as thirty thousand people worked for the agency—it was a big tip, hinting at the breadth the CIA had attained over the previous decade.

The very fact that the building was being publicly unveiled said more about the CIA circa 1959 than did the building itself. Specifically, it spoke volumes about the complicated, even schizophrenic relationship in the United States between the principles of a free society and the existence of a federal agency devoted to secrecy. The CIA was engaged in what could be at times a murky and dangerous business. Disturbing hints occasionally emerged from its vaults. At the very moment the cornerstone ceremony was commencing on the bluff above the Potomac, for example, the body of a thirty-two-year-old CIA analyst named James Woodbury was floating lifelessly in the river below. A week earlier, Woodbury, recently returned to Washington from a two-year assignment in Germany, had committed suicide by throwing himself into the rapids at Great Falls, Virginia, a few miles upriver. The suicide, Woodbury's wife implied, had something to do with his work for the agency. "They wanted to put him in a psycho ward," she told reporters. Woodbury's battered body would be found by a fisherman, downriver of Langley, on November 7.

One of Allen Dulles's finer qualities as director of Central Intelligence was his facility for making you forget the body in the river. With his tweedy, avuncular manner, his white brush mustache, bushy white eyebrows, and twinkling blue eyes, he looked more like the proprietor of a candy shop than "America's master spy," as magazines liked to call him. But even those magazines portrayed him as a genial, decent sort of fellow. The press admired him, and his agency made good copy—and Dulles made sure of it. Pipe in hand, the director frequently invited reporters into his smoke-filled office to weave captivating stories of intrigue and patriotism, while showing off architectural drawings of the new building in Langley. The CIA, as rendered by Dulles, was not the antithesis of an open society, but its protector. The biblical epigraph he'd ordered engraved over the main entrance of the new headquarters said it all: *The Truth Shall Set You Free.* An odd slogan for an agency devoted to subterfuge, but Allen Dulles meant it without irony. It was gospel.

> *As in this high hour we come with our fallible hands to lay the cornerstone of the noble structure which is here to rise as witness to Thy truth which makes men free . . .*

As the Reverend Frederick Brown Harris, the heavy-browed chaplain of the U.S. Senate, began his invocation, Dulles could look out over the mounds of dirt and steel columns and take pride in his efforts. He'd been working toward this occasion from the moment Eisenhower named him director of Central Intelligence in 1953. The CIA had been making do with a collection of poorly insulated, vermin-infested buildings scattered around Washington, from the headquarters in Foggy Bottom to Quarters Eye on the Mall, and including dozens of other nondescript government structures. Arguably, the dreariness of the CIA's offices suited an agency whose business was—on most days—to blend in. But as a matter of functionality as well as prestige, the arrangement was unsatisfactory. Dulles wanted a home worthy of his agency. He'd lobbied Congress for the funds—$65 million—then helped design the new building himself, including the office of the director on the seventh floor, complete with private dining room. He probably suspected he would never occupy the office himself. He was sixty-six years old, serving under a president soon entering his last year in the White House, and the building would not be habitable for many months to come. But Dulles would be here in name: *Allen Welsh Dulles*. There it was, engraved in the cornerstone that he and the president had come this morning to lay.

> *As we lay this stone conscious that others have put the torch of freedom and of human dignity in our hands, we pray for a new resolve now that the precious gains of Christian civilization are threatened by sinister forces without pity or conscience . . .*

If not Allen Dulles's crowning achievement, this building would be at least a suitable palace for the empire he had built under President Eisenhower. When complete, the Langley complex would be second in size only to the Pentagon among government agencies. And why should it not be? Over the course of its thirteen-year history, and especially during Dulles's seven years as director, the CIA had become every bit as essential to the defense of the United States as the Pentagon. Arguably, what it had to offer was more useful. This included, of course, the agency's intelligence-gathering unit, the Directorate of Intelligence. But even more significant was the CIA's dedication to covert action, represented by the Directorate of Plans.

In spite of our own shortcomings which we confess with contrition, in this hour of global crisis Thou has summoned us as trustees of Thy truth to defend our birthright . . .

The Directorate of Plans had flourished under Dulles and Eisenhower. The president had come to understand that the Cold War made overt operations—that is, U.S. military actions—fraught with risk. Once upon a time, it may have been enough to charge up San Juan Hill, as Theodore Roosevelt had done before he became president, or storm the beaches of Normandy, as General Eisenhower had ordered before he became president. But the Cold War demanded new and more subtle tactics: thus, the Directorate of Plans. For a mere fraction of the cost incurred by the Pentagon, the CIA could advance American interests without ever requiring the president to declare war, send U.S. troops into harm's way, chance the fragile nuclear peace, or, for that matter, put his own prestige on the line. That was the theory, anyway. So far, on available evidence, it had been proven mostly correct. As Dulles and Eisenhower stood there in the sunshine listening to the reverend's solemn utterances, they could count their shared successes. There had been Operation Ajax, in 1953, when CIA agent Kermit "Kim" Roosevelt (grandson of the Rough Rider himself) managed to overturn the government of Iranian prime minister Mohammad Mossadegh and replace him with the shah, a leader more to the administration's liking. A year later, the CIA had engaged in the much larger and more ambitious Operation Success to overthrow Jacobo Arbenz, the president of Guatemala suspected by the United States of Communist leanings. Time would prove that both Ajax and Success—not to mention covert operations in Syria, Hungary, Indonesia, and elsewhere—were more damaging than beneficial, but in the fall of 1959 they still looked like victories.

In this dear land of our love may we close our national ranks in a new unity, as principalities of darkness seek to destroy the precious things we hold nearest our hearts . . .

On droned the reverend, painting a world of light and shadow in which tribes of righteous Christians defended America against the godless onslaught. His theme closely mirrored the view both Allen Dulles and his late brother, John Foster Dulles, took of the Communist threat.

Descended from a long line of Presbyterian ministers, the Dulles brothers approached the Cold War with Manichean zeal. John had run the overt side of America's anti-Communist foreign policy as Eisenhower's secretary of state; Allen, as director of Central Intelligence, had handled the covert. John may have distinguished himself as the greater and more serious intellect of the two, but most people preferred Allen's livelier company. (It was of John whom Winston Churchill once joked, "That man makes a beautiful declension: 'Dull, Duller, Dulles.' ") Earlier in the decade, too, Allen had won admirers by standing up for his agents when Joe McCarthy came knocking on the CIA's door in search of Communists. For all his own deep revulsion for communism, Allen saw McCarthy as the witch-hunter he was and sent him packing. John Foster had not been half as stalwart in defending his men in the State Department.

All this was water under the bridge now. Five months before meeting to lay this cornerstone, Allen and the president had stood on another bluff over the Potomac River, downstream, at Arlington National Cemetery—a muggy late-spring day—to lay John to rest. Since then, friends and colleagues had noticed a change in Allen. He had become more distracted, more distant from daily operations at the agency. His wife, Clover, was encouraging him to step down, and he seemed ready to do so.

But not quite yet. First there was this building to complete. And, though he did not know it yet, there was one more big operation, the grandest ever conceived by the CIA, and the ultimate test of the organization Allen Dulles and President Eisenhower had cultivated over the past seven years.

> *In this titanic struggle of the ages may this building whose cornerstone we now lay with a prayer to the God Who hath made and preserved us a nation, be a cathedral of truth, an arsenal of freedom, an armory for battalions marshaled against deceit and falsehood . . .*

When it was his turn at the podium, Eisenhower spoke briefly and vaguely. He told the CIA men standing before him that the nation depended on their successes—even if these could never be measured in public. "In the work of intelligence, heroes are undecorated and unsung, often even among their own fraternity." Eisenhower and Dulles were handed silver trowels to spread the ceremonial first layer of mortar on the cornerstone. Before the stone was set in place, a copper box was placed under it. The box contained a time capsule from the year 1959.

"What's in it?" the president asked Dulles.

The director raised his bushy eyebrows and grinned.

"It's a secret."

4

"Program of Covert Action"

December 1959–March 1960

Washington, D.C., December 1959

THE CIA'S OPERATION to overthrow Fidel Castro was launched in fits and starts over the last weeks of 1959, between the Langley cornerstone ceremony and the Christmas holidays. There would later develop a myth that, as one history put it, the CIA "originated the plan to overthrow Castro and pushed it on the president." Actually, the CIA came relatively late to the conclusion that Castro had to go. The State Department had for months been laying a political foundation for Castro's ouster, arguing that his continued presence would have "serious adverse effects on the United States position in Latin America and corresponding advantages for International Communism." At the same time, the CIA's deputy director General Charles P. Cabell was testifying to Congress, on November 5, that while the profile of Communists had increased since Castro came to power, Castro himself was *not* a Communist. The following day, an internal CIA "Related Mission Directive" stipulated that "For the moment, CIA operations should be carried out on the assumption that the revolutionary government is basically non-Communist, with legitimate reform goals that deserve US respect and support." And as late as December 10, 1959, the CIA's intra-agency publication, *Current Intelligence Weekly Review*, conjectured that while Castro would probably continue to drift to the left, he was tolerating Communists rather than embracing them.

Just one day later, though—December 11, 1959—a remarkable top-secret memorandum landed on the desk of Allen Dulles at CIA headquarters. Drafted by the chief of the CIA's Western Hemisphere Division, J. C. King, the memo, for the first time, plainly laid out the case, and offered a prescription, for ridding the world of Fidel Castro. Ironically, King had a reputation within the agency for preferring slow-footed espionage to action-packed operations. But he also was a fierce anti-Communist who enjoyed long ties to American businessmen invested in Latin America. Many of his acquaintances worried that if Cuba were allowed to catch the Communist bug, it would spread throughout the region and billions of American dollars would be lost.

In his memo, King recommended "the overthrow of Castro within one year." As to means, King's memo offered two specific suggestions. First, that an anti-Castro group "establish by force" a beachhead within Cuba from which a new junta could be put in place. Second, that "thorough consideration be given to the elimination of Fidel Castro." The CIA frequently employed euphemisms when discussing the most unsavory aspects of its trade, but it did not take an agency-issued thesaurus to interpret King's meaning. He was suggesting that Fidel Castro be assassinated.

After reading the memo, Allen Dulles penciled out the word "elimination" and substituted "removal." Later in the memo, where King observed that "many informed people believe that the disappearance of Fidel would greatly accelerate the fall of the present government," Dulles again crossed out the loaded word—"disappearance"—and scratched in the more neutral "removal." For the moment, the assassination of Fidel Castro was put on the back burner.

Washington, D.C., January 1960

BECAUSE IT IS the nature of covert operators to cover their own tracks, what remains of the gestational phase of the plan to overthrow Fidel Castro is an incomplete paper trail. Some of the surviving documents are preserved in the whopping volumes of *Foreign Relations of the United States* (*FRUS*), the selected papers of the U.S. State Department. Others are tucked into internal histories of the CIA, or in postmortems, or in file boxes in the John F. Kennedy Library in Boston. They are like cairns in an ancient field: the path they marked may be long gone, but here it once ran. Taken together, they show an administration moving swiftly, if sometimes fitfully, to reorient itself from an attitude of regretful tolerance of Fidel Castro to angry resolve.

A partially declassified history of the Bay of Pigs, written in the 1970s by CIA historian Jack Pfeiffer, points to January 8, 1960, as the "beginning of the serious anti-Castro programs by the Central Intelligence Agency." Late that Friday morning, in a conference room at the Pentagon, General Cabell represented the CIA in a meeting that brought together leading State Department officials and the Joint Chiefs of Staff. Only two months had passed since Cabell assured Congress that Fidel Castro was not a Communist. Now he told a very different story. Communist ideology was increasing its hold on Castro's government, he told the group, and action was required.

Whatever subtle distinctions CIA analysts might still be drawing in the pages of *Intelligence Weekly*, the agency's official position was now clear: Castro had to go.

THAT SAME FRIDAY morning, in a regularly scheduled meeting at CIA headquarters on E Street, Allen Dulles instructed his deputy director for plans, Richard Bissell, to set up a task force to begin orchestrating an operation to overthrow Castro. Five days later, January 13, 1960, Dulles went to the Special Group of the National Security Council to request conditional approval to take covert action against Castro. The request was granted.

Appreciating the purpose and authority of the Special Group is essential to grasping the mechanics of covert activity during the Eisenhower administration. Sometimes known as Committee 5412, the Special Group had been created by Eisenhower in 1955 with a presidential directive (NSC-5412/2)—"one of the most secret documents in the U.S. government," Allen Dulles later described it. A subcommittee of the National Security Council, its members included the president's national security adviser, the assistant secretaries of state and defense, and the director of Central Intelligence. The explicit task of this group was to monitor and authorize covert actions. So it was the Special Group that gave Dulles approval to carry on with "covert contingency planning" against Castro on January 13. And it was the Special Group that would oversee much of the planning throughout the remainder of the Eisenhower administration.

The unstated but fundamental purpose of the Special Group was to provide a buffer of "plausible denial" between the president and covert actions. Politically and diplomatically it would have been unseemly, and potentially inflammatory, for the president to order coups, assassinations, and other mischief. The Special Group acted as his proxy. But in the end, its actions—its decisions, its approvals—were taken on behalf of the president, with his full knowledge and consent.

Eisenhower's popular image was—and remains—that of a benign and (so said his detractors) ineffectual chief executive who delegated responsibility and stayed out of the nitty-gritty of administration, escaping whenever possible to the golf links—one hand loosely clasping the tiller of state, the other clutching a nine iron. If this image suited his opponents' political aims, it also suited Eisenhower's. The old general understood that when the world seemed to be teetering on the brink of apocalypse, presidential calm, even presidential relaxation, was reassuring. But the image hid a more complicated truth. Enough evidence survives Ike's self-imposed veil of plausible denial to establish that he was thoroughly hands-on when it came to applying the force of the CIA. It was Eisenhower who ordered the overthrow of Mossadegh in Iran, of Arbenz in Guatemala, of Sukarno in Indonesia—and others. And there is little doubt Eisenhower fully participated in planning the overthrow of Fidel Castro. In fact, he was the prime mover.

A hint of Eisenhower's tendencies is found in a note his national security adviser, Gordon Gray, wrote regarding a meeting at the White House on January 11, 1960. Allen Dulles attended, along with Vice President Nixon and Secretary of the Treasury Robert Anderson. Dulles brought along "schematic drawings" to illustrate a CIA plan to sabotage some sugar refineries in Cuba, the sort of low-level harassment the CIA was generating in the early stages of its campaign against Castro. "At the conclusion of the presentation," Gray wrote, "the President said that he didn't object to such an undertaking and, indeed, thought something like this was timely." Eisenhower's only concern, wrote Gray, was that the plan was too timid: "he felt that any program should be much more ambitious, and it was probably now the time to move against Castro in a positive and aggressive way which went beyond pure harassment."

Eisenhower was not alone in urging the CIA to explore more ambitious plans. Vice President Richard Nixon likewise became an enthusiastic advocate for strong action as 1959 ran into 1960. He was no longer ambivalent about Castro, as he had been the previous April. Chairing an NSC meeting on December 16, 1959, Nixon opined that the United

States "needed to find a few dramatic things to do with respect to the Cuban situation in order to indicate that we would not allow ourselves to be kicked around completely." Nixon also began a dialogue with William D. Pawley, an American businessman with long ties to Cuba and a powerful antipathy for Castro. In early January 1960, Nixon assured Pawley he was in the middle of "intense discussions" with both governmental and nongovernmental parties regarding Castro's removal.

Nixon was acting in his role as vice president, of course, but he was also, by the start of 1960, an aspiring Republican candidate for president. A man possessed of acute political instincts, he understood that Castro was likely to be either a big problem or a big opportunity for him. When Senator John F. Kennedy took to the floor of the Senate caucus room on January 2, 1960, to announce his intention to seek the Democratic nomination for the presidency, Nixon knew at once that Kennedy would be the man to beat come November, and that his chances of beating him would depend in no small part on the future disposition of Fidel Castro.

Havana, Winter 1960

HOW STRANGELY THE future came to pass. For months, Castro had been predicting that the United States intended to invade his country. For months, American officials had been predicting that Castro was falling into the Communist embrace of the Soviet Union. At the moment each side began to suspect the worst of the other, its suspicions were ill-founded, even paranoid. That was no longer the case by the start of 1960. Each had transmogrified into the very demon the other had prematurely vilified. From this point forward, every step of the dance between the two governments seemed prechoreographed, a pas de deux swirling inexorably to the edge of a cliff.

Late that January of 1960, decrying "the stepped-up campaign of calumny against the United States Government by the Government of Cuba," the State Department led the dance a step closer to the edge by recalling Philip Bonsal to Washington. Bonsal hated to abandon his post in Havana, still hoping to somehow salvage relations between the nations, but Secretary Herter was adamant. It was necessary to send Castro a firm message—a shot across the bow—that the United States would not tolerate his obnoxious behavior any longer. Bonsal flew home to Washington on January 24. The following day, he visited Eisenhower in the Oval Office, where he found the president frustrated and snappish. Declaring that Castro had begun to look like a "madman," Eisenhower said he was considering a blockade of Cuba. "If the Cuban people are hungry, they will throw Castro out." Bonsal respectfully contended that the Cuban people did not deserve to be starved for Castro's sins. The president cooled down and agreed.

Bonsal's absence from Havana did nothing to bring Castro to his senses. On the contrary, it appeared to make him only more determined to thumb his nose at America. Castro got his chance to do so on February 4, when Anastas Mikoyan arrived in Havana from Moscow. A veteran of the Russian revolution and onetime Stalin henchman, Mikoyan was a first deputy premier in the Kremlin and one of the most powerful members of the Soviet Presidium. He came to Cuba officially to accompany a trade exhibition of Soviet culture and technology. Less publicly, he came to negotiate an alliance with Fidel Castro. Stepping off an Aeroflot jet with a box of Russian caviar, he might have been mistaken for a suitor courting the belle of the ball. The belle in question was all too willing to be wooed.

The Soviets were no more sure of Castro's motives than the Americans at the time. They puzzled over his politics and his personality—was he a Communist? was he sane?—nearly as fretfully as their counterparts in the United States. But they also recognized the extraordinary strategic and propaganda value of an alliance with Cuba and believed that pursuing it was worth the risk. Castro was reluctant to submit to Soviet dominion—he did not want *anyone* telling him how to run his country—but he, too, saw the value of the alliance. The Soviets could offer the new regime what no other country could, both in material sustenance and, if it came to it, military protection. In return, Castro would allow Cuba to become a pawn in the Cold War. And a very well-positioned pawn the little island would be.

As far as the U.S. government knew, Mikoyan's arrival in Havana marked the first official state visit by a Soviet representative to Cuba. There had been the earlier undercover mission by Alexander Alexeyev, but Mikoyan represented a whole new level of interest from the Soviets. He had the authority to make promises. On February 13, Castro and Mikoyan signed a "trade agreement," in effect a hefty package of Soviet aid to Cuba. The Soviets pledged to buy hundreds of thousands of tons of sugar from Cuba and granted a $100 million low-interest loan. Both Mikoyan and Castro made clear there was more of the same to follow, and the United States got the message. "Mikoyan's visit marks definite espousal of Castro regime by Soviet Union," read notes prepared for Allen Dulles's briefing to the National Security Council on February 18. "USSR has shifted from cautious attitude to one of active support." Though not entirely surprising, the revelation that the Soviets and the Cubans were now officially allied—the very alliance the United States had so greatly feared—landed as a bombshell that February.

Then, in early March, came the explosion—a real explosion. A French freighter, *La Coubre*, had steamed to Havana Harbor from Antwerp, carrying seventy-six tons of Belgian artillery shells, grenades, and small-arms ammunition for Castro's army. On the afternoon of March 4, just after 3:00 P.M., something, or somebody, ignited *La Coubre* and the ship went up in a series of blasts, sending lethal fragments of steel hurling across the harbor. Nearly a hundred people were killed outright; three hundred more were wounded. The following day, at the funeral for those killed in the explosion, Castro accused the United States of blowing up the ship as a pretext to invading his country, just as the United States—so he claimed—had blown up the *Maine* sixty-three years earlier as a pretext for entering the Spanish-American War. No evidence has ever been produced to prove that the United States blew up *La Coubre* (much less the *Maine*). Then again, there is no question the CIA was in the market for something "positive and aggressive," as President Eisenhower had put it, to rattle Fidel Castro and the Cuban people.

If the United States was behind the *Coubre* explosion, the violence of the act would have been matched only by its sheer stupidity. Castro had made abundantly clear by March 1960 that he was much like his friend the caged tiger. Antagonizing him only made him more dangerous.

Washington, D.C., March 1960

THE CIA SPENT the late winter of 1960 fetching about for suitable methods of removing Castro. Most of these relied on garden variety sanctions and sabotage, sticks and stones to weaken the government of Cuba by breaking the back of its economy. Some efforts, though, were aimed more pointedly at Castro himself. Two days before *La Coubre*, in a briefing to the vice president titled "What We Are Doing in Cuba," Allen Dulles told Nixon about a drug "which, if placed in Castro's food, would make him behave in such an irrational manner that a public appearance could have very damaging results to him." (Dulles did not specify the drug's pharmacology, but it is well established that the CIA experimented with LSD in the 1950s.)

If using a hallucinogenic food additive to oust a foreign leader sounded like something inspired by James Bond, that is because it may have been. Allen Dulles, like many other in-the-know Washingtonians at the time, was besotted with Ian Fleming's Bond series. He'd been a fan of 007 ever since the pretty young wife of the junior senator from Massachusetts handed him a copy of *From Russia with Love*. "Here is a book *you* should have, Mr. Director," said Jacqueline Kennedy. Dulles later shared a dinner with Fleming in London and became an avid fan. He made no secret of his envy for some of the tools the author invented for Bond. "I recall in particular one device," Dulles would write, "a special kind of homing radio outfit which Bond installed in cars his opponents were using and which permitted him, with an appropriate radar type of gadget, to follow the hostile car and home in on it from his own car even at many miles' distance." Dulles encouraged CIA technicians to create such a device, but their efforts never amounted to anything.

In mid-March, days before the CIA was to present President Eisenhower with a plan to oust Castro, Ian Fleming happened to visit Washington. The British author attended a dinner party at the Georgetown home of Jacqueline and John Kennedy on the evening of March 13. The guests were sipping brandy and coffee after dinner when Senator Kennedy (or, in another version of the anecdote, columnist Joseph Alsop) turned to Fleming and asked him what he would do to get rid of Castro. "Ridicule, chiefly," was Fleming's off-the-cuff advice. He suggested a few fanciful ploys. One was to drop leaflets over Havana warning residents that atomic tests had poisoned the Cuban air with radiation. Radiation was known to sap men's virility. Since radiation lingered in beards, and since Cuban men prized their virility above all else—according to Fleming—all the barbudos would hastily shave their facial hair, including the great Castro himself. Unmasked, shorn of mystique, Castro and the revolution would be effectively neutered and would sputter to a collapse.

The morning after the Kennedys' party, a CIA officer who had been a guest told Allen Dulles of Fleming's comments. Dulles was intrigued. He tried to get hold of the Bond author to solicit more serious advice. Or perhaps he thought Fleming's advice about the beards *was* serious. After all, it wasn't far beyond some of the anti-Castro solutions the CIA was already researching in its Technical Services Division, in addition to the hallucinogenic food additive. One of these was a depilatory powder that could be sprinkled into Castro's shoes and would cause his hair, beard and all, to fall out. In any case, Dulles was too late. Fleming had already left town.

At a meeting of the Special Group later that afternoon, March 14, Dulles made no mention of hallucinogens or depilatory powders, but the group did entertain assassination—*triple* assassination, in fact—to take out not only Castro but also the two men likely to replace him. As recorded by J. C. King, the man who had first raised the issue of assassination in his December 11 memo, the discussion turned to "What would be the effect on the Cuban scene if Fidel and Raúl Castro and Che Guevara [sic] should disappear simultaneously."

The formal plan to overthrow Castro, titled "A Program of Covert Action Against the Castro Regime," was presented to President Eisenhower in the Oval Office on the morning of March 17. The presentation was attended by more than a dozen top administration officials, including Vice President Nixon, Secretary of State Herter, and Admiral Arleigh Burke from the Joint Chiefs of Staff. Representing the CIA were Allen Dulles, Richard Bissell, and J. C. King. The president listened carefully, interrupting occasionally to ask questions, as Dulles laid out the general elements of the plan. Dulles deferred to Bissell to handle the more detailed questions. Neither man, so far as the record shows, said a word about drugs or powders or assassinations.

"The purpose of the program outlined herein," began the CIA brief, "is to bring about the replacement of the Castro regime with one more devoted to the interests of the Cuban people and more acceptable to the U.S. in such a manner as to avoid any appearance of U.S. intervention." To achieve this, the program called for the creation of four assets:

1. A political opposition group—"responsible, appealing, and unified"—of Cuban defectors who could plausibly take over from Castro.
2. Intensive anti-Castro propaganda to be broadcast into Cuba by a medium-wave radio station located outside of Cuba, mostly likely on the CIA-owned property of Swan Island in the Caribbean.
3. A covert force of anti-Castro Cubans that could gather intelligence and carry out missions inside Cuba.
4. An "adequate paramilitary force" that could be trained outside of Cuba and later deployed against Castro.

There was no mention at this stage of a large-scale invasion. Rather, the plan envisioned a small force, trained by the CIA in guerrilla tactics, that could surgically infiltrate Cuba, then serve as instructors for new recruits. But the important precept of using Cuban exiles to remove Castro, without ever revealing direct American involvement, was established.

The CIA estimated that the program would take six to eight months to put into action and require a budget of $4.4 million. Eisenhower agreed to it at once. His only condition, he told the men in the Oval Office, was that the operation remain covert. "The great problem is leakage and breach of security," the president said. "Everyone must be prepared to swear he has not heard of it."

Thus, with little fanfare and even less apparent foreknowledge, the American government launched the most ambitious covert operation in its history, one that would alter the course of the Cold War and the lives of a great many people involved. For some, the change would be for the better—Fidel Castro being the primary beneficiary—but more often, it would be for the worse. Among the latter cases fell Richard Bissell, the CIA's fifty-year-old deputy director for plans, for whom the Cuba operation would be the challenge of a lifetime—and the end of a very good ride.

5

"A Question of Propriety"

1954, 1960

RICHARD BISSELL DID not, in the beginning, promote the plan to overthrow Fidel Castro, nor did he ask to carry it out. But over time no man in American government would come to be more associated with the effort and its eventual failure. Afterward, Bissell's role as the plan's Dr. Frankenstein only grew in the telling, taking on more gothic tones with the passing years. He was "the deus ex machina" of the Bay of Pigs, one scholar would suggest after his death in 1998. Others called him worse: "ruthless," "deceitful," "contemptuous," "petulant," and "Ivy-Leaguer schemer" are a few of the choice words describing him in books. The portrait would no doubt have shocked Bissell, but applying his famously rational mind to it, he might have recognized it as a clearer reflection of late-twentieth- and early-twenty-first-century attitudes than of his own mid-twentieth-century self. A full understanding of the Bay of Pigs operation must include a fair description of Richard Bissell, who was, for better and for worse, a creature of his own time.

By most accounts, Richard Mervin Bissell Jr.—Dick to his colleagues, Dickie to his friends—was a remarkable man. Before Cuba came along and rerouted his life, he was the spymaster with the golden briefcase, regarded as brilliant by nearly all who knew him. And many very important people knew Richard Bissell. This was true both in the Eisenhower administration, when he began his CIA career, and later in the Kennedy administration, in which great things were expected of him. It wasn't just the Connecticut blue-blood upbringing, with summer sailing off the coast of Maine and annual excursions to Europe, that made him a natural fit in the CIA of the 1950s and the New Frontier of the 1960s. Nor was it the schooling at Groton and Yale, though such provenance certainly did not hurt among either crowd. Rather, it was the way his exceptional intellect combined with a bold predilection for *action*. As the tough-talking Kennedys would have put it—Bissell himself was too polite to use such language—he combined *brains* with *balls*.

That Bissell was something of a paradox was obvious even in his youth in Hartford, where his father worked as an insurance executive and where young Bissell lived in the large, gabled house Mark Twain had once called home.* Bissell was a physically awkward lad with crossed eyes (later corrected by surgery) whose idea of fun was reading railroad timetables and rate schedules from around the world, many of which he committed to memory.

His lifelong interest in railroads, sparked by his maternal grandfather—a railroad company president—betrayed a deep fascination for grand systems and complex logistics that appealed to his prodigious intellect. Had he chosen to continue pursuing an academic life at a university such as Yale or MIT, both of which had employed him as an instructor after he completed graduate work in economics at the London School of Economics and Yale, he would no doubt have enjoyed an illustrious career of abstract thought in the comforts of the ivory tower.

But Richard Bissell did not have the temperament for life in the academy. His rangy six-foot-four frame rebelled against quiet contemplation. Forever fidgeting, rolling his large hands over each other, torturing paper clips with his fingertips, pacing before office desks, or suddenly striding down office corridors as assistants trotted to keep up, Bissell was seldom still. Stillness and passivity were modes he abhorred. His sharpest rebuke for any man, his daughter Ann later recalled, was to call him "bovine."

Bissell himself chewed no cud. As his love of railroads suggested, he craved adventure along with intellectual challenge. All the better should the adventure involve risk. He'd gone out of his way to court physical danger as a young man. In college he made a nocturnal sport of climbing

* Now a museum, the house is where Twain wrote *Tom Sawyer* and *Huckleberry Finn*.

onto the lethally pitched rooftops of Yale's dormitories, crawling over the slippery slates like a cat burglar to appear unannounced at the windows of friends. He liked to climb rocks, too. On one occasion he nearly got himself killed in a fall from a cliff near New Haven. He lost his grip, plummeted thirty feet, then tumbled another forty feet, tearing his collarbone from his sternum.

The most telling fact about young Richard Bissell is that as soon as he healed, he returned to the same cliff and climbed it again, and this time reached the top. He accomplished what he intended with a tenacity that bordered on obstinacy. He liked to do things his way, which meant he often pressed his will upon others, albeit with his best aristocratic manners. "Dick was and is one of the truly remarkable people I have known," wrote the columnist Joseph Alsop, with whom Bissell attended Groton and remained friends for life, "but when he was young he was also one of the most domineering people I have ever known."

Bissell's confidence in his convictions made him formidable, but it was also, possibly, his greatest vulnerability. McGeorge Bundy, who had been a student of Bissell's at Yale and counted him as a friend, would write to Kennedy shortly before the Bay of Pigs, "if Dick has a fault, it is that he does not look at all sides of the question."

Following a stint teaching economics at Yale, during which his students included not only McGeorge Bundy but others who would go on to play prominent roles in the Kennedy administration—including McGeorge's brother, William Bundy, an undersecretary of defense, and Walt Rostow, the deputy national security adviser—Bissell joined the nation's effort in World War II. He worked for the War Shipping Administration in the unglorified but vital area of merchant shipping. His assignment was figuring out how to get war matériel where it needed to be when it needed to be there. It was work that suited his intellect, and he proved to be very adept at it.

His first real taste of administrative clout came after the war, when he joined the Economic Cooperation Administration. This was the agency responsible for implementing the Marshall Plan. Though relatively low in the hierarchy—his title was assistant deputy administrator—Bissell controlled the purse strings for the dollars used to rebuild postwar Europe, earning the sobriquet of "Mr. Marshall Plan." The Marshall Plan was seminal to Bissell's career not only because it made him, at a young age, a man to see in Washington, but also because it provided lessons in the deployment of power. The first lesson was practical: the men with true clout were not necessarily the cabinet-level figureheads who spent half their time getting hauled before Congress to testify. Rather, they were the well-placed functionaries with the ability to make things happen—which was, in the end, the only power that really mattered.

Lesson number two was more philosophical; it pertained to the morality and efficacy of American intervention, and it was one lesson Bissell and many of his midcentury compatriots never forgot. The Marshall Plan was the greatest act of peaceful intervention America, or any nation, had ever undertaken—"the most unsordid act in human history," Winston Churchill called it—and it opened Bissell's eyes to the possibilities, and the justification, for other kinds of American intervention. Bissell would draw little distinction between the intervention of the Marshall Plan, which sought to promote prosperity (and capitalism) throughout Western Europe, and the intervention of operations perpetrated by the CIA, which sought to quash communism through Eastern Europe and elsewhere. These were, as Bissell saw it, two sides of the same coin. "Some people argue that such intervention is benign," he said of the Marshall Plan, "but restoring law and order can be benign, too." This included circumstances when doing so might seem "distasteful." Bissell summed up his perspective in an interview a few years after the Bay of Pigs: "The question of propriety or impropriety comes down to this: 'Is it ever justifiable to intervene against a lawfully established government?' I think there are bound to be occasions when it is." Meddling in the affairs and sovereignty of other nations may have been at times "distasteful," but it was not, in Bissell's opinion, immoral. He was far from alone in believing this.

Bissell emerged from his work on the Marshall Plan as a power player in Washington. He and his wife, Annie Bissell, mixed with the most brilliant society the capital had to offer. They were part of the Georgetown Set, a group of well-bred, serious-minded, hard-partying writers, journalists, artists, State Department officials, and CIA men. The years of the Eisenhower administration are usually recalled as a sleepy, provincial time in Washington, particularly compared to the coming dazzle of Kennedy's Camelot, but for the Georgetown Set Washington after the war was glamorous and thrilling. The men were smart and ambitious, launched in interesting careers of great importance. The women were talented and in some cases as ambitious and talented as their husbands.* Together, they were intellectually enlivened by the emergent new conflict against the Communists. They tended to be fairly liberal on domestic issues and shared a revulsion for the petty viciousness of Joseph McCarthy—"the domestic enemy," Bissell called him—but when it came to international communism, they were uniformly unyielding. The fight against communism was a challenge as serious to them as the fight against Nazism. There were differences, of course, and one of them was that the Cold War could be waged from the comfort of offices and cocktail parties.

Bissell joined the Ford Foundation after the Marshall Plan but soon became restless there. The work was too academic, too theoretical—too dull. It was at about this time that Allen Dulles, recently appointed director of the CIA, began asking Bissell to do consulting work for the agency. Dulles had gotten to know Bissell socially, and he shared the opinion that Bissell was one of Washington's more able men. A happy relationship developed. For several years Bissell served Dulles as a sort of freelance adviser to the agency. With every assignment, he found himself more drawn into the realm of covert action, more convinced of its value. There was this, too: the work was fun.

Bissell's first real taste of the more "distasteful" form of American intervention came in the spring of 1954. He was still freelancing at the time, but at Dulles's urging he now immersed himself fully in the agency. He joined his old Groton classmate the veteran CIA officer Tracy Barnes on an all-consuming project: to coordinate the overthrow of Guatemala's president, Jacobo Arbenz, and replace him with a man more favorable to U.S. interests.

President Arbenz had been democratically elected in 1951 but recently had started to sound increasingly, alarmingly, like a Communist to the ears of the Eisenhower administration. Though he had little power of his own to harm the United States, Arbenz's flirtation with communism could not be countenanced—so the thinking went—or else Guatemala would become a beachhead for Soviet expansion in Latin America. Thus, with strong backing from President Eisenhower, and with no apparent appreciation of the irony involved in overthrowing a

* One talented young wife in the Georgetown Set was Julia Child, who met regularly with Annie Bissell to try out new creations, including, on one occasion, Child's twenty-six-page recipe for lobster.

democratically elected leader to promote democracy, the CIA moved to take Arbenz down.

As Tracy Barnes oversaw the propaganda side of the operation, Bissell drew upon his considerable logistical talents and ordered up a small rummage-sale air force to fly over Guatemala City and drop explosives. The bombs were mostly harmless—many were nothing more than empty Coca-Cola bottles that whistled when they fell and exploded with a jarring *pop* when they hit the ground—but in conjunction with the flame-fanning anti-Arbenz rhetoric CIA operatives were broadcasting over the local radio, they created waves of panic that soon caught up with Arbenz and washed him out of power at the end of June. The CIA's handpicked successor, Carlos Castillo Armas, was installed in his place. The whole operation had taken a few months. Allen Dulles beamed with pride, President Eisenhower offered his personal congratulations, and Richard Bissell was hooked.

In retrospect, Operation Success did more harm than good. Guatemala may have been saved from the evils of communism (such as they were), but the country would go on to suffer decades of political unrest, dictatorship, and civil war under a sequence of corrupt and inept governments. Short-term, though, the work was all Bissell could have desired. As an intellectual challenge, it was a high-stakes chess match, with a three-card Monte hustle on the side. As an exercise in power, it was a heady pageant. The CIA gave its men the opportunity—without the requirement of campaigning for elected office or rising through military ranks; without answering to Congress or the press or red-tape-entangled bureaucrats; without having, really, to justify themselves to anyone beyond their CIA superiors and the president—to lead armies and install governments, to create small air forces and devise wondrous chimeras, to break and make rules as needed, and to do all of this in the name of a cause they sincerely believed to be noble and just. For a man like Richard Bissell, there was simply no place better.

Along with the work, the society suited him. The top echelon of the agency was the last flowering of the East Coast WASP aristocracy from which Bissell hailed. These were men who had grown up with privilege and the noblesse oblige that called them to government service rather than more enriching careers in banking or law. They had family money but lived in ramshackle houses and drove old cars; they wore the best suits but owned just a few; they disdained country clubs but spent their summers in exclusive enclaves on the New England coast and knew their way around the best restaurants in Europe. They went to government offices and carried briefcases, but enjoyed lives that were more engaging, more intense, more remarkable—and riskier—than those of their fellow bureaucrats in gray flannel suits.

Late in the summer of 1954, shortly after the Guatemala operation had wrapped up, Bissell sat on his beloved fifty-four-foot sailboat, *The Sea Witch*, in Bar Harbor, Maine. He was preparing to embark on a well-earned summer voyage along the Maine coast. But first he stole a moment to write a letter to Allen Dulles. *"Yawl Sea Witch, Bar Harbor; Fri. Aug 6,"* he penned in the upper right-hand corner of the stationery. He began his letter by informing Dulles that the last thing he had done before leaving Washington was turn down a serious job offer from another agency. Then he gave Dulles the good news. "I will therefore be with you for some time at least. May I say that I look forward to the prospect with pleasure and hope there will be useful work to do."

A few days later, before embarking on his own summer sojourn, Dulles responded to Bissell, telling him that his letter was "the pleasantest bit of news that I have received to speed me on my way." Then Dulles added, "I sincerely hope you won't regret it."

BISSELL'S JOB WAS vaguely defined at first. He was Allen Dulles's "special assistant," a position that allowed him to graze over projects and get up to speed on the workings of the agency. Soon he landed on a project for which his talents were uniquely suited. He was the man at the CIA charged with the development of a top-secret high-altitude reconnaissance aircraft. This plane would come to be known as the U-2.

Bissell had no previous experience in building airplanes, but he was a quick study and immersed himself in the finer points of airframe construction, avionics, and camera optics. Working with the brilliant engineer Kelly Johnson at Lockheed Aircraft and Edwin Land of the Polaroid Corporation, Bissell oversaw the creation of an aircraft the likes of which had never existed. The U-2 combined a featherweight fuselage with an extremely wide wingspan—it was really more of a glider than a plane—that allowed it to fly in the thin atmosphere of seventy thousand feet, beyond the reach of Soviet missiles. From these great heights, the U-2's stunning new cameras could capture high-resolution images of the Earth and read the Soviet Union like an open book.

Almost as remarkable as the plane itself was the schedule under which

Bissell was able to get it produced. The air force, which originally tried to control the development of the U-2, had predicted a six-year timetable for its development. Bissell delivered the plane in fewer than twenty months—and $3 million under budget.

The plane's first flight over the Soviet Union, on July 4, 1956, marked one of the greatest leaps in the history of intelligence gathering. From seventy thousand feet, its cameras brought back photographs of extraordinary clarity. CIA analysts could make out the Winter Palace in Leningrad and the Kremlin in Moscow. They could count the number of automobiles on the streets. More important, as the U-2 began to fly regularly under Bissell's direction, the U.S. government could know the number of missiles the Soviets had deployed; where troops were moving; what sites were under construction; and, most important, whether they had any surprises up their sleeves.

One of the plane's early revelations was that the missile gap was a myth. The Soviets were not ahead of the Americans in missiles. They were, in fact, well behind. This was good news, of course, but because its source was a top-secret aircraft, the Eisenhower administration could not publicly share it.

Allen Dulles was already impressed with Bissell. The triumph of the U-2 convinced him that Bissell was the ablest man in the agency. At the end of 1958, he named Bissell his new deputy director for plans, replacing the legendary Frank Wisner—who had succumbed in his latter years to alcoholism and dementia—and passing over seasoned veterans such as Richard Helms. The job made Bissell the lord of the agency's underworld, overseer of a vast realm of fifty CIA stations and hundreds of active operations around the world. He stepped into his new role on January 1, 1959—the very same day, as it happened, that Fidel Castro became the new leader of Cuba.

Washington, D.C., Spring 1960

MARCH 1960: now fifteen months deep into their respective positions, Richard Bissell and Fidel Castro were both very busy men. Castro was charting a daring and risky new alliance with the Soviet Union. Richard Bissell was preparing to launch the most ambitious covert operation in the CIA's history—against Castro.

The year 1960 was a remarkable one in Richard Bissell's life. His power to make things happen in Washington—in the world—was at a high point. Though his name did not appear in the newspapers as often as Allen Dulles's or Charles Cabell's, Bissell's domain—the Directorate of Plans—was the heart of the CIA, the place, literally, where the action was. Dulles's focus had been drifting lately, winding down, and Bissell, in his prime at fifty, was heir apparent at the agency. General Cabell, the deputy director, technically outranked Bissell, but his role was somewhat ornamental—a touch of military spit and polish to impress Congress. Cabell was the guy they sent to the Hill to do the testifying; all the better, then, that he not know too much. Bissell spent little time before Congress, but lots of time with the president in off-the-record meetings. What happened in those meetings no one knew, but it was likely to be interesting. Many believed that next to President Eisenhower, Richard Bissell had more raw power—power to make things happen, power to change the shape of the world—than any man in Washington.

Socially, the Bissells moved among the city's elite. They entertained often, dinners mostly. "It was a very gay time," recalls their daughter Ann. Once or twice a month, the house filled with important men in black tie, attractive and smart women in long dresses, the sound of ice clinking in glasses, people laughing. "We would be attempting to go to sleep, and the noise would come up the stairs," said Ann Bissell. "We'd sit on the staircase and listen and watch. The men would smoke cigars, and the women would go off to a special room—it was very old-fashioned."

Sometimes the men would go off to a special room, too, and it was clear serious matters were being discussed behind closed doors. During one of the parties, Bissell's eldest son, Richard III, contrived with a friend—the son of columnist Stewart Alsop—to drop a microphone down the chimney from an upstairs fireplace and eavesdrop on the talk. They even managed to broadcast the signal, via walkie-talkie, to the Alsops' house. The KGB could have done no better. When the boys were discovered, the Alsops were mortified but Bissell laughed it off. "I think my father was just pleased with my brother's ingenuity," recalls Ann Bissell. "I don't think he was in the least upset."

Bissell's home was lively but held its share of burdens. The previous year, his first as DDP, he and his wife had made the heart-wrenching decision to commit their mentally disabled son, William, to residential treatment, resigned that they were no longer able to care for him properly at home. That same year, another son, Thomas, was born, bringing a squalling new infant into the house. Meanwhile, Bissell's all-consuming work was becoming even more demanding. As he continued to oversee the U-2 flights and other operations around the world, he now had to devote increasing attention to the "Program of Covert Action" to remove Fidel Castro.

BISSELL'S FIRST STEP in implementing the program was to staff an entirely new section of the agency, the so-called Cuba Task Force. On January 18, 1960, Bissell delivered to Dulles a table of organization for what would be known as Branch 4 of the Western Hemisphere Division, or simply WH/4. In time, WH/4 would have nearly six hundred noncombatants on its payroll, but it was born with a modest staff of just forty. Eighteen of these staffers would work out of Quarters Eye in Washington, with the remaining twenty-two operating covertly from within Cuba.

Bissell and his WH/4 colleagues intended to use the "Guatemala scenario" as a template. They apparently believed, in these early days, that overthrowing Fidel Castro would be not significantly more difficult than overthrowing Jacobo Arbenz had been, although at least one anonymous and undated memorandum that circulated in the CIA at the time compared the Cuba plan unfavorably to the Guatemala plan. The memo pointed to several key differences. The deposed Guatemalan leader had enjoyed little popular support, for example, whereas Castro was a hero to most Cubans. The memo also underscored the "unique coincidence of favorable factors" and "unbelievable luck" that had contributed to the Guatemalan operation. None of this, the memo presciently warned, could be taken for granted in the Cuban plan.

The men Bissell chose to help him run the operation were all veterans of the Guatemala venture. His right-hand man was to be Tracy Barnes, his old friend from Groton and Yale. Bissell and Barnes were an interesting and, in many ways, odd couple. Bissell was the more cerebral and reserved, Barnes the more charismatic and personable—the nattier dresser, but the sloppier thinker. At Groton, Barnes had been the better athlete and more social of the two, and higher in the pecking order. Now the tables had turned—Bissell was Barnes's boss—but both men were too polite to let this intrude on their friendship, and Bissell, in any case, still admired the social skills that had made Barnes so popular at Groton.

With his aristocratic good looks, his ready smile, and his urbane manner, Barnes was a world-class lubricator, which often came in handy when the CIA rubbed up against other government agencies. Bissell also respected the fact that Barnes, who began his career in intelligence during the war, had been at the agency longer than he had been. He often used him as a sounding board—perhaps too often, he later acknowledged. "I know fair and neutral colleagues who felt that he knew little more about tradecraft than I did," Bissell later wrote ruefully. "Some might argue that for me to rely on his judgment to support my views was to rely on ignorance to support ignorance." Everybody liked Tracy Barnes, but many of his fellow CIA men thought he was in the wrong line of work. "Like those who no matter how great their effort seemed doomed never to master a foreign language," Richard Helms later wrote, "Barnes proved unable to get the hang of secret operations."

Richard Helms should have played a role in the Cuba operation, given his position, but did not. Later, after the Bay of Pigs, Helms would take over from Bissell the job of deputy director for plans, and eventually would be named the CIA's director (from which position he would suffer his own fall from grace in the 1970s). But in 1960, Helms worked under Bissell as chief of clandestine operations—Bissell's number two—and was not happy about it. Allen Dulles had conspicuously passed over Helms to tap Bissell, a circumstance which led to a "cool relationship," according to Bissell. Their offices were just thirty-five feet apart, but the two men seldom talked if they could help it. Not only was Helms working under the man whose job he wanted, but also he fundamentally disapproved of Bissell's approach to the clandestine service. Helms preferred quiet espionage—spying—to the kind of big, dramatic operations Bissell and Barnes favored. Such productions looked to him like boyish antics. When Bissell talked about the Cuba operation in meetings, Helms listened carefully, studying his fingernails, but stayed quiet and steered clear.

One of those who would later come to wish he had steered clear was Jacob Esterline. Another Operation Success veteran, Esterline came into the Cuba venture as task force commander—the man who would run daily operations. He did not fit the usual profile of a CIA officer. A product of rural Pennsylvania and a graduate of Temple University, he lacked the Ivy League pedigree and polish of men such as Bissell and Barnes and Helms, and seldom minced his words for the sake of manners. If a bit rough around the edges, though, he was not uncultured. In earlier days he had trained to be an opera singer, and he still maintained a deeply resonant, albeit plainspoken, baritone. The start of 1960 had found Esterline serving as station chief in Caracas, Venezuela, a place for which he had no great affection. When headquarters called and invited him to lead the Cuba task force, he jumped at the chance, eager to participate in what he believed would be "a very simple little kind of an operation."

Another player reprising his role in Guatemala was David Atlee Phillips, a handsome thirty-seven-year-old former stage actor who spoke fluent Spanish. Phillips had been something of a dilettante before joining the CIA. In addition to acting, he'd tried his hand at newspaper publishing and public relations. His hidden talent turned out to be psychological warfare. During Operation Success, he had used radio broadcasts to create an illusion of great rebel hordes marching against Jacobo Arbenz. The real rebel army had been a few hundred poorly trained men who probably could have been turned away by a stiff breeze, but Arbenz fell for it. Following his work in Guatemala, Phillips had gone to live in Cuba. He was in Havana at the moment of Castro's victory. In fact, he was the first American to report Batista's hurried departure to the CIA station chief in the early hours of January 1, 1959, a scoop he owed not to diligent spy work but to a lawn chair with a view of the Havana sky. He was lying on the chair, sipping champagne after a New Year's Eve party, when he saw a large commercial airplane flying low over his house. Commercial air traffic did not fly out of Cuba at 4:00 A.M. Correctly surmising the plane held Batista and his fleeing cronies, Phillips shared his news.

Phillips reported to Quarters Eye in late March 1960 to take the job of director of propaganda for the Cuba operation. He quickly developed a plan to open a fifty-kilowatt medium-wave radio station to broadcast into Havana from the tiny, CIA-owned, guano-caked Swan Island, about ninety miles off the coast of Honduras. Plans also included funneling agency money into anti-Castro newspapers and leaflet campaigns. In April 1960, Phillips confidently told Bissell he could create "the proper psychological climate" within six months. Bissell told him to get Radio Swan up and running within a month.

Along with the military and propaganda challenges of overthrowing Castro came the problem of installing a new government to succeed him. There was no shortage of would-be leaders among the exiles who had already fled Castro's Cuba. As many as 184 different groups would arise from the exile community over the next year. The job of organizing a political body that represented some sort of consensus, and that could eventually be forwarded as a plausible government to replace Castro, went to two of the most colorful members of the team. The political affairs officer was to be Gerry Droller. Better known by his nom de guerre "Frank Bender," Droller was the same rumpled, German-born, cigar-chomping "Latin America expert" who had been smitten by Castro in New York in 1959. He was a figure who tended to produce amusement and irritation in many of his fellow officers by combining obtuseness with arrogance. He had been an odd choice to interview Castro, and he was an even odder fit for this new assignment. In the tart words of a CIA postmortem, his "linguistic accomplishments did not include Spanish." Nor did his personal accomplishments include much in the way of political acumen or even tact, an unfortunate deficit in a man charged with bringing together squabbling Cubans.

Working with Droller would be a political officer named E. Howard Hunt. A decade later, the name would become infamous, after Hunt masterminded—if that is the term—the Watergate break-in. But in 1960, Howard Hunt was still known mainly as an enthusiastic, imaginative, but somewhat flighty operative who had served in a number of stations in Latin America. In addition to his duties in the CIA, Hunt carried on a lucrative sideline as an adventure novelist. He had written dozens of James Bondish genre novels and film scripts, many with intrigues more plausible than his real-life plots. "Listen to his music," a fellow CIA officer warned David Phillips of Hunt's propensity for outlandish ideas, "but ignore his lyrics."

Whatever else you could say about the group of men Bissell gathered around him, they shared a notable flair for the performing arts. Hunt had demonstrated talent as a scriptwriter. Esterline was a trained singer, Phillips a trained actor. Droller did not perform, but he was descended—as his fellow CIA officers came to learn of him—from a long line of East European circus clowns.

Together, they probably could have put on a pretty good show. The production they had in mind, of course, was something quite different.

6

"The End Justified the Means"

May–August 1960

Washington, D.C., Spring 1960

THROUGHOUT THE SPRING of 1960, as the Cuba operation was gearing up, Richard Bissell continued to oversee his spy plane's reconnaissance flights. The U-2 had been flying for four years now, accumulating a trove of images and data about the Soviet Union. In early May, this extraordinary project suddenly came to a crashing halt. Though no one apparently made the connection at the time, the U-2 imbroglio of 1960 contained warning signs about the nature of covert activity, and the nature of Richard Bissell, pertinent to the still embryonic Cuba operation.

The U-2 flights over the USSR were ostensibly covert. In fact, though, the Soviets had been able to track the plane's incursions into their airspace from the start. They knew about the U-2, and the Americans knew they knew—and yet neither whispered a word. Within the peculiar rules of Cold War politics, it served both sides to carry on as if the spy plane did not exist. This way the Americans could plausibly deny any knowledge of the craft should the truth ever be made public. And the Soviets could avoid disclosing the embarrassing fact that their airspace was being routinely violated and they were unable to do anything about it.

The problem for the Americans in the spring of 1960 was that the Soviets were getting more determined to shoot the U-2 out of the sky and end this complicity. If and when the Soviets succeeded, they could reveal the truth of the U-2 on their own terms, as its slayer rather than its subject. Though Soviet fighter jets could not fly in the thin atmosphere of seventy thousand feet, they were creeping ever higher in pursuit of the U-2. Meanwhile, U.S. Air Force intelligence was picking up evidence that the Soviets were on the verge of deploying new surface-to-air missiles that could reach the altitude of the U-2.

President Eisenhower considered grounding the spy plane that April. He was preparing for a mid-May summit in Paris with Khrushchev and did not wish to provoke the Soviets. And yet the U-2's intelligence was extremely valuable and could very well come in handy at the summit; the better he knew what the Soviets were up to inside their borders, the stronger his position in negotiations. He found himself hung on the horns of a dilemma: to fly or not to fly. This is where Richard Bissell came in.

Bissell was famously persuasive. The "great expositor," McGeorge Bundy would call him during the Kennedy administration, high praise from a man who was no slouch himself when it came to briefing presidents. Bissell made a compelling case to President Eisenhower for continuing the flights. Soviet missiles were still inaccurate above sixty thousand feet and would almost certainly miss the plane. Even if the Soviets got lucky, the diplomatic damage would be limited. Neither the plane nor the pilot would survive a shootdown in a form easily identifiable as American. The paper-light plane would dissolve into scraps. And the pilot, assuming he managed to eject in time, would not be likely to survive a parachute jump from seventy thousand feet. In the unlikely event he did survive, he had been furnished a small poisoned pin. Pricking himself with the pin was not mandated, but it was an option the pilot was invited to consider.

Bissell's briefings during the U-2 incident pointed to a potential flaw in the great expositor. When he took on a project, he tended to see it as a personal crusade, advocating for it rather than advising impartially. Bissell "argued for weeks" and "pleaded" with Eisenhower to resume flights, according to one history of the affair. Bissell himself admitted that he pressed the president. Since presidents rely on their advisers to give them complete pictures, not just best-case scenarios, Bissell's tendency amounted to a kind of negligence. Then again, as Eisenhower biographer Stephen Ambrose has pointed out, Bissell was really just confirming what the president already believed. Sending the U-2 over the Soviet Union was ultimately Eisenhower's choice, not Bissell's.

Eisenhower agreed to let the flights continue. First, he approved a two-week window, from mid to late April, for the U-2 to overfly the Soviet Union. When clouds prevented a mission within that window, he agreed to extend the deadline by one week. On the last approved day—May 1, 1960—the clouds finally cleared. A pilot named Francis Gary Powers took off from Adana, Turkey, and flew over the Soviet Union. The first sign something had gone wrong came several hours later, when Powers failed to appear at the landing site in Norway.

For two days, the whereabouts of pilot and aircraft were unknown. Finally, on May 5, Khrushchev announced in a speech before the Supreme Soviet that missiles had shot down a U.S. spy plane. The United States did not deny that an American plane had gone down; rather, it trotted out a ready-to-go cover story that the downed plane was nothing more than a NASA weather craft that had strayed off course on a routine flight over Turkey. Two days later, on May 7, Khrushchev, clearly enjoying himself, revealed that he had not only the plane in his possession, but also rolls and rolls of high-altitude reconnaissance film that had been recovered from the plane—very odd for a weather craft, no? And one other thing: he had the pilot, an American, "quite alive and kicking." Francis Gary Powers had somehow survived the crash, as well as any urge to martyr himself with the poison pin.

The president's advisers tried to keep Eisenhower at arm's length from the U-2 embarrassment, hiding him behind the cloak of plausible denial. But this only begged the question: who, if not the president, had authorized American spy planes to fly over the Soviet Union? The president was either a scoundrel who stood behind a lie or a fool who was ignorant of the machinations of his own government.

There was no happy resolution. Khrushchev pulled out of the Paris summit. Eisenhower considered resigning. His government had run a secret operation, lied when the operation was revealed, and had then been caught in the lie. All of which, come the spring of 1961, would have a familiar ring to it.

Florida, Spring 1960

NOBODY IN THE spring of 1960 was anticipating comparisons between the U-2 crisis and the operation to overthrow Fidel Castro. Even as the former unfolded, the latter quickly gathered steam. Dulles and Bissell had promised Eisenhower they could have the necessary elements in place within six to eight months. This put them on a tight schedule.

The first challenge for the CIA was to organize the political opposition to Castro. This meant cobbling together an anti-Castro coalition from among the numerous and thorny branches of Cuban exiles and defectors who had been flooding into Florida since 1959. Some of these were former Batistinos fleeing Castro's vengeance. Others were once-wealthy Cubans whose property had been confiscated by the new government. Increasingly throughout 1960, the hunted and the dispossessed were joined by the disillusioned. This included former supporters and allies of Castro, some of whom had even fought alongside him and now found themselves repelled by his drift into communism and authoritarianism. All the exiles shared a conviction that Castro had to go, but beyond that their views had little in common.

CIA hands had a name for the task of joining the factions in a unified front: "putting in the plumbing." The term was an acknowledgment of the fact that until there was a viable political infrastructure, there could be no operation. The men chosen to lay the pipes, Gerry Droller and Howard Hunt—better known to Cubans by their aliases, "Frank Bender" and "Eduardo"—plunged into the rapidly growing neighborhoods of Cuban exiles in Miami, scouting for talent. Hunt also spent quite a bit of time among the community of Cuban exiles in Mexico City. The exceeding difficulty Droller and Hunt met in their efforts to identify potential leaders who did not outright despise one another or lean too far to the left or the right was a hint of greater difficulties to come.

The Cuban Revolutionary Front—Frente Revolucionario Democrático, as it was known in Spanish, or simply Frente—would serve as the body under whose auspices the coup against Castro was initiated. Frente was to be a "front" in the political sense, as a unified opposition, but also in the covert sense, as a facade for the CIA. The agency would operate behind the scenes, paying the bills and pulling the strings, as Frente drummed up Cuban support and pretended to lead a legitimate homegrown rebellion.

The political and personal bickering among the Cubans was reflected in the sniping between Droller and Hunt. Each man found the other ridiculous and incompetent, for good reason. Hunt charged around Florida and Mexico dispensing cash to Cubans—and, at one point, misplacing a briefcase of valuable secret documents. He reveled in the plotting and hush-hush but had no real aptitude for it. While staying in a house in Coconut Grove, he shuttled Cuban men in and out so indiscreetly that his next-door neighbors, a woman and her comely daughter, became convinced he was a promiscuous homosexual (but not before, Hunt hastened to add, the mother tried to set him up with the daughter). Droller, or rather "Bender," made frequent visits from Washington to stir up the pot, blowing cigar smoke and boasting that he "carried the counterrevolution around in his checkbook." Some of the Cubans were impressed with his brashness, others taken aback. Especially disconcerting was his habit of referring to himself—or rather, his pseudonymous self—in the third person, as in "Bender wants this done."

As for the operatives' cover story—that they were working for "a powerful company that wants to fight communism"—it fooled no one. The Cubans realized the men were from the CIA, or, as they took to calling the agency, the "Cuban Invasion Authority."

ALONG WITH SETTING up the political front, the CIA began recruiting the military personnel who would do the actual fighting. These few dozen early recruits would form the nucleus of the brigade. As plans stood in the spring and summer of 1960, they were to be placed in small paramilitary units that were to be discreetly infiltrated into Cuba. Preferably the recruits for these units had already obtained military training, either inside Cuba or (as was true in some cases) in the U.S. armed forces, but this was not a requirement. Many were former Havana University students, including young men who had participated in a Catholic underground group known as Agrupación Católica Universitaria.

Castro and his government would later belittle the men who served in the brigade as "mercenaries," as if they had joined up for a fistful of U.S. dollars. At the same time, invariably, they would be portrayed by Castro as the spoiled sons of the rich. In fact, the men of the brigade, at least in the form it ultimately took, represented a broad swath of the Cuban population. About 135 of them were former soldiers. Another 240 were students, the largest segment. But there were also farmers and fishermen, lawyers and doctors and certified public accountants, rich and poor, black and white. Evidently, these men were not representative of their fellow Cubans in one important respect: they left their homeland while their former compatriots stayed, then chose to return with guns. In some cases, their impulse to fight Castro was personal and vengeful, seeded in the bloody early days of the revolution, when friends were killed or vanished, or when the revolutionary government "expropriated" a family farm. Some chose to fight Castro for political ideals, sickened by his rapid descent into totalitarianism. Many of the Catholics who participated would later explain that it was their faith that roused them to stand against a leader who was carrying the nation into godless communism. This was, for them, a religious war.

Naturally, the early recruits, much like the political leaders meant to represent them, did not always like or trust one another. The students tended to suspect the military men of being former Batista loyalists; the military men suspected the students of being closet Communists. Differences aside, they tended to be highly motivated. From their ranks would come future leaders of the brigade, such as Hugo Sueiro, a twenty-one-year-old who would command the brigade's Second Battalion, and José Pérez San Román—known as Pepe—a twenty-nine-year-old former captain in the Cuban Army who would lead the invasion into the Bay of Pigs the following spring.

Starting in late May 1960, in best cloak-and-dagger fashion, the recruits were whisked out of Miami in the middle of the night. Small convoys of sedans sped west across the quiet dark of central Florida to the Gulf Coast. Still under cover of night, they were ferried by powerboat to Useppa Island, a speck of beachy terrain where the CIA had taken over a golf resort. The recruits lived at Useppa for about a month, undergoing batteries of tests—lie detector tests, Rorschach inkblot tests, intelligence tests—to measure their trustworthiness and competence. Between tests, they were given military training by American instructors. The Americans taught them demolition and guerrilla warfare, radio operating and cryptography, and supplied them with M-1 carbines and Thompson submachine guns—all the while insisting that the U.S. government had nothing, *nothing*, to do with any of this. The largesse, said the Americans, came by way of a rich anti-Castro Cuban who wished to remain anonymous. None of the Cubans questioned the claim out loud, but none really believed it, either. Who was rich enough to take over an island and fund a revolution? The answer was obvious: the Americans.

WHAT THESE FEW dozen men probably could not have guessed as they ran through their drills and tests on Useppa is how truly committed the American government was already to their mission. Eisenhower's green light on March 17 had made the overthrow of Fidel Castro official U.S. policy. In time, the operation would receive, in addition to the considerable resources of the CIA, cooperation from the State Department, the Department of the Treasury, the Office of the Attorney General, the Immigration and Naturalization Service, the Federal Aviation Administration, and the U.S. Coast Guard. Most consistently, it would draw upon the resources and counsel of the Department of Defense.

As Pentagon generals would frequently insist later, they never owned the plan—it was run out of the CIA—but the plan could not have gone forward without the Pentagon's early and consistent cooperation. The army lent military camps and personnel. The air force donated surplus aircraft. The Marines provided several of the operation's key staffers. Even the National Guard would become deeply involved, providing the operation with American pilots.

No branch of the U.S. military played a larger role, start to finish, than the navy. The navy had the most at stake, as Guantánamo Bay Naval Base was at the eastern end of Cuba and made a potential target for Castro. The navy also had at its head Admiral Arleigh Burke, probably the most anti-Communist of the Joint Chiefs—no small superlative, given the competition. As a destroyer squadron commander, Burke had earned himself the sobriquet "31-Knot Burke" for his tendency to run his ships at boiler-bursting speed. He remained, at fifty-nine, a hard-charging, barrel-chested man, and he was gung-ho to see Castro's demise.

Burke later insisted that he and the other chiefs were brought late into the planning. In fact, the CIA kept him, especially, well apprised from the start. He had been present in the Oval Office on March 17, when Eisenhower approved the plan, then again on April 8, when Richard Bissell, accompanied by General Cabell, J. C. King, and Jake Esterline, crossed the river to the Pentagon and fully briefed the Joint Chiefs. None objected to what he heard, least of all Burke. According to the CIA history of the Bay of Pigs by Jack Pfeiffer, Burke "emerged as the principal 'hawk' " among the Joint Chiefs and offered to do whatever he could to help the CIA remove Castro.

Summer 1960

RELATIONS BETWEEN THE United States and Cuba continued to deteriorate over the summer of 1960, now following a familiar sequence of tit for tat. At the end of June, Soviet freighters loaded with Russian oil arrived in Cuba. Castro demanded that American oil companies on the island refine the oil, but after consulting with the Eisenhower administration, the companies—Esso and Texaco, among others—refused. Castro responded by nationalizing the oil companies' property in Cuba—that is, confiscating it and putting it in the hands of the Cuban government. The U.S. Congress retaliated on July 3 by drastically reducing the sugar quota, the amount of sugar the United States would import from Cuba. Castro, in turn, nationalized more U.S. property in Cuba. President Eisenhower further reduced sugar imports from Cuba. Without missing a beat, Castro brokered a deal to sell his sugar to the Soviet Union.

And so it went. Every move the United States made against Castro only pushed him deeper into the embrace of the Soviets while embittering the Cuban masses against the Yankees. A July 15 memorandum to Allen Dulles from Sherman Kent, the CIA's highly regarded chairman of the Board of National Estimates—the branch of the agency responsible for analyzing intelligence and publishing the authoritative *National Intelligence Estimate*—observed that recent events had only "strengthened Castro's hand in Cuba over the short term" and "given new life to Castro's strident anti-US campaign." Though moderate Cubans had been turning against the Castro regime in greater numbers, "Castro's popularity is still widespread and we see little likelihood of the emergence in the near future of an opposition Castro cannot control."

Sherman Kent saw the danger of punitive measures against Castro, but U.S. domestic politics virtually required these by the summer of 1960. Congress was calling for action, and the voices belonged not just to the usual right-wing suspects. Democrats, looking forward to a presidential election in the fall, were smacking the incumbents over the head with Castro. See how the Republicans took their eye off the ball? See how Eisenhower and Nixon had allowed a Communist weed to grow in America's backyard? The last thing Eisenhower and Nixon could do under the circumstances was appear soft on Castro. Nixon suspected, and polls confirmed, that American voters would not stand for it. By May 1960, 81 percent of Americans had developed an "unfavorable" view of Castro, according to Gallup (compared to just 38 percent in July 1959). Sixty percent described their feelings for the Cuban as "highly negative," a number that would climb through the summer of 1960, reaching 71 percent by August. Another Gallup poll, conducted in July 1960, found that 50 percent of Americans believed Castro would be gone within a year.

Meanwhile, Castro grew ever bolder in his alliance with the Soviets. The Kremlin was moving to support Cuba not just with trade agreements now, but also with arms—and Castro's arms were open to receive them. The Soviets would send small weapons to Cuba, free of charge, with the promise of greater tools, such as MiG fighter jets, to follow. Khrushchev, in a hostile mood after the U-2 shootdown, made his position explicit in a speech on July 9. "We shall do everything to support Cuba in her struggle," he told a meeting of schoolteachers in Moscow. Lest anyone miss the threat in the word *everything*, he advised the Americans "not to forget that, as shown at the latest tests, we have rockets which can land precisely in a preset square target 13,000 kilometers away."

"This, if you want," added Khrushchev, never one to waste subtlety on a threat, "is a warning to those who would like to solve international problems by force and not by reason."

Hyannis Port, Massachusetts, July 1960

JOHN F. KENNEDY was nominated as the Democratic candidate for president on July 13. "Communist influence has penetrated into Asia, it stands in the Middle East, and now festers some ninety miles off the coast of Florida," Kennedy told the Democratic delegates inside Los Angeles Memorial Coliseum. "The world has been close to war before, but no man, who's survived all previous threats to his existence, has taken into his mortal hands the power to exterminate his species seven times over."

The rising threat of communism would be the backbone theme of Kennedy's presidential campaign, one he would hit again and again over the next months. Though no doubt reflecting Kennedy's genuine concern, this also was a political calculation. Kennedy seemed to understand from the start that the only way to beat Richard Nixon was to outflank him as an anti-Communist hawk. It did not take a genius to figure this out in 1960, but it would require rare political skill to pull it off.

Ten days after Kennedy's nomination, on Saturday, July 23, Allen Dulles, accompanied by two aides carrying small hand cases, flew into Hyannis, Massachusetts, aboard a CIA-operated Aero Commander. Dulles came by order of the White House to deliver to Senator Kennedy a top-secret intelligence briefing. Presidential candidates had been entitled to these since 1952, when President Truman instructed the CIA to brief both the Republican candidate, Dwight Eisenhower, and the Democratic candidate, Adlai Stevenson. The goal was to ensure that whichever candidate won would have a good handle on national security issues before he took office.

Dulles arrived in Cape Cod on a perfect summer day in the middle of the pandemonium that had been building around John Kennedy since his nomination. The usually sleepy seaside village of Hyannis Port had been deluged by giddy, sunburned tourists who pressed against police barricades to get a glimpse of the candidate on his way into or out of the compound. Kennedy was now more than a candidate for president; he was a full-blown celebrity, a deeply tanned sex symbol in Wayfarers.

Dulles, one younger brother of a famous fraternal duo, was met at the Hyannis airport by another, Robert Kennedy, who drove him through the summer crowds in a convertible. Accompanying the two men were a couple of freckled Kennedy children, as if the man coming to visit were a beloved uncle rather than the director of Central Intelligence. (The Kennedys, like Dulles, knew a bit about mixing the dark arts of statecraft with generous dollops of sunshine.) In fact, Dulles was no stranger to the Kennedy family. He and his wife, Clover, took frequent holidays in Palm Beach and had socialized with the Kennedys there. Though a Republican and Eisenhower loyalist, Dulles was never so partisan as to turn down a perfectly useful friendship with a promising young Democratic senator.

Today the men did no socializing; this visit was strictly business. The briefing lasted more than two hours. According to a memo Dulles later prepared for President Eisenhower, they roamed over the Cold War landscape, lighting on such trouble spots as Berlin and the Congo and, of course, Cuba. When it was over, Dulles and Kennedy came out onto the lawn to smile for photographs. "The United States is faced with a good many serious problems around the world," Kennedy told the press waiting on the lawn, "and we discussed them in some detail." Before heading off to nearby Cotuit for a weekend of tennis at a friend's house, Dulles downplayed the briefing: "I just told Kennedy what he could've read in the morning *Times*."

Exactly what Allen Dulles *did* tell John Kennedy that day on Cape Cod would later become an issue of great significance, at least in the mind of Richard Nixon. Indeed, Nixon would come to suspect that the Hyannis Port briefing—and specifically information Dulles gave Kennedy about the CIA's covert operation in Cuba—cost him the 1960 election.

Washington, D.C., Summer 1960

NIXON WAS STILL the front-runner in the race against Kennedy that July, but Cuba made him exceedingly anxious. The vice president wanted Castro gone before the November election. This would turn Castro from a liability into a victory, one Nixon could claim at least partly as his own. But here it was midsummer and little discernible progress had been made. "Are they falling dead over there?" he asked an aide about the CIA. "What in the world are they doing that takes months?" The vice president and his allies hoped the "Institute," as Nixon liked to call the CIA, would hurry things up. "How the hell are they coming?" he wondered aloud to aides.

"From the start of the 1960 campaign many of us were convinced that Cuba could be the deciding issue in a close election," Nixon's press secretary, Herbert G. Klein, would tell the *San Diego Union* in a 1962 interview. "For a long time, as we campaigned across the country, we held the hope that the training would go rapidly enough to permit the beach landing. The defeat of Castro would have been a powerful factor for Richard Nixon."

THERE'S NO EVIDENCE that Richard Nixon was ever so eager to get rid of Castro that he pushed the CIA to pursue assassination to speed him on his way. But somebody wanted Castro dead, and in the summer of 1960, the specter of assassination, first raised back in December by J. C. King, was revived within the CIA. It would remain a vital, if little recognized, element of the Cuba operation through the following spring and beyond.

Most histories of the CIA's assassination gambit, including the "Family Jewels" documents released by the CIA in 2007, state that Richard Bissell approached Sheffield Edwards, director of the CIA's Office of Security, in August 1960 to discuss methods of killing Castro; but according to Bissell's memoir (and his testimony before a presidential commission in 1975), Edwards approached *him*. More broadly, Bissell later claimed, he did not conceive the plan to kill Castro but simply signed off as a link in a chain of command—a chain that led up to Allen Dulles; the Special Group; and, almost certainly, the president. "It is true, however," Bissell acknowledged, "that when the plan was presented to me I supported it."

The plan was to hire the Mafia to kill Fidel Castro.

On the very face of it, the plan was mad. On second thought, it actually made a good deal of sense. That was before you realized that it really was mad.

The Mafia had an incentive to cooperate in a plan to kill Castro: vengeance against the man who had confiscated its lucrative Havana rackets. From the CIA's perspective, giving the job to the Mafia kept the agency's hands clean. Should the hit get traced back to organized crime, so much the better. It would hardly raise an eyebrow. And who would ever believe that the CIA was behind it? Some men other than Bissell—Richard Helms, for instance—would not have looked twice at such a scheme, but Bissell, peremptory as he could sometimes be, was a man who kept an open mind about such matters. If it could work, he was interested.

Sometime in August, the CIA's Office of Security initiated contacts with the Mafia by way of a middleman named Robert Maheu. A former FBI agent, Maheu lived in Las Vegas, where he worked for Howard Hughes, watching over the reclusive billionaire's assets and interests in that city. Maheu also was on a CIA retainer of $500 per month. Through his Las Vegas contacts, Maheu had inroads to the Mafia, and in late summer he met with mobster Johnny Rosselli at a bar, the Brown Derby, in Beverly Hills.

Rosselli was a fifty-five-year-old silver-maned, diamond-cuff-linked mobster known to friends as "Handsome Johnny." He handled the Las Vegas and Los Angeles ends of business for the Chicago mob, originally working under Al Capone, more recently under the syndicate boss Sam Giancana. Rosselli's career had been long and varied, mixing off-the-books work with semilegitimate enterprises. He'd produced a few movies, and was famous for having used his clout—and perhaps a few threats—to land his friend Frank Sinatra a role in *From Here to Eternity* (for which Sinatra won an Academy Award). Perhaps his most lucrative business—perfect for a man who loved diamonds—was Las Vegas ice. In the language of a government report, he "controlled all the ice-making machines on the Strip."

At the Brown Derby, Rosselli initially laughed at Maheu—"Me? You want *me* to get involved with Uncle Sam?"—but quickly warmed to the idea of a mob hit on Castro. A man thought by the FBI to be personally guilty of at least thirteen murders, Rosselli was not opposed to violence on principle, and in this case, Maheu told him, he'd be helping his country. This appealed to Rosselli. He may have had ice in his veins, but his blood ran red, white, and blue. He just needed some assurance this was on the level—not some phony setup by the feds. Maheu promised to introduce him to someone from the CIA who could confirm the deal's authenticity. Rosselli agreed to cooperate. And so began one of the stranger episodes in the history of the CIA.

Putting aside the Mafia for a moment, the broader question of using assassination to achieve foreign policy goals deserves serious attention, because it got plenty of serious attention in 1960. Indeed, assassination enjoyed quite a vogue at the time, when no fewer than three national leaders—Castro of Cuba, Patrice Lumumba of the Congo, and Rafael Trujillo of the Dominican Republic—were targeted for death by the CIA. The use of euphemisms for assassination, instead of "bad words," as Bissell called them, suggests an understanding that state-sponsored murder was a subject unfit for public discourse, yet it seems to have induced no real shame. "My philosophy during my last two or three years in the agency," Bissell wrote in his memoir, "was very definitely that the end justified the means, and I was not going to be held back."

Bissell's views must be judged in the context of 1960. Rather than some personal aberration in his character, they were shaped by his times. Bissell and his contemporaries were of a generation that had fought against Adolf Hitler—and what reasonable person would not have welcomed Hitler's assassination? They had experienced war as an all-or-nothing proposition. Indeed, if ever there had been an argument for ends justifying means, it was the Second World War—and it was the United States that had pursued the argument to its most horrifying conclusion. American planes firebombed German and Japanese cities and killed tens of thousands of civilians, literally burning and suffocating them to death. Dwight Eisenhower's predecessor, Harry Truman, approved the use of atomic bombs on two large Japanese cities, killing hundreds of thousands more civilians. Winning the war had trumped every other moral consideration. Next to Dresden and Hiroshima, what was the assassination of a single man in Havana, or even three, if it might prevent the menace of communism from threatening the homeland?

Among those who shared Bissell's view, unsurprisingly, was Dwight Eisenhower. Despite denials later issued by his supporters, there can be little doubt that Eisenhower approved the plan to assassinate Castro. No gun smokes in Ike's hand to link him directly to the Castro assassination plot, but there is evidence he had the stomach for this sort of thing. Enough evidence, for example, for a Senate committee in the 1970s to draw a "reasonable inference" that Eisenhower ordered the assassination of Patrice Lumumba, the prime minister of the Congo.* As for Castro, in a meeting on May 13, 1960, Eisenhower told advisers he wanted the Cuban prime minister "sawed off," an evocative choice of words.

According to Richard Bissell's testimony in a 1975 Senate hearing, Allen Dulles would never have told him that President Eisenhower had personally approved an assassination. He would have said something like, "this has been approved in the highest quarter." And, added Bissell, "I would have known what he meant."

"Eisenhower was a tough man behind that smile," Bissell wrote in his memoir.

Some historians and journalists believe that assassination was a critical component of Bissell's planning—the "lynchpin of the overthrow," as one historian recently put it. Bissell's task force chief, Jacob Esterline, who learned of the plan to assassinate Castro just before Kennedy's inauguration, later came to believe that the "magic bullet" worked against the invasion because it gave Bissell license to cut corners and pliantly accept restrictions placed on it by President Kennedy. "There's no question about it," Esterline told author Don Bohning in a 1997 interview. "If that whole specter of an assassination using the Mafia hadn't been on the horizon, there would have been more preparation."

Richard Bissell insisted on several occasions that he never intended assassination to be more than a corollary to the plan to overthrow Castro. "I do remember my own feeling that the Mafia plot had a very modest chance of success," he told CIA historian Jack Pfeiffer in a 1975 interview, "and that it was not something to be depended on in any way." Certainly it would have been foolhardy for Bissell to have placed a large bet on so unpredictable a wild card. Then again, it was pretty foolhardy to go along with such a foible-laden scheme in the first place.

In any case, assassination remained isolated from the efforts of WH/4. The task force devoted itself to overthrowing Castro by more conventional means of subterfuge.

---

* Lumumba would, in fact, be killed on January 17, 1961, three days before Kennedy took office. The United States was apparently not directly involved in his murder.

Guatemala, Summer 1960

IN EARLY JULY, the first recruits of the anti-Castro paramilitary arrived in a remote corner of southwestern Guatemala to continue their training. The CIA had cut a deal with Guatemala's president, Miguel Ydigoras Fuentes, the successor to the CIA-installed Carlos Castillo Armas (who had been killed in a coup). In exchange for unspecified favors, Ydigoras allowed the CIA to take over part of a large *finca*, or plantation, of a wealthy coffee grower named Roberto Alejos, brother of the Guatemalan ambassador to Washington. The finca was named Helvetia. It was spread across five thousand acres on the flanks of a volcano in the Sierra Madre, near the Pacific coast, and could be accessed only by a single rutted and winding dirt road. The CIA christened the place Base Trax and began moving in American trainers and Cuban recruits.

Following their stay on Useppa, the recruits, now numbering about 150, had trained for two months at a U.S. military base in the Panama Canal Zone. Then they were flown to Guatemala. Before they could resume training at Base Trax, they had to build it. They were put to work pouring cement foundations and hammering together the barracks, latrines, mess hall, chapel, and assorted other structures. Military drills in those early weeks waited until night, after construction hours.

Meanwhile, new men were entering the brigade's ranks every week. That summer, as Castro turned increasingly leftward, a flood of right-wing and, increasingly, centrist Cubans were defecting from the island in ever-greater numbers by boat and plane, an exodus of one hundred thousand émigrés by the end of 1960. Most ended up in Florida. Among them were men eager to join the effort to overthrow Castro. After signing up at the Frente office in Miami, the fresh recruits were given background checks and psychological tests similar to those the earlier recruits had received at Useppa. A few days or weeks later, the phone would ring and they would be mustered at an appointed hour at the Frente office. They would be issued uniforms and some equipment, then driven in darkness to Opa Locka air base to board an unmarked C-54 with darkened windows and piloted by men of vague East European background (Polish, in fact). Neither the pilots nor the Americans who ran the show ever said where they were going, but the duration of the flight—seven hours—suggested it was far from Florida. "Welcome to the Dominican Republic," somebody at the landing strip would inevitably greet them when they arrived—a joke, of course, as they soon discovered. They were in Retalhuleu, Guatemala, a small city in the lowlands, thirty miles from Helvetia. The CIA had built a $1.8 million landing strip in Retalhuleu to serve as home base to the brigade's little air force. For many of the men in the brigade, this was the first stop on the long journey that would eventually take them back to Cuba.

The men's second surprise, after realizing they were in Guatemala, was discovering how few others were there with them. In Miami, Frente officers gave recruits the impression that hordes of exiles were already at the camp. That turned out to be an exaggeration. "When I got there," recalled Máximo Cruz, who arrived in August, "I realized they did not have thousands of people. There were probably three or four hundred." Cruz was disappointed. "But I said, 'Well, I'm here.'" He would go on to distinguish himself as one of the most remarkable young men in the brigade.

Conditions at the camp were rustic and difficult. The men slept in the hastily constructed barracks. No showers had been installed yet, so bathing was done in the finca's swimming pool. The food was uniformly tasteless. Drinking water was in short supply when the weather was dry. When it rained—and sometimes it did nothing but rain—the volcanic soil under Base Trax turned to slop. Days were devoted to training, dawn till dusk. The men submitted to a grueling schedule of drills and lessons: firearms practice, radio operations technique, calisthenics. Often they took fast marches up the side of the volcano to the summit at seven thousand feet, where the air was perpetually misty and thin enough to leave them gasping for breath.

It was on one of these long marches that the brigade earned its name. Each man had been given a serial number upon his arrival. To fool possible Castro spies into thinking the brigade was larger than it was, the serial numbers began at 2500. On September 7, on a hike with his platoon, one of the earliest recruits, a well-liked young student named Carlos Rafael Santana, slipped off a rain-soaked escarpment and fell fatally into a ravine. The brigade honored his death, the first, by appropriating his serial number. They were now Brigade 2506.

7

"Shock Action"

Autumn 1960

New York, September 1960

SUDDENLY HE WAS BACK. On the stormy afternoon of September 18, 1960, Fidel Castro returned to America for the first time since April 1959. He came on short notice to attend the fifteenth session of the General Assembly at the United Nations. In the first moments after his arrival at New York's Idlewild (now Kennedy) International Airport, this visit bore a striking resemblance to the last. Castro stepped out of the Cubana Airlines Britannia and strolled down the ramp to the awaiting microphones. "My English, the same as last time, is not so good." He had perhaps aged a little, was a little thicker around the waist, but otherwise appeared much the same: still attired in his battle fatigues; still accompanied by his hirsute entourage; still running two hours behind schedule. Adoring crowds were there, too, cheering from behind barricades. Castro waved and clasped his hands over his head.

But there was little real joy this time around. Castro's smile, so quick to show in 1959, had to be coaxed out of him by the photographers on the tarmac. His vast American security detail, willing to humor his escapades seventeen months earlier, had turned grimly purposeful. The airport crowd was never given a chance to get closer than five hundred yards to the object of its affection, nor was Castro given a chance to get close to the crowd. When he tried to stop the motorcade to greet a flock of admirers along the route to Manhattan, policemen literally *pushed* his car to keep it moving. Castro later claimed that an "uncivil and violent" security agent shoved his arm back into the car as he attempted to wave through the open window. This was just one of many affronts that would cause him to describe New York to his fellow Cubans as "a city of persecution."

The persecution only intensified when Castro's motorcade rose from Queens Midtown Tunnel into the gauntlets of Manhattan. Fidel Castro, prime minister of one island, became de facto prisoner of another. By instruction of the State Department, he would not be permitted, "on security grounds," to leave Manhattan during his stay in the United States. No side trips to universities and boarding schools this time. No impromptu excursions to outer boroughs to pet caged tigers. Feeling perhaps like a caged animal himself, Castro sulked in his rooms at the Shelburne Hotel on Lexington Avenue and did not show himself for twenty-four hours.

Just as it was starting to look as if the pool of reporters assigned to cover the Cuban delegation would have to endure an entire news cycle without so much as a peep from Castro, he suddenly appeared in the Shelburne's lobby. The hotel's management was subjecting the Cubans to "unacceptable cash demands," he angrily told reporters—an up-front deposit of $10,000. Outraged by this de facto "eviction," Castro and his delegation were leaving the Shelburne at once for fairer pastures. They would camp out in Central Park if necessary. "We are a mountain people," Castro told reporters, yanking a hammock out of his pack. "We are used to sleeping in the open air." The Shelburne's management declared there had been a misunderstanding and asked the Cubans to return, but in truth the hotel was not sorry to see them go. Word spread that the Cubans left behind empty milk cartons on tabletops and cigar burns in the carpets. One room, number 806, was filled with chicken feathers. Apparently a member of the delegation—the Maximum Leader himself?—had plucked and boiled a chicken in the room.

They did not sleep in Central Park after all. Late on the night of their exodus from the Shelburne, Castro led his caravan to Harlem. The Cubans had managed to secure forty rooms in the three-hundred-room Hotel Theresa (or, as the partially burned-out neon sign had it, HOTEL THE——) on 125th Street and Seventh Avenue. Hundreds of Harlem locals, tipped off to Fidel Castro's arrival, were out on the streets to greet the Cubans as they pulled up to the hotel at 12:30 A.M. Castro looked genuinely happy for the first time since arriving in New York. After waving to the crowd, he repaired to an eighth-floor suite. The paint was peeling, the toilets were in disrepair, but where others saw squalor, Castro saw an opportunity to make new friends. That very night, he opened his door to leaders of the black community in Harlem, holding court until the wee hours of the morning. Among his visitors was a handsome and somber-looking young man described by the *New York Times* as "a leader of the so-called Muslim movement among United States Negroes who calls himself Malcolm X."

The following afternoon at the Theresa, Castro received a visitor who needed no introduction to readers of the *Times*: Nikita Khrushchev. Also in town for the General Assembly, the Soviet premier traveled to Harlem to pay his respects. The tall Cuban and the squat Ukrainian hugged like obedient son and doting, if somewhat captious, father. "He bent down and enveloped me with his whole body," Khrushchev later wrote. "While I'm fairly broad abeam, he wasn't so thin either, especially for his age."

Khrushchev found the Hotel Theresa oppressively shabby ("Except for Negroes, no one would live in a place like this"), but he liked what he saw of the not-so-thin Cuban. Following their twenty-minute meeting, he publicly hailed Castro as "a heroic man." Privately, he told aides he thought Castro would make a good Communist in the end, but was "like a young horse that hasn't been broken. He needs some training." At the United Nations a few hours later, Khrushchev made a point of finding Castro in his seat on the floor of the General Assembly hall. The men hugged for the second time that day. And then, as news photographers snapped and flashbulbs flashed, they hugged again and again, just in case anyone missed the shot.

A romance was blooming between Khrushchev and Castro inside the General Assembly, but there was little love in the city beyond. Opposing bands of Cubans armed with placards and baseball bats flung themselves at one another. Spontaneous egg fights broke out in front of Hotel Theresa. More seriously, on September 21, a gun battle erupted in an Eighth Avenue restaurant between pro-Castro and anti-Castro Cubans. A nine-year-old girl was hit in the back by a stray bullet and killed.

In Cuba, Raúl Castro and Che Guevara monitored reports from New York and grew agitated. Raúl, acting prime minister in his brother's absence, threatened to take over Guantánamo Bay Naval Base if Fidel were not treated more civilly in New York. Guevara publicly accused the United States of imprisoning Castro on Manhattan with the aim of assassinating him while they had him in their sights. Though Guevara had no specific information of an American plot, Castro's assassination was a serious concern among the Cubans even before Castro's departure for New York. Castro's mother had wept while bidding him farewell at the airport in Havana, certain she'd never see him alive again. "Ay! Don't worry, Old Woman," Castro admonished her. "I've taken worse trips than this, and nothing's happened to me yet."

He might not have been so insouciant had he known that just four days before his arrival, Robert Maheu, the man charged by the CIA with arranging his liquidation, had met again with Johnny Rosselli, this time at the Plaza Hotel in midtown Manhattan. Maheu had brought along a representative of the CIA's Special Service Division, James O'Connell. Maheu and O'Connell made a formal offer of $150,000 to Rosselli. The mobster told them he could not take the money. He was a patriot. He'd arrange the job gratis.

AS ROSSELLI WENT to work on Castro's assassination, the lovefest continued in New York. On September 23, Khrushchev spoke before the General Assembly for two and a half hours. Most members of the audience found the Soviet premier astoundingly dull, but Fidel, his pep restored by his stay at the Theresa, repeatedly jumped to his feet to applaud, Khrushchev's *número uno* fan. Khrushchev returned the compliment a few days later, September 26, when Castro took his turn at the rostrum. After promising to keep it short, Castro went on to deliver a four-and-a-half-hour speech, the longest in U.N. history. The speech was the usual litany of anti-U.S. slogans and charges of American aggression, peppered with newly inserted paeans to the Soviet Union. Khrushchev beamed with pride and applauded frequently. When Castro disparagingly referred to a comment that had been made by Admiral Arleigh Burke—that the Soviet Union would never be so foolish as to launch rockets at the United States to aid Cuba—Khrushchev raised his fist and gallantly shouted, "He is mistaken!"

Khrushchev aside, Castro's logorrhea put a large part of the General Assembly into a stupor. Twice, though, the audience was aroused when Frederick Boland, president of the General Assembly, brought down his gavel. Once Boland's gavel fell when Castro chastised Spain's president, Generalissimo Francisco Franco, a clear breach of U.N. protocol. The other whack was prompted by Castro's description of John F. Kennedy, the Democratic candidate for president, as an "illiterate and ignorant millionaire."

New York, October 1960

JOHN F. KENNEDY really could not have asked for a better endorsement. To be personally insulted by Fidel Castro was, in that political season of 1960, a kind of benediction. In fact, the whole timing and drama of the General Assembly—two weeks of Communist shenanigans six weeks before the national election—added up to great political fortune for John Kennedy.

Kennedy was campaigning in America's heartland as the General Assembly convened in New York. Richard Nixon had suggested that the candidates (i.e., Kennedy) lay off criticizing the Eisenhower administration's national security policies during the General Assembly, but Kennedy was having none of it. At every whistle-stop, from Nashville, Tennessee, to Sioux City, Iowa, he raised the subject of Fidel Castro early and often. How was it possible that the Republicans had lost Cuba and permitted "a Communist satellite ninety miles off the coast of the United States"? Kennedy asked the crowds. "Those who say they will stand up to Mr. Khrushchev," he jabbed, "have demonstrated no ability to stand up to Mr. Castro."

Kennedy's opinions of Fidel Castro had evolved dramatically over the previous year. As recently as the start of 1960, he had cheered Batista's ouster and scolded the Eisenhower administration, both in private and in public, for not giving Castro a better welcome during the Cuban leader's 1959 visit. "I don't know why we didn't embrace Castro when he was in this country in 1959," he told a friend. "Instead of that, we made an enemy of him, and then we get upset because the Russians are giving them money, doing for them what we wouldn't do." There would be no more such sentiments from Kennedy. He had undergone a change of heart. Perhaps more to the point, so had the American people. As Kennedy told his friend Senator George Smathers, "voters asked him more often about Cuba and Castro than any other foreign issue." He came back to the who-lost-Cuba theme relentlessly. The presence of Fidel Castro in the flesh in the General Assembly, insulting Americans daily—insulting Kennedy *personally*—only helped make his case. For a candidate with a few strikes against him—youth, inexperience, Catholicism, rumors of philandering, rumors of ill health—Castro was his ticket.

By another happy coincidence (for Kennedy), the same Monday evening that Castro stood at the dais in the General Assembly of the United Nations delivering (still) his speech, Kennedy and Richard Nixon met in a CBS television studio in Chicago for the first of their four debates—and the nation's first-ever presidential debate on live television. More than seventy million Americans tuned in for the historic event. Castro was not on-screen, but the drone of his voice was the background music for the candidates' performance.

The focus of this first debate was domestic policy, but the body language of the candidates added to an impression that Kennedy had the stuff to handle a fellow like Castro. He looked cool and composed next to a ghoulish Nixon, who was suffering from a knee infection and a bad case of five o'clock shadow. Given the mood of the country—and the newly prominent role of television—appearances mattered in the 1960 election. "The threat of nuclear war will probably continue the tendency in Presidential elections to vote for the man rather than the party," the managing editor of the Gallup poll wrote in anticipation of the election. "The voters will continue to want a man whose personality inspires their confidence and calms their fears."

The first Kennedy-Nixon debate is the one most frequently recalled by history, but there were three more to follow. In the second and third debates, Nixon acquitted himself well and even managed to get Kennedy on the ropes a few times. Then, on October 21, came the fourth and final debate, held in New York City.

In his classic profile of the 1960 election, *The Making of the President, 1960,* Theodore H. White dismissed this last debate as "the dreariest" of the four, since the candidates repeated a lot of what they'd said before. But it was this debate, and its heated exchange on Cuba, that may have mattered most in the end. This was the one Richard Nixon would come to rue—the one in which Nixon made what he later called "the most difficult and, as it turned out, the most costly decision of my political career."

The ground for the fourth debate had been laid over the previous several days, both in private meetings and public comments. Four days earlier, on October 17, Nixon, frustrated as he watched the Castro issue slip away from him, had urged President Eisenhower to "take some action with respect to Cuba at an early date" and proposed that "he be tied into the President's action in Cuba in some way." Time was short, with just a month to go before the election, and Nixon needed a boost.

Eisenhower agreed to arrange something. What Nixon really hoped for, of course, was a striking and definitive move, such as an attack, but it was getting late for that. Instead, on October 19, the State Department issued an embargo on most forms of trade with Cuba.

The following afternoon, October 20—now one day before the fourth debate—Nixon was preparing in a suite at the Waldorf-Astoria in New York City when the afternoon papers came out. He was stunned to see one of the headlines:

KENNEDY ADVOCATES U.S. INTERVENTION IN CUBA
CALLS FOR AID TO REBEL FORCES IN CUBA

The Kennedy campaign had released a statement ridiculing the Eisenhower administration's new trade embargo as "too little too late, a dramatic but almost empty gesture." The statement then went on to make a bold proposal: "We must attempt to strengthen the non-Batista democratic anti-Castro forces in exile, and in Cuba itself, who offer eventual hope of overthrowing Castro. Thus far these fighters for freedom have had virtually no support from our Government."

"I could hardly believe my eyes," Nixon wrote in his 1962 book *Six Crises.* Kennedy seemed to be advocating exactly what the Eisenhower administration was doing. A coincidence? Nixon thought not.

"Now the question was," Nixon wrote, "*did* John Kennedy know of the existence of the project?" Nixon was aware that Allen Dulles had briefed Kennedy about CIA matters back in July. He also knew there had been another impromptu briefing at Kennedy's home in Georgetown, on the morning of Monday, September 19. Had Dulles told Kennedy about the Cuba plans in either of these briefings?

Nixon summoned an aide, Fred Seaton, to his hotel room. He directed Seaton to call the White House on a secure telephone line and inquire whether the CIA briefings had touched on the subject of Cuba. The answer came back: they had. Nixon's blood boiled. "For the first and only time in the campaign, I got mad at Kennedy—personally." Furthermore, he added, "my rage was greater because I could do nothing about it."

As Nixon saw it, Kennedy was playing a cunning game of dirty pool. Knowing full well that the Eisenhower administration was already backing a covert operation in Cuba, since Dulles had told him so, Kennedy had the nerve to criticize the Eisenhower administration for *not* backing an operation—and thereby put Nixon in a bind. The vice president could not very well defend the administration—and himself—without publicly acknowledging that plans were, in fact, under way.

The fourth debate may have seemed a dreary rehash to Theodore White, but for Richard Nixon it was more like a bad dream. Among other mishaps, an unfortunate phrase popped out of his mouth while he was discussing the nation's need to move forward to meet new challenges. Nixon advised viewers that "America cannot stand pat"—not the choicest of phrases when "Pat" is the name of your wife. Whatever marital woes Nixon caused himself that night, they probably did not equal the damage he inflicted on his campaign in his bizarre exchange with Kennedy about Cuba.

It was Nixon who first raised the subject, and he did so near the start of the debate. He'd decided he needed to respond to Kennedy's statement of the previous day. In retrospect, one can imagine a number of possible responses Nixon might have given—or no response at all, which might have been the best tactic. As Nixon saw it, though, "I had only one choice: to protect the security of the program, I had to oppose Kennedy on his position of advocating that the United States openly aid anti-Castro forces inside and outside Cuba." Thus:

> I think that Senator Kennedy's policies and recommendations for the handling of the Castro regime are probably the most dangerously irresponsible recommendations that he's made during the course of this campaign. . . . I do know this: that if we were to follow that recommendation, that we would lose all of our friends in Latin America, we would probably be condemned in the United Nations, and we would not accomplish our objective. I know something else. It would be an open invitation for Mr. Khrushchev to come in, to come into Latin America and to engage us in what would be a civil war, and possibly even worse than that.

A sensitive, probing, and prophetic critique this may have been, but it was also precisely contrary to the policy Nixon had been supporting and encouraging for months. Nixon later acknowledged that the lie he told in the fourth debate—his "uncomfortable and ironic duty," as he put it—probably cost him the presidency in 1960, but he believed that lying was his moral and patriotic obligation. "The position was right from the standpoint of the country. It was wrong politically." Incredibly, Richard Nixon, a man who had made his reputation quashing Reds—who had been the self-appointed anti-Castro watchdog inside the White House—emerged from the debate looking softer on Fidel Castro than his Democratic opponent. And in "the closest presidential election in history," Nixon later mused, "our positions on the Cuban issue could well have been the decisive factor." He had allowed himself to be sandbagged. It was a mistake he'd never make again. "From this point on I had the wisdom and wariness of someone who had been burned by the Kennedys," he wrote. "I vowed that I would never again enter an election at a disadvantage by being vulnerable to them—or anyone—on the level of political tactics."

Richard Nixon learned his lesson all too well.

WAS NIXON RIGHT to suspect John Kennedy? Did Kennedy know about the Cuban operation before the election of 1960, then use the information to outwit Nixon? Both John Kennedy and Allen Dulles later claimed that the candidate was never given more than a vague picture of anti-Castro efforts in the July briefing in Hyannis Port or in the September briefing in Georgetown. The young campaign aide who wrote the statement that caused all the fuss, Richard Goodwin—later a key player in Kennedy's White House—insisted that he had been given no specific orders to draft the statement and that its recommendation to strengthen support to "fighters for freedom" had been drawn out of his own head, based on his intuition that this was the kind of thing Kennedy would say and Americans would like to hear. That term, "fighters for freedom," was of his own invention. He just liked the sound of it.

"There has been, I believe, an honest misunderstanding," Allen Dulles would write in 1962 in response to Nixon's charge that he divulged the plan to the Democratic candidate. "The Cuban situation was, of course, dealt with in the briefings I gave to Senator Kennedy," but these briefings "did not cover our own Government's plans or programs for action—overt or covert."

Dulles's statement notwithstanding, some historians and journalists who have studied the matter hold, with Nixon, that Kennedy was told plenty. The journalist and author Seymour M. Hersh, in his book *The Dark Side of Camelot*, insinuates that Allen Dulles, in the spirit of friendship and self-interest, *did* reveal the Cuban operation to Kennedy in

July. Dulles's reward for his intelligence, in Hersh's view, was reappointment as CIA chief under Kennedy. Hersh's chief evidence of Dulles's divulgence is that if Dulles had kept the "make or break information" about the invasion from Kennedy, there is no way Kennedy would have reappointed him. Reasoning backward, Dulles probably told Kennedy everything.*

This is a fairly specious line of thought, founded on the premise that Allen Dulles, a sixty-six-year-old Republican and longtime Eisenhower loyalist, sold out his own party, committed a breach of national security, then lied about it—repeatedly—to retain a job he was not sure he wanted to keep in the first place. Even if we suppose Dulles *had* wanted to help Kennedy, it is far from certain that telling him about the invasion would have been more to the candidate's advantage than not telling him. The syndicated columnist Ted Lewis, writing during the same 1962 dustup that produced Allen Dulles's response, made exactly this point. Taking Dulles at his word, Lewis described the CIA director's failure to mention the invasion to Kennedy in the briefing as "a phenomenally lucky break" for then candidate Kennedy. "If Dulles had informed Kennedy of what was going on, Kennedy, as the Presidential campaign reached a climax, would have been forced to soft-pedal the Cuban issue. . . . Instead, it was an issue Kennedy, out of ignorance, made one of his most effective."

But let us for a moment suppose, with Hersh, that Kennedy knew about the invasion. The next question becomes: what use did he make of his knowledge, other than to create political and moral turmoil for Richard Nixon? According to Hersh, Kennedy did much more than this. Knowing how damaging an invasion (a successful one) could be to the Democrats' hopes, "the Kennedy campaign had to find some way to stall the invasion." Hersh's implication, never stated directly nor substantiated, is that the candidate asked his friends at the CIA to delay the operation until after the election, and they agreed.

In the end, what is indisputable—whatever Kennedy's familiarity with the CIA plan—is that with every word the candidate uttered against the scourge of Fidel Castro, with every argument he made for the need to expel Castro from power, he was paving a road he would have to follow if and when he became president.

---

* For more on similar theories, see the notes for this chapter.

Havana/Base Trax, October 1960

FIDEL CASTRO BECAME convinced that his country was about to be invaded that fall. This was hardly a new concern, but as the season progressed, his suspicions were nourished by the increasingly strident rhetoric flung about in the American presidential campaign. He was also picking up signals from contacts in Central America. He knew that Cuban exiles had started training in the mountains near Retalhuleu, Guatemala, while others were being recruited in Miami. On October 27, 1960, six days after the final Kennedy-Nixon debate, concerned that Eisenhower might try to arrange a preelection surprise in Cuba, Castro put the Cuban military on high alert and posted sentries along the entire southern coast.

As in the past, Castro had misconstrued the threat he faced in the present—the United States was nowhere near mounting an attack—while uncannily foretelling the threat to come. Until the moment Castro put his nation on alert for a full-scale invasion in late October 1960, the CIA had been pressing forward with its program of training and infiltrating paramilitary units into Cuba. Within days of Castro's order, though, the CIA was transforming its operation into a full-blown amphibious invasion, much like the one for which Castro was already preparing.

The ground for the change had been laid back on August 18, when President Eisenhower approved a new budget of more than $13 million for the expansion of the Cuba program. By the fall, it was clear the CIA's original infiltration plan was a dud. Training had proceeded too slowly at Base Trax, but that was just part of the problem. The groups of in-country rebels into which the paramilitary trainees were supposed to be inserted—the Cuban underground, as it were—turned out to be sketchier than the CIA had anticipated. "The more we learned about active dissident groups," Richard Bissell recalled in a 1975 interview, "the more it appeared these were small, virtually powerless, primitive groups, the leadership of which, and the loyalty of which, were very difficult to ascertain." The already thin ranks of armed dissidents had been further culled by Castro, who knew a thing or two about choking off and destroying rebel bands, having led one of his own. When the CIA tried to put men onto the island by boat, Castro's troops had picked them up within a day or two. And when brigade pilots began flying air drops from Guatemala to Cuba to support anti-Castro rebels, the missions tended to fail, due either to pilot error or poor communication with the guerrillas. The first delivery, a pallet of arms and radio equipment missed its designated drop zone by seven miles.

Beyond these practical challenges, the larger problem with the guerrilla concept, Bissell had come to believe, was that it "would not produce a psychological effect sufficient to precipitate general uprisings or widespread revolt among disaffected elements of Castro's armed forces." To do that—to create the "shock action" that could rouse Castro's own minions to take up arms against him—they needed to think big.

Birmingham, October 1960

ONE OF THE earliest indications that Bissell and the CIA were looking to dramatically widen the scope of the operation came the October day that Major Harry "Heinie" Aderholt flew into the municipal airport at Birmingham, Alabama. A Birmingham native and a former Korean War USAF pilot, Aderholt was now working with the CIA. He came to pay a visit to the headquarters of the Alabama Air National Guard.

Aderholt was an old friend of the AANG commander, Brigadier General George Reid Doster, better known to his men as "Poppa." Aderholt came to Poppa Doster to make a request on behalf of the CIA. Would the general consider lending the services of his 117th Tactical Reconnaissance Wing to an operation to overthrow Fidel Castro? Among the reasons the CIA approached the AANG was the wing's familiarity with B-26 bombers; the AANG had been among the last Air Guard units to fly the vintage bombers, and that experience might come in handy. It didn't hurt that Doster was the sort of gung-ho, better-dead-than-Red military man likely to welcome such a project. "You're finally going after that commie son of a bitch," he boomed back to Aderholt. "Mister, you've got yourself an air force."

Sometime that October, a delegation of CIA officials flew to Nicaragua to meet with General Luis Somoza, that nation's dictator, to request use of the landing strip at Puerto Cabezas. Somoza happily consented. Now the air force had an air base.

CIA headquarters informed Base Trax of the change in a Halloween cable, then sent the finalized plan on November 4. Henceforth, according to the new orders, no more than sixty men would participate in infiltration teams. The focus now would shift to creating an "assault force" consisting of "one or more infantry battalions each having about 600 men." The object of the mission would no longer be to quietly enter

Cuba as guerrillas, but "to seize and defend lodgment in target by amphibious and airborne assault." In short, the operation to overthrow Castro had become an invasion.

Four days later, thanks in no small part to the man this plan was intended to overthrow, John F. Kennedy was elected president of the United States.

8

"No Easy Matters"

November 9, 1960–January 19, 1961

Palm Beach/Washington, D.C., November 1960

"ALLEN, I'D LIKE YOU to stay on as director of Central Intelligence when I take over next January twentieth."

On November 9, 1960, one day after narrowly beating Richard Nixon to become president, John Kennedy called Allen Dulles from Hyannis Port. Kennedy wanted to announce that Dulles, along with J. Edgar Hoover, director of the FBI, would remain in position in his administration. For Kennedy, this was a part of a "strategy of reassurance," as Arthur Schlesinger put it. Hoover and Dulles were both "national ikons." Both were also consummate Washington insiders, the kind of men who knew where the bodies were buried. For a president who had a few skeletons in his closet such men were best held close.

Dulles had just returned from vacation in Europe when he received Kennedy's call. He later claimed he was surprised by it. He'd assumed his tenure was up now that the Republicans were out. "Senator, I'm beyond retiring age," Dulles responded modestly. "There are a lot of young men in this shop that are coming along and a lot of able people. . . . But if you want me to stay on, I'll certainly stay on for a period . . . and then I think I probably ought to retire." They could discuss retirement later, Kennedy told him. The president-elect made the announcement at a news conference in Hyannis Port later that same day. Dulles told reporters he was "gratified."

Ten days after the election, on November 18, Allen Dulles paid a visit to Kennedy to deliver him another, and more complete, briefing on Cuba and other issues. By this time, Kennedy had moved from one of his father's seaside estates, in Hyannis Port, to another, in Palm Beach. Dulles brought Richard Bissell along to Florida to handle the finer points of the briefing. The CIA men arrived at the Kennedy estate just before nine-thirty that morning, carrying two large folders stuffed with maps. Kennedy had them ushered to an outdoor terrace, where they sat at a table by the swimming pool. Dulles spoke first, touching on various covert operations around the globe, but he soon turned the briefing over to Bissell and the subject most immediately at hand: Cuba.

Dulles, as mentioned, had been to the Kennedy home often, dropping by to socialize whenever he visited his friend Charles Wrightsman, who owned a house just down the beach from the Kennedy estate. It was here in Palm Beach that the soon-to-be First Lady had introduced him to James Bond novels. Now he was back for business, but the briefing, by the pool under the Florida sun, was "very relaxed," Dulles later recalled. "It was not the purpose of the briefing to ask the President's approval or disapproval of the program at this stage, but merely to acquaint him with the planning which was in progress," wrote Dulles. "November 18th was the first time that President-elect Kennedy had ever been briefed about the operation, (and) as far as I could tell, had never heard any details about it before."

This was also Richard Bissell's first opportunity to officially brief Kennedy. Bissell had voted for Kennedy and had met him a few times previously. He was pleased his man had been elected. A few days earlier, he'd written to a friend that Kennedy's victory would probably have "considerable influence" on his work, "but I have not the faintest idea what it will be." In any event, "I think Kennedy is surrounded by a group of men with a much livelier awareness than the Republicans of the extreme crisis we are living in. . . . My guess is that Washington will be a more lively and interesting place in which to live and work."

Using the maps spread on the poolside table, Bissell gave the president-elect a brief history of the operation as developed under Eisenhower, including its original conception as a small paramilitary infiltration. He informed Kennedy that the CIA, after determining that paramilitary action alone would not be "successful in sparking a successful revolt," was now putting together a "strike force" intended to act as a catalyst for Castro's overthrow.

The truth is that the operation Bissell described to Kennedy that day was still very much in flux. It was expanding rapidly. CIA staff for the operation, just 40 men the previous March, now included 308 dedicated positions. The number of invaders, 600 when Bissell addressed Kennedy, was growing all the time. Meanwhile, though, some members of the Eisenhower administration were questioning every detail and premise of the operation, including whether it should continue at all. A few weeks earlier, in a Special Group meeting, Gordon Gray, President Eisenhower's national security adviser, had wondered if a better alternative to the covert program might be to devise some sort of fake attack on Guantánamo Bay Naval Base, blame it on Castro, then use it as a pretext for invading Cuba, overtly, with U.S. military forces.

The role of overt military participation was a persistent variable in the Eisenhower administration's plans for Cuba, and would remain a matter of debate in the Kennedy administration. Indeed, it remains a matter of debate among historians today. Some find in the record indications that the CIA always expected the invasion to include a U.S. armed services component but failed to inform either Eisenhower or Kennedy of this expectation—that this was really the most secret aspect of their secret plan. A commonly cited proof of the CIA's intentions is an internal memorandum that came out of a mid-November CIA meeting just prior to, and in preparation for, Bissell's briefing to Kennedy in Palm Beach. Written by Richard Drain of WH/4, the memorandum is a pessimistic appraisal of the Cuba operation, not only in its originally conceived guerrilla version but also in its new life as an amphibious landing. The memo reads, in part:

> Our second concept (1,500–3,000 man force to secure a beach with airstrip) is also now seen to be unachievable, except as a joint Agency/DOD action. Our Guatemala experience demonstrates we cannot staff nor otherwise timely create the base and lift needed.

Jack Pfeiffer, the CIA historian who uncovered this memo in the 1970s, found it "strange and contradictory." Others, such as author Tim Weiner, cast it in a more nefarious light. Weiner interprets the memo as an admission at the highest levels of the CIA that "to overthrow Castro, the United States would have to send in the marines." Bissell, charges Weiner, "never breathed a word."

If Weiner is correct, Bissell and his colleagues at the CIA were guilty of stunning malfeasance and duplicity. They knew their covert operation was doomed as planned, that it could not possibly succeed without significant overt intervention, and yet went ahead anyway, either resigned to failure or assuming that when the time came, the president would do what was necessary and lend U.S. military firepower to the invasion.

This is an electrifying charge, but it needs to be taken with a grain of salt. For one thing, a single memo makes a flimsy foundation for an indictment. What about all the other memos and papers produced by the CIA before and after that assumed and asserted the invasion plan *could* succeed without overt help from the marines? Don't they need to be weighed, too? And does it make sense that the CIA, an agency known to jealously guard its turf, seriously intended to hand over the reins of an operation to the Pentagon? What would the fourteenth-century logician William of Occam have to say about this?

Occam's time-tested rule of thumb—popularly known as Occam's Razor—is that the simplest explanation is usually the best explanation. Applying Occam's Razor to Drain's memo, the most obvious interpretation is that its author was *not* suggesting the CIA would have to "send in the marines" when he referred to a joint agency/DOD action, but rather restating a long-established and widely shared opinion that the CIA needed personnel and logistical support from the Pentagon if the "strike force" operation was to succeed—the sort of "limited additional help from DOD" that Jacob Esterline, Drain's superior, called for in a report he filed later that fall. Support from the Pentagon had *always* been assumed, from the earliest days of the operation when navy Seabees helped the CIA prepare Swan Island. Now that the operation had become much bigger, it required a good deal more support. Richard Bissell and his WH/4 colleagues knew they did not have enough real estate on their Guatemalan mountain perch to train the growing brigade, for example, so they were looking for U.S. military bases to take up the slack. They also were looking for about 150 military trainers to quickly bring the brigade up to speed, and expecting the army to lend these from its Special Forces Division. Moreover, they knew they did not have the airpower to lift the men to Cuba or the manpower to do it in a timely manner. The CIA had always expected the Pentagon to come into the picture *after* the invasion to offer support to the brigade, and explicitly stated this expectation in its plans.

The memo may simply have been acknowledging the obvious: there was no way the CIA was going to be able to land hundreds of infantrymen on the shores of Cuba without a lot of help from its friends in the Pentagon.

THE NATURAL COROLLARY to the question of whether Allen Dulles and Richard Bissell knowingly misled the incoming president about the Cuban operation is whether they deliberately misled the outgoing president, too. Tim Weiner again makes a case against the CIA. He notes that President Eisenhower never approved any written plan for the Cuba operation after the March 17 "Program of Covert Action." The Program specifically called for small paramilitary units, not a word in it anticipating the kind of invasion the CIA was now planning. "Eisenhower had never approved an invasion of Cuba" is how Weiner puts it. "But Kennedy did not know that."

The implication is that Eisenhower went along believing the plan he'd approved in March was the plan the CIA was still pursuing in November—and that nobody ever disabused him. But that is far from the truth. Eisenhower knew very well that the plan had changed, and gave every indication that he did not object. To the contrary, he embraced the strike force proposal; if anything, he wanted the invasion bigger than the one Bissell envisioned. In a meeting on the morning of November 29, 1960, Eisenhower raised the possibility of increasing troop levels to two thousand or more, which was about fifteen hundred greater than the number in Guatemala at the time. "Are we being sufficiently imaginative and bold," he asked, "subject to not letting our hand appear?" He did not share the concern of the conservative State Department about "shooting from the hip," he told his advisers.

"The President made it clear he wanted all done that could be done with all possible urgency," Bissell reported to his CIA colleagues after the meeting, "and the President led a discussion as to how best to organize the total US effort against the target." For Eisenhower, as always, *"The main thing was not to let the U.S.' hand show."*

Why Eisenhower, in his last two months in office, exhibited what Jack Pfeiffer referred to as a "sudden resurgence" of interest in the Cuba project is unclear. Part of the answer may lie in the fact that with the election now behind, he no longer had to worry about the operation flopping on his watch and hurting Nixon's chances. "I will say this, it probably had a political basis," said Jacob Esterline, the CIA's task force commander. "They [the Eisenhower administration] realized that they had lost, and they realized that they were going to have to brief a new administration. . . . I suspect they didn't want to brief on something that would emerge that they hadn't been giving anything other than their full support."

Washington, D.C., December 1960

ON DECEMBER 6, Eisenhower hosted Kennedy at the White House for an "informal" one-on-one discussion about the state of the world and the workings of the White House. This meeting could not have been a happy one for Eisenhower, a proud man who had been personally devastated by Nixon's loss to Kennedy. "Including my military career, I have never suffered a greater hurt of defeat," he told an aide after the election. With swallowed pride came the taste of sour grapes. "I want to call this a turnover, not transition," he instructed staff members. "Transition implies gradual infiltration and I'm not going to share executive responsibility—this administration is going to maintain absolute control until January twentieth."

When Kennedy arrived at the North Portico of the White House, he bounded out of the limousine before it had come to a complete stop, then hurried up the stairs to grab Eisenhower's hand. If the president-elect's puppylike eagerness confirmed Eisenhower's impression that Kennedy was too callow to be president—"Little Boy Blue," he called him—this was soon gainsaid by Kennedy's behavior inside the White House. The president-elect was appropriately solicitous to the old general and listened carefully and politely, striking Eisenhower as "a serious, earnest seeker of information." Both men had drawn up a list of discussion topics before the meeting. At the top of each of their lists was Cuba. Nothing specific about the CIA operation was on the agenda, but it is unlikely they avoided it. Before they parted, Eisenhower gave his successor a word of warning: "No easy matters will ever come to you as President."

Washington, D.C., January 1961

EISENHOWER SPENT HIS last weeks in office making his admonition come true for Kennedy, at least regarding Cuba. It would be cynical to suggest that his actions were taken other than in the best interest (in his opinion) of the nation, but Kennedy loyalists could be forgiven for wondering if Eisenhower did not, at some level, enjoy tightening the Gordian knot before bequeathing it to Kennedy.

Eisenhower's farewell actions against Cuba were precipitated by Castro's decision, on January 2, 1961, to order nearly the entire staff of the U.S. embassy out of Havana. Giving the Americans forty-eight hours to leave, Castro told reporters that "ninety percent of functionaries are spies anyway." He had to know his move would provoke a response from Eisenhower, and it did. The following morning, January 3, the president held an emergency high-level meeting at the White House. Along with the secretaries of state, defense, and treasury, he invited Allen Dulles, Richard Bissell, and Tracy Barnes of the CIA to attend. The chairman of the Joint Chiefs, Lyman Lemnitzer, was there as well, taking notes. Eisenhower told his advisers that the United States "should not tolerate being kicked around" by Castro. According to Richard Bissell, the president and his councilors went on to discuss—again—the possibility of exploiting some sort of made-up event to invade Cuba with U.S. forces, such as a fake attack on Guantánamo. This went to show that the CIA was not alone in its willingness to "create" history, as Richard Bissell put it. Indeed, the CIA plan seemed almost scrupulous in comparison to actions Eisenhower and others considered that morning.

In the end, the gathered parties agreed that the ongoing CIA operation was the best course, and the sooner it was undertaken the better. Proceed, Eisenhower told Bissell and Dulles, instructing them at the same time to increase the size of the force training in Guatemala. General Andrew Goodpaster, Eisenhower's chief of staff, interjected to warn—presciently—that the CIA's operation was gathering a momentum that would be difficult to stop. Eisenhower dismissed Goodpaster's concern. The expanding force in Guatemala would merely be an "asset" for the next president. It committed the United States to nothing.

Later that day, the United States informed Cuba it was breaking diplomatic relations entirely and requested that all Cuban personnel leave Washington "as soon as possible."

ON JANUARY 4, 1961—the day after Eisenhower broke ties with Cuba—Colonel Jack Hawkins addressed an in-house memorandum to his superior, Jacob Esterline, regarding the "current status" of the CIA's operation to overthrow Castro. The memo is a snapshot of where the operation stood in the weeks before Kennedy took over. In some respects preparations were quite advanced. For example, Cuban crews were already in Vieques training to operate the landing craft that would be used to transport the Cuban Expeditionary Force to shore. In other areas, though, the operation was woefully lagging. Ten B-26s had been procured, but only five Cuban pilots were capable of flying the planes. The brigade was undergoing rigorous training in Guatemala, but just five hundred men had been successfully recruited.

In addition to describing the preparations under way, Hawkins's memo, without mentioning specific tactics or landing points for the amphibious invasion, clearly states the goals and expectations of the operation's planners as they stood before Kennedy entered office. The memo is worth quoting at length:

> The concept envisages the seizure of a small lodgment on Cuban soil by an all-Cuban amphibious/airborne force of about 750 men. The landings in Cuba will be preceded by a tactical air preparation, beginning at dawn of D-1 Day. The primary purpose of the air preparation will be to destroy or neutralize all Cuban military aircraft and naval vessels constituting a threat to the invasion force. . . .
>
> The primary objective of the force will be to survive and maintain its integrity on Cuban soil. There will be no early attempt to break out of the lodgment for further offensive operations unless and until there is a general uprising against the Castro regime or overt military intervention by United States forces has taken place. . . .
>
> It is expected that these operations will precipitate a general uprising throughout Cuba and cause the revolt of large segments of the Cuban Army and Militia. The lodgment, it is hoped, will serve as a rallying point for the thousands who are ready for overt resistance to Castro but who hesitate to act until they can feel some assurance of success. A general revolt in Cuba, if one is successfully triggered by our operations, may serve to topple the Castro regime within a period of weeks.

Several important expectations and stipulations are packed into this document. First, the brigade's function will not be to invade Cuba and keep moving, but rather to land, secure a beachhead, and *hold tight*. Second, if the force *can* hold its ground, either internal uprisings or overt military assistance will be forthcoming; these actions, not the invasion itself, will topple Castro. Perhaps most notable, in light of future events, is how pointedly Hawkins emphasizes the need for aerial dominance. He writes almost as if anticipating exactly what would occur three and a half months later:

> The question has been raised in some quarters as to whether amphibious/airborne operation could not be mounted without tactical air preparation or support or with minimal air support. It is axiomatic in amphibious operations that control of air and sea in the objective area is absolutely required. The Cuban Air Force and naval vessels capable of opposing our landing must be knocked out or neutralized before our amphibious shipping makes its final run into the beach. If this is not done, we will be courting disaster.

A possible disaster of another kind came calling on the morning of January 10, when Hawkins and his fellow CIA planners awoke to find their Guatemalan training facility featured in the *New York Times* under an ominous headline: U.S. HELPS TRAIN AN ANTI-CASTRO FORCE AT SECRET GUATEMALAN AIR-GROUND BASE. The story was not the first in the American press to mention the brigade training camps—the *Nation* magazine had run a brief article in November noting their existence—but the front-page *Times* article promised a whole new level of scrutiny. "In the Cordillera foothills a few miles back from the Pacific," reported *Times* correspondent Paul P. Kennedy, "commando-like forces are being drilled in guerrilla warfare tactics by foreign personnel, mostly from the United States." Reading on, it turned out the CIA had no reason to worry. Paul Kennedy had been duped by his Guatemalan sources. The commandos were Guatemalan soldiers, Kennedy was told, and their training was a purely defensive measure, undertaken in anticipation of a possible attack—from Cuba.

The CIA itself could not have devised a better cover story.

THE OFFICIAL CHRONOLOGY of Joint Chiefs' activity in Operation Bumpy Road, as the Pentagon would prophetically name the Cuba plan, gives Wednesday, January 11, as the first time "working level officers" of the military staffs were brought into the planning for the invasion of

Cuba. The chiefs themselves had long been acquainted with the program, but now lesser officers would become closely involved. Major General David W. Gray, chief of the Joint Subsidiary Activities Division, would act as liaison between the agency and the Pentagon, becoming from this point on an engaged partner with the CIA.

Gray's first step was to undertake an evaluation of the CIA's invasion plan. Starting with its estimate of Castro's forces—200,000 to 300,000 militia members and a trained Revolutionary Army of 32,000—this first JCS assessment was not optimistic. "To hold a lodgment for any appreciable period without massive popular support would require a minimum force of 5,000," which would have to be trained, the report concluded, for at least seven months. At the moment, the CIA had barely 750 men and hoped to invade in March at the latest.

THE DAY BEFORE he was sworn in as president, as the city of Washington underwent last-minute preparations for his inauguration, John Kennedy paid another visit to Dwight Eisenhower. The sky was leaden over the White House when Kennedy arrived through the northwest gate off Pennsylvania Avenue at 9:00 A.M. The weather forecast called for snow. The lawn of the Rose Garden was brown stubble.

For forty-five minutes, Kennedy and Eisenhower sat alone in the barren Oval Office. Most of Eisenhower's personal effects had already been packed up. Despite the gray weather and glum spirits weighing on many in his administration, Eisenhower sat at his desk looking "very fit, pink cheeked and unharassed," Kennedy recorded in a note later that day. Eisenhower was intent on teaching Kennedy what to do in case of nuclear attack. This was in many ways what being president during the Cold War boiled down to—anticipating end-of-the-world scenarios. Eisenhower showed Kennedy the "football," the briefcase containing the nuclear codes required to launch an attack. Then Eisenhower picked up a telephone and said three words into it: "Opal Drill Three." Fewer than five minutes later, a Marine Corps helicopter appeared from the sky and hovered over the White House lawn—then turned back to wherever it came from. In the event of a real emergency, the helicopter would have evacuated the president to a secure location. Kennedy was impressed.

At nine forty-five, they adjourned to the cabinet room. Waiting for them were the outgoing and incoming secretaries of state, defense, and treasury—Eisenhower's men and Kennedy's counterparts sitting side by side at the long table. For the next two hours, the presidents and their advisers roamed over the world's hot spots. First up was Laos, where the Pathet Lao, in alliance with the Communist bloc, was threatening the U.S.-backed government. Then they spoke of Cuba.

"Should we support guerrilla operations in Cuba?" inquired Kennedy.

"To the utmost," replied Eisenhower, reminding the president-elect that it was about to become his "responsibility to do whatever is necessary." Before Kennedy departed, Eisenhower came back to Cuba: "We cannot have the present government there go on."

Kennedy stepped back outside before noon. Snow was already falling. The next time he returned to the White House, the city would be a winter palace blanketed in white, and this, and all that came with it, would be his.

PART III

GOLDEN INTERLUDE

January 20–April 14, 1961

9

"A Grenade"

Winter 1961

Washington, D.C., January 20

MAYBE THE SMOKE should have been some kind of warning. It rose from the wooden lectern, swirled around the tousled white head of Richard Cardinal Cushing, then wafted over the steps of the Capitol into the icy air. The cardinal went on reciting his invocation as if nothing were the matter—as if the smoke were just the usual High Mass stagecraft—but the men and women seated on the steps rising behind him began to stir with concern. For a few moments—could it be?—the cardinal himself appeared to be on fire, smoke billowing out from beneath his clerical robes and heavy overcoat. But no, it was not the cardinal; it was the lectern behind which he stood and where, in a few moments, John F. Kennedy would take the oath of office to become the thirty-fifth president of the United States.

The inauguration of John F. Kennedy had arrived on the back of an unexpected winter storm. The flakes had begun to fall shortly before noon of the previous day, at about the time Kennedy left his White House conference with President Eisenhower. By late afternoon, the familiar contours of buildings and monuments were dissolving behind a white scrim. Traffic sputtered to a halt, forcing drivers to abandon their vehicles by the hundreds and trudge home in the falling dark. But with the chaos and inconvenience came a kind of magic—Kennedy magic. "Great floodlights around the Washington Monument glittered through the white storm," Arthur M. Schlesinger would write in his book *A Thousand Days*. "It was a scene of eerie beauty." The poet Robert

Frost was on hand for the inauguration, but you didn't need a poet to appreciate the metaphorical implications. The city was being made new again under this virgin snow: a fresh sheet onto which a new chapter of history would be written.

Now, the following day, January 20, was simply breathtaking. The storm had moved off to the north, leaving behind eight inches of powder, cold temperatures, and a cloudless sky. As stiff breezes whipped the flags atop the Capitol dome, sunlight danced off the snow and marble. At ten minutes past noon, the Marine Corps band struck up "Hail to the Chief." Eisenhower and Nixon walked out of the Capitol rotunda and down the steps to their seats. Lyndon Johnson followed a few moments later. At last came John F. Kennedy, carrying a top hat in his hand and smiling casually. He took his seat next to Eisenhower, completing the semicircle of once and future presidents: Eisenhower, Kennedy, Johnson, Nixon; the thirty-fourth, thirty-fifth, thirty-sixth, and thirty-seventh presidents of the United States. All but Eisenhower would leave the office under circumstances of tragedy or dismay. But, of course, that was years away.

For the moment, John Kennedy glowed in the cold sunlight, the very picture of immortal vitality. His hair was thick and wavy, his face newly tanned from a recent visit to Palm Beach. The hue of Kennedy's face may have owed something, too, to the Addison's disease from which he had long suffered—one of Addison's symptoms is hyperpigmentation, or browning of the skin—but Kennedy and his confidants had managed to keep his ailment secret. No one would have guessed that the young man sitting there in the arctic air that January day was actually in far poorer health than the elderly man sitting next to him.

As they waited for the ceremony to begin, Eisenhower seemed to be lecturing the president-elect, sweeping his right hand out before him, like a father about to hand over the keys of the new Cadillac Fleetwood to his teenage son, reminding him how to play the clutch and not to flood the engine, and for goodness' sake watch out for where the road curved and narrowed. "It would be a most delightful thing to have a microphone between former president Eisenhower and President John F. Kennedy," Chet Huntley told the audience watching on NBC. Kennedy listened, nodding obediently if a little distractedly. Perhaps he was starting to suspect that he was being handed something he did not especially want. "A grenade," as Pentagon undersecretary William Bundy would later describe it, "with the pin pulled."

* * *

EXACTLY WHEN THE lectern began to smolder is not clear. Judging from television footage, smoke was already rising as Kennedy and Eisenhower stood for "America the Beautiful," but these first wisps were easily confused with the collective breath of the cold people standing below the platform. By the time the proceedings finally got under way, generous gray puffs, smelling of toasted rubber, were venting from the flanks of the podium, and there could be no mistake. The fire had been caused by a short circuit in the wiring under the podium. "They're trying to preserve some of the cables for fear it may shut off communication," Huntley told viewers as the cardinal finished with his blessing. "The great danger is that some of the cables are going to burn out."

It would be a reach to assign great significance to a small electrical fire. But just as the preinaugural snow offered metaphorical possibilities to the poetically minded, the burning podium fairly begged for soothsaying. Was it an omen of greater conflagrations to come? The immediate practical question was what would happen if fire gutted the wiring. The public address system and broadcast audio would be lost. John F. Kennedy's inaugural address, destined to be one of the best-remembered and most quoted in American history, would be delivered in cold silence.

That, of course, is not what happened. A few more preliminaries—a prayer, Robert Frost's poem, the swearing in of Vice President Johnson—and then John F. Kennedy slipped off his overcoat and stepped up to the podium. "Let every nation know, whether it wishes us well or ill, that we shall pay any price, bear any burden, meet any hardship, support any friend, oppose any foe to assure the survival and the success of liberty."

Fifty years later, Kennedy's inaugural speech is best recalled for its stirring oratory. But what made it immediately arresting was how succinctly it addressed the very peculiar and difficult circumstances in which the United States found itself in 1961. This was a nation at the height of its powers yet profoundly concerned for its future. The *New York Times* columnist Wallace Carroll quoted Dickens to capture the paradox of American life in January 1961: "It was the best of times, it was the worst of times," wrote Carroll. "In its arsenals the nation had more destructive power than all the armies from Genghis Khan to Adolph Hitler. Yet for the first time since the Emperor Maximilian set foot in Mexico a century ago, an unfriendly power seemed to be gaining a foothold in the hemisphere, across the narrow straits of Florida."

Nobody would have missed the allusion in Carroll's column to Fidel Castro. Nor could anyone have missed it in Kennedy's speech: "Let all our neighbors know that we shall join with them to oppose aggression or subversion anywhere in the Americas. . . . And let every other power know that this Hemisphere intends to remain the master of its own house."

The speech was over almost before it began. To the tens of thousands watching from the lawn of the Capitol, and to the millions at home, the reaction was uniformly positive. Hard-line anti-Communists who had doubted the new president's resolve beforehand applauded the tough language. "I have never heard a better speech," said Admiral Arleigh Burke. "It's the best statement of policies in which I believe that I have ever heard." Doves, too, found much to praise, including a desire by Kennedy to break the Cold War stalemate and work with the Soviets to achieve peace.

One other man who liked what he heard that day was Fidel Castro. The speech was broadcast in Cuba with a simultaneous Spanish translation. Later that afternoon, Castro went in front of the Presidential Palace in Havana and declared that he, too, pledged to "begin anew" in building relations with the United States. "We have no resentment of the past, but we will wait for the action of the Kennedy Administration." To show that he meant what he said, he ordered his army to demobilize. "Let us hope that no Yankee invasion comes," said Castro. "If, in place of invasion, they offer friendship, we will accept it, but with the condition they treat us with respect."

Washington, D.C., Winter

IF CASTRO SERIOUSLY expected the Kennedy administration to look favorably upon his regime, he was in for a rude awakening. What President Kennedy intended to do about Castro he did not yet know, but friendship was not among the options on his table.

On Saturday, January 28, just over a week into the "golden interlude," as Arthur Schlesinger would later describe the first heady months of the Kennedy administration, President Kennedy convened a high-level meeting in the cabinet room to discuss Cuba. Vice President Lyndon Johnson joined the president, along with Secretary of Defense Robert McNamara, Secretary of State Dean Rusk, General Lyman Lemnitzer of the Joint Chiefs, and assorted undersecretaries and aides. Allen Dulles, accompanied by Tracy Barnes, briefed the group on the CIA operation.

Working from notes prepared by Richard Bissell and the WH/4 staff, Dulles told the president that the CIA believed "the present plan can establish a beachhead on Cuban soil and maintain it for a period of two weeks, possibly as long as thirty days." Once this had been accomplished, there would be "a basis for an overt, open U.S. initiative to institute a military occupation of the island," preferably by forces that would include Latin Americans from the Organization of American States. "There is a reasonable chance that the success of the above plan would set in motion forces which would cause the downfall of the regime."

At this first full-dress White House briefing, Dulles also sounded the theme that would become a kind of CIA mantra over the next weeks: the time to overthrow Fidel Castro was now or never. Not only was Castro's grip on the island tightening, but arms shipments would soon be arriving in Cuba from the Eastern bloc, making his regime a far more formidable foe. Most alarmingly, CIA and Pentagon intelligence suggested that the Soviets were about to supply Castro with jets—MiGs—which would instantly transform Castro's air force from a secondhand, third-rate smorgasbord into a state-of-the-art fleet. Finally, there was the weather to consider. The rainy season in Cuba began in April. Any operation would be far more difficult once the drops began to fall.

In previous briefings, both as a candidate and as president-elect, Kennedy had enjoyed the luxury of considering the operation in the abstract, as somebody else's problem and not especially pressing in light of the hundreds of other decisions big and small he had to make before assuming office. Not until the moment he became president, wrote Schlesinger, did Kennedy "realize how contingency planning could generate its own momentum and create its own reality." Just a week into his administration, reality was fast approaching, no time to spare.

When Dulles finished, Kennedy turned to General Lemnitzer of the Joint Chiefs. Lemnitzer expressed his reservations that such a small force as the CIA was preparing could effectively hold its ground against Castro's army. This would be one of the rare times Lemnitzer or any of his fellow chiefs spoke out against the plan in the president's presence.

"Have the Joint Chiefs done a careful evaluation of this operation?" Kennedy asked. "I want that done as the very next step."

* * *

MAJOR GENERAL GRAY, again, oversaw the JCS evaluation. Unlike the report earlier in the month, which had considered several different scenarios for overthrowing Castro, this was to be a critique specifically of the CIA plan as it stood at the end of January. Gray and his staff of four were given just three days to complete their first draft. The CIA did not make the job easy. When the five Pentagon men went to Quarters Eye, they were met by half a dozen CIA officers who briefed them orally. For reasons probably owing as much to the fluidity of the planning as to its secrecy, little had been committed to paper; the men running the operation—Bissell, Barnes, Esterline, Hawkins, Drain—were essentially carrying it around in their heads. The first thing the Pentagon staffers did after receiving the "verbal rundown," as Gray put it, was return to their offices across the river, collate their notes on a conference table, then write up a twenty-five-page version of the CIA plan so they could evaluate it.

Gray and his team presented a draft of their report to the Joint Chiefs on Tuesday, January 31. This was revised and forwarded, with Chairman Lemnitzer's signature, to Secretary McNamara on February 3, under the title "Military Evaluation of the CIA Para-Military Plan, Cuba."

The plan the JCS considered in this report came to be known as Operation Trinidad, named after the then intended landing site on the south-central coast of Cuba, near the small city of Trinidad. Operation Trinidad would differ from the plan the CIA ultimately adopted in several important respects, including its location and the fact that it was scheduled for daylight hours rather than night. But many of the report's conclusions would apply to one as well as to the other.

Making sense of these conclusions was not easy. The JCS evaluation was, as Arthur Schlesinger put it, "a peculiar and ambiguous document" laced with provisos and caveats. It began with a strong note of caution, stipulating that the success of the operation was "dependent on the degree of local Cuban support" and suggesting that without such support, the invasion would fail. But the overall tone was positive. "The amphibious assault should be successful even if lightly opposed," the report stated. Assuming local support came through, and assuming that Castro's small air force could be destroyed in preinvasion air strikes, the operation "would not necessarily require overt U.S. intervention."

"In summary, evaluation of the current plan results in a favorable assessment," the report concluded. "[T]he Joint Chiefs of Staff consider that timely execution of this plan has a fair chance of ultimate success and, even if it does not achieve immediately the full results desired, could contribute to the eventual overthrow of the Castro regime."

The use of that innocuous word "fair" to describe the operation's chances had been inserted at the direction of General Earle Wheeler, Gray's immediate superior. Wheeler believed the evaluation had to include some kind of overall, easy-to-grasp assessment. It turned out to be the most misunderstood word in the entire report, a one-syllable triumph of bureaucratic equivocation over clarity. Just what did "fair" mean? Gray later offered that, in his opinion, it meant the operation had about a 30 percent chance of success—that is, a 70 percent chance of failure. "We thought other people would think that 'a fair chance' would mean 'not too good.'" But Gray's 30 percent figure never made it into the report. And contrary to his expectation, most of the document's readers did not interpret the word "fair" to mean "not too good." The entire report, on balance, came off as an endorsement of the CIA's plan.

Guatemala, Winter 1961

AS THE ADMINISTRATION and Joint Chiefs considered the plan to overthrow Castro, the operation lurched forward, gathering speed one moment, stumbling the next. It nearly collapsed altogether at the end of January when the internecine squabbles that had been simmering among the Cuban exiles came to a boil at Base Trax. About 230 of the men, nearly half the total force encamped in Guatemala, abruptly resigned from the brigade. The mutinous faction had become convinced that the brigade's leadership was taking a starkly rightist, pro-Batista turn. This concern combined with the impression held by some of the Cubans that their American trainers at the camp were behaving as overlords, as if the Cubans were there to assist them in overthrowing Castro, not the other way around. Nearly all the mutineers eventually agreed to stay, but a dozen of the more disruptive instigators were flown out of Trax by helicopter to a makeshift prison in the middle of the Guatemalan jungle, where they would remain until after the invasion—exiled from their own exile.

The drama at the camps was short-lived but served to remind Bissell and his colleagues that the glue binding the brigade was thin despite a year of effort by Droller and Hunt to forge an alliance. The message, to anyone listening, was disturbing. Even if the invasion initially succeeded, its aftermath was likely to be knotty. If a few hundred men joined in the common cause of overthrowing Fidel Castro could not agree on a post-Castro Cuba, what hope was there that a nation of six million Cubans would agree?

Dulles and Bissell drew a different lesson from the mutiny; namely, here was another compelling reason to mobilize the brigade as quickly as possible, before it fell apart completely. First, though, they needed more men. The CIA redoubled its recruiting efforts. Earlier, the agency had been choosy about the men admitted into the brigade. No longer. Nearly nine hundred would be added to the rolls between early January and mid-April 1961.

The original recruits had tended to be young men drawn from the Cuban military or student leagues. The 1961 models were different. Many were older. They had careers; some were accomplished lawyers or doctors. They also had families. Joining the brigade often meant tearing themselves away from wives and children one day, finding themselves sweating in the wilds of Guatemala the next.

A typical experience was recorded in the diary of Manuel Penabaz, a thirty-seven-year-old lawyer, married with two children. On January 24, 1961—four days after Kennedy's inauguration—Penabaz received the call from the Frente's office on Nineteenth Street in Miami. He had already registered with the Frente to indicate his interest in joining the brigade, but the call nonetheless took him by surprise. "Your mobilization has been ordered," he was told. "Be ready at 5:00 P.M. at our office in Miami for your orders." When he told his wife, Leo, that he was leaving, she begged him not to go. "I wave good bye," Penabaz wrote in his journal. "Leo tries to smile. The children were at her side, the girl saddened, the boy proud without even understanding what is going on." That same evening, Penabaz was taken to Opa Locka, where he and sixty other recruits boarded an unmarked C-46 with darkened windows. Seven hours later, the plane landed. The joke was still the same. "Gentlemen, welcome to the Dominican Republic," a priest from the brigade greeted them when they filed out of the plane. "Generalissimo Rafael Trujillo sends you his regards."

AT ABOUT THIS TIME, in those early weeks of 1961, Grayston Lynch entered the picture. Brought in by the CIA to help assemble its growing maritime fleet and prepare the brigade for the landing on Cuba's beaches, Lynch was a veteran of the U.S. Army's Special Forces, recently retired after twenty-two highly decorated years in the military. He was a formidably built, tough-talking Texan who knew his way around secret and dangerous missions, and the CIA had scooped him up the moment he retired. Called to Quarters Eye in early January 1961, Lynch was given a physical exam and a three-hour psychological evaluation and polygraph, then rushed through processing at the CIA, all in a day. He was introduced to his future partner, William "Rip" Robertson, another paramilitary veteran, and another brawny, take-no-prisoners Texan who had cut his teeth (as a marine) in World War II. Robertson had worked for the CIA in the past, most notably during the Guatemala operation, where he had demonstrated a disconcerting tendency to shoot first and ask questions later. He had, in fact, caused a near disaster by ordering a plane under his command to bomb a ship he believed to be transporting Soviet arms to Guatemala. When the destroyed vessel turned out to be a British freighter delivering grain, the CIA was charged $1.5 million in compensation and Robertson was, for a time, persona non grata around headquarters. But now he was back. The East Coast Ivy Leaguers knew that planning a military operation was one thing; going into battle was quite another, and required a different sort of man.

As Lynch and Robertson worked to put the brigade's little navy into shape, the air wing, too, came together. This was accomplished with the help of the Alabama Air National Guard. General Reid Doster and two of his best men, Riley Shamburger and Joe Shannon, oversaw the recruitment of pilots and ground crews. They drew mostly from the men who belonged to the Air National Guard, but they reached out to other pilots with combat experience—men, that is, such as Albert "Buck" Persons.

"How much four-engine time you got, Buck?" his old friend Shamburger asked him one day at the airport. At the time, Persons was flying for a Birmingham construction company. "We need some four-engine drivers with military experience. It's out of this country. I can't tell you where at the moment. All I can tell you is that it's legitimate and shouldn't last more than a couple of months."

Another thing: the job would start right away. And one more thing: he would not be permitted to tell anyone where he was going, not even after somebody told *him* where he was going. But at least he'd be well compensated for his troubles. The pay was $2,800 a month—a fairly princely sum in 1961—plus bonuses and a good offer on a life insurance policy.

10

"A Stone Falling in Water"

February 8–March 15, 1961

Washington, D.C., Early February

ON A WINTER evening in early February, after the inaugural snow was melted but before the new administration lost its piney freshness, Allen Dulles hosted a get-to-know-you dinner for top CIA and White House officials. A dozen men from each group convened at Dulles's private club, the Alibi, a snug retreat tucked into a narrow brick row house on Eye Street in downtown Washington. The Alibi did not look particularly distinguished on the outside, but inside its bric-a-brac-filled rooms was one of the most exclusive sanctums in the city. Since the club's founding in 1884, members had included presidents, cabinet secretaries, and generals. Its very name hinting at intimacy and stealth, the Alibi was an ideal setting to bedazzle New Frontiersmen with "the alchemical magic of the clandestine"—as White House aide Richard Goodwin described CIA activities—and give them a taste of what the agency had to offer.

The small party mingled in the wood-paneled dining room, enjoying, in the words of one guest, a "pleasant three-cocktail dinner." After dinner, the discussion turned serious. One by one, the CIA officials took the floor to explain their work to the White House staffers, giving a "sort of *New Yorker*-ish précis." The hit of the evening was Richard Bissell. Standing to address the group, Bissell introduced himself, with a hint of a grin, as a "man-eating shark," cleverly mocking his prowess in the black arts even as he asserted it. This was exactly the sort of ironic tough talk the men of the New Frontier devoured. Many of them already knew and respected Bissell, if not personally then by reputation. They also knew President Kennedy considered him to possess one of the keenest minds in Washington and intended to name him as Dulles's replacement. He was their kind of man.

The same could be said of the CIA as a whole: it was their kind of agency. The Kennedy administration and the CIA were cut from the same cloth. They cherished the same qualities of good breeding and fine education (Groton and Yale; Choate and Harvard), of high intelligence matched with boyish swagger. Eisenhower had valued the agency for what it could do, but to Kennedy the CIA was a model of what he wanted his White House to be—virile and daring, fast on the draw, pragmatic. Especially in comparison to the cumbersomely hierarchical Pentagon or the ponderous, ever-cautious State Department, the CIA was the can-do branch of government. "By gosh, I don't care what it is," President Kennedy had told his national security adviser, McGeorge Bundy, "but if I need some material fast or an idea fast, CIA is the place I have to go. The State Department takes four or five days to answer a simple yes or no."

Above all, the CIA's capabilities comported perfectly with the new president's strategy for waging the Cold War. The generals at the Pentagon had their nuclear arsenal to offer, while the Foreign Service folk put their faith in toothless remedies such as economic sanctions. But the CIA got it: victory against the Communists would be won not by threatening nuclear obliteration or by engaging in mealymouthed diplomacy, but by prevailing in far-flung regional conflicts where communism was gaining ground. The Congo. Laos. Vietnam. Cuba. These were the small theaters where the great drama of the late twentieth century would be played. Here the means of victory would have to be surgical, shrewd, and, very often, covert.

"HAVE WE DETERMINED what we are going to do about Cuba?" President Kennedy inquired in a note to McGeorge Bundy on Monday, February 6. "If there is a difference of opinion between agencies I think they should be brought to my attention." Kennedy had been in office seventeen days and had found little time to devote to Cuba since the meeting in the cabinet room on January 28. His query to Bundy on this Monday morning, with its implied assumption that there might *not* be a difference of opinion between agencies—that the Cuba situation might be easily revolved—is almost touching in its soon-to-be shattered innocence.

Two days later, on Wednesday, February 8, Bundy, still getting up to speed on Cuba himself, responded to the president with a preview of troubles ahead. In preparation for a White House meeting that afternoon to discuss the just-completed JCS evaluation of the CIA's plan, Bundy wrote Kennedy a memo distilling the two broad positions already taking root in the administration: "Defense and CIA now feel quite enthusiastic about the invasion from Guatemala," Bundy wrote from his desk in the Old Executive Office Building. "State Department takes a much cooler view, primarily because of its belief that the political consequences would be very grave both in the United Nations and in Latin America." Bundy ended with his own recommendation "that there should certainly not be an invasion adventure."

Having a man like Mac Bundy on the case no doubt gave Kennedy confidence in these early days that a solution to the problem of Cuba was at hand. Everything about Bundy inspired confidence in the president, and not a little awe in others. A trim man of average stature, Bundy was not physically imposing but he packed the wiry strength and springy quickness of a middleweight wrestler. (Actually, his sport was tennis.) He looked younger than his forty-two years, his cheeks perpetually pink, his thinning hair swept back as if only moments ago he had stepped off a bicycle—which had been, in fact, his primary mode of transportation during his previous life in Cambridge, Massachusetts. The glasses with the clear plastic rims might have looked donnish or fey on another man, but on Bundy they only added to the impression of lucid intelligence. "You can't beat brains," President Kennedy once said of Bundy to their mutual friend Ben Bradlee. In fact, Bundy had been pretty much unbeatable his whole life—from his birth into Boston's Brahmin elite, to the top of his class at Groton, to Phi Beta Kappa at Yale. A stint in the army during the war had been followed by an appointment at Harvard, where, at the astonishing age of thirty-four, he was named dean of the faculty of arts and sciences. The *Harvard Lampoon* had honored his meteoric rise with a pithy verse:

McGeorge Bundy
Born on Monday
Groton on Tuesday
Yale on Wednesday
Army on Thursday
Harvard on Friday
Dean on Saturday
God on Sunday

The *Lampoon* had his birthday off by a day—Bundy was born on a Sunday—but otherwise hit the mark.

Despite a few of his own budding concerns regarding Kennedy's management style, Bundy in many ways personified it. Kennedy eschewed the layers of formal hierarchy that had weighed down the Eisenhower administration, including, in his opinion, the National Security Council. The recipe for good decisions, thought Kennedy, was not cumbersome protocol and time-consuming meetings, but smart, adroit men responding efficiently to hard facts. That was Bundy in a nutshell. Whether in person, when he was informed and incisive, or in his punchy memos, signed with a breezy "McB," or in his handwritten notes composed in a neat but recondite script ("so small you almost needed a magnifying glass to read it," according to Kennedy's secretary, Evelyn Lincoln), Bundy's every word and action conveyed the style John Kennedy hoped to achieve in his administration. "He was the brightest light in the glittering constellation around the President," author David Halberstam would later write of Bundy—the man who proved "that sheer intelligence and rationality could answer and solve anything."

By the time Halberstam wrote those words in *The Best and the Brightest*, his bestselling book about the Vietnam War, they would be tinged with irony and regret. But in February 1961, they were the creed of the realm.

THE WHITE HOUSE meeting that Wednesday afternoon brought together many of the same top administration officials who had attended the January 28 meeting. Secretary of State Dean Rusk came with Assistant Secretaries Thomas Mann and Charles Bohlen. Secretary of Defense Robert McNamara was flanked by Assistant Secretary Paul Nitze and Assistant Deputy Secretary William Bundy (McGeorge's brother). The chairman of the Joint Chiefs of Staff, General Lyman Lemnitzer, was there, too, as were Allen Dulles and Richard Bissell.

Dulles let Bissell do most of the talking. Peering through his bullet-proof-thick horn-rimmed glasses, Bissell reviewed the CIA plan and the Pentagon's evaluation of it. He noted that the Joint Chiefs had given the plan a "fair" chance of success. Letting that innocuous word "fair" drift away without comment, Bissell defined "success" as the brigade's ability "to survive, hold ground, and attract growing support from Cubans." He closed by reiterating Dulles's earlier call for prompt action. As recently as January, the CIA had been planning for a strike date of March 1. This was now unlikely. But the sooner the better.

After Bissell, it was the State Department's turn to present its case. Secretary Rusk spoke dispassionately of the "grave effects" such an operation could have on the United States' position in Latin America. In a soft rebuttal to Bissell's call for fast action, he urged caution and restraint. U.S. policy "should not be driven to drastic and irrevocable choice by the urgencies, however real, of a single battalion of men." Rusk stopped short of recommending cancellation. This was a model of the secretary's approach to the operation as it would develop over the next several months. He would chip away with objections while never clearly stating—on the record, anyway—exactly what he hoped the president would do instead. He was not alone in evading clarity on the subject, but he seemed to have special knack for it.

Bissell had to expect carping from Rusk; he knew State's concerns going into the meeting. The State Department always talked like this: subjunctive phrases laced with prudent clauses. More surprising to Bissell was the conspicuous silence of Secretary McNamara and Chairman Lemnitzer. Neither man from the Pentagon weighed in with an opinion, for or against the CIA plan. The way Bissell saw it, McNamara, still new to his job and lacking military experience, was reluctant to opine on a military operation in the presence of Lemnitzer. In fact, McNamara never played more than a minor role in the planning. As for why General Lemnitzer kept quiet—who knows? He did not hold his tongue because he thought the plan was flawless. McGeorge Bundy had characterized the Joint Chiefs' view as "enthusiastic" in his memo to the president, but that overstated the case, as Bissell knew. So why did Lemnitzer not take this opportunity to address some of the deep concerns he and the other chiefs later admitted to having about the operation? Apparently, like McNamara, he was wary of overstepping his bounds. This was the CIA's operation, not the Pentagon's. Who was he to criticize it in front of the president?

Well, he was the chairman of the Joint Chiefs, for one thing. High among the list of mystifying lapses leading up to the Bay of Pigs was the persistent failure of Lemnitzer and his fellow chiefs to insert themselves forcefully into the debate about the military prospects of the operation. Later they would all admit to having harbored serious doubts, but none seemed to think it his place to share these with the president. The fact was, Kennedy *wanted* their opinions; he *needed* them. Unlike Eisenhower, who knew more about amphibious invasions than any of his chiefs, President Kennedy's own war experience, as the lieutenant of a PT boat, had not prepared him to gauge the merits of military invasions. When Lemnitzer and the other chiefs were silent, they may have intended merely to acknowledge the CIA's priority. To Kennedy, though, they appeared to be tacitly endorsing it.

Perhaps it was the responsibility of Richard Bissell to mention the JCS's concerns about the plan. Both he and Dulles later came under a good deal of fire for failing to flag the pitfalls, giving the president only the rosiest view. "They fell in love with the plan and ceased to think critically of it," as one administration official would later put it. Said another: "Allen and Dick didn't just brief us on the Cuban operation; they sold us on it."

This is a charge neither Bissell nor Dulles entirely denied; nor did either quite apologize for it. Asking them to assess their own plan objectively would be like expecting a playwright to review his own play. "Obviously, you present a plan and it isn't your job to say, well, that's a rotten plan I've presented," said Dulles. "You can only say, here are the merits of the plan, and in presenting the merits of the plan the tendency is always—because you're meeting a position, you're meeting this criticism and that criticism—to be drawn into more of a salesmanship job than you should." Bissell, too, admitted that he and Dulles "edged into the role of advocates," but this, Bissell suggested, was inevitable given the countless hours and effort he and his staff had invested in the plan. The job of the "operator," wrote Bissell, is to make the operation work; this is what consumes his nights and days. "His eyes are going to be fixed on the success of the operation." It is not the operator's tendency, nor even his prerogative, to question his own operation; that task is better left to others. Ultimately it is for the president alone to weigh the pros and cons. "There is always going to be this incredibly difficult choice, and if it is an important issue, it is going to be in every case, as it was then, the President's choice."

Kennedy addressed his advisers before the meeting adjourned that Wednesday afternoon. He was clearly still finding his bearings. He seemed taken aback by the size of the operation he'd inherited, yet uncertain of his alternatives. "Could not such a force be landed gradually and quietly and make its first major military efforts from the mountains—then taking shape as a Cuban force within Cuba, not as an invasion force sent by the Yankees?" he wondered aloud, describing what sounded less like an invasion and more like an infiltration or an insertion—a venture, in other words, very much like the one the CIA and President Eisenhower had discarded back in the fall. The problem, more than four months later, was that the invasion train had left the station. Not even a president could easily call it back.

Washington, D.C., Mid-February 1961

THE FAILURE OF the Joint Chiefs and the CIA to raise red flags notwithstanding, the president did not have to look hard to find serious critiques of the Cuba operation. Even in those early days of the administration—*especially* in those early days—there were plenty around.

Among the operation's earliest and most consistent critics was Kennedy aide Arthur Schlesinger. Starting in early February, Schlesinger drafted a series of memos that would stand out, in retrospect, as perceptive and prescient. Schlesinger was by no means the first to raise concerns about the Cuba project to the president—Bundy and Rusk had already done so in some measure—but no one in the White House stated his position as frequently or as unequivocally. Schlesinger would later distinguish himself as chief apologist for Kennedy's mistakes during the Bay of Pigs, placing blame on those advisers (mainly CIA) who failed to warn the president adequately of the operation's risks. Ironically, Schlesinger was among those who did warn him, and in no uncertain terms.

It took some courage on Schlesinger's part to take a stand against an ongoing endeavor within weeks of coming to work for Kennedy. He was operating from a flimsy perch at his office in the low-status East Wing of the White House—"with the women," as Dean Rusk put it. His official job title in the administration was special assistant to the president, an omnibus assignment with an open-ended portfolio and no real power base. Though in later years he would come to be identified as the quintessential Kennedy insider, Schlesinger was in those early days a bit of an odd bird in the administration. He had once written speeches for Adlai Stevenson, a mark against any Kennedy Democrat, and was suspiciously tight with other left-wingers in the party, such as Eleanor Roosevelt. Furthermore, his preference for bow ties and his former employment—history professor at Harvard—reeked of the lofty intellectualism that was anathema to the steely men of the New Frontier.

But Arthur Schlesinger was no ivory tower egghead. Within his bantamweight frame and bespectacled cranium lived a healthy ego stoked by family connections (his father had been a celebrated scholar) and early accomplishments (he'd won his first Pulitzer fourteen years earlier, at twenty-nine). And despite the relationship with Stevenson, his credentials as a tough-minded Democrat were unimpeachable. Indeed, when it came to tough-minded Democrats, he wrote the book. *The Vital Center*, penned by Schlesinger twelve years earlier, had preached exactly the sort of pragmatic anti-Communist liberalism that John Kennedy was putting into practice. Arthur Schlesinger had every reason to believe himself entitled to an opinion; and on the subject of Cuba, he did not hesitate to share it.

"As you know, there is great pressure within the government in favor of a drastic decision with regard to Cuba," he wrote to Kennedy in a February 11 memo. "There is, it seems to me, a plausible argument for this decision if one excludes everything but Cuba itself." Schlesinger continued:

> However well disguised any action might be, it will be ascribed to the United States. The result would be a wave of massive protest, agitation and sabotage throughout Latin America, Europe, Asia and Africa (not to speak of Canada and of certain quarters in the United States). Worst of all, this would be your first dramatic foreign policy initiative. At one stroke, it would dissipate all the extraordinary good will which has been rising toward the new Administration through the world. It would fix a malevolent image of the new Administration in the minds of millions.

ANOTHER VOCAL OPPONENT of the invasion in the early days of the administration was Thomas Mann, assistant secretary of state for inter-American affairs. A holdover from the Eisenhower administration, Mann was about to take the post of ambassador to Mexico. Before cleaning out his desk at the State Department, though, he felt compelled to share some reservations. "I'm a team man," Mann liked to say, but in this case he worried the team was about to make the wrong play. In mid-February he committed his concerns to writing.

McGeorge Bundy gave Mann's five-page paper to the president on February 18. At the same time, Bundy handed Kennedy a recently composed eight-page paper by Richard Bissell, so that Kennedy might weigh the opposing arguments adjacently. "Since I think you lean to Mann's view, I have put Bissell on top," Bundy wrote in a cover note to the president, adding, not very helpfully, "[o]n balance I think the gloomier parts of both papers are right."

Bissell's paper rehearsed the by now familiar litany of arguments for going ahead with the operation, and soon. Unless action were taken to remove him, Castro was here to stay. Bissell then introduced an additional argument no U.S. politician could wisely ignore, certainly not one who had gained a narrow victory over his opponent by trumpeting a hard-line policy against Castro. This was the "dissolution" problem or, as it also came to be known, the "dispersal" or "disposal" problem. If the brigademen were not used within the next four to six weeks, they would have to be let go. This would unleash many hundreds of restive Cubans into the population to share their pent-up grievance with anyone who cared to listen. "The resettlement of the military force will unavoidably cause practical problems. Its members will be angry, disillusioned and aggressive with the inevitable result that they will provide honey for the press bees and the U.S. will have to face the resulting indignities and embarrassments."

Now came Thomas Mann's paper. Like Arthur Schlesinger, Mann had taken his analysis of the operation upon himself, not under any State Department mandate or guidance. In fact, he later stated, he never had any idea what the State Department's position *was*, since Dean Rusk never clearly articulated one. His own view was not that Castro was acceptable; rather, it was that a covert military operation was the wrong way to go about ousting him. Mann attacked what he took to be the operation's underlying assumption, as stipulated in the JCS report. An operation pitting an army of fifteen hundred against an army of two hundred thousand made sense only if a mass uprising against Castro occurred; and the kind of mass uprising required was unlikely.

There was one other major problem as Mann saw it: the CIA invasion was against the law. Both international and U.S. statutes forbade it.

Mann had no idea if Kennedy read his paper. He never heard anything back after Bundy delivered it to Kennedy. "It was," said Mann, "like a stone falling in water."

THE FACT IS, John Kennedy did not really need Schlesinger or Mann or anyone else to tell him that the plan was risky. As president, he had to consider risks, including some well beyond the scope of those they addressed. How, for instance, would the Soviets react to an American-backed invasion of Cuba? Kennedy's greatest worry was that Khrushchev would retaliate by making good on his oft-expressed vow to isolate West Berlin by shutting off access through East Germany. If the Soviets retaliated in Berlin, American prestige would require that Kennedy retaliate in kind. Every move was either a step back or a step forward in the dangerous game with the Soviets; and always there was the risk the game would spiral out of control.

Less potentially lethal but nearly as worrisome was the possible reaction by Latin American countries. Kennedy had entered office determined to strengthen economic ties between the United States and its neighbors to the south, primarily by means of a reform and aid program called the Alliance for Progress (Alianza para el Progreso). He had unveiled the Alliance in March, promising the start of a new and happier chapter in U.S.–Latin American relations. An invasion could instantly spoil the Alliance; if Latin Americans suspected a U.S. hand behind the invasion, many would denounce it as a return to the despised gunboat diplomacy of earlier eras. "We might be confronted by serious uprisings all over Latin America if U.S. forces were to go in," worried Secretary Rusk.

But if invading was risky, so was *not* invading. Yes, backing an enterprise to overthrow Castro would make Kennedy look like an aggressor and possibly stir up a world of trouble. Not backing it, though, would cast him as a wimp, a hypocrite, and a fool. "If he hadn't gone ahead with it, everybody would have said it showed that he had no courage," Robert Kennedy later reflected, imagining the scenario: "Eisenhower's people all said it would succeed—and we turned it down." The Kennedy administration would have appeared, said McGeorge Bundy, as "this antsy-pantsy bunch of liberals." All that talk about losing Cuba and fighters for freedom and eight jet minutes would come back to haunt them. Kennedy would have had to eat his words, and Fidel Castro would still be in power, still ninety miles from the coast of Florida, still mouthing off and thumbing his nose at America as he gathered arms from the Soviet Union and other Communist nations.

Kennedy had himself mainly to blame for his predicament. He had backed himself into a corner with his anti-Castro statements during the campaign, tenaciously and profitably exploiting the issue of Cuba and the previous administration's missteps. The fact that he and his men had been handed a time-sensitive operation by Eisenhower—a grenade, a ticking time bomb; choose your metaphor—only made the predicament more pressing. "You can't mañana this thing," Bissell told the president, running again through the urgencies. Richard Goodwin, the young adviser who had helped put Kennedy in this mess with the statement he wrote the previous October, recalled that when President Kennedy told Dulles he needed time to think and discuss, Dulles responded, "That's understandable, Mr. President, but there isn't much time."

Dulles later took issue with the suggestion that Kennedy was forced to make his decision about the Bay of Pigs under extreme constraints of time. "In a sense, there never is adequate time in government, but one rarely has had more time than was given in this particular case," Dulles contended in an unpublished draft of a magazine article he wrote a few years after the invasion. Not only did Kennedy have two months to consider the matter between his first briefing (in Palm Beach) in November and his inauguration in January, but he also had three additional months in office—a total of five months to ruminate before making a go/no-go decision. "To picture this as something into which the President was rushed or hurried or stampeded is unrealistic," wrote Dulles.

The CIA was only telling the truth when it warned Kennedy that the opportunity to make a move on Castro was fast closing. Given the rate at which Soviet bloc and now Chinese arms were pouring into Cuba that winter and spring, a delay of months, even weeks, could change circumstances dramatically. In March 1961, Castro's armed forces were little better than those of an average banana republic. By the end of April, thanks to Communist beneficence, the Cubans would be in possession of 125 tanks, about 500 artillery pieces, nearly 1,000 large machine guns, another 1,000 antiaircraft guns, and 167,000 pistols and rifles, ammunition included. Forty-one Soviet MiGs were just months from being operational, and Cuban pilots had been sent to Czechoslovakia to learn to fly the jets.

Nonetheless, Dulles himself was ignoring reality if he meant to imply that Kennedy could have seriously considered the invasion before January. It would have been awkward for the president-elect to insert himself too probingly into what was, after all, still his predecessor's project. (As Dulles knew, there was a carefully observed etiquette regarding such matters.) Nor would Kennedy have been able to consult with his non-CIA advisers before the inauguration because none yet were privy to top-secret intelligence. Thomas Mann later recalled that when he went to discuss the operation with Dean Rusk during the transition, he was informed that the outgoing and incoming administrations "had an understanding that they would not discuss any pending problems until after the inauguration." Mann would look back on this as a serious mistake "because it gave the President very, very little time to really focus on this thing."

11

"Too Spectacular"

March 1961

Washington, D.C., Mid-March

BY TEN IN the morning of Saturday, March 11—fifty days after Kennedy's inauguration, thirty-five days before the first strike on Cuba—the president's men were crowded into the cabinet room awaiting his arrival. Arthur Schlesinger sank into a leather chair, taking mental notes for the book he would one day write about his time in the White House, and starting to realize, perhaps, that the first chapter of Kennedy's presidency was already taking a dramatic turn. As he looked around the long, bullet-shaped table, he saw before him "an intimidating group," including the vice president, three of the Joint Chiefs of Staff, the secretaries of defense and state, and the usual assortment of assistant secretaries, deputy secretaries, and high-ranking military personnel arranged in chairs behind their principals. There was Richard Bissell, too, pointer in hand, ready to walk the group through the plan to invade Cuba. It was Bissell who had requested this meeting, no doubt hoping to get a decision one way or the other.

A few minutes after ten the president entered and the meeting began. Working off a written report, Bissell brought Kennedy and his advisers up to speed on the preparations for the invasion. The brigade now numbered 850 men and continued to grow, supported by an air force of more than 30 combat and transport planes and a navy of more than 12 vessels. Reviewing once again the time pressures they faced, Bissell stressed the need to put the men into action as soon as possible. "It will be infeasible to hold all these forces together beyond early April," his report read.

"Their motivation for action is high but their morale cannot be maintained if their commitment to action is long delayed."

As Bissell spoke, waving his pointer like a wand over a map of Cuba, Arthur Schlesinger was newly struck by Bissell's "swift and penetrating" mind. Skeptical as Schlesinger was of the operation, he found himself falling, along with the others in the room, under Bissell's spell, "transfixed . . . fascinated by the workings of this superbly clear, organized and articulate intelligence." McGeorge Bundy had not tagged Bissell the "great expositor" for nothing. The compliment had an edge, though; what Bundy meant was that Bissell was so good, he fooled people into agreeing with him.

McGeorge's brother William Bundy, also present at the meeting, later took up the question of whether Bissell pushed too hard as he exposited. He thought not. "None of us looked as hard as we might have, but the agency did not sell the project and Dick Bissell did not mislead us." Schlesinger more or less agreed. He would have plenty of hard words for the CIA later, but he never accused Bissell of being a charlatan. On the contrary, he wrote, Bissell straightforwardly warned his listeners to "discount his bias."

There is little question, though, that the CIA was actively advocating the operation by early March. Having invested a great deal in it, Bissell and his colleagues in WH/4 were anxious to see it go forward. The best evidence of this is found in several memos written by Tracy Barnes before the March 11 meeting. As concerns mounted within the agency that Thomas Mann's anti-invasion view was gaining traction in the White House, Barnes wrote to Bissell, on March 1, "there is no doubt in my mind that our only chance is to be very firm in our position and be very strong in urging the need for the proposed action. This means, as I see it, persuading the Boss that this must be done." Barnes urged Bissell to have a "very frank talk with Mac Bundy, explaining not only the need for decision but laying it on hard as to why we feel a favorable decision for the Project is the best solution." He also hoped Bissell would talk to Chairman Lemnitzer and elicit his strong support.

In a memo written on March 10, in preparation for the March 11 White House meeting, Barnes had run through several talking points that might sway the president. These included the fact that air strikes would be limited to "specific targets," not "indiscriminate bombing," and that the invasion was "NOT a U.S. operation" but a Cuban endeavor. "Surely there are and will be allegations of and evidence of U.S. support. The operation, however, is by *Cuban* volunteer patriots, operating entirely from non-U.S. bases."

"In conclusion," wrote Barnes, "I believe that we must not undersell what we have carefully prepared and on which a favorable DOD reaction has been obtained after detailed review."

The DOD reaction to which Barnes referred was the newest, just-completed evaluation by the staff of the Joint Chiefs. This contained a firsthand report by three colonels who had traveled to Guatemala in late February and spent three days observing the brigade training camps and the airstrip near Retalhuleu. The colonels had come back from Guatemala convinced the brigade was ready, willing, and able to fight in Cuba. In nearly every category of training, from weapons handling to leadership to morale, the evaluators gave the brigade soldiers marks of "good," "excellent," or "superior." Lieutenant Colonel D. W. Tarwater of the U.S. Air Force stated that the Cuban pilots he observed were well trained—indeed, had more training hours under their belts than the average USAF pilot had before going into combat in World War II. The report concluded that both the infantry and air force of the brigade would, by mid-March, "have achieved adequate military effectiveness" to successfully carry out their missions.

Like Bissell, the evaluators repeatedly stressed the need to move with haste. Indeed, they did so in starker terms than anyone at the CIA had done: "An early decision to proceed with this operation is imperative. The point of no return has been passed and a decision to abandon the scheme is untenable." Cancellation would probably result in a revolt among the Cubans at the camps, "with dire consequences both for the US trainer personnel and for US interests abroad."

Altogether, the JCS evaluation appeared to be a glowing appraisal of the brigade and an endorsement of the CIA's argument for sending the men to Cuba as soon as possible. But, like earlier JCS reports, this one contained incongruously ominous warnings of hazards beneath the surface. Most alarming were several sentences buried in the middle of the report, at the conclusion of Lieutenant Colonel Tarwater's discussion of the air element. If surprise was achieved, Tarwater believed, the brigade air force could accomplish its mission. Without surprise, it was doomed to fail. "The odds against achieving surprise, however, are believed to be about 85 to 15." In other words, for all the positive remarks elsewhere in their report, the evaluators were giving the brigade air force a *15 percent* chance of success.

Not surprisingly, Bissell side-stepped this detail and focused, instead, on the plan he hoped the president would approve. After running through several lesser alternatives—including a quiet night landing, which he dismissed as courting "unacceptable military risks"—he came to the so-called Trinidad plan. Kennedy and others in the room were already familiar with its contours from earlier meetings. The key element was a large daytime amphibious assault, a low-budget version of the Allied invasions carried out in World War II. (Bissell compared it to the 1944 landing at Anzio, Italy—an inauspicious comparison, as Anzio was a disaster.)

The aim of an invasion, as Bissell saw it, was not simply to place men in Cuba; it was to administer a dramatic psychological blow to Castro—"a demoralizing shock." Shock was integral to the strategy; the invasion would send reverberations through Cuba and possibly arouse the Cuban people to turn on Castro and scare him from office, much as the CIA's bag of psychological tricks had scared Jacobo Arbenz out of Guatemala in 1954. Never mind that Castro was an entirely different creature than Arbenz, far more personally and politically secure; never mind that the previous day, March 10, Bissell's friend Sherman Kent, chairman of the CIA's Board of National Estimates, had written in a memo that "Castro remains firmly in control of Cuba and that his position is, if anything, likely to grow stronger rather than weaker as time goes on." The more indomitable the CIA could make the invasion appear—the more inevitable its success—the better the chances that Cubans would flock to its side.

In the meantime, the invaders would have secured a beachhead on the coast of Cuba. The United States could then fly in the provisional government the CIA had been busily assembling in Florida, which "could be recognized and a legal basis provided for at least nongovernmental logistic support." The beachhead would be a foot in the door for the United States; the provisional government would constitute a proper invitation.

There was an escape hatch built into the operation, just in case none of the above worked, Bissell explained. The rebels could "fade" to the nearby Escambray Mountains, where they could hide out and continue to harass the Castro government for the foreseeable future, "exerting continuing pressure on the regime."

Many who were in the room that day said it was this last aspect of the plan that sold it. The invasion was not an all-or-nothing proposition that depended entirely on conventional military success; between the possibility of uprisings among the Cuban populace and the chance for the brigade to go commando in the mountains, as Robert McNamara put it, "We were led to believe that the cost of failure would be small."

Kennedy was in—but only up to a point. "Too spectacular," he told Bissell. "It sounds like D-Day. You have to reduce the noise level of this thing."

This was not what Bissell wanted to hear; less noise meant less shock, and shock was part—no, it was the whole point. "You have to understand—," Bissell started to interject, but the president cut him short. Kennedy understood well enough to know he wanted the landing to be more discreet than the one Bissell proposed. The bigger the invasion, the more American it would appear. Tone it down, he told Bissell, and come back in a few days with the new plan.

Given that the president was rejecting one of the key elements out of hand, this might have been a good moment for Bissell to withdraw his own commitment to the operation and inform the president that, in his opinion, it would fail if so modified, especially considering that the modifications would have to be carried out in days. "It is hard to believe in retrospect that the President and his advisers felt the plans for a large-scale, complicated military operation that had been ongoing for more than a year could be reworked in four days and still offer a high likelihood of success. It is equally amazing that we in the agency agreed so readily."

STARTING WORK THAT same Saturday and going day and night through the following Tuesday, the men of WH/4, in consultation with staff officers of the Joint Chiefs, went back to the drawing board. They studied maps of Cuba to identify landing sites suitable for a less noisy enterprise—and also happened to have an airstrip that could accommodate a B-26. This was a condition Kennedy and Dean Rusk had imposed to enforce the impression that the invasion was homegrown. The brigade's planes needed to land and then take off on Cuban soil. The fact that Trinidad lacked a strip long enough to handle a B-26 was one of the reasons the president had rejected it.

The CIA planners quickly settled on an area of the southern coast of Cuba, 130 miles southeast of Havana, along a narrow, deep bay—the Bahía de Cochinos—that gave out onto the Caribbean Sea and faced

Central America. Just inland of the bay was a vast and nearly impenetrable swamp, the Ciénaga de Zapata.

The location had much to recommend it. Not only did the shoreline offer a number of sandy beaches that appeared ideal for amphibious landings, it also included a B-26-ready landing strip just inland of the coast. The population was very sparse, so the landing would indeed be quieter than in Trinidad—less public, less noticed, less chance for civilian casualties, and less resistance from Castro's militia during the landing phase. The barrier of the Zapata Swamp would have been a deficit for a World War II–type invasion, in which the goal was to advance after landing. But in this case, by limiting access, it served the CIA's strategy of securing and holding a beachhead while awaiting the arrival of the provisional government. For these reasons and others, Tracy Barnes, for one, had come to prefer the new plan "after cogitation," as he wrote in a March 16 memo. The marine specialist Jack Hawkins shared this opinion, at least originally. And when the plan was shown to the Joint Chiefs for a quick evaluation, they indicated that while they preferred the old site of Trinidad, they considered the new site a viable alternative, possessing "all the prerequisites necessary to successfully establish the Cuban Voluntary Task Force."

But there were problems with the site, evident to some CIA men from the start. David Phillips, the propaganda chief, saw the redrawn map of the invasion at headquarters a few days after the change was made and immediately noticed a crucial difference between the old site in Trinidad and the new one at the Bahía de Cochinos. The new site was now too far away from the Escambrays for any invaders to plausibly escape.

The second thing he noticed was that name: Bahía de Cochinos. Phillips spoke fluent Spanish and knew the translation: Bay of Pigs. As chief propagandist, with an appreciation for the effects of language, he saw a problem. "How can we have a victorious landing force wading ashore at a place with that name?"

MCGEORGE BUNDY WAS impressed when Bissell handed him the new plan on Wednesday, March 15. "They have done a remarkable job of reframing the landing plan so as to make it unspectacular and quiet, and plausibly Cuban in its essentials," he wrote to President Kennedy in advance of that afternoon's meeting to review the revised plan. "I have been a skeptic about Bissell's operation, but now I think we are on the edge of a good answer."

Bissell returned to the White House that afternoon to present the revised plan, which would henceforth be known as Operation Zapata. Kennedy agreed it was an improvement. But he was still looking for an invasion that would be less invasionlike. "The President did not like the idea of the dawn landing," according to notes taken by General Gray, "and felt that in order to make this appear as an inside guerilla-type operation, the ships should be clear of the area by dawn." Since November, Bissell and his colleagues had been preparing a *strike force* to hit Cuba with a frontal assault; now here was Kennedy, just a month before the launch, still talking about an *inside guerrilla-type operation*, just as he had at the February 8 meeting.

The language indicates how far apart the CIA and the president remained in their conceptions of what they were trying to accomplish. At this point it would have made sense for either man—or anyone else in the room—to step in and point out that they were trying to marry opposing and essentially incompatible goals. But they pushed on, Kennedy trying to make Bissell's operation more like a guerrilla infiltration, Bissell trying to appease the president while holding on to his strike force objective.

On the afternoon of Thursday, March 16, Bissell returned yet again to the White House. The CIA task force had spent another long night trying to tailor the plan to the president's specifications. In this newest iteration, the landing was to occur at night, and the ships, per Kennedy's wishes, would be gone by dawn. Forget that only a few days earlier Bissell had dismissed a night landing as difficult and impractical. If the president wanted a night landing, a night landing he would have.

What the president really wanted, it seems, was for the CIA to pull off the neat trick of invading Cuba without actually invading it: an immaculate invasion, as it were, in which the end result—fourteen hundred men arriving on a beach with tanks, mortars, bazookas, trucks, and jeeps—was somehow achieved without all the messy business along the way. When informed that the attack would be preceded by air strikes to dismantle Castro's air force and communications, Kennedy wondered whether the air strikes were really necessary. They absolutely were, he was repeatedly told, but, according to Bissell, "he wouldn't take yes for an answer."

In the meantime, Kennedy and his advisers seemed not to notice that the new plan, while ostensibly getting the president closer to his stated objective, actually took him farther from it. What the operation had gained in discretion it lost in potential for popular uprisings, since there were very few people in the neighborhood to rise up. Furthermore, as David Phillips noted when he looked at the map of Cuba, the possibility of the brigade going into the mountains was pretty much gone. The Zapata Swamp, with its boot-sucking glop and impenetrable tangles of mangrove, made a poor substitute as a guerrilla hideout.

Richard Bissell later wrote that if there was one sin of omission for which he was most guilty, it was neglecting to tell the president that the safety valve built into the old plan did not exist in the new one. "It must be admitted that we either encouraged or allowed the president and his advisers to believe that in the event of uncontainable pressure at the beachhead the brigade could retire and thereby protect the guerrilla option." Nobody had the heart to tell Kennedy that he himself had killed the guerrilla option when he ordered the new plan.

Miami, Mid-March

SO WHY DID Richard Bissell let the operation move forward after Kennedy began to meddle with it? The simplest answer—applying Occam's Razor again—is that he (and, for the moment, his colleagues in WH/4) still thought it could succeed, and genuinely *wanted* it to succeed because he believed its success was important. Personal pride and ambition, too, may have encouraged Bissell to accept mounting modifications. His reputation in the CIA and the Kennedy administration was riding on this operation, as was his position as Allen Dulles's heir apparent. To cancel would be equivalent to a forfeit. Nothing in Bissell's character suggests this would have been an acceptable outcome to him.

Another possible reason, as discussed earlier (and later) in these pages, is that Bissell assumed President Kennedy would not let it fail—would do, that is, whatever was necessary to make it succeed, even if that meant sending U.S. military forces to the rescue. Yet another possibility: Bissell assumed the Mafia would finally get its act together and take out Castro before, or coincident with, the invasion. So far there was little evidence to support that assumption.

This is not to say that the Mafia had been inactive. The previous September, while Castro was in New York at the United Nations, Johnny Rosselli and Robert Maheu had followed up their meeting at the Plaza Hotel with a trip to Miami Beach. There, at the Fontainebleau Hotel, Rosselli had introduced Maheu to two associates who would be able to help them out with the Castro problem. The men agreed to lend their support. Not until a couple of weeks later, when photographs of these men appeared in an issue of *Parade* magazine, did Maheu realize that Rosselli's associates were two of the Mafia's most powerful and dangerous bosses, Salvatore "Sam" Giancana, from Chicago, and Florida's own Santo Trafficante.

Despite the bosses' involvement, the assassination plot had yielded no results—Castro remained alive and kicking. What it had produced, instead, was a farcical round of complications and headaches. It turned out that mob bosses were less discreet than CIA officers (even the likes of Howard Hunt) and their love lives more complicated. Sam Giancana had bragged to anyone who would listen about the plan to kill Castro. Then, in October, he'd somehow convinced Maheu to pull the CIA into resolving a personal matter. Giancana had come to suspect that his girlfriend, the singer Phyllis McGuire (of the McGuire Sisters trio), was cheating on him with the comedian Dan Rowan (of the Rowan and Martin comedy team). The CIA agreed to bug Rowan's hotel room, perhaps as a return favor to Giancana or perhaps to find out if the mobster had been chatting with Miss McGuire about the Castro plot. After the bug was discovered by a hotel maid, the FBI had gotten involved, only dropping its investigation when the CIA requested it to do so.

Richard Bissell preferred to keep his distance from all of this. During the months leading up to the invasion, the phone would occasionally ring at the CIA, a shady underworld figure on the other end wanting to talk to the deputy director personally. Bissell never took the calls. "I don't know how they got the inside telephone number even," Bissell's secretary recalled. "He just didn't want to have any part of it."

But he did nothing to stop it, either. The same mid-March week that the CIA was reconfiguring its plan to suit the president, the agency's Castro assassination plot, after languishing for months, took a significant step forward.

A batch of six pills containing botulinum toxin, prepared by the CIA's Technical Services Division, had been delivered from the CIA to Robert Maheu. This came after an earlier batch was rejected because the pills failed to dissolve in water. The new batch "did the job expected of them" when tested on monkeys. The victim would die slowly, over the course of a few days, allowing the killer to make a clean getaway. Not the sort of gangland, guns-blazing hit the mob usually favored, but what hit man would take the kamikaze job of gunning down Fidel Castro in Cuba?

Maheu handed the pills to Rosselli in mid-March, just over a month before the invasion, at the Fontainebleau. They met in the company of Sam Giancana and Santo Trafficante, as well as Joseph Shimon, a Washington, D.C., police detective who moonlighted for Maheu. They were in town ostensibly to watch a heavyweight fight between Floyd Patterson and Ingemar Johansson.

Rosselli introduced Maheu to a Cuban exile named Tony Varona, who was going to arrange the job inside Cuba. Already well known to the CIA, Varona was one of the leaders of Frente, the exiled Cubans' leadership council that had been acting as a front for the agency in Miami. A man of considerable clout among the Cubans in Miami, Varona was also, as the CIA believed, an unscrupulous character—"a scoundrel, a cheat, and a thief," Jacob Esterline would call him—who was cozy with the Mafia because he hoped someday to return to Cuba and join them in business. For the moment, he had come to offer his services. He knew a waiter who worked in a Havana restaurant frequented by Castro. The waiter would drop a pill into Castro's drink. Varona just needed $10,000 to get the ball rolling.

Johnny Rosselli later testified that he saw Maheu dump the cash from a briefcase onto a bed in the Fontainebleau. Maheu and Rosselli then went downstairs to the lobby, where they met Varona in front of the Boom Boom Room and handed him the cash and the pills.

A few days later, Joseph Shimon, the Washington cop, got a call from Maheu, who had just read in a newspaper that Castro was feeling poorly. "Did you see the paper? Castro's ill. He's going to be sick two or three days. Wow, we got him." Maheu was wrong; the poison was never delivered to the target. In one version, the waiter/assassin chickened out; in another, the "go signal" from the CIA never came.

Just as circumstantial evidence suggests that President Eisenhower knew of the CIA plots to assassinate Castro, it seems likely that Kennedy, too, was aware of the continuing effort, though he may have been spared the grittier and more ridiculous details. Kennedy's old friend and confidant Senator George Smathers of Florida—the man with whom he had visited Cuba in his younger days—recalled a conversation he had with Kennedy while strolling the White House grounds sometime in March. Kennedy told Smathers that the CIA had led him to believe Castro would be assassinated. Smathers despised Castro as much as any American politician, but he was taken aback. He told Kennedy it was a bad idea. If Castro was killed, the United States would be blamed for it, and Kennedy would be personally held accountable. Kennedy, according to Smathers, agreed.

THE REAL CONCERN for the CIA in the weeks before the invasion was not Castro's assassination, nor was it even the military operation itself. It was the part that came after: the part regarding the provisional government under whose auspices the United States would enter Cuba. After a year of concerted effort by the CIA, the hoped-for coalition of exiled Cuban leaders—liberals, moderates, and conservatives joined by love of country and hatred of communism—remained unrealized. Gerry Droller (aka Frank Bender) and Howard Hunt had struck out. Hunt had become so disgusted with what he perceived as pressure from the new administration to make the coalition leftist—he favored a more conservative element—that in mid-March he threw up his hands and asked Bissell to give him a new assignment. Hunt flew back to Washington and joined David Phillips in the propaganda arm of the operation.

Bissell replaced Hunt with the former CIA station chief in Havana, James Noel. "We've only got a week to put them together," Bissell told Noel. "You go down there and do whatever is necessary."

Noel invited the exiled leaders to the Skyways Motel, near Miami International Airport. On the evening of Saturday, March 18, twenty-two Cubans passed under the cantilevered, wing-shaped awning and into the Skyways' banquet room. The meeting began with a scolding from Noel. There would be no more sweet talk, he told them; while they were squabbling over petty differences in Miami, they were losing Cuba. "If you don't come out of this meeting with a committee, you just forget the whole fuckin' business, because we're through."

The threat worked. By Monday morning, the Cubans managed to agree to a coalition of left, right, and center. They also issued a list of goals and principles, starting with the overthrow of Fidel Castro and a "return to law and order," and including the establishment of general elections within eighteen months and the adoption of "economic policies designed to increase the national income and raise the standard of living." Dr. José Miró Cardona, a moderate who had briefly served as the first prime minister of Cuba under Castro, was elected chairman of the committee. The name of the exile coalition was changed from the Frente (FRD) to the Cuban Revolutionary Council (CRC).

The new council made its debut in New York City on Wednesday, March 22, at a press conference at the Biltmore Hotel. Dr. Cardona announced confidently that the CRC would move to "secure a piece of Cuban soil," then serve as the provisional government of Cuba. When his chief lieutenant, Tony Varona—the same Tony Varona who just over a week earlier had met at the Fontainebleau with Maheu and Rosselli and had walked off with a briefcase containing $10,000—was asked whether the council was receiving any support from the United States, financial or moral, he shook his head emphatically. "Definitely no!"

12

"Albatross"

Late March–Early April 1961

Washington, D.C., Late March

"WHAT DO YOU think of this damned invasion?" Arthur Schlesinger asked President Kennedy at the end of a meeting about Cuba.

"I think of it," responded Kennedy, "as little as possible."

Certainly John Kennedy had plenty else to occupy his thoughts that Tuesday near the end of March. He'd just announced an increase in defense spending. In Laos, the Communist insurgent Pathet Lao were making steady gains and threatening to become a bigger headache than Castro. Kennedy was increasingly worried about developments in Vietnam, "the worst one we've got," he called it. He was initiating a large aid program, the Alliance for Progress (Alianza para el Progreso), to spur economic growth in Latin America, while establishing the Peace Corps to promote American goodwill throughout the world. There were pressing domestic matters, too. Race relations were boiling over in the American South. Freedom Riders were on the move.

But whatever else interceded, there was no real chance of Cuba drifting from his mind that spring. It was a subject he returned to again and again. It was, he told one journalist, his "albatross."

The morning after his exchange with Schlesinger, March 29, Kennedy welcomed former secretary of state Dean Acheson to the White House. A silver-haired man with thick eyebrows and a thin mustache, Acheson still maintained, at sixty-seven, his dashing good looks and rapier wit. One of the original anti-Communist "wise men" of the Cold War, Acheson had retired from public life after serving under Truman, but Kennedy wanted him back into the fold, at least unofficially. He valued Acheson's counsel. Like most people, though, he also found the old wise man to be prickly and condescending.

That morning Acheson (and his son-in-law, William Bundy, married to Acheson's daughter) sat in with the president for a National Security Council meeting. Afterward Acheson and Kennedy retired to a bench in the Rose Garden for a private moment in the sun. "I want to talk with you about something else," Kennedy said when they were alone. "Do you know anything about this Cuba proposal?"

"A Cuba proposal? I didn't know there was one."

As Kennedy explained the plan to get rid of Fidel Castro, he may have expected a nod of approval from Acheson; few Democrats were as wary of communism's spread as the former secretary of state; surely Acheson would support a move to send Fidel packing. But when Kennedy was finished, Acheson could barely contain his scorn. "Are you serious?"

"I don't know if I'm serious or just—I've been thinking about it," the president sputtered.

Acheson thought the plan was idiotic. "It doesn't take Price Waterhouse to figure out that fifteen hundred Cubans aren't as good as twenty-five thousand."

That afternoon, President Kennedy met again with his advisers to review the Cuba plans. Along with the usual roster—Bissell and Dulles, the Bundy brothers, McNamara, and Lemnitzer—Chester Bowles attended. Bowles, as undersecretary of state, was sitting in for Dean Rusk, who was attending a conference in Bangkok. Until this moment, Bowles had been out of the loop on Cuba and only barely aware of the planning. He was now getting a crash course from Bissell.

Like others in the room—Schlesinger, the Bundys—Chet Bowles had a long history with Dick Bissell, both personal and professional. They were old friends and fellow sailors from Connecticut; Bowles often borrowed Bissell's sailboat, the *Sea Witch*, for his own voyages along the Maine coast, and the two men sometimes sailed together. Back in January, Bowles had tried to convince Bissell to join him at the State Department as deputy undersecretary for political affairs, a notion that seemed to interest Bissell until President Kennedy put an end to it. "You can't have him," the president told Bowles. "He's going to take Allen Dulles's job on July first."* Now Bowles listened with growing dismay as his old friend spoke.

According to notes later drafted by Major General David Gray, Bissell began with a discussion of photoreconnaissance that had been conducted over Cuba, presumably by one of his own U-2 spy planes. Kennedy peppered Bissell with questions. How much did Castro know about the invasion? Had Castro said anything that would indicate he'd guessed it was coming? No, replied Bissell, he had not. Kennedy returned to his pet peeve. "Do you really have to have these air strikes?" he asked. Yes, said Bissell, they did.

Before the meeting broke up at five-thirty, the president told the group to plan on meeting again on Tuesday, April 4. They would hold off on the final decision until then.

"I have the impression that the tide is flowing against the project," Arthur Schlesinger recorded in his diary. The president was growing "steadily more skeptical."

IF SCHLESINGER WENT away hopeful that the operation was dying on the vine, Chester Bowles returned to his office at the State Department astonished that it was even being considered. Allen Dulles, said Bowles later, should have been "thrown out of the office, by either Eisenhower or Kennedy," simply for suggesting it. Like Schlesinger and Thomas Mann before him, Bowles felt compelled to share his objections. He sat down at once and drafted a memo, addressing it to Dean Rusk: "On Tuesday, April 4th, a meeting will be held at the White House at which a decision will be reached on the Cuban adventure," Bowles wrote. "During your absence I have had an opportunity to become better acquainted with the proposal, and I find it profoundly disturbing."

Chester Bowles was a peculiar figure in the Kennedy administration, in some ways already a doomed Cassandra—a fate this memo would help seal. A week shy of sixty, Bowles was deep into his second career as a statesman. In his previous life, he had cofounded the advertising agency

---

* McGeorge Bundy supported moving Bissell to the State Department, as he'd written to JFK on February 25. "One final argument in favor of this shift is that Bissell and the State Department would be good for each other: if Dick has a fault it is that he does not look at all sides of the question, and of course the State Department's trouble is that it is usually doing that and not much else."

Benton & Bowles and made himself rich enough by age forty to retire. Since then, he'd served a term as governor of Connecticut and had been President Truman's ambassador to India. During the 1960 presidential campaign he had served as Kennedy's chief foreign policy adviser and worked tirelessly to bring home to the candidate that faction of the party he best represented, the liberals.

Here was part of the problem with Chester Bowles. He was another liberal egghead, hatched from the same shell that produced Adlai Stevenson. Kennedy had wooed him when he needed him, and duly rewarded him for his efforts with the not-too-shabby spoils of undersecretary (after considering him, briefly, for secretary). But Kennedy did not, in the end, have any more time for Bowles than he had for Stevenson. Bowles was too soft, too much of a principled do-gooder, when what Kennedy wanted in a man was brass-tacks pragmatism. Bowles further suffered from the lamentable condition (in Kennedy's mind) of prolixity. He was a fellow who gave "long answers to short questions," as David Halberstam once wrote of him. No surprise, then, that Bowles launched his memo with a wordy, highly principled preamble:

> In considerable degree, my concern stems from a deep personal conviction that our national interests are poorly served by a covert operation of this kind at a time when our new President is effectively appealing to world opinion on the basis of high principle.
>
> Even in our imperfect world, the differences which distinguish us from the Russians are of vital importance. This is true not only in a moral sense but in the practical effect of these differences on our capacity to rally the non-Communist world in behalf of our traditional democratic objectives.
>
> In saying this, I do not overlook the ruthless nature of the struggle in which we are involved, nor do I ignore the need on occasion for action which is expedient and distasteful. Yet I cannot persuade myself that means can be wholly divorced from ends—even within the context of the Cold War.

Had Bowles's memo ever found its way in front of Kennedy's eyes—it almost certainly did not—they would have glazed over by this point. Kennedy had little interest in Bowles's "deep personal conviction."

Bowles handed his memo to Rusk in person on the evening of Friday, March 31, immediately upon the secretary's return to Washington. He urged Rusk to read it promptly and, if he agreed, to share its views with the president. "I think you can kill this thing if you take a firm stand on it," he told Rusk. "But if you can't, I want to see the President."

As time would tell, Rusk did not kill it. Nor did he evidently pass Bowles's memo on to Kennedy or arrange a face-to-face between Bowles and the president. Sometime later, Rusk sent the memo back to Bowles, as if it were a piece of mail that had accidentally come his way. In the corner, in tiny letters, were the secretary's initials, indicating that he had read, digested, and disposed of it: D.R.

EVEN BEFORE BOWLES handed his memo to Rusk that Friday night before Easter, Kennedy, on Thursday morning, heard from one last serious opponent to the invasion. This was J. William Fulbright, a long-serving senator from Arkansas and powerful chairman of the Senate Foreign Relations Committee. If Mann's and Bowles's objections never made it to the president, Senator Fulbright's certainly did.

A week prior to Easter, while he and Kennedy were exchanging pleasantries at an evening "coffee hour" for members of Congress, Fulbright happened to mention that he was going to Florida for the holiday weekend. Kennedy, who was flying down to Palm Beach, offered the senator a lift on *Air Force One*. Fulbright accepted. Realizing this would be a perfect opportunity to address an issue that had been troubling him, he got to work.

Fulbright was aware of the invasion in general terms. He was privy to rumors, of course, and Dulles and Cabell had been keeping Congress vaguely informed of the plan in intelligence briefings. Fulbright knew enough about the invasion to recognize it as a betrayal of every principle of foreign relations he held dear. Commonly acknowledged as one of the most authoritative voices on international affairs in the Democratic Party (the Fulbright scholarship would bear his name), he was, like Chester Bowles, a man who valued moral standards alongside practical goals. Nobody was likely to mistake this southern Democrat for a pushover or a softie, but he took a more nuanced view of communism than most of his fellow politicians. Yes, communism was bad, but it was not the devil's work, and certainly did not merit the kind of witch hunt stirred up by Joseph McCarthy. One of Fulbright's finer moments had come when most senators, including John F. Kennedy, were quailing before McCarthy; Fulbright was one of the lonely voices who stood up to the bully from Wisconsin. McCarthy vindictively took to calling him Senator Halfbright, but the pun had no traction. Fulbright had been a Rhodes scholar, and nobody seriously questioned his intellectual gifts.

Fulbright had backbone and decency, but he was, like many complex thinkers—particularly those who make their living as politicians—a frequently disappointing man. His principles seemed to fail him, for example, when it came to civil rights. Enlightened as his views were on international relations, his views on desegregation were no more, and perhaps less, progressive than those of his fellow southern Democrats. This was one reason why Kennedy had passed him over as secretary of state, a job he wanted and most Washington insiders assumed he would win even over strong contenders such as Stevenson, Bowles, and Rusk. Naming Fulbright to his cabinet would have instantly poisoned Kennedy's relations with African-American voters, 70 percent of whom had supported him at the polls. Fulbright had been magnanimous when the job went to Rusk, but friends knew the rejection stung. Perhaps giving the senator a lift to Florida was Kennedy's way of saying sorry.

On the morning of Thursday, March 30, Fulbright boarded *Air Force One* along with a number of other guests and White House staffers to begin the Easter weekend early. He and the president chatted cordially for a while; then, about an hour into the flight, Fulbright told Kennedy he had something he wanted to show him. He pulled a four-thousand-word memorandum out of his jacket pocket and handed it to the president. "I'd like you to read this."

Fulbright had prepared the memo over the previous several days with the aid of Pat Holt, the Latin American expert on the staff of the Senate Foreign Relations Committee. Some of its arguments would have been familiar to anyone who had read Mann's or Bowles's or Schlesinger's memos. Where Fulbright's was particularly effective was in pointing out that *even if the invasion succeeded* it would do incalculable harm to America's reputation, since it would be "of a piece with the hypocrisy and cynicism for which the United States is constantly denouncing the Soviet Union." In Latin America, the action would be "denounced from the Rio Grande to Patagonia as an example of imperialism." In the meantime, America would have assumed responsibility for governing Cuba, an "endless can of worms."

An implied question screamed out from between the lines: how on earth could the same man who had delivered those stirring words on the steps of the Capitol in January, who had since promised time and again to strengthen reason and civility in international relations, go forward with an action of such bald aggression? The memo concluded by reminding the president that Castro could well fall without a push from the United States. And if he did not, the world would not end: "the Castro regime is a thorn in the flesh; but it is not a dagger in the heart."

Before *Air Force One* landed at 11:20 A.M. at West Palm Beach, Kennedy had read the memo. "What do you think of it?" Fulbright asked. Kennedy's response was noncommittal. Some fellow passengers interrupted them, and the conversation turned to other matters. The senator and the president went off to enjoy their respective weekends. Fulbright assumed his arguments had missed the mark.

EVEN AS THE president grappled with his decision regarding Cuba that last week of March, the machinery of the U.S. government began gathering steam in preparation—though, as yet, nobody in charge was clear what exactly they were preparing *for*. It was something like a war, yet a war in which no U.S. military personnel were expected to fire a shot. In certain respects the task resembled nothing so much as a very elaborate job of chaperoning.

On March 23, an intra-agency coordinating committee known as the Working Group circulated a to-do list among the CIA, Department of Defense, and State Department. Counting back from D-Day, the list spelled out chores for each agency in day-by-day detail. For example, on D–9 (nine days before the invasion), the State Department was to "provide Working Group with Policy Statement as to what 'recognition' really means." That same day, the Pentagon would "complete logistics plans for DOD follow up support," while the CIA would "complete review of Psychological Warfare Plan for D-Day and post D-Day phase."

The State Department and the CIA both had plenty on their plates in these weeks before the invasion, but it was the Pentagon—specifically the Atlantic Fleet of the U.S. Navy—that was called upon to perform the most complex set of tasks. The navy was expected to prepare for a role the likes of which it had never before played: shadowing the brigade's small flotilla and offering logistical support, close enough to help if necessary, but not *too* close and not *too* much help. As the six ships and fifteen hundred men of the brigade landed on the shores of Cuba, one U.S.

aircraft carrier and seven U.S. destroyers, carrying among them nearly five thousand sailors, were to hide beyond the horizon and pretend they only just happened to be there, the way an elephant just happens to be in the room.

On March 24, General Lemnitzer sent to Admiral Robert Dennison, commander in chief of the Atlantic Fleet, a list of the navy's responsibilities. Dennison had been briefed about the operation in broad terms five months earlier at his office in Newport, Virginia, when Richard Bissell, accompanied by Jacob Esterline and Jack Hawkins, paid him a visit. An irascible sort of man, Dennison had not liked anything about this sketchy, half-baked scheme when he first heard of it in November, and his taste for it had not improved much since. Orders were orders, though, and on March 28 he sent back a response to Lemnitzer. "I will be prepared to execute the missions directed."

Dennison informed Lemnitzer that the aircraft carrier *Essex* and its complement of seven destroyers were scheduled to conduct routine antisubmarine warfare (ASW) exercises in the Gulf of Mexico from April 3 to April 18. After boarding two thousand marines and landing a squadron of Skyhawk A-4s on the *Essex* (the carrier would have to be modified to accommodate the navy jets), the admiral would divert the carrier and destroyers to the Caribbean. Nearly twenty other navy ships would already be conducting routine training operations off Guantánamo, bringing an extraordinary U.S. naval presence to the area. Just in case Castro tried to attack Guantánamo—a constant concern of the navy—Dennison would send in a marine battalion landing team to reinforce the base.

Admiral Dennison assigned Rear Admiral John A. Clark to command the American armada. At Dennison's office in Norfolk, Clark listened with growing dismay as several CIA visitors explained the operation. "You mean," he asked, turning to Dennison, "I'm to go down there armed to the teeth, but I'm not supposed to do anything?" Just so, replied Dennison, none too thrilled with the idea himself.

The operation was to be conducted in absolute secrecy. Ship logs were to be kept brief and would be destroyed afterward. No one was to whisper a word—a condition that held not only while the operation was ongoing but in perpetuity. To this day, official Bumpy Road records tell only part of the story of the U.S. Navy's involvement in the invasion of Cuba.

Aboard the USS *Essex*, Late March–Early April

ONE DECIDEDLY UNOFFICIAL document adds to the surviving history. This is the journal a young enlisted man named Don Roberts kept in the spring of 1961, when he was serving aboard the *Essex* as an aircraft maintenance technician. Don Roberts was by his own admission an unworldly lad when the operation began, fresh from boyhood in Noblesville, Indiana. He and the other seamen were told almost nothing about the *Essex*'s mission during the month or so the carrier was engaged in the Bay of Pigs operation. He only knew what his eyes and ears could tell him, which was that something significant and strange was happening around him. In brief notes, sometimes just a word or two per entry, Roberts jotted down day-to-day events. He mentioned his journal to no one, worried it might get him court-martialed. "Three navy commanders got us together and said you will never talk about what we're doing for the rest of your life or you're going to federal prison," he later recalled. "So I kept my mouth shut for thirty-five years." But a few years after the Bay of Pigs, back in Noblesville and teaching American history at the local public high school, realizing that he had obtained his own small but privileged glimpse of American history, Roberts sat down and expanded some of the entries slightly, while his memory was fresh. Still, he told no one other than his wife of his adventure aboard the *Essex*.

Don Roberts first understood he was going to be part of something unusual around his twenty-fourth birthday, on March 24, 1961. A few days earlier, the *Essex* had docked in Norfolk, Virginia, after sailing down from Quonset Point, Rhode Island. Usually the *Essex* patrolled the Atlantic on ASW drills. From the day the carrier arrived in Norfolk, though, it was evident the next mission was to be different. The tip-off was not just the three barges' worth of 250-pound bombs the ship took on that night. More disquieting were the 200 aluminum caskets.

The following day, a large contingent of high-ranking naval officers boarded the *Essex*. Then, on March 23: "Lots of new people on board, wearing civilian clothes. We were instructed not to talk to any of these people." Later Roberts came to realize that the civilians must have been from the CIA.

On March 26, at 1:00 A.M., the *Essex* took on several hundred more of the unnerving metal caskets. "Division officer can't tell me what's going on but he said we'll be the closest to war we've been since Korea," Roberts wrote. "People were asking me what was going on and I did not know." On March 29: "Everyone is uneasy. Something big is in the works." On April 2, Easter Sunday, Roberts simply wrote, "Lonely Day."

The *Essex* departed from Norfolk the following morning, April 3. "I have never seen the ship like this before. It is weird. No one talks. We're headed south."

Palm Beach, Easter Weekend

THE PRINTED SCHEDULES of John Kennedy's activities in Palm Beach give away none of his thoughts over the long Easter weekend, nothing to explain what arguments or considerations might have swayed him. Was it a conversation he had with one of his golf partners—Bing Crosby? Peter Lawford?—during the hours he spent on the links at the Palm Beach Country Club? On the afternoon of April 2, his golf foursome included Earl T. Smith, a Florida businessman who had served as ambassador to Cuba during the last years of the Batista regime and had strongly opposed the rise of Fidel Castro. Had Smith made a strong case for action to Kennedy? (Smith would see Kennedy several times over the weekend.) Or was it a prayerful notion that came over the president during the hours he spent in St. Edward's Church between Good Friday and Easter Sunday, Jacqueline at his side in her blue straw pillbox hat? An awakening during one of his walks on the beach? An epiphany while watching movies with his family? (What message might he have taken from *All in a Night's Work* and *Posse from Hell*?) The Secret Service had picked up rumors that some pro-Castro Cubans intended to kidnap Caroline, but there is no sign that Kennedy took these seriously or that they weighed on him.

Not all the president's time was spent in relaxation and worship. Dean Rusk came down to meet him bright and early on Saturday and stayed for nearly two hours. On Easter Sunday General Chester Clifton, his military adviser, visited for half an hour. Both men surely touched on plans for Cuba. Possibly these consultations persuaded the president.

Some of the president's advisers "darkly suspected," as Arthur Schlesinger put it, that the real persuader was his father, Joseph P. Kennedy. The elder Kennedy was a man who never stepped down from a fight and probably would have urged his son not to do so, either, certainly not from a fight against Communists, whom Joseph Kennedy loathed.

Whatever the reason, the president underwent some kind of conversion in Palm Beach. His advisers noticed it when he returned. As McGeorge Bundy would put it, "He went down there and something happened that made him come back and say, 'We're going ahead.'

"If I'd known him and had the kind of relationship with him that we both developed, I would have said, 'What the hell has happened to you on the weekend?' But I didn't say that. I said, 'Yes, sir.'"

BEFORE JOHN KENNEDY left Palm Beach for Washington on Tuesday, April 4, he put in a call to Senator Fulbright. He invited the senator and his wife to join him for the return trip. Again, Fulbright accepted. The senator met the president at the West Palm Beach airport in midafternoon and boarded *Air Force One*. Kennedy did not raise the subject of Fulbright's memo until the flight was nearly over. "I'm having a meeting to discuss the subject of your memorandum," he told Fulbright, almost as an afterthought. "I'd like you to come along." Fulbright could hardly decline. When they touched down at Andrews Air Force Base at 4:30 P.M., a chilly afternoon in early April, the senator walked across the tarmac with Kennedy to *Marine One*, the president's helicopter. They lifted off for Washington.

At the State Department that evening, Fulbright stood near the back of an auditorium as Kennedy gave a brief address to the Conference of Foreign Policy. It was six o'clock when the president led Fulbright to a small conference room off Dean Rusk's office, on the seventh floor of the State Department Building. According to the president's schedule, the next two hours and eighteen minutes he "conferred with Hon. Dean Rusk." This was deliberately misleading. To further throw off reporters and snoops, the president's counselors had arrived at the State Department separately and at staggered times.

Entering the conference room, Senator Fulbright was stunned to find himself amid the better part of the military and civilian leadership of the United States. Kennedy motioned for Fulbright to take the chair to his right. Despite his many years as a senator and frequent adviser to presidents, the senator found himself feeling uneasy as he sat. "God, it was tense," he later said. "I didn't know quite what I was getting into." It did not help that some of the fifteen or so men in the room were glaring at him. As surprised as he was to find himself among them, they were perhaps more surprised to find him, a U.S. senator, at a high-level, top-secret meeting of the executive branch. By now the president's advisers and senior military officers were becoming acquainted with Kennedy's predilection for flouting hierarchy and protocol, but to some of those present, this was simply too much. Fulbright had not asked to come here—he'd been invited—but they resented his presence.

Richard Bissell handled the briefing for the CIA with his usual aplomb, summarizing the latest tweaks and adjustments to the plan. Colonel Jack Hawkins had been brought along to attest to the fitness of the brigade; they were ready to go. Others in the room interrupted with questions. Bissell seemed to have an answer for all. "Suppose they can't establish a beachhead?" someone asked, according to the recollection of Richard Goodwin.

"It's unlikely, but we have a contingency plan." He turned to Hawkins, who handed him a document. Bissell pointed at the Bay of Pigs on a map. "If they can't hold on here, they'll move into the mountains here"—he pointed to the Escambrays—"and form guerrilla units which we can resupply by air. That's the worst that can happen."

"How do we know the Cuban people will support the rebels?"

Bissell turned to Hawkins again. "We have an NIE on that, don't we?" An NIE was a national intelligence estimate from the CIA's Board of National Estimates. In fact, the estimates regarding Cuban support for an overthrow of Castro were ambiguous at best, but according to Goodwin, Hawkins nodded affirmatively. "It was an unforgettable moment," Goodwin would write in his memoir.

In his own memoir, Bissell remembered the unforgettable moment differently. "I believe it was made clear that no immediate wave of rebellion among the population was expected."

Senator Fulbright could hardly believe his ears in any case. For all he had picked up about the invasion, he had no idea until now that planning was so far advanced and so near consummation. He was still absorbing what he had learned when the president turned to him and asked him to share his thoughts with the room. Fulbright had been given no opportunity to prepare his comments, but he did have the points of his memo freshly collated in his mind. Emboldened by his assumption that he'd been brought to speak because Kennedy shared his views, and more certain than ever that the CIA's plan was a grave error, Fulbright enumerated his arguments against the invasion. Above all, he told the group, it was immoral. "If one has faith in the human values of the United States, and if that faith is supported by vigorous and intelligent action, then there is no need to fear competition from an unshaven megalomaniac."

By the time he finished talking, Fulbright had delivered, in Arthur Schlesinger's words, "a brave, old-fashioned American speech, honorable, sensible, and strong." Unfortunately, added Schlesinger, "he left everyone in the room, except me and perhaps the President, wholly unmoved."

The problem was that most of those present found Fulbright's sermon more irritating than convincing. Who was he to come in and criticize a plan the administration had been considering for more than two months? His dismissal of the operation as immoral and absurd tacitly condemned the men sitting in the room, including the president. If the operation was so immoral and absurd, what were they doing talking about it? Some of those present, such as Deputy Secretary of Defense Paul Nitze, found the entire argument Fulbright presented—an argument from principle rather than practicality—fundamentally and irksomely off-point. "In my mind, our moral right to try to stop the Communist menace from invading our hemisphere was not the issue," Nitze later wrote. On the contrary, the United States had every right—indeed, an obligation—to excise communism from Latin America as if it were "a spreading cancer." Weeks earlier, Nitze had told Tracy Barnes that in his opinion, the CIA "should go ahead and do it."

When Fulbright was done speaking, Nitze tore into the senator's argument. This, he later realized, was a mistake. In doing so, he let himself get off-point, too, and neglected to mention his overriding concern: that he had come to believe the plan would probably fail as constructed. "I took the opportunity to attack Bill Fulbright's ideas and didn't bring up what was my worry, and that was, would the goddamn thing work?"

Nitze's deputy Bill Bundy shared his boss's irritation with Fulbright. He thought the senator's speech at this late date was counterproductive and turned the meeting into a kind of "charade." The moment had passed for moral debate; in the limited time that remained they should have been concentrating on practical questions: would it achieve what it was meant to do? "Damn it to hell," Bundy thought in frustration, "these are bridges we crossed long ago."

In retrospect, Senator Fulbright unwittingly acted as a kind of foil that evening, causing those present to close ranks and defend an operation about which many had their own grave doubts. Rather than take advantage of these critical minutes with the president to conduct a last-minute vetting, they came together in common cause and collectively supported the plan.

"What do you think?" asked the president, who had heard enough of speeches. "Yes or no."

Nearly every non-CIA man present would later claim that he knew the operation was badly flawed. Yet when the president went around the table and asked for their verdicts, not one spoke against it. McNamara, Nitze, and Mac Bundy all cast votes in favor. Bill Bundy did not approve of the president reducing a complex discussion to a yes-or-no vote—"This is not the right way to do it," he thought—then voted yes. When Kennedy came to Adolph Berle, a veteran Latin America specialist at State, Berle launched into a windy speech. Kennedy cut him short. "Adolph, you haven't voted."

"I'd say, let 'er rip!"

Perhaps the most surprising vote of the evening was the one cast by Thomas Mann, the assistant secretary of state who had argued so forcefully against the invasion back in February. Mann's memo had included many of the same points as Fulbright's, but Mann nonetheless now voted with the others for going forward. He did so because, unlike Fulbright, he believed Castro had to be dealt with one way or another; and since no one had come up with a better solution than the CIA's invasion, he concluded "that it was probably the last chance we would have" and threw in his support. Like Bill Bundy and others, Mann was not happy with the way the meeting was conducted—he found it both rushed and shallow—nor was he happy with the way the entire issue had been handled in the State Department. No one seemed to know exactly what the department's policy was on the invasion. Dean Rusk had been of no help. "I don't know what his feelings were," Mann said years later. "It created uncertainties . . . as to what the government line was, what the decision was."

With the possible exception of Kennedy himself, Rusk was the most inscrutable of the major participants in the weeks prior to the Bay of Pigs. A former Rhodes scholar who came to the State Department from running the Rockefeller Foundation, he was smart, industrious, decent, and possessed the hushed equanimity of a librarian. He also was a fairly colorless fellow, a man one would not notice in the room were he not secretary of state.

Even as Kennedy badgered the others for an up-or-down vote, Rusk remained firmly noncommittal. In fact, he remained mostly silent. For his own reasons, he, too, disapproved of the way the president was handling the meeting, throwing together men of various ranks and positions—cabinet secretaries and deputies and speechwriters—into a free-for-all, then asking everyone to weigh in as if their opinions were of equal value.

But Rusk's reserve went deeper than a concern for protocol; it was rooted in his whole approach to the job of secretary of state. Whatever his personal feelings on an issue, he believed that he was there in service to the president. "With large numbers of people sitting around the cabinet room talking with the president, I felt that my role was to penetrate weak points and raise searching questions about assumptions taken for granted," he later wrote. Not to express his own opinions, but to assist the president in reaching his.

In the interest of confidentiality, Rusk usually waited until he was alone with Kennedy behind closed doors before divulging any thoughts that might be construed as contrary to the president's. There was some doubt among the Washington cognoscenti as to whether "the silent secretary," as he was coming to be known, ever really opened up. One joke making the rounds in Washington placed Kennedy and Rusk alone together in the Oval Office; when the president asked the secretary for an opinion, Rusk demurred. "There's still too many people here, Mr. President."

Rusk later admitted he knew the plan to invade Cuba would not work. He had served enough time in the army, as a colonel in the Far East during World War II, to understand "that this thin brigade of Cuban exiles did not stand a snowball's chance in hell of success." He also shared, with other critics of the operation, a concern that it violated international law and that the fingerprints of the United States would be all over it, no matter how hard the CIA tried to erase them. But he did not tell Kennedy this. In the end, as he later came to realize, all his efforts at loyalty and solicitude backfired. "I served President Kennedy very badly," he wrote. "I didn't oppose it forcefully. . . . I was too busy sitting on my little post of responsibility."

OVER THE PAST fifty years, a good deal of ink has been poured into explaining how a roomful of extraordinarily smart and able men allowed themselves to support a disaster. Indeed, like another infamous incident a few years later—the 1964 murder of Kitty Genovese in Queens, New York, when thirty-eight people supposedly witnessed the crime but failed to report it—the communal lapse of the president's men became a case study in the psychology of group dynamics, inspiring, among other texts, the classic 1972 book *Groupthink* by Irving Janis. For Janis, the explanation for why Kennedy's advisers went along with the plan and committed "among the worst fiascoes ever perpetrated by a responsible government" came down to "concurrence seeking," a condition in which "amiability and esprit de corps" trump all other motives. Better to be loyal to the group than to be right. According to Janis, the presence of a contrary interloper—Senator Fulbright, in this case—only exaggerates the tendency toward groupthink among the others.

In addition to naturally occurring human dynamics that might affect any group, the men in the Kennedy administration were perhaps doubly at risk of concurrence due to the privileged backgrounds that many of them shared. They likewise shared a respect, inculcated by boarding school boyhoods and the fraternal experience of war, for toughness—those "balls" that every good New Frontiersman was supposed to haul around with him. Nobody in the Kennedy administration wanted to look like a guy unwilling to fight. As Theodore Sorensen would write of the lead-up to the Bay of Pigs, "doubts were entertained but never pressed, partly out of fear of being labeled 'soft' or undaring in the eyes of their colleagues." And though they were tough, they were also, probably, a little tentative, still new to their jobs, anxious to fit in and please the president and impress each other. They went along to get along, even if they knew they were headed for failure.

Or maybe the prospect of failure did not occur to them. Afterward, yes, they would claim they knew better, but possibly at the time they actually thought it would work. John Kennedy, as Chet Bowles would write, "had never failed at anything." The men who worked under him were not used to failure, either. People well acquainted with failure seldom end up in presidents' cabinets. Certainly they did not end up in John Kennedy's.

"I liked all the young men, but my God they were cocky," the presidential adviser Clark Clifford later reflected. "And that made the Bay of Pigs situation more cataclysmic than it might have been, because I think they felt that this was a real pike—that if Eisenhower and that bunch of mossbacks could do the job, they were really going to. . . ." Clifford did not complete the thought, but his point was clear. As smart as Kennedy and his men were, they were maybe too smart—too blessed by brains and breeding, too confident in their collective brilliance—for their own good.

* * *

BEFORE THE MEETING adjourned that evening, John Kennedy said something that should have given everyone in the room pause. "The President again indicated his preference for an operation which would infiltrate the force in units of 200–250 and then develop them through a build up." Bissell let Colonel Hawkins, his military expert, respond. Hawkins told Kennedy these smaller groups were considered a bad idea because they would be eliminated by Castro one by one, just as other guerrilla groups inside Cuba had been eliminated. "The President indicated that he still wished to make the operation appear as an internal uprising and wished to consider the matter further the next morning."

Kennedy's desire to break down the brigade into smaller units may have been sensible. But was it not alarming that just ten days before the brigade ships left Puerto Cabezas for Cuba, the president was still tossing out ideas that were completely at odds with the operation the CIA had been planning for months? The man who would ultimately make the key decisions, the commander in chief, was evidently still profoundly uncomfortable with essential elements of the plan. He and the CIA were not on the same page. They were possibly not even reading the same book.

The president stood. The time was a quarter past eight. The men had been meeting for more than two hours and had resolved little. "We better sleep on it," Kennedy said as the men began to file out. Then Kennedy turned to Fulbright. "You're the only one in the room who can say, 'I told you so.'"

Arthur Schlesinger had told him so, too, in so many words. But that had been in written form, in a memo. At this meeting, Schlesinger failed to speak up. A staff man, he believed he was too junior to register his opinion in such a setting. "It is one thing for a Special Assistant to talk frankly in private to a President at his request," Schlesinger explained later, "and another for a college professor, fresh to the government, to interpose his unassisted judgment in open meeting against that of such august figures as the Secretaries of State and Defense and the Joint Chiefs of Staff, each speaking with the full weight of his institution behind him." Nor would it have helped—to underline the point Ted Sorensen made—that Schlesinger would have been in the unenviable position of arguing, like Senator Fulbright, *against* a military action. While the advocates of the venture could "strike virile poses and talk of tangible things" such as air strikes and landing craft, the naysayer was left with wimpy-sounding abstractions such as "morality" and "other such odious concepts." So he sat back and watched Fulbright fail to make the case for the opposition and bit his tongue.

Schlesinger was about to slip out of the conference room when Kennedy called him over. He asked the young professor what he thought now of the invasion. Speaking quickly and, he later thought, incoherently, Schlesinger replied that he felt pretty much the same as he had all along: it was a bad idea. Kennedy nodded but said nothing.

AFTER THE MEETING, Chester Bowles paid Dean Rusk a visit in the secretary's office to find out how things had gone. Was the invasion still on? Had Rusk given Kennedy the memo? Should he talk to the president himself?

No need, Rusk responded. He told Bowles not to worry about the matter. "It isn't going to amount to anything."

"What do you mean, 'amount to anything'?" asked Bowles. "Will it make the front page of the *New York Times*?"

"I wouldn't think so."

13

"Infinite Trouble"

April 5–April 11, 1961

On the morning of Wednesday, April 5, Arthur Schlesinger rose early and hurried to his office. His quick, stilted conversation with President Kennedy immediately after the meeting the previous evening had left him feeling frustrated. He wanted to try, once again, to marshal his arguments against the invasion. He was at his typewriter by 6:30 A.M., tapping away as early light slanted through the windows of the East Wing.

"When you asked me after the meeting yesterday what I thought about the Cuban proposal, I am afraid that I did not give a properly ordered answer," wrote Schlesinger. He went on to enumerate the "hazards," as he saw them. First of all, no matter how "Cuban" the invasion was supposed to look, everybody on earth would assume that the United States was behind it.

> If we admit involvement, we admit action taken in violation of the basic characters of the hemisphere and of the United Nations. If we justify such violation by pleading a higher law, we place ourselves thereafter on the same moral plane as the Soviet Union. If we deny involvement, few will believe us; and we invite a repetition of the U-2 episode, which made us look absurd before the world.
>
> Whatever we do, the effect will be to spoil the new US image—the image of intelligence, reasonableness and honest firmness which has already had such an extraordinary effect in changing world opinion about the US and increasing world confidence in US methods and purposes.

Practically speaking, the United States would not be able to allow a defeat in Cuba, which would mean "the logic of the situation could well lead us, step by step, to the point where the last step would be to dispatch the Marines." If this was done, "Cuba will become our Hungary," warned Schlesinger, recalling the Soviet Union's bloody and ignominious assault on that country in the autumn of 1956.

When Kennedy saw Schlesinger later in the day, having presumably read the memo, he assured him that the invasion was not a done deal. "You know, I've reserved the right to stop this thing up to twenty-four hours before the landing. In the meantime, I'm trying to make some sense of it. We'll just have to see."

The next couple of mornings, with Schlesinger in attendance, Kennedy continued to hold meetings on the operation with his top advisers. Despite his assurances to Schlesinger, the president allowed the operation to move forward and gather steam. The discussion no longer revolved around *whether* the invasion should occur, but around *how* it should proceed.

Kennedy and his advisers ran through several CIA-generated ruses meant to fool both Castro and the general public about the real nature and origin of the attack on Cuba. One of these called for fake defections from Castro's air force—the "defectors" would actually be brigade pilots—timed to correspond with the opening bombing sallies, so that the attack would appear to come from inside Cuba. The CIA also informed the president of plans to stage a diversionary landing on the eve of the first air attack, intended to draw Castro's attention from the real landing site at the Bay of Pigs to another province of the country.

After the April 6 meeting, Schlesinger was aware that the time to halt the operation was slipping away. He wrote in his journal, "We seem now destined to go ahead on a quasi-minimum basis—a large-scale infiltration (hopefully) rather than an invasion."

Schlesinger's visit to the president late the following afternoon, April 7, only confirmed the sinking feeling. "It is apparent that he has made his decision and is not likely now to reverse it." Schlesinger quoted the president in his journal entry that day: "If we have to get rid of these 800 men, it is much better to dump them in Cuba than in the United States." To Schlesinger, the statement "suggested how much Dulles's insistence on the disposal problem had influenced the decision, as well as how greatly Kennedy was himself moved by the commitment of the Cuban patriots." That was one way to interpret Kennedy's words. But blaming the decision on Dulles's "insistence" made Kennedy look more like a passive sap than he really was. It was a stretch, too, to hold up Kennedy's statement about the exiles as evidence of how "moved" he was. On the contrary, Kennedy's choice of words—*dump them in Cuba*—sounds almost callous.

Most disturbing of all, at least from a strategic point of view, was that Kennedy apparently believed only eight hundred men served in the brigade. The actual number by early April, as the president should have known, was closer to thirteen hundred. The eight hundred number was apparently lodged in Kennedy's brain from briefings of the past. The error may have been a slip of the tongue, but, like other comments made by Kennedy in the weeks before the invasion, it called into question his basic grasp of the operation. If he miscalculated the number of men involved by nearly five hundred, what else did he have wrong?

NEW YORK TIMES reporter Tad Szulc miscalculated the number, too—he thought as many as six thousand recruits were preparing to invade Cuba—but otherwise he had a better handle on the Cuba operation than many men in the administration. Szulc's reporting on the CIA operation would become an important episode in the final lead-up to the Bay of Pigs. At the very least, it would mark a significant moment in the history of the *New York Times*. When Szulc died forty years later, his Bay of Pigs article, above hundreds of others he wrote, would headline his obit in the *Times*: TAD SZULC, 74, DIES; TIMES CORRESPONDENT WHO UNCOVERED BAY OF PIGS IMBROGLIO.

Szulc was thirty-four years old in the spring of 1961 and one of the bright stars in the newspaper's constellation of Latin American correspondents. He was Polish by birth but, more to the point, a born reporter, endowed with rapacious curiosity and bottomless stores of energy. A chain-smoker with a taste for trench coats and "a passion for meeting odd strangers in ill-lighted bars in ill-frequented parts of town" (as his *Times* colleague Harrison Salisbury wrote), Szulc was known in the halls of the newspaper's Times Square headquarters as an unrelenting, if somewhat mysterious, dervish of productivity. In addition to his other qualities and abilities, he possessed that indispensable gift of every great reporter: being in the right place at the right time.

So it was that he had happened to be in Miami at the end of March—the same Easter weekend President Kennedy flew to Palm Beach—taking a quick break after filing a long string of stories from Rio de

Janeiro and Lima, among other places, when the story about the invasion of Cuba fell into his lap. His tip came from a Cuban acquaintance he bumped into while sipping a martini at a hotel bar. Like most people, Szulc had heard the rumors (and read the articles, including those in his own paper) about training camps filled with Cuban exiles. But what he learned now, as he pieced together an account of the Cuban operation, was that an invasion was, as he would put it, "imminent." Smelling a scoop, he jumped.

Even before Szulc's article ran it began to stir up trouble. On Wednesday, April 5, two days before publication, Szulc was in Washington to share breakfast with his friend Donald Wilson, a former hotshot journalist for *Life* magazine who had recently joined the administration as deputy director of the U.S. Information Administration. Under the assumption that the USIA would oversee the flow of information once the invasion of Cuba began, Szulc asked Wilson what sort of arrangements might be made to brief reporters covering the invasion. Szulc hardly expected Wilson's stunned response: *What invasion?*

Don Wilson was a well-connected young man in Washington. His recently arrived boss, Edward R. Murrow, was even better connected. Murrow, fifty-three, had been the most respected and celebrated television journalist in America before joining the administration as director of the USIA. As recently as January, he had reported on Kennedy's inauguration for CBS. Murrow's understanding with Kennedy as he accepted his new job was that both the agency and its director would be brought closer to the hub, and kept more in the loop, than they had been in previous administrations.

When Wilson burst into his boss's office after breakfast and announced what he had picked up from Szulc, Murrow was "totally taken aback," Wilson later recalled. The fact that anti-Castro training camps had already been mentioned in newspapers had not prepared either man for Szulc's revelation that the invasion was about to occur. "You read a lot of junk in the newspapers," Wilson explained. "We read the newspapers avidly, of course, but that doesn't mean you're filled in. The newspapers really didn't tell you it was coming. We were smart boys, but we didn't really figure it out until we were told." As Wilson filled his boss in, Murrow's surprise turned to anger. How had it come to pass that he, director of the USIA, was learning such critical information by way of a newspaper reporter? "Get me Allen Dulles," he snapped.

It is a measure of the respect Ed Murrow commanded in Washington that within hours he and Don Wilson were sitting in the office of the CIA director at agency headquarters. They got little out of Dulles. As they peppered him with questions, the director sucked on his pipe and responded with polite nonsense. "It was a remarkable meeting," Don Wilson said. "Here's Allen Dulles, one of the smartest men in the world, and he answered us with non sequiturs. We'd ask him a question, and he'd go on another tack, so we realized right away he could not answer us."

Later that day, back at his USIA office, Murrow got a call from Mac Bundy at the White House. Bundy filled Murrow in on the invasion. Murrow had calmed down and was a good sport on the phone with Bundy, but when he hung up he was still upset. Not because he had been left out of discussions regarding a major foreign policy move. Rather, because invading Cuba was a "stupid, stupid idea," as Don Wilson would later recall his boss's view; "not only foolish, but immoral, wrong."

PERHAPS IT WAS Bundy who first brought Tad Szulc's article to John Kennedy's attention. Somebody—it's not clear who—apparently read a draft over the phone to Kennedy that Thursday. Kennedy was furious; it would be "treason" for the *Times* to publish the story. According to several accounts, Kennedy personally tried to get the *Times* to kill it, on the grounds that it would compromise a secret government action and put human lives at risk. In one version, he called the newspaper's publisher, Orvil Dryfoos. In another, Dryfoos called Kennedy. Whoever called whom, the publisher got the message. On April 6, Dryfoos came down from the fourteenth floor of the Times Building for a rare visit to the third floor. He crossed through the newsroom to have a word with his managing editor, Turner Catledge. According to the man who succeeded Catledge as the *Times*' managing editor, Clifton Daniel, Dryfoos "was greatly troubled by the security implications of Szulc's story. He could envision failure for the invasion, and he could see his *New York Times* being blamed for a bloody fiasco." Catledge shared the publisher's concern, at least to an extent, and went to work toning down Szulc's account. "I was worried not so much about protecting the government," Catledge later explained, "as about protecting the *Times*. . . . I was willing to say an invasion was planned but not that it was imminent." Should the invasion never materialize, he did not want the newspaper to look foolish.

So the word "imminent" was removed from Szulc's description of the invasion. References to the CIA were struck. The headline was shrunk from an emphatic four columns to a coy one column, and the article's placement was shifted from the top of the front page to a less prominent position lower down. None of this was done lightly or without vehement protest. Theodore Bernstein, an assistant managing editor, and Lewis Jordan, a news editor, both argued that allowing White House concerns to dictate front-page news was an abdication of the paper's journalistic responsibility. Some *Times* men threatened to quit over the incident. None ever forgot it.

THE SAME THURSDAY that Orvil Dryfoos visited the *Times'* third-floor newsroom, Arthur Schlesinger arranged to kill another story about the invasion without ever leaving his office in the East Wing. This one was set to appear in the *New Republic* magazine. As a courtesy, the magazine's editor and publisher, Gil Harrison, had sent galleys of the article to his old friend Schlesinger. The article was titled "Our Men in Miami" and had been written by a pseudonymous author. It was, according to Schlesinger, "a careful, accurate, and devastating account of CIA activities among the refugees." As a scholar and writer, Schlesinger felt uneasy in the role of censor, but as a White House aide he was alarmed. He forwarded the article to Kennedy with a note attached. "I think he would withdraw the article if we asked him to do so. I am not sure we should ask him to do so."

Kennedy did not share his aide's scruples. "Stop it," he instructed Schlesinger. So Schlesinger held his nose and called Harrison back later in the day. "I must ask you on the highest authority not to publish this piece." Harrison capitulated.

"Gil Harrison came through like a gentleman and a patriot," Schlesinger wrote to Kennedy. "He asked no questions and said he would drop the piece, though it must have done violence to his journalistic instinct."

The identity of the pseudonymous author of "Our Men in Miami," it should be noted, was Karl E. Meyer, an editorial writer for the *Washington Post*. The reason Karl Meyer was writing about the invasion for the *New Republic* and not his own publication was apparently that he had been unable to convince his bosses at the *Post* to carry the story. The newspaper's publisher, Philip Graham, a close friend of the president, had personally killed a few pieces on the Bay of Pigs.

In some respects, the Kennedy administration marked a high point for American journalists. Seldom had ink-stained editors and reporters been given so much attention by those in high office. Kennedy, once an aspiring journalist himself, invited men such as Ben Bradlee of *Newsweek*, Charles Bartlett of the *Chattanooga Times*, and the syndicated columnist Joe Alsop into his home. He sailed and watched movies and dined with them; he counted them as friends. This was all very cozy and glamorous and gave all journalists, whether they rubbed elbows with the president or not, a boost in stature and pride. But it was also, of course, toxic for the trade of journalism. Like the legions of women who lifted their skirts for John Kennedy (never mentioned in the press at the time), many newspapermen lost their heads in his presence and let him have his way. "Kennedy, after all, was so likable, so charming about his connections with publishers and reporters, he made it easier for journalists to believe in his essential good will," David Halberstam would later write. "It was impossible for important journalists of that era to believe that such a man would carry America on a course into darkness."

Tad Szulc's edited story appeared in the *New York Times* on the morning of Friday, April 7. "For nearly nine months," the article began, "Cuban exile military forces dedicated to the overthrow of Premier Fidel Castro have been training in the United States as well as in Central America." Even in its attenuated form, the article angered Kennedy. "I can't believe what I'm reading! Castro doesn't need agents over here. All he has to do is read our papers!"

Havana, April 8

BUT, OF COURSE, Castro did have agents in the United States, and probably in the training camps in Guatemala, and he did not need the *New York Times* to tell him what he already knew. He had so much intelligence coming in from the Cuban exile community in Florida, in fact, that his greatest difficulty was sorting truth from rumor.

In addition to reports from his own agents, Castro may have learned the specific invasion date—April 17—from Soviet intelligence. Jacob Esterline, the WH/4 task force chief, would be informed sometime after the invasion that CIA counterintelligence agents had intercepted a "cable of this Russian diplomat who had gotten this information in Washington, and had gone to Mexico." Apparently somebody in the

U.S. government had leaked the date to the Soviet diplomat, who had then notified the KGB from the Soviet embassy in Mexico City in early April. "I know that within a few days of his [Kennedy's] giving the word, the Soviets had it from Mexico," Esterline told CIA historian Jack Pfeiffer in a 1975 interview. It is not clear what use, if any, the KGB made of this intelligence, nor if the Soviets bothered to pass it on to Castro. Like the Cubans, the KGB was having a difficult time distinguishing fact from fiction amid the surfeit of incoming intelligence. Some histories, and at least one Hollywood movie (*The Good Shepherd*), have ascribed great significance to this leak, but even if it did reach Castro's ears—by no means certain—it's unlikely it was decisive. Castro was already about as primed for an invasion as he could possibly be. Nearly every day in the first weeks of April he spoke of the coming "mercenaries," as he called them, exhorting his people to prepare for war.

On Saturday, April 8, as the CIA was sending its first U-2 forays over Cuba to collect reconnaissance on Castro's air fleet, Castro was yet again speaking of the coming invasion. "Really, rather than Central Intelligence Agency, it should be called the 'Central Agency of Yankee Cretins,'" he told a meeting of the Confederation of Cuban Workers. "For months the 'Central Agency of Cretins' has been preparing—on the soil of Guatemala and the soil of other countries ruled by puppets of imperialism—military bases and armies of mercenaries to attack our country. . . . We will submit to any sacrifices but we will not submit to the Yankee yoke, or to the gangsters and thieves of imperialism. The terrorists will be exterminated."

Castro's security apparatus had already begun to arrest suspected dissidents, rounding up and throwing into jail many thousands of Cubans, summarily executing some of them. Castro understood, perhaps better than the CIA, that no invasion would succeed without internal support. He was ruthless in making sure there would be none.

New York, April 8

THAT SAME SATURDAY found Arthur Schlesinger pressing on with his campaign to halt the invasion. First thing that morning he visited Dean Rusk at the State Department. Like Chester Bowles before him, he hoped Rusk might embrace his concerns and prevail upon the president. Rusk listened "quietly and mournfully," then told Schlesinger that he intended to write a "balance sheet" laying out the pros and cons of the project over the weekend and present this to Kennedy on Monday. Schlesinger never learned if Rusk actually accomplished this.

After leaving Rusk's office, Schlesinger hurried to National Airport and caught the Eastern Airlines shuttle. Landing in New York, he went directly to the U.S. Mission to the United Nations, on Park Avenue in midtown Manhattan. He had been sent by Kennedy to partake in a briefing of Adlai Stevenson on the operation to invade Cuba.

It made a good deal of sense that Stevenson, the nation's ambassador to the United Nations, should be informed, if not consulted, about this development in U.S.-Cuba relations; particularly so given the fact that the ambassador was at that moment preparing for a previously scheduled U.N. debate regarding long-standing charges by Cuba against U.S. aggression. "The integrity and credibility of Adlai Stevenson constitutes one of our great national assets," Kennedy had told Schlesinger the previous afternoon. "I don't want anything to be done which might jeopardize that." The quote makes Kennedy sound as if he cared more for Adlai Stevenson than he did. But he was a smart enough politician to realize he could not afford to lose Stevenson's support at a moment when he would need it most. Twice nominated as the Democratic candidate for president (beaten in both 1952 and 1956 by Eisenhower), Stevenson still commanded a great deal of respect from many in the party, particularly its liberal wing, and was highly regarded by leaders around the world.

Tracy Barnes handled the briefing for the CIA. According to a number of people who were present at the U.S. Mission that Saturday, Barnes earned his reputation as "the soul of vagueness," the sobriquet by which some of his fellow CIA officers knew him. He left out many key details of the operation, omissions that would cause Stevenson grief the following Saturday.

One of those sitting in the meeting, Francis T. P. Plimpton, then deputy U.S. representative to the United Nations (as well as a founding partner of the New York law firm Debevoise & Plimpton and the father of writer George Plimpton), later recalled that while Barnes "guardedly indicated" an attack was coming, the overall impression the CIA man gave was of a gradual buildup funded entirely by Cubans, with "no hint of a frontal assault." According to Plimpton, the briefing, on the whole, demonstrated "a great lack of candor."

Arthur Schlesinger recalled the meeting with Stevenson a little differently. "We told him about the exile group. We told him we were training them, supplying weapons," Schlesinger recounted. "We told him that the Cubans were armed by us and the money had come from the United States, and it was going to take place." Still, Schlesinger acknowledged, there was "a failure of communication." He and Barnes neglected to mention that the operation was commencing in just over a week—that the landing of the American-backed brigade, in fact, had been scheduled for the morning of Monday, April 17, the very day Adlai Stevenson was supposed to take the floor of the General Assembly and tell his fellow delegates how wrong the Cuban government was to accuse America of aggression. "I fear we inadvertently left him with the impression that it would not take place until the General Assembly adjourned," Schlesinger wrote. Even by the standards of top-secret intelligence briefings, this one was "unduly vague."

The vagueness seems not to have arisen from any sinister intent. Indeed, Tracy Barnes's decidedly unsinister personality was probably more to blame than deliberate obfuscation. Barnes was kind, outgoing, genteel, utterly likable, and immeasurably charming. But he was not a man known to let hard facts spoil an otherwise pleasant occasion. "Tracy was one of the sweetest guys that ever lived," said Jacob Esterline, "but he couldn't ever draw a straight line between two points."

"Knowing Tracy, I've always had severe doubt that Tracy made it very clear to the Ambassador," said Richard Drain, who worked under Esterline in WH/4. Drain thought Barnes probably handled Adlai the way he handled most people—"lots of smiling and graciousness, interjection of completely non-connected events, shook hands, laughed, and said what a great time he'd had." And neglected to mention that Stevenson's life was about to get turned upside down.

In any case, Stevenson heard enough from Barnes and Schlesinger to express alarm. "Look, I don't like this," he said when the briefing was done. "If I were calling the shots, I wouldn't do it. But this is Kennedy's show." When Schlesinger had a moment to himself later that day, he noted in his journal that Stevenson "wholly disapproves of the project . . . and believes it will cause infinite trouble."

Washington, D.C., April 9

A BRIGHT EARLY-SPRING day was blooming that Sunday, and Richard Bissell was at home in Cleveland Park enjoying a rare moment with his family. The bell rang. At the door were Jacob Esterline, the buzz cut, powerfully built task force chief of the CIA's Cuba operation, and Jack Hawkins, the marine colonel who had been overseeing the military planning. Esterline and Hawkins were formidable-looking men, but as they stood at Bissell's front door that Sunday, they were gray-faced and red-eyed, depleted by anxiety and exhaustion. Esterline had called ahead, so Bissell knew why they were here. Still, he greeted them warmly and escorted them to his living room.

Life in the Bissell home had become particularly hectic that spring. Richard Bissell's daughter, Ann, then a sophomore at the nearby Sidwell Friends School, recalls how the pace and intensity of her father's work picked up in the weeks before the invasion. He was seldom home, and when he was home he brought his work with him.

"Things were going on in our house. You know when you have red telephones and white telephones, when you have a safe in your house where you've never had a safe before. And he was spending less and less time [at home]. There were some weeks there where he was coming home very, very late, and we didn't see him very often. He knew that I was aware. Rather than have me be confused and maybe upset by this, I think he wanted us to understand why. That it wasn't us. That there wasn't anything wrong with the marriage. That it was very important work he was doing."

Bissell had already talked with his children, in very general terms, about what was happening. He did not share specifics of the Cuba operation, of course, but he addressed it elliptically, thematically. He spoke of risk, of how great accomplishments require taking chances, which in turn requires courage. Later, Ann Bissell came to understand that he was preparing them—and perhaps preparing himself, too—for what might be coming. "I just remember that conversation so well, and it stuck with me. And then as things began to come apart, shall we say, I understood what he was saying."

Richard Bissell had achieved a great deal with his life. In his time at the CIA, particularly with the U-2 program, he had done important, even history-making work. Now he was in charge of an effort to overthrow a Communist dictator, a covert operation that was unlike anything ever attempted by the CIA. Under him in WH/4 was a staff that had ballooned from the original forty men to nearly six hundred—and that was just a small part of his dominion. He personally commanded a military, complete with army, navy, and air force, that rivaled that of some nations.

The question, by early April, is whether Bissell still believed he had a firm grip on the Cuba operation. Later, in interviews and in his memoir, he would revisit many of the choices made or conceded by the CIA in those final weeks and see clearly how they went wrong. But that was in hindsight.

Bissell was at his most opaque in these days leading up to D-Day. He had to be aware that the operation was degenerating daily. The Joint Chiefs' evaluation had warned that the invasion required surprise to succeed, but there could be little surprise when the *New York Times* was publishing accounts of the operation on the front page. The Joint Chiefs also advised that the operation would require popular support, but how would the invasion in its quiet new location rouse the Cuban people to action? Worst of all, the president was giving every indication that he had a different operation in mind than the one Bissell and the men of WH/4 had been preparing. Yet Bissell, perhaps in a sincere expression of his faith in the plan, or perhaps reflecting his coy conviction (as some have suggested) that a deus ex machina—a hired assassin, a platoon of U.S. Marines—would come along and take care of Castro before the operation could fail, or perhaps because he simply believed it was too late to go back, seemed almost sanguine.

Whatever the reason for Bissell's show of confidence, Jacob Esterline and Jack Hawkins did not share it. In fact, on this Sunday morning, they had come to tell him they believed the operation was in serious jeopardy and wanted no more of it. Sitting there in Bissell's living room, the two men, in obvious distress, spilled out frustrations and concerns that had been accumulating between them (and among many of their subordinates) over the previous weeks. The operation had undergone too many changes, had been compromised in too many ways. It was no longer the operation they had signed on to, nor one they believed would succeed. Rather, it had the makings of a "terrible disaster."

Esterline and Hawkins were particularly distressed about the hasty change of landing site from Trinidad to the Bay of Pigs. In Hawkins's case, this concern was belated, since he initially indicated satisfaction with the new site, but it was real and urgent. Both men worried the air support so necessary to the operation's success was being compromised by the president's compulsion for deniability. Without sufficient airpower, the brigade would be trapped on the beaches behind the swamp, unable to hold its turf, unable to break out and nowhere to go if it could. The operation had to be canceled, they told Bissell. If not, they wanted to resign.

Bissell listened attentively. He was not, in the end, a man immune to pressure; he seemed, rather, to channel it into the movements of his large hands, rubbing and rolling them over each other as the rest of him sat still. "The atmosphere was calm, serious, polite and mutually respectful," Hawkins would write years later of the meeting in Bissell's living room. "In all my dealings with Bissell I found him to be courteous and friendly, never abrupt, abrasive or overbearing." None of which would prevent either Hawkins or Esterline from feeling very bitter toward Bissell later on.

Bissell agreed that the operation had been compromised. But he also believed it was too late to stop it and they had to see it through. "He earnestly asked us not to abandon him at this late date," wrote Hawkins. Somewhat mollified, the men agreed to stay, but only after exacting "a promise from him that he would take immediate action with the president to use more aircraft and increase the power of the attack on the opposing air force."

THE NEXT DAY, Monday, April 10, Richard Bissell went to the Justice Department to meet alone with Robert Kennedy. Ordinarily, attorneys general do not receive CIA briefings on overseas covert operations. In this case, of course, the attorney general happened to be the president's brother and the president wanted him briefed, so he was. Bissell gave the younger Kennedy what he considered a "straightforward" rundown of the operation. It was obvious to Bissell from Robert Kennedy's reactions that he was more skeptical about the operation than his brother was. Kennedy asked Bissell what he thought the chances were for success. Two out of three, Bissell responded. "I hope you're right," said the attorney general.

"Usually such a remark implies that the speaker hopes you're right," Bissell later wrote, "but is by no means sure you are."

Straits of Florida, April 9–April 10

THAT WEEKEND THE aircraft carrier USS *Essex* and its complement of seven navy destroyers were somewhere in the Straits of Florida, between the Keys and the western end of Cuba, bearing south for the Yucatán Channel. Officially designated Special Task Group 81.8, this formidable fleet would in days rendezvous discreetly with the brigade's little armada and escort it toward the southern coast of Cuba. For the moment, though, the sailors aboard the navy ships could only guess their location, as the commanding officers told them nothing. It did not take much to figure out they were not navigating the common course of their ASW drills. "Usually when we went into the channel we headed north," explained Billy Houston, then a nineteen-year-old gunner's mate aboard the destroyer USS *Murray*. "That time we went into the channel and headed south." Off the starboard side they could see land; one night they made out the lights of Miami. What geography suggested, temperature confirmed. "Instead of freezing," said Houston, "all of a sudden we're sweating."

"When I saw the coast of Florida when we were going by at night, I figured it out then," said Jim Padgett, a twenty-year-old gunner's mate aboard the destroyer USS *Eaton* at the time. On the whole, though, they did not spend a lot of time speculating. "We were trained sailors. We did what we were told. There wasn't a lot of grumbling."

Sailors on the aircraft carrier *Essex* were given a cover story for the operation. "We were instructed today to tell our folks that we were here to do a large study of water tides—currents and the Atlantic drift," wrote Don Roberts, the twenty-four-year-old aircraft maintenance technician, in his journal on April 5. "Scientists were on board."

Most of the men realized something bigger was afoot than oceanography. One sure sign was the squadron of A-4 Skyhawks that arrived out of the sky one day and alighted upon the deck of the carrier. Usually, prop planes flew off the *Essex*; Skyhawks were fighter jets.

The atmosphere fairly crackled with preparations, even as their meaning remained undisclosed. "Everybody knows something big is going to come off," wrote Don Roberts on April 7. "Marines are everywhere with loaded .45s. All watches are doubled." That Saturday, April 8, reports circulated among the men that a U-2 spy plane was flying overhead, "photographing everything that is going on." These were the only photographs that would be taken of the *Essex*; all hands were ordered to turn over cameras.

"The weather is perfect," Roberts wrote on April 9. "It is very hot."

The men aboard the retinue of destroyers were, like Roberts, struck by the unusual activity: strange men with briefcases and .45s prowling the ships; helicopters dropping down to whisk away executive officers for conferences aboard the *Essex*. On Monday, April 10, the USS *Murray* performed search-and-seizure drills with the USS *Eaton*, "a very unusual thing to do," recalled Bruce King, then a twenty-two-year-old self-described country boy from Alabama and leading yeoman aboard the *Murray*. "By that time it had become obvious that something was going on."

Nothing made so indelible an impression on the men as what happened soon after. The ships came to a stop and several men were lowered over the sides to paint over the numbers on the bow, as a bosun hung a piece of gray canvas over the ship's name on the fantail. Then, most remarkably, the U.S. flag was lowered from the mast. "You tell people that happened," said Bruce King years later, "and they say, 'Oh, no, the United States did not do that.' But they did."

ON THE MONDAY a week before D-Day, listed on Pentagon schedules as D–7, Admiral Dennison sent a revised Rules of Engagement to Rear Admiral Clark, commander of the task force. In the main, the rules covered actions the navy vessels might take in response to an attack on the CEF (Cuban Expeditionary Force) while en route from Nicaragua to Cuba. Although the U.S. ships were to stay as far from the brigade ships as possible to avoid any appearance that they were "screening" them, and were to avoid any engagement with an enemy unless absolutely necessary, they were authorized to defend the CEF ships if they came under attack. Should such an intervention become necessary, the remainder of the operation would be automatically canceled and the CEF ships immediately withdrawn to a designated port (probably Vieques) outside of Cuba.

Washington, D.C., April 10 (D–7)

ARTHUR SCHLESINGER WROTE one last long memo about the hazards of the Cuba invasion that Monday. This final effort was a study in resigned prognostication, every sentence laden with the assumption that the invasion would go forward and would, in all likelihood, go badly. Even if the military effort was successful, Schlesinger fretted, it "may be to a considerable degree nullified by seriously adverse results in the political, diplomatic and economic areas."

Schlesinger's primary purpose in writing this memo was not to once again argue against the invasion. Rather, it was to prepare the president for the aftermath, when the U.S. government would have to tell a number of lies with a straight face. These lies would have to be handled delicately, and none more delicately than those it would fall to the president to tell. The highest priority was to protect him, President Kennedy, from the embarrassment. Though Schlesinger did not use the term coined in the Eisenhower administration—"plausible denial"—his memo was a prescription for its techniques: "When lies must be told, they should be told by subordinate officials. At no point should the President be asked to lend himself to the cover operation. For this reason, there seems to me merit in Secretary Rusk's suggestion that someone other than the President make the final decision and do so in his absence—someone whose head can later be placed on the block if things go terribly wrong."

The following evening, as millions of Americans sat in their living rooms to watch a decorous hour-long NBC special about the photogenic new president and picturesque First Family, Schlesinger drove with his wife out to Robert Kennedy's large, rambling house on the Virginia side of the Potomac River to enjoy a different perspective of the Kennedy clan. There at Hickory Hill the younger Kennedy was throwing a party to celebrate the thirty-third birthday of his wife, Ethel. The party, like many held in those days at Hickory Hill, was "messy, disordered, chaotic . . . always trembling on the verge of total disintegration," as scores of Kennedy children and dogs ran wild through the house. "In certain respects it was a terrible party," recorded Schlesinger in his journal, "but it was also tremendous fun."

Amid the havoc, the attorney general pulled Schlesinger aside for a private word about the Cuba invasion. "I hear you don't think much of this business," said Robert Kennedy. "You may be right or you may be wrong, but the president has made his mind up. Don't push it any further. Now is the time for everyone to help him all they can."

14

"A Fanatical Urge to Begin"

April 12–April 14, 1961

Washington, D.C., April 12 (D–5)

A FEW HOURS after the party at Hickory Hill ended, and after the television networks had gone off the air and gray static took their place, U.S. monitoring stations thousands of miles from Washington began picking up signals indicating that the Soviets had fired some sort of rocket toward the stratosphere. The time was 1:35 A.M. in Washington. Approximately eighty minutes later—just before 3:00 A.M. EST—a Soviet cosmonaut named Yuri Gagarin, having orbited the Earth once, returned to it and landed gently in a Russian wheatfield. Man, for the first time, had gone into space.

News of Yuri Gagarin's flight was delivered to Kennedy first thing in the morning by his press secretary, Pierre Salinger. By 10:00 A.M., the president was in his office with a team of science advisers and the vice president, determined to best the Russians in outer space. Later that Wednesday, after sending the obligatory note of congratulations to Moscow, Kennedy traveled to the State Department to give his ninth press conference since becoming president. Nearly every question went to the issue of America's standing in the Cold War. Several focused on Yuri Gagarin's flight. Others went to Red China and Laos. But the primary attention was on Cuba.

"Mr. President, has a decision been reached on how far this country will be willing to go in helping an anti-Castro uprising or invasion of Cuba?" asked a reporter shortly after the press conference began at four o'clock. "What could you say with respect to recent developments as far as the anti-Castro movements in Cuba are concerned?"

"First, I want to say that there will not be, under any conditions, an intervention in Cuba by the United States Armed Forces," responded Kennedy. "This Government will do everything it possibly can, and I think it can meet its responsibilities, to make sure that there are no Americans involved in any actions inside Cuba."

Uttered three days before brigade planes set out to bomb Cuba, these words formed as clear a public statement as Kennedy had made on the subject. The president was drawing a line for all to see: he did not intend to commit U.S. forces *militarily*. Nor did he intend for any Americans to participate *inside* Cuba.

If there was deceit laced through the president's statement—and there was, of course—it was by omission, not commission. He neglected to mention, for instance, that a large contingent of the U.S. Atlantic Fleet was steaming into the Caribbean at that very moment to support the Cubans. Nor did he let on that directly after leaving the press conference he would be returning to the White House for one last review of the American-backed invasion of Cuba.

THE LAST MEETING began at 5:45 P.M. and lasted less than an hour. The usual team of high government and military officials came together one more time in the cabinet room. The occasion was the final briefing by Richard Bissell.

That afternoon's edition of the *Washington Evening Star* happened to carry an account of Kennedy's appearance on NBC the previous night. The article highlighted one of Kennedy's comments regarding his administrative style. He disdained cabinet meetings as a waste of time and preferred more informal jousting among his advisers, to generate a "clash of ideas" on issues before him. Unfortunately, if there was one thing that Kennedy had not been receiving from his advisers on Cuba, it was a clash of ideas. Perhaps at this last meeting the advisers would speak out. Would Rusk forcefully articulate his concerns? Would McNamara or Lemnitzer raise red flags? Surely, someone would take this as an opportunity to warn the president. But no one did.

The topic of air strikes was foremost on Bissell's mind that evening. His briefing notes, handed out to the participants, specified that "plans for air operations have been modified to provide for operations on a limited scale on D–2 and again on D-Day itself instead of placing reliance on a larger strike coordinated with the landings on D-Day." The briefing notes do not indicate whether Bissell stressed this point verbally at the meeting. They do clearly show, though, that the president, Rusk, and all others were given, in writing, a clear timetable of the air strikes three days before they were supposed to begin.

Away from the president's presence, the question of when to carry out the strikes had been debated at length among all the players, including the CIA, the Pentagon, and White House officials. (Mac Bundy had weighed in several times.) There was never any question among the planners in the CIA or the Pentagon that the air strikes were a prerequisite for the success of the invasion. Those same planners, like Esterline and Hawkins, had come to worry that this message had been diluted—hence the visit to Bissell's house over the weekend.

General David Gray, on the staff of the Joint Chiefs, shared Esterline's and Hawkins's concern that air strikes might be compromised in the days before the launch. In the car on the way to this last meeting, driving over the river to the White House with Chairman Lemnitzer and Secretary McNamara, he made a point of reiterating to his superiors how important air dominance would be during the invasion. He hoped they would emphasize this to the president. Later, when Gray arrived at the White House, he found Tracy Barnes and warned him that the principals did not adequately understand the issue. "For Christ's sake, Tracy, this is the last chance."

It may have been just before this same meeting that Gray also took Bissell aside for a quick word. According to Bissell (he does not provide the date of the exchange), Gray told him about a Joint Chiefs meeting that he (Gray) had attended at which "several of the chiefs admitted their doubts about the absolute essentiality of air cover." General Gray was concerned that the Joint Chiefs might be privately expressing this sentiment to the president. Later, Bissell would wonder if Kennedy had been negatively influenced by the chiefs' casual attitude regarding airpower.

In retrospect, Bissell might have taken it upon himself to level with Kennedy and set him straight, even at this late hour. But Bissell seemed determined to say nothing that would upset the president and cause him to rethink the operation. He told Kennedy what he knew Kennedy wanted to hear, not quite misrepresenting the operation but coloring it in terms likely to find favor with the president:

> The present concept of the operation being mounted to overthrow Castro is that it should have the appearance of a growing and increasingly effective internal resistance, helped by the activities of defected Cuban aircraft and by the infiltration (over a period of time and at several places) of weapons and small groups of men.

The meeting, like all the meetings before, ended inconclusively. If the participants realized they had slipped over a final threshold, none acknowledged it. The president never gave explicit approval for the mission. He did ask Bissell what the deadline was for killing the operation. Bissell told him he had until noon of Friday, April 14, to halt the first air strikes, and noon of April 16 to cancel the landing.

At some point during the day, Kennedy mentioned the Cuban operation for the first time to his speechwriter Ted Sorensen. "I know everybody is grabbing their nuts on this."

Happy Valley, April 13 (D–4)

THE BRIGADE PILOTS and air crews woke to another infernal tropical morning on the coast of Central America that Thursday before the invasion. The air base at Happy Valley, on the outskirts of Puerto Cabezas, Nicaragua—the launchpad for the air and sea attack on Cuba—was jumping with activity. The first planeloads of infantry had started to land, a stream of C-54s flying in from Guatemala and depositing brigademen on the hot tarmac. The men filed out into the sun, looking around with blinking eyes before boarding the railcars that would take them to the pier and their respective ships.

In addition to the other planes, an unfamiliar Lockheed Super Constellation, with U.S. Air Force markings peeking from behind a coat of fresh paint, landed at Happy Valley early that morning. About a dozen men, Americans in civilian clothing, stepped onto the tarmac. They were immediately driven to the operations tent. As they vanished into it, the flaps were lowered.

Inside the tent, Lieutenant Colonel Frank Egan, the CIA man who had been in charge of the ground training for the brigade in Guatemala, conducted a briefing for the brigade's Cuban commanders, also freshly arrived from Guatemala. As Egan spoke, he glanced over now and then at the Americans who had flown in that morning. One of these was Colonel Jack Hawkins, the marine who had devised the paramilitary plan on which they were being briefed. Hawkins had come down to Nicaragua for a final review of the troops. The briefing inside the stifling tent lasted for the better part of the morning, broke for lunch, then resumed for another long session. At one point Colonel Hawkins was called away to receive an "emergency" cable from CIA headquarters. It was from Jacob Esterline, and it was two sentences long.

> (a) Please advise Emergency precedence if your experiences during the last few days have in any way changed your evaluation of the Brigade.
> (b) For your information: The President has stated that under no conditions will U.S. intervene with any U.S. forces.

Hawkins promptly cabled back his response, which was nothing short of a rave: "My observations the last few days have increased my confidence in the ability of this force to accomplish not only initial combat missions but also the ultimate objective of Castro's overthrow." Only four days earlier Hawkins had gone with Esterline to Richard Bissell's house to tender his resignation because he believed the invasion was doomed to failure; now he wrote of the brigade and its chances in glowing language, all doubt swept away by what he witnessed and heard of the troops as they moved through camp that day on their way to the ships in Puerto Cabezas.

"These officers are young, vigorous, intelligent and motivated with a fanatical urge to begin battle for which most of them have been preparing in the rugged conditions of training camps for almost a year," he wrote. "Without exception, they have utmost confidence in their ability to win. . . . I share their confidence." The brigade ground forces were "more heavily armed and better equipped in some respects than U.S. infantry units." As for the air wing, "aircraft are kept with pride and some of the B-26 crews are so eager to commence contemplated operations that they have already armed their aircraft." Hawkins ended by declaring that the brigade did not expect help from U.S. armed forces. They only wanted to get going and take care of Castro themselves. "This Cuban Air Force is motivated, strong, well trained, armed to the teeth, and ready. I believe profoundly that it would be a serious mistake for the United States to deter it from its intended purpose."

Cuba, April 14 (D–3)

FIDEL CASTRO HAD been sleeping little and smoking a great deal. Kennedy's press conference on April 12, with the president's pointed restrictions on U.S. involvement in any attack on Cuba, signaled to Castro that an attack must be truly imminent. As he remained in the capital, bunking up at his command post, Punto Uno, he sent his brother Raúl to the eastern provinces of the island to command the forces there. Che Guevara was put in command of the army of the western provinces. Sentries and troops were positioned along the coast, concentrated near areas Castro considered likely to host a landing, such as Trinidad (the site of the original CIA invasion plan). Wherever the attack came, the Cuban military would be ready. So ready, in fact, Guevara informed the Soviet ambassador that Friday, "the danger of invasion . . . has now in all likelihood receded," for it was "unlikely that the forces of the counterrevolution would undertake such a risk now."

Washington, D.C., April 14 (D–3)

AMID A HEAVY schedule of meetings, John Kennedy took a break from the pressures of the presidency to stroll the White House south lawn with his wife, enjoying the early-spring sunshine as Caroline played nearby with some ducks. He even found a few moments to work on his golf game, treating tourists to the sight of the president of the United States "swinging golf balls," as the lady from Ohio put it.

At some point that Friday Richard Bissell showed Kennedy a copy of Jack Hawkins's cable from Happy Valley. The colonel's words struck just the right note of optimism to allay any outstanding doubts in the president's mind. Robert Kennedy later singled out Hawkins's cable as critical in tipping the balance in favor of the invasion. But there was a catch. Almost as an afterthought, Kennedy asked Bissell how many planes were going to be used in the first air strike on Cuba, now less than twenty-four hours away. Sixteen, Bissell told him. Kennedy thought this too many. He told Bissell to cut it down. "As far as I know," Bissell later wrote, "he made this decision without consulting either the Joint Chiefs or the Secretary of Defense. I was simply directed to reduce the scale and make it 'minimal.' He left it to me to determine exactly what that meant, and I responded by cutting the planned sixteen aircraft to eight."

President Kennedy went to the Executive Mansion before eight o'clock that evening. As he retired, the ships carrying Brigade 2506 were steaming on their way to Cuba, shadowed by a sizable contingent of the U.S. Navy, and the planes at Happy Valley were just hours away from takeoff. By dawn, the air attack would be under way.

PART IV

D-DAY

April 15–April 19, 1961

15

"This Is the Aggression"

Saturday, April 15: D–2

Over the Caribbean, 4:30 A.M.

IN MOST CASES of military aggression, the objective is fairly straightforward: to overpower the enemy by force. In the Bay of Pigs invasion, this objective was complicated by a secondary and, at times, fundamentally conflicting intention: to hide the hand applying the force. The attack was meant to appear as an entirely Cuban-on-Cuban affair, as if it had been conceived, planned, and supported by Cuban exiles and insurgents and not by the CIA, Department of Defense, State Department, and the president of the United States. To succeed at the first task—the *real* war—the Americans required a plausible military force and strategy. To succeed at the second—the *pretend* war—they needed a fictional construction worthy of Potemkin's village.

In the real war that Saturday morning, eight Douglas B-26 Invaders, each heavily laden with bombs and missiles, had taken off from Nicaragua in the first dark hours of April 15 and were now halfway to Cuba, flying eight thousand feet above the Caribbean under a moonless, star-filled sky. The planes flew in three distinct formations, or "flights," each of these locked on a different target. The first, Gorilla Flight, included Captain Gustavo Ponzoa and his navigator, Rafael García Pujol, in *Gorilla One* and, in *Gorilla Two*, pilot Gonzálo Herrera and navigator Ángel López. Behind them came Linda Flight and Puma Flight, each comprising three planes and six crew members. Ponzoa and Herrera flew northeast, toward the southeastern coast of Cuba. Their target was Antonio Maceo Airport in the city Santiago de Cuba. Linda Flight and Puma Flight flew almost due north, toward the western end of the island. The three planes of Linda Flight were to hit San Antonio de los Baños, an air base south of Havana. Puma Flight's three planes aimed for Libertad, a heavily guarded military base just west of central Havana, near Castro's command post.

Based on U-2 aerial reconnaissance photographs taken over the previous week, the CIA knew Castro had thirty-six combat aircraft scattered among the three airfields, and believed that half of these planes were operational and battle-ready. This included six Lockheed T-33 jet trainers, six British-made Sea Furies, and six B-26s, all armed with machine guns and, in the case of the T-33s, wing-mounted rockets. The mission was to destroy as many of Castro's planes on the ground as possible. By the time the brigade ships landed on the beaches of Cuba, Castro would have no planes to repel them. That was the plan, anyway, in the real war.

THE EIGHT B-26 Invaders were about two hours into their flights when a ninth Invader taxied onto the runway at Happy Valley. Like the eight that had gone before, this plane was marked to resemble one of Fidel Castro's own, right down to a serial number—933—that corresponded to the sequence used by Castro's air force. A close observer would have noticed something else about this B-26. One of the cowlings—metal engine covers—was riddled by bullet holes, as if damaged in combat. In fact, the plane had been nowhere near combat. Hours earlier, a CIA operative had taken the plane into a hangar, removed the cowling, shot it up with a machine gun, then replaced it.

After takeoff, "Special Aircraft" B-26 no. 933 banked to the north and followed the flight path of Linda and Puma flights, heading roughly in the direction of Havana. Unlike those planes, this one would blaze fast and low over Cuba without pausing, and continue northward toward Miami, to play a supporting role in the CIA's elaborate ruse.

Cuba, 5:45 A.M.

FLYING LEAD IN *Gorilla One*, Gus Ponzoa was still more than a hundred miles from land when he saw the hills of the Sierra Maestra rising around Santiago de Cuba. He intended to circle around Santiago, passing over nearby Guantánamo, and approach the air base from the east, out of the rising sun. Ponzoa would be the first pilot to arrive over Cuba.

His chiseled, hawklike face, accentuated by stripes of white hair blazing over each temple, was the visage of a man born for aviation, and his preternatural calm made the former Cubana Airlines captain a natural fighter pilot. The next minutes would take all the calm he possessed.

Unbeknownst to Ponzoa, earlier that morning a group of 160 Cuban defectors under the command of Nino Díaz, who took his orders, in turn, from the CIA, had attempted a diversionary landing thirty miles east of Guantánamo, but the landing had been aborted at the last minute. This was probably to Ponzoa's advantage; had Díaz's landing succeeded, Castro's forces would already be on high alert and antiaircraft batteries would be combing the skies for invaders. As it was, Ponzoa spied what appeared to be a Castro patrol boat on the water about twenty miles from the coast. Fearing that the Cubans might identify him as an enemy aircraft and send an alert ahead to the airport, he decided on a more direct approach. The sooner they made their attack, the better.

Minutes from the target, Ponzoa dropped down to five hundred feet to evade radar, then down again to two hundred feet, skimming in over the water, as Herrera followed in *Gorilla Two*. The air strike would be straightforward but exceedingly dangerous. On the first pass, the pilots would have the element of surprise on their side. By the second pass, the artillery nests would be active, spewing bullets into the sky. By the third pass, Castro's pilots would be clambering into whatever aircraft remained intact, and by the fourth pass those planes would be airborne and giving chase—which would mean the brigade pilots were in trouble. The Douglas B-26 Invader had many fine attributes as a bomber, but it was slow and cumbersome in air-to-air combat. The brigade Invaders were at particular risk. To lower weight and conserve fuel consumption, the CIA had removed the tail gun turrets that normally defended the rear of the plane. Head on, the Invaders were formidable killing machines; from behind, they were waddling ducks.

The pilots had been briefed extensively on the mission by their American instructors. They had studied the target maps and reconnaissance photographs. They had practiced their gunnery skills on tin drum rafts floating in mountain lakes near their training camp in Guatemala. But Guatemala was behind them now, Cuba was ahead, and none of the pilots had ever flown in combat.

In addition to excitement and apprehension, they were likely to experience something like regret. This was not a foreign land they would soon be bombing. It was their country, their homeland, a place they loved well enough to risk death to save. Some of them, such as Gus Ponzoa, had supported Fidel Castro when he first came to power. Then Castro began to turn to communism, and disenchantment set in. Ponzoa had flown out of Cuba for the last time in July 1960. This was his first trip back since defecting.

Ponzoa and Herrera dropped to fifty feet, close enough to the water to drizzle the cockpit window with salt spray. They could see the rugged shoreline, its escarpments rising beyond the breakers. Abruptly, the planes reared into a steep climb, to six thousand feet, then parted for the attack. Ponzoa banked to the northeast, Herrera to the east. The time was fifteen minutes before six. Below, Santiago was catching the first rays of sun. Its old, narrow streets were still quiet.

From reconnaissance photographs and maps, Ponzoa knew the location of every target to destroy, every artillery nest to avoid. Even without the photographs and maps, he knew Antonio Maceo Airport like his own backyard, having flown into it hundreds if not thousands of times as a commercial airline pilot. As he went into his dive, he recognized a Cubana Airlines DC-3 refueling near the runway, preparing for its daily 6:00 A.M. flight. He had piloted the plane himself many times.

Ponzoa opened the bomb bay and released a five-hundred-pounder. An instant later, a fireball leaped up from the tarmac and the DC-3 exploded. Ponzoa rose for his second pass. By this time men below were already at the batteries, populating the air with tracer bullets. Now it was Herrera's turn to dive. *Gorilla Two* came in from the east, spraying machine gun rounds, banked out to sea to escape return fire, then turned back to deliver its payload of fragmentation bombs. More planes shattered on the ground. An airplane hangar splintered with magnificent pyrotechnics.

It was time to go. Gorilla Flight hightailed it for open sea. Ponzoa had come through the attack with hardly a nick. Herrera had been pelted by antiaircraft fire, puckering his fuselage and opening a leak of hydraulic fluid. But they were both alive, airborne, and heading back to Happy Valley.

AT ABOUT THE same time Gorilla Flight was turning back, the three planes of Linda Flight appeared over the airport at San Antonio de los Baños, the FAR's main air base. A Cuban control tower operator at the base later recalled that when he heard the B-26s approach, he glanced up from his copy of *Bohemia* magazine, registered the planes' markings as friendly, and went back to reading. Seconds later, bombs were falling and flames were leaping from the runway. Linda Flight made several passes over the airfield, then, like Gorilla Flight, turned back for Happy Valley.

Puma Flight was less fortunate than Gorilla and Linda. Its target was Libertad, twenty-five miles northeast of San Antonio, in a suburb of Havana. As the planes roared in, residents of the city awoke, startled from sleep, and rushed to their windows and balconies. Then, as bombs began to fall with shrill whistles and the first tracer bullets began to hiss across the sky, people dove under their beds for cover.

Among those who witnessed the air strike on Libertad that morning was Fidel Castro. The Cuban prime minister had spent the night at his command center, Punto Uno, a two-story villa half a mile from the air base, where he had been spending most nights in anticipation of an attack such as this. "What are these planes?" he asked an aide when the first B-26 roared by low overhead. An instant later, the sound of exploding bombs reverberated from the direction of Libertad, and he had his answer. "This is the aggression."

Libertad was defended by a battery of newly acquired four-barreled Czechoslovakian antiaircraft guns, and the Puma bombers came under heavy, sustained fire. *Puma One* was hit and turned across the Straits of Florida to make an emergency landing. *Puma Two* also was pelted but remained sound; it turned off for open sea, heading south, back to Happy Valley.

Puma Three was on its second pass over Libertad when a battery of guns on the northern side of the base opened up. Pilot Daniel Fernández-Mon, a red-haired twenty-nine-year-old, flew over Havana Harbor to escape the hail of bullets and perhaps make a run, like *Puma One,* for Key West. Fernández-Mon was well liked by his fellow pilots. Among his celebrated virtues back at the training camp was the fact that he owned a record player; when you wanted to hear music, you visited Daniel. He also organized the raffles in camp; when you got lucky, you went to Daniel to collect.

On this day, he and his twenty-five-year-old navigator, Gaston Pérez, met the worst kind of luck. Their plane burst into flames, lost altitude, and slammed into the ocean. Fernández-Mon and Pérez became the first combat casualties of the invasion.

Miami, 8:20 A.M.

CAPTAIN MARIO ZUNIGA had flown nearly eight hundred miles since leaving Puerto Cabezas in B-26 no. 933. At 8:00 A.M. he was thirty miles south of Miami. Zuniga reached for the switch that controlled the right engine—the engine, that is, beneath the bullet-riddled cowling. It feathered and died. Flying now on just one engine, Zuniga slowly descended to Miami International Airport. He radioed ahead to let the control tower know he was coming.

Zuniga was a proficient and serious young pilot, and he did not especially relish the role he was about to play. But he had volunteered for it, and had been picked by his superiors because he was quick on his feet—a natural improviser. He was eager to contribute in any way he could to the effort to overthrow Castro. All he asked was that as soon as he was done with his playacting in Miami, he be permitted to return to Happy Valley and join his fellow pilots in combat.

On the flight from Nicaragua, Zuniga had rehearsed in his head the lines written for him in CIA headquarters. He brought along a baseball cap with a "Made in Cuba" tag inside and carried a pack of Cuban cigarettes. Even the white T-shirt he wore had been carefully selected for its Cuban make. All were props to support the story he was about to tell.

Zuniga landed in Miami at 8:20 A.M. and stepped out of the plane into the hands of two Dade County police officers, who disarmed him and handed him over to officials from the U.S. Immigration and Naturalization Service. The officials quickly whisked him away for questioning. Almost certainly, INS had been contacted by the CIA and already knew why Zuniga was there, but they played gamely along. While refusing to divulge the name of the pilot, the INS soon released his statement: "I am one of the twelve B-26 pilots who remained in the Castro air force after the defection of Pedro Luis Díaz Lanz and the purges that followed," the statement began. "Three of my fellow pilots and I have planned for months how we could escape from Castro's Cuba." That morning, after becoming concerned that their plot was about to be revealed, the conspirators had decided to act. At 6:00 A.M., Zuniga's statement claimed, he had taken off from San Antonio de los Baños and flown over to Libertad, where he and the other pilots dropped bombs and strafed planes with machine guns, taking on fire from ground artillery. As he returned to strafe his own airfield at San Antonio, his coconspirators attacked other Cuban airfields.

Mario Zuniga's story had been contrived to convince the world that the air attack on Cuba that morning was the work of Castro's own pilots flying Castro's own B-26s. As soon became apparent, the story was as riddled with holes as the cowling on Zuniga's plane. The first obvious question—though no one asked it—might have been how Zuniga had spent the two hours that had presumably passed since the attack; the flight from Cuba to Miami could be made in half an hour, which would have left the pilot nearly two hours to kill after his air raid. But there were more troubling questions, and these were asked. One reporter noticed tape sealing the barrels of Zuniga's machine guns. Tape was a commonly used prophylactic to keep dust out of the barrels, but how could the tape remain if the guns had been fired? Another reporter, conversant in Cuban aviation, observed that the nose of Zuniga's B-26 was solid metal, while the noses on Castro's B-26s were Plexiglas. And one final discrepancy: Zuniga's guns were mounted in his plane's nose; Castro's were mounted under the wings.

Happy Valley, 9:30 A.M. (10:30 A.M. EST)

ZUNIGA WAS STILL being interviewed by officials in Miami when the Cuban and American pilots who had stayed behind at Happy Valley gathered near the runway to greet the returning airplanes. Nobody had bothered to go back to sleep after the eight B-26s left for Cuba. Sleep was impossible. Some of the men had formed groups around radios to listen to Radio Havana, cheering when they heard the first reports of explosions. At about 9:00 A.M. they began to gather near the runway, squinting into the sky over the Caribbean. "Here they come," somebody called out at nine-thirty. A gray spot appeared on the horizon, followed by another. The dots slowly revealed themselves to be the B-26s flown by Ponzoa and Herrera, the first planes to return, as they had been the first to leave. Ponzoa came in seamlessly, landing softly, his plane hardly nicked from battle. Herrera's plane was in worse shape. Bullet holes pierced the fuselage, and the right wing panel was torn. The tires blew out as the landing gear hit the runway. But Herrera and his navigator were safe, the plane salvageable, their bombing mission an apparent success.

Over the next hour, three more planes straggled in. One of these, *Puma Two*, had taken part in the raid on Libertad near Havana; two others, *Linda One* and *Linda Two*, were returning from the attack on San

Antonio de Los Baños. This left three planes still absent. As the men waiting at Happy Valley would come to learn, one of these planes had made an emergency landing at Boca Chica field in Key West, Florida, after sustaining combat damage. Another was temporarily grounded in Grand Cayman, where its pilot had paused to refuel. The third, *Puma Three*, had burst into flames and fallen into the sea near Havana.

The returning crews were picked up by jeep and ferried directly to the Air Command shack at Happy Valley. There they were debriefed by the CIA's air base commander, a thirty-three-year-old former smoke jumper from Montana named Garfield Thorsrud. Nobody called him by his full name. More than six feet tall, with a buzz cut, gruff manner, and bad temper, he was known simply as "Gar," pronounced like a quiet growl. He had a few gold teeth, which showed when he smiled. He did not smile often.

Still, Gar had to be pleased. With the tragic exception of *Puma Two*, the news the pilots delivered was positive. The pilots from the Libertad raid reported that 50 percent of tactical aircraft had been destroyed. The Linda Flight pilots believed they had knocked out 75 to 80 percent of the aircraft at San Antonio de los Baños. The Gorilla pilots, Ponzoa and Herrera, were pretty sure they had destroyed 100 percent of Castro's serviceable air force at Santiago de Cuba, including two B-26s and a T-33. If these initial estimates were accurate, they added up to an extraordinary success rate. Castro would still have a few planes, but they could easily be handled in the mop-up raids slated for that afternoon and the following morning.

Gar Thorsrud transmitted the results by flash cable from Happy Valley to Quarters Eye. In Washington, the exhausted men in the CIA's war room congratulated one another with slaps on the back. They would dispatch a U-2 to confirm the pilot reports with overhead reconnaissance photographs, but so far, so good.

Just yards away from the windowless war room where the CIA men were celebrating the good news, tourists strolled the Mall near the Lincoln Memorial, enjoying the pleasures of the nation's capital on a pleasant Saturday in April. "The air is balmy, the cherry trees blossom and the girls are prettier," David Halberstam, still an unknown young journalist, had written in the *New York Times* a few days earlier. "Springtime in Washington is a wonderful and patriotic time."

New York, 10:30 A.M.

SPRINGTIME WAS WONDERFUL in New York, too, particularly from the perspective of the forty-second floor of the Waldorf-Astoria Hotel on Park Avenue. Sunlight poured through the high windows. Outward, the view was a Technicolor panorama of the city stretching north to the budding greenery of Central Park and south to the glittering waters of New York Harbor. A man could feel on top of the world here. Unless, that is, the man happened to be Adlai Stevenson, current tenant of suite 42-A.

As a two-time candidate for president, Stevenson had once aspired to greater heights. These days, he woke up tired and heavy. He'd been going to too many parties, eating too much rich food. He'd been sleeping poorly, too, and only "with the help of God and Seconal," as he'd written to a friend earlier that April. He was frustrated with his work, restless in his life, depressed by the series of humiliations he had suffered since John Kennedy relieved him of the Democratic nomination and the party's leadership in 1960. The worst of these humiliations had been Kennedy's failure to appoint him secretary of state, the post Stevenson had desired and expected as his due. Instead, Kennedy had offered him this consolation prize: permanent representative to the United Nations. Three months in, Stevenson was still not sure he wanted the job. "It won't work," he told a friend. "I'm on the wrong end of the telephone."

The problem with permanent representative to the United Nations was that the position came with all the trappings of power (suite 42-A, for example) but none of the levers. Stevenson had hoped to make policy; this job required him to defend the policies of others. To make matters worse, the man on the other end of the telephone did not appreciate the gifts of eloquence and probity that so many others had admired in Stevenson over the years. President Kennedy found Stevenson to be wordy, ineffectual, indecisive—all fine attributes in a U.N. diplomat, but not the stuff of the New Frontier. "Stevenson was miscast in the New Frontier," a journalist and friend of Stevenson named John Steel would later write. "The men of John F. Kennedy were flat-stomached; Stevenson was paunchy. They talked in cryptic, often barely understandable phrases; Stevenson talked in long sentences, comma-struck with parenthetical, often qualifying phrases. He was epigrammatic, enjoyed discourse for discourse's sake. The New Frontiersmen were grim, passionate men with their own brand of acidic humor."

The president did admire some of Stevenson's qualities. There was the swooning adoration, for instance, Stevenson could still inspire among American liberals and some foreign leaders. Kennedy also considered Stevenson to be personally affable and paid him the compliment of asking him occasionally to squire the First Lady around town. Just two days earlier, in fact—Thursday evening, April 13—Adlai had flown to Washington to accompany Jacqueline Kennedy to the opening of *Carmen* at the Opera Society of Washington.

But even this honor carried a whiff of insult. While Stevenson was escorting the First Lady to *Carmen*, the New Frontiersmen of the Kennedy administration were attending a stag party for West German chancellor Konrad Adenauer, just then finishing a trip to the United States. McGeorge Bundy, Arthur Schlesinger, Theodore Sorensen, Dean Rusk, Bobby Kennedy, Robert McNamara, Paul Nitze—they were all there. But not Adlai Stevenson. He was at the opera with the women.

ADLAI'S BAY OF PIGS ordeal began at 10:30 that Saturday morning, after he traveled from the comfort of the beaux arts Waldorf on Park Avenue to the austerely contemporary U.N. building near the East River. Inside the cavernous General Assembly hall he took his place among the other delegates. On the agenda this morning was, first, a round of congratulations to the Soviet Union for putting a man into orbit—such blandishments were pro forma in the United Nations—followed by a long-overdue debate on a deteriorating situation in the Congo.

Stevenson would have known of the overnight bombing of Cuba by the time he took his seat in the General Assembly hall. The air raid was being reported on the wires. And so, by now, was the story of the B-26 pilot who had defected to Miami. Another Cuban FAR B-26 had reportedly landed at the Boca Chica Naval Air Station in Key West, also apparently a defector. (In fact, this plane was *Puma One*, coming in for emergency repairs.) Despite the briefing from Tracy Barnes and Arthur Schlesinger the previous week, Stevenson had no prior knowledge of the bombing raid, or any reason to believe that the defectors who landed in Florida that morning were flying under CIA command. As far as he knew, they were real Cuban Air Force pilots who had actually defected and taken it upon themselves to bomb their own airfields.

No sooner did Frederick H. Boland of Ireland, acting president of the General Assembly, bring the meeting to order than Raúl Roa, foreign minister of Cuba, demanded the floor. Roa was a sallow man with sharp features, a thin mustache, and thinning, greased-back hair—a whippet profile accompanied by terrier personality. When he spoke, he tended to gesticulate with one hand while pinching a lit cigarette between the fingers of the other. "I should like to inform this Assembly, which is the supreme forum for the expression of the international conscience, that this morning, at 6:30, United States aircraft—"

Boland interrupted with a bang of the gavel. Roa paused. Stevenson probably already guessed where he was headed with his complaint. For months now, Cuba had been accusing the United States of aggression against its government, including supposed attacks. A meeting devoted to these charges had already been scheduled for the following Monday. No doubt Roa was going to tie the morning's raids to the other supposed offenses perpetrated by the United States against Cuba.

"Thank you, Mr. President," Roa responded testily after Boland remonstrated him for speaking out of order. "But really I do not know which is of greater interest to the United Nations General Assembly, a purely procedural question or a breach of international peace. I have made my point and shall withdraw." Just then, Ambassador Zorin of the Soviet Union jumped to his feet to "discuss immediately the question of the aggression against Cuba." When Boland pointed out, again, that the rules did not permit this, Zorin insisted the matter be taken up in an emergency meeting of the Political Committee that very afternoon.

Stevenson had been baited by Roa and Zorin but remained silent for the moment. The discussion turned to more predictable business. One by one, delegates stood to congratulate the Soviet Union for Yuri Gagarin's flight with varying heaps of praise. Stevenson joined in with his own perfunctory compliments, made some comments regarding the Congo, then went off to eat lunch and prepare for what promised to be a lively afternoon.

Washington, D.C., Noon

PRESIDENT KENNEDY'S PUBLIC schedule betrayed nothing out of the ordinary that morning. As was his habit, he had come down from the domestic quarters to the West Wing of the White House at about nine o'clock, pausing at the desk of his secretary, Evelyn Lincoln, to glance over the day's schedule—a light one this Saturday, since he'd be leaving town early in the afternoon. His first meeting, at nine-thirty, had been his daily intelligence briefing with McGeorge Bundy. Precisely what Bundy told the president is not recorded, but it's safe to assume they spoke of the air strikes that had been launched on Cuba earlier. No reliable intelligence had come in regarding the raid yet, so Bundy's information would have been sketchy.

The remainder of the morning was consumed by a meeting with George Meany of the AFL-CIO, a brief exchange of pleasantries with a group of physicians visiting the White House, and a three-minute catch-up with an old friend. Shortly before noon, Kennedy traveled to Foggy Bottom, where the State Department was hosting a reception for African diplomats. "We are also a revolutionary country," Kennedy assured the Africans. "Your brightest days are still ahead. I believe ours are, also."

While at the State Department, Kennedy took care of another matter, one that went largely unmarked. He named Philip Bonsal as the new American ambassador to Morocco. That the president should reassign Bonsal, former ambassador to Cuba, on this of all days was no doubt another coincidence. But it was also a pointed reminder of how far diplomacy had fallen short closer to home.

By noon, six hours or so since the air strikes, Kennedy was back at the White House to meet with five of his top advisers to discuss the progress of the Cuba operation. Along with McGeorge Bundy, the attendees included Secretary of State Dean Rusk, State Department adviser Adolph Berle, and Arthur Schlesinger. Also present was Richard Bissell. Altogether they made an extraordinarily well-educated group: Bundy and Schlesinger, both fresh from careers at Harvard; Rusk, a Rhodes scholar; Berle, a graduate of Harvard and professor of law at Columbia University; and Bissell, another Yalie, and perhaps the best educated of the group. "Mr. President," Bundy said as the meeting began, "do you realize you are surrounded by five ex-professors?" Everyone laughed. The line was funny enough to break the tension, but also reassuring. Given the academic pedigree of his brain trust, everything was "bound to be all right," Bundy told Kennedy.

Like Kennedy's morning conversation with Bundy, this meeting was not recorded, but some of the discussion can be surmised. The advisers would have gone over what they knew of the morning's air strikes on Cuba and discussed what was coming next. Early pilot reports had made their way from Puerto Cabezas to Washington. These had to be considered skeptically, as pilot reports were notoriously optimistic, but pending confirmation from photoreconnaissance the men in the Oval Office could take heart from the pilots' confidence. Richard Bissell would have reminded the president that he had until noon on Sunday—twenty-four hours hence—to cancel the amphibious landing of the exile brigade. After that, it would be too late to call them back.

Middleburg, Afternoon

THE PRESIDENT LEFT town after the meeting, lifting off from the White House lawn at 12:40 P.M. for a twenty-minute helicopter ride to Middleburg, Virginia. Later he would tell his old friend Lem Billings that leaving Washington that weekend was probably a mistake, for it removed him from his advisers at a critical moment. But staying at the White House might have raised red flags by suggesting something out of the ordinary was in the works. Kennedy had made a practice of going away on weekends to join his family at Glen Ora. This weekend was no time to break a habit.

Glen Ora was the country estate the Kennedys had been leasing for $2,000 a month near Middleburg. A large six-bedroom colonial surrounded by six hundred acres of field and woodland, the estate was a "salvation" for Jacqueline, who loved horses and fox hunting almost as much as she disliked Washington politics. To the president, Glen Ora was more of an obligation. He agreed to come for his wife's sake but had little fondness for the place. He was a beach man, an ocean lover, a sailor. The fields and trees of the bucolic Virginia hunt country held no appeal for him, nor did the old house stuffed with French antiques. Jackie had purchased him a horseback riding outfit, but the president had no interest in horseback riding. "Can you imagine me ending up in a place like this?" he asked Billings and other chums he brought along to keep him entertained.

There was always company at Glen Ora. The houseguests this weekend were his sister Jean and her husband, Stephen Smith. Following a quick lunch, the Kennedys and the Smiths motored to nearby Middleburg Racetrack to watch the steeplechase races. "That was an interesting race," Kennedy told reporters after watching the first race. "First time I've ever seen these steeplechases." He did not, in fact, appear interested. A photograph taken of him at the racetrack that afternoon shows him dressed stiffly in a dark gray business suit, standing alone, looking off to the side at nothing in particular, distracted, restive. Fewer than forty minutes after he arrived, he left to return to Glen Ora. "I've got to get back and do a little work," he told reporters. The First Lady remained at the track, according to the newspapers, attired in a black turtleneck, a gray plaid skirt, and large sunglasses, which she removed only when clouds began to gather.

New York, 3:00 P.M.

AT ABOUT THE same time President Kennedy left the Middleburg Racetrack, Adlai Stevenson took his seat for the afternoon session of the Political Committee of the United Nations. Stevenson had gone back to the Waldorf for lunch after the morning session, leaving his staff to gather the facts of the morning air raid on Cuba. The story was getting more complicated by the hour. The first wire reports out of Miami had been mostly credulous, but by the time Mario Zuniga emerged from his four-hour "interrogation" with immigration officials, the press was asking questions. In addition to wondering about the tape over the gun barrels and the metal nose cone of Zuniga's plane, reporters now demanded to know why immigration officials would not release the pilot's name. The answer—that doing so might endanger the pilot's family back in Cuba—made no sense. As Cuba's president Osvaldo Dorticós put it to reporters in Havana, "If any of our planes or pilots were missing, don't you think we would know who they were?" And if the pilot's identity were a secret, why allow photographers to snap his picture? Zuniga's wife, who was living in Miami, had recognized him in the photographs. Surely Castro and his henchmen could do the same.

In Cuba, government officials were conducting their own investigation and sowing doubts as best they could. Pieces of made-in-U.S.A. shells—shrapnel of the bombs, claimed the Cubans, that had fallen on Cuba that morning—were exhibited to reporters. The shrapnel proved little, since Castro was assumed to have American-made ammo in his stocks. More difficult to dismiss were the auxiliary fuel tanks that had been recovered near the bombed airfields. The tanks had evidently been jettisoned from aircraft. Only planes from outside of Cuba would need auxiliary fuel tanks. If their presence did not prove American involvement, it reinforced the impression, already taking hold, that the air raids had not originated from within the ranks of the Cuban Air Force.

At the White House, the president's press secretary, Pierre Salinger, denied any knowledge of the air raids beyond what he had seen in news reports, but he promised to look into the matter more deeply. "We are naturally interested in what is going on in a country only ninety miles off our shores."

Adlai Stevenson came to the United Nations that afternoon with the findings of his staff in hand. Their work had been thorough. Leading the lunchtime investigation were Harlan Cleveland, assistant secretary of state for international organization affairs—the State Department official who served as Stevenson's liaison—and an assistant named Joseph Sisco. These men had spent the early afternoon trying to piece together the story of the bombardment. They contacted the State Department's Inter-American Affairs Bureau, which then contacted the CIA. Word came back: the planes that had landed in Florida that morning were in fact Castro defectors—*real* defectors—not pretenders, as Raúl Roa had charged that morning and as the news wires were beginning to suggest. This intelligence in hand, Cleveland called Stevenson on a secure phone line and filled him in as Sisco hurriedly drafted a speech for Stevenson. The speech was approved by Secretary Rusk, then dictated by phone to Stevenson's secretary at the United Nations just in time for the three-o'clock session.

Fifty years after the fact, with most of the key players long deceased, it is impossible to say who misled whom that afternoon. Did the CIA knowingly lie to the State Department officials about the origins of Mario Zuniga's plane? Did the State Department lie to Stevenson? Most of the players at the State Department, including Cleveland and Sisco, seem to have genuinely believed the version they delivered to Stevenson. Even Secretary Rusk, who approved Sisco's speech before it went to Stevenson, claimed that when he did so, he was unaware the defectors were fakes. "I thought I was giving Stevenson the truth," Rusk said years later. "If he was fooled so was I." How this could be so is hard to fathom. Rusk had been privy to the planning of the operation; moreover, he had attended the noon meeting in the Oval Office with the president and Richard Bissell. Surely somebody in his presence had mentioned to him that the B-26s that landed in Florida were piloted by men under American command.

Whatever the truth, Adlai Stevenson took his seat in the Political Committee that afternoon prepared to defend what was, unbeknownst to him, a bald-faced lie.

Raúl Roa was the first to speak. He began by denouncing (as recorded in the language of official U.N. minutes) the "act of aggression carried out that morning against the territorial integrity and political independence of the Republic of Cuba." For this, his government "solemnly accused the United States."

The minutes of Roa's speech continue: "Official United States propaganda was cynically attempting to distort the truth by asserting that the attack had been carried on by members of the Cuban Air Force in revolt against their government." The attack was "undoubtedly the prelude to a large-scale invasion organized, equipped, and financed by the United States government."

So far Roa's interpretation had been correct. He clearly knew more about the morning's events than Adlai Stevenson did. Given all that he had right, the principal circumstantial evidence he brought against the United States that afternoon was bizarre: *sunspots*. The attack on Cuba, he announced dramatically, had "coincided with sunspot disturbances which had interfered with radio communications." Surely this could be no coincidence but rather "indicated that the bombing had been timed on the advice of the technical experts of the Central Intelligence Agency." It took a country as diabolical as the United States, Roa seemed to imply, to time its misdeeds in a country ninety miles off its shores to an astronomical anomaly ninety million miles away.

Roa wrapped up after about twenty minutes. Now it was Adlai Stevenson's turn to respond. He worked from the speech dictated by Joe Sisco earlier that afternoon. Few politicians had Stevenson's ability to deliver a prepared speech, a speech he had not written, with as much gravitas as Adlai Stevenson. Reading slowly and deliberately from the text on the desk in front of him, sounding out each word as if he'd weighed it carefully on the scales of human justice before releasing it from his lips, he told the committee that everything they had just heard was false. The United States had nothing to do with the air raids that morning.

"We have heard a number of charges by Dr. Roa and now, if I may, I should like to impose on the committee long enough to report a few facts," he began.

"No United States personnel participated. No United States Government airplanes of any kind participated. These two planes, to the best of our knowledge, were Castro's own air force planes and, according to the pilots, they took off from Castro's own air force fields." Stevenson held up a photograph of Mario Zuniga's B-26, no. 933. It had been taken that morning and grabbed off the wires by his staff. "It has the markings of Castro's air force on the tail, which everyone can see for himself. The

1

Fidel Castro arrives at Washington National Airport on the evening of April 15, 1959, exactly two years before the start of the CIA-backed attack on Cuba, to launch a charm offensive on America. "I hope the people of the United States will understand better the people of Cuba, and I hope to understand better the people of the United States," he tells reporters, then breaks away from his security detail to greet a crowd of fans.

2

Castro met Vice President Richard Nixon on the afternoon of Sunday, April 19, after touring the monuments of Washington, D.C. Nixon tried to warn the young rebel away from communism. "This man has spent the whole time scolding me," Castro later told an aide.

3

Castro enjoying himself at the Bronx Zoo on the afternoon of April 24, near the end of his whirlwind New York visit. Having less fun were the police assigned to protect him from possible assassins. "The hell of it is you never know when, where, or how he's going," said one officer. "He just decides every once in a while to go for a walk and talk to people."

4

Fidel Castro (left) and Ernesto "Che" Guevara (center) lead a funeral procession through Havana on March 5, 1960, following the explosion of *La Coubre* in Havana Harbor. In his eulogy at Colon Cemetery, Castro angrily accused the United States of sponsoring the attack. "*¡Patria o muerte!*" he cried out. *Homeland or death!*

5

Now one of the most reproduced images in the world, this photograph of Che Guevara was taken on March 5 during the memorial service for *La Coubre* victims.

6

Richard M. Bissell, having taken over as the CIA's deputy director for plans on January 1, 1959—the same day that Fidel Castro became leader of Cuba—helmed the Cuba operation. He began making formal arrangements for Castro's demise on March 17, 1960, when President Eisenhower approved "A Program of Covert Action Against the Castro Regime."

7

John F. Kennedy and CIA director Allen Dulles in Hyannis Port, Saturday, July 23, 1960, following Dulles's intelligence briefing to the then candidate for president. "I just told Kennedy what he could've read in the morning *Times*." Later, Richard Nixon would come to believe that Dulles told much more than that regarding the CIA's plans for Cuba.

8

Fidel Castro and Nikita Khrushchev engaged in a round of conspicuous hugging at the United Nations on the afternoon of September 20, 1960. "He bent down and enveloped me with his whole body," Khrushchev later wrote. "While I'm fairly broad abeam, he wasn't so thin either, especially for his age." Six days later, Castro delivered a defiant four-and-a-half-hour speech to the General Assembly, the longest oration in U.N. history.

9

Castro was still talking at the United Nations on the evening of September 26 when John Kennedy and Richard Nixon met at a CBS studio in Chicago for the first of four presidential debates. No issue would loom larger in the debates than Castro's Cuba. Nixon believed Kennedy used top-secret intelligence from Dulles's briefing on the CIA plan to sandbag him.

10

11

On December 6, 1960, President Eisenhower hosted John Kennedy at the White House. Kennedy bounded out of the car before it came to a full stop, confirming Eisenhower's impression of the president-elect as immature. Inside the Oval Office, though, JFK struck Ike as a "serious, earnest seeker of information." Eisenhower's advice to Kennedy regarding Cuba before handing over the reins of power was blunt: "We cannot have the present government there go on."

Allen Dulles trudges through the snowy capital to John Kennedy's inauguration, January 20, 1961. "I probably made a mistake in keeping Allen Dulles on," Kennedy would later confess. "I can't estimate his meaning when he tells me things."

12

13

National security adviser McGeorge Bundy arriving at a meeting at the White House days before the invasion, April 1961. "You can't beat brains," Kennedy said of Bundy.

Arthur Schlesinger, special assistant to the president, tried on several occasions to warn of the hazards of the plan to invade Cuba. "You know, I've reserved the right to stop this thing up to twenty-four hours before the landing," Kennedy assured him. "In the meantime, I'm trying to make some sense of it."

14

The airfield in Santiago de Cuba after the air strike on the morning of April 15, 1961, the opening salvo of the CIA-backed attack on Cuba. The wreckage is from a Cubana Airlines plane. The brigade pilot who bombed it, Gustavo Ponzoa, had flown the plane many times in his former life as a Cubana pilot.

15

The B-26 flown by Mario Zuniga from Nicaragua to Miami on the morning of April 15. Zuniga posed as a defector from Castro's air force, but his ruse did not last long. For one thing, reporters noticed that the machine-gun barrels on his plane were in the nose. On Castro's B-26s, they were mounted on the wings.

16

Six hours after the landing began, on the morning of April 17, 1961, the brigade ship *Houston* was attacked by a Cuban Sea Fury. Another ship, the *Rio Escondido*, would be sunk off Playa Girón later in the morning, taking critical ammunition and supplies down with it.

17

Adlai Stevenson at the United Nations on April 17, 1961, insisting that the United States was not behind the invasion of Cuba. "These charges are totally false and I deny them categorically." Later, Stevenson will tell a friend he has no choice but to resign as U.N. ambassador.

Fidel Castro jumps out of a tank at Playa Larga on April 18.

18

Wreckage of a brigade plane, shot down by a Sea fury.

19

Cuban antiaircraft artillery near the beach.

20

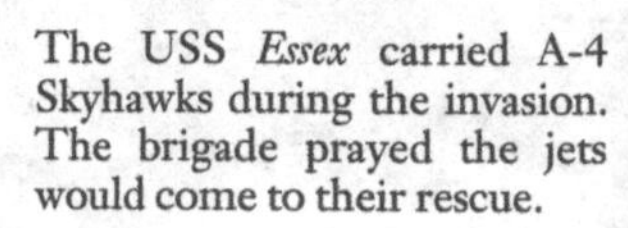

The USS *Essex* carried A-4 Skyhawks during the invasion. The brigade prayed the jets would come to their rescue.

21

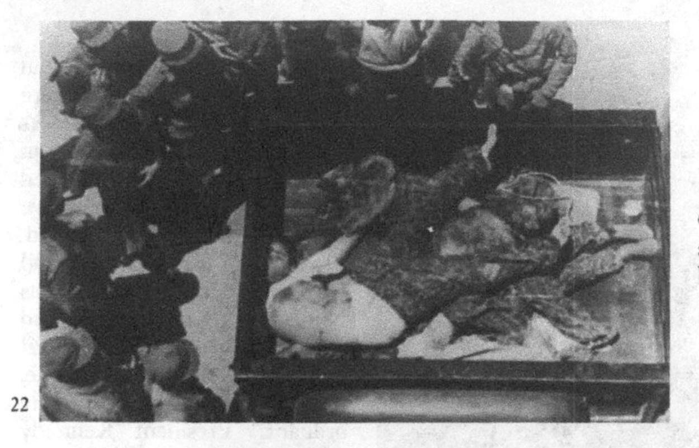

22

Cuban soldiers gather around the bodies of brigademen.

23

April 20, 1961. Captured brigade soldiers, flushed from hiding places in the swamps, begin a twenty-month ordeal of imprisonment.

24

On April 22, former president Eisenhower visits Camp David to discuss the Cuba debacle. Eisenhower was largely unsympathetic to his successor's plight. "I believe there is only one thing to do when you go into this kind of thing," he chided Kennedy. "It must be a success." (This photograph won the 1962 Pulitzer Prize.)

25

"The president thinks you should swing your axe elsewhere for a while," Richard Bissell was told after the Bay of Pigs. On March 1, 1962, Bissell returned to the White House to receive the National Security Medal. Allen Dulles, left, who had received the medal the previous November, attended, as did the new director of Central Intelligence, John McCone, right. "Your father is truly brilliant," President Kennedy told Bissell's daughter that morning.

26

After the brigade's release on Christmas Eve of 1962, President and Jacqueline Kennedy visit the Orange Bowl on December 29 to welcome them. The First Lady tells the men that when her infant son grows up she will tell him their story. "It is my wish and my hope that someday he may be a man at least half as brave as the members of Brigade 2506."

27

Playa Girón on April 18, 2010, looking west from where the first boats came ashore. The two-story structure in the distance, left of center, is a sentry post manned by the Cuban military, still diligently guarding the beach half a century after the invasion.

Cuban star and initials FAR, Fuerza Aérea Revolucionaria, are clearly visible."

Among those watching Stevenson on television that afternoon was David Phillips, the man at the CIA responsible for crafting the propaganda effort in the Bay of Pigs. It was Phillips who had devised the "charade"—his word—involving Mario Zuniga and B-26 no. 933, the very charade Adlai Stevenson was now unwittingly propping up at the United Nations. Phillips was a great admirer of Stevenson, and as he watched his hero speak on a television in the war room at Quarters Eye, a terrible thought occurred to him. "Was it possible," he asked his CIA colleague Dick Drain, "that Stevenson had not been briefed?"

"It's possible, I guess." Drain told Phillips that Tracy Barnes had gone to New York the previous weekend to see Stevenson. "But you know Tracy. He can be charming and urbane and talk around a subject until you don't know what he means to say." Perhaps Barnes had given the ambassador "the flavor but not the facts."

"As I watched Stevenson defend the deceitful scheme a chill moved through my body," Phillips later wrote. "What had we done? *Adlai Stevenson had been taken in by a hoax!*"

Middleburg, 4:05 P.M.

AT THE VERY moment the emergency meeting of the Political Committee ended at the United Nations, President Kennedy put down his golf club at Glen Ora. For forty minutes he had been standing at the back of the house with Stephen Smith, hitting balls into the west pasture. The sky had clouded over; rain was coming. Golf balls littered the long grass. Kennedy and Smith walked back to the house.

Caribbean, En Route to Cuba, Evening

THE SKY WAS clear, the temperature hot. The sun, spots and all, dropped off the port side of the brigade's rusty vessels as they chugged north toward Cuba. Since leaving Puerto Cabezas, the six ships of the Cuban Expeditionary Force had been following divergent courses so as not to appear as a single armada. The *Houston*, *Río Escondido*, *Caribe*, and *Atlántico* were commercial freighters that had been chartered by the CIA from the García Line, a shipping company owned by a family of anti-Castro Cubans. These carried most of the men of the brigade. The two other ships, the *Blagar* and *Barbara J*, were converted LCIs (landing craft, infantry) of World War II vintage, purchased by the CIA for $240,000 apiece. These were the flagships, from which the commanders of the operation, including two American CIA operatives, would direct the action.

Aboard the freighters, the fourteen hundred men of the brigade passed the time playing cards and talking. Because they were sitting atop dormant infernos of gasoline and explosives, they were forbidden to smoke, but some lit up anyway. Aboard were lawyers and doctors and students, men who had known little of military life until their arrival at the training camp in Guatemala months, or in some cases, just days, earlier. They were naturally apprehensive. Who could begrudge them a smoke?

Nerves had been at least temporarily steeled that morning when news of the air attack on Cuba was broadcast over ship radios. The men had responded with cheers. An even better morale booster was the occasional glimpse of U.S. Navy destroyers on the horizon. Each of the brigade's ships had its own dedicated naval escort accompanying it from Puerto Cabezas to Cuba. Though the U.S. vessels kept their distance, the men knew why they were there. To protect them. To watch over them like guardian angels.

That second evening out, a terrible accident occurred on one of the ships. A gunner was practicing with one of the mounted .50-calibers on the deck of the *Atlántico* when the gun broke loose from its mount and sprayed bullets across the deck. Two men were wounded and a third was killed. "The death was very difficult," Jorge Silveira, a radioman aboard the *Atlántico*, recalled decades later. "We were very close as a group. We wanted to bring the body to Cuba to bury it, but conditions on the ship did not allow for that."

Later that night, a U.S. destroyer pulled up alongside the *Atlántico* and took away the wounded and the dead. The accident was tragic, but it confirmed what most of the men already believed: the Americans were there when you needed them.

16

"The Air Will Be Yours"

Sunday, April 16: D–1

Washington, D.C., Morning

SUNDAY DAWNED GRAY and dreary along the eastern seaboard. A cold drizzle fell over Washington. In New York, hard rain and wind blew a flock of seagulls into Central Park and forced the cancellation of a Yankees doubleheader against Kansas City. The Midwest awoke to a late-season cold front. Heavy snow fell across the Great Plains. Duluth was buried under eighteen inches. Four inches fell in Chicago, where forty-five-mile-per-hour wind gusts piled up drifts and made city roads impassable. Air traffic faltered east of the Mississippi under heavy skies and low visibility.

Over Cuba, the skies were clear and calm. Perfect flying weather. Perfect weather for aerial reconnaissance.

The first poststrike U-2 photographs were in hand that morning at the CIA's National Photographic Interpretation Center. Pending construction of the new headquarters at Langley, and notwithstanding its elaborate title, the center was housed in a plain seven-story building in a run-down neighborhood in downtown Washington, at Fifth and K streets. The ground floor of the building was an automobile showroom. Upstairs, occupying four floors, was the most advanced photo intelligence laboratory in the world.

CIA technicians studied the U-2 photographs of the Cuban airfields hit by the brigade B-26s the previous dawn. The results were disappointing. The damage to Castro's air force was not nearly as severe as the returning pilots had reported. Instead of a total hit ratio of about

75 percent, the true figure appeared to be closer to 50 percent. Of the original eighteen deemed operational by the CIA, only five of Castro's planes had been "definitely destroyed." A few others were damaged but intact. At least seven were still airworthy. This included two B-26s; two Sea Furies; and, most dangerously, three or four jet-powered T-33s.

But the pictures delivered some good news, too. Rather than disperse or conceal his surviving aircraft, as common sense and practice would seem to dictate, Castro had apparently left them clumped together at San Antonio de los Baños, making them easy to destroy.* Which is exactly what the CIA intended to do to them. Another round of air strikes was scheduled to hit Cuba the following morning—D-Day—as the brigade was completing its landing but before Castro's air force could be alerted and airborne. Six planes, maybe seven. With any luck, they would all be gone tomorrow.

AT 9:00 A.M., the nation's top military brass assembled in a briefing room inside the Pentagon. The secretary of defense, Robert McNamara, was there, along with Deputy Assistant Secretary of Defense William Bundy. The Joint Chiefs of Staff, too, were in full attendance: Admiral Arleigh Burke, chief of naval operations; General David Shoup, commandant of the Marine Corps; General Curtis LeMay, vice chief for the air force; and General Lyman Lemnitzer, chairman of the Joint Chiefs. An unnamed CIA official was present, too, and later wrote a memorandum describing the meeting.

First to speak was Major General David W. Gray, the staff officer who had been serving as the Joint Chiefs' liaison to the CIA and point man for the Cuba operation. He now briefed the secretary and the chiefs on Saturday's air strikes, cautioning them that full results would not be available until later in the morning, following further photo analysis by the CIA.

As Secretary McNamara listened, he displayed little interest in the assault itself. He seemed to take success for granted. True to the New Frontier model, the forty-four-year-old former president of Ford Motor Company was a tremendously confident man, forceful and firm in his opinions. He had voted to proceed with the operation at the April 4 meeting and was in no mood now to second-guess it. He was looking to

* Castro claimed that his planes were, in fact, dispersed after the April 15 attack.

the future, after the beachhead had been won and the new provisional government installed. He wanted U.S. Navy ships as close to Cuba as possible, he told the chiefs, so that when the time came, they could move in quickly and begin unloading massive amounts of equipment to assist the brigade. The equipment, noted the unnamed CIA scribe, included "48 two and one half ton trucks and 24 jeeps, eight M-51 tanks and mechanized graders." McNamara returned several times that morning to the question of support *after* the invasion, including the provision of hospital facilities for the wounded. "It became apparent," wrote the CIA man, "that it was Secretary McNamara's understanding that a great amount of the equipment to be provided was predicated on the fact that a Provisional Government holding Cuban territory would be supported by the U.S. and supplies furnished overtly."

Happy Valley, Morning

WHATEVER SECRETARY MCNAMARA'S understanding, the intentions of the U.S. military—indeed, of the entire U.S. government—were a growing mystery at the brigade's Happy Valley air base that Sunday. The jubilation that had greeted the returning brigade pilots the previous morning sagged under a queasy suspicion that something was amiss. First, follow-up strikes the pilots had expected to run on the afternoon of April 15 had been scrapped. Then came news that there would be no strikes on April 16—today—either. This left only the strikes scheduled for dawn of April 17 to destroy Castro's air force.

As ground crews prepared the airplanes for flight, the pilots whiled away the day on horseshoes, beer, and speculation. They could not begin to fathom the logic of reducing air strikes. Why not keep the pressure on Castro? Why give him this long interval to prepare for what was coming? The American commanders at Happy Valley who might be expected to answer such questions, such as Gar Thorsrud, were holed up in the air command shed and not available to field such queries, and could not have answered them anyway. Their silence, combined with the idleness of the airplanes, produced "growing evidence of consternation," the American pilot Albert "Buck" Persons later wrote, "as the atmosphere of foreboding increased in the compound."

Edward Ferrer, a Cuban pilot for the brigade, shared Albert Persons's unease but remained hopeful. Partly it was his job to remain hopeful; in addition to his flying duties, he was the camp's morale officer. As he went around boosting the spirits of the other pilots, he held faith in his own words. "I had been assured many times in private conversation with the advisers that the invasion would not fail . . . that the American armed forces would be standing by." He particularly recalled a comment one of the Americans had made to him on the evening of April 14 as they watched the brigade ships steam away from Puerto Cabezas. "We're gonna have Cuban pilots who don't speak Spanish and who have blond hair and blue eyes taking care of us," the adviser told Ferrer. "We can't lose."

The clear message Ferrer and his fellow pilots had been receiving from their CIA commanders was that U.S. jets would provide whatever air cover was necessary to fill in the cracks. Though never explicitly promised, a safety net was implied. Or, rather, its geometric converse: a safety "umbrella," as the commanders called it, of American fighter jets that would swoop in from above to assist. Meantime, there were still Monday morning's D-Day strikes; after these destroyed what remained of Castro's air force, the skies over Cuba would belong to the brigade. It never occurred to any of the pilots, "not in our wildest imagination," as Buck Persons put it, "that an all-out attack with everything we had would not be flown on Monday."

Caribbean, En Route to Cuba, Morning

THE MEN OF the brigade suffered through another sleepless night on the decks of the ships, and now the sun rose on a hot, still day. The ships chugged slowly across a glassy sea. "You could catch a fish with your hands," recalled Máximo Cruz, then a twenty-three-year-old company leader aboard the *Houston*. The fish were starting to look good, too. There was little to eat for breakfast—little food of any sort aboard the ships, and none of it tempting: crackers, biscuits, cold sausages. Not that the men could have done anything with a fish if they caught one. Cooking, like smoking, was prohibited aboard the highly combustible ships.

An empty stomach had its advantages on at least one ship, the *Atlántico*. That is because another amenity not available on board was a toilet. Instead, a wooden plank had been rigged to the stern. The contraption provided an even more nerve-racking experience than the scorpion-infested latrines at Happy Valley. A man hoping to relieve himself was faced with the challenge of scooting out on this plank, trousers at knees, and obtaining an unsteady purchase directly over the ship's propeller. One false move and he would be pulverized into shark chum by the blades. An empty stomach kept a man off the plank.

Máximo Cruz used the time to talk to his men about the battle and steady their morale. For the moment, morale was pretty good despite the hunger, the heat, the anxiety; despite the fact that what they were doing was, if they thought about it, absurd. They in their rusty buckets, fourteen hundred men, many of whom until two or three weeks earlier had never held a gun, sailing off to meet a professional army of nearly thirty thousand, with another two hundred thousand militia supporting it. If their situation made them afraid, it also gave them hope, because it convinced them that they were not alone—they could not *possibly* be alone. The only way this made any sense other than as a suicide mission was that they were not alone, that the vessels they occasionally glimpsed in the distance were not mirages but real U.S. destroyers there for a purpose, and that purpose was to help.

The ships' radios picked up Cuban broadcasts. The men listened for news of more air strikes and wondered why none came. Late in the morning, Grayston Lynch, the CIA case officer aboard the *Blagar*, got the answer. He was in the ship's communications room when he learned from incoming cables that follow-up raids had been canceled for "political considerations." Many years later he'd still vividly recall the "sudden sinking sensation that came to the pit of my stomach." To the Cubans, Gray Lynch was the exemplar of flinty, squinty-eyed, tough-talking, can-do Americans they knew from movies and newsreels—a real-life John Wayne. He exuded the confidence and strength of a man who had been there before, and, in fact, had been. A veteran of Omaha Beach and the Battle of the Bulge, where he was wounded, Lynch later served in Korea. His last assignment had been in the jungles of Laos as captain in the 77th Special Forces Group. It was exactly this extensive combat experience that made Lynch so concerned now. He knew the golden rule of amphibious landings: to control the beach, you must first control the air. Canceling follow-up strikes made no sense.

Lynch kept his concerns to himself. And like the Cubans serving alongside him, he believed in the power, the goodness, of his country. "Until April 1961," he wrote, "the United States had never lost a war, and above all had never deserted a friend."

Middleburg, Late Morning

PRESIDENT KENNEDY SPENT the gray morning inside the house at Glen Ora. His stomach was bothering him. Medical records from his personal physician, Dr. Janet Travell, indicate that he was suffering "acute" diarrhea and a urinary tract infection that weekend. Such afflictions were nothing new to Kennedy. Despite his appearance of vigor, he was often beset by illness. Months of his life had been spent in hospital beds. Twice he had come so near to death that a priest had administered him last rites. Now, at age forty-three, he took a dozen medications a day, including antispasmodics for his colon, codeine and Demerol for pain, and hormone replacement shots to treat his Addison's disease.

The Addison's was the chief culprit behind Kennedy's maladies. Characterized by a progressive failure of the adrenal glands, Addison's produces an array of symptoms, including abdominal discomfort, nausea, dizzines, muscle cramping, and, until the advent of synthetic steroids in the 1930s, almost certain death. Kennedy had been taking steroids to treat the disease since he was thirty. Other drugs muted the pain, but they could not make it go away. Kennedy was a man who lived in a nearly constant state of physical discomfort, including, perhaps worst of all, back pain from osteoporosis, which may have been directly attributed to the Addison's or indirectly caused by the long-term use of steroids.

The role of pain and illness—and prescription medications—in Kennedy's life and presidency has been the subject of historical scholarship and medical scrutiny. Of particular interest is how these factors might have affected Kennedy during moments of crisis such as the Bay of Pigs. Might pain have disturbed his ability to concentrate? Might narcotic painkillers have clouded his judgment? Did steroids, including small daily doses of testosterone, make him more prone to aggression and risk-taking? Did any of these influence his actions before and during the invasion of Cuba?

The answer to all such questions appears to be no. The dose of testosterone he ingested, for example, was too low to have affected his personality. And even if he seemed at times to be on a quest to prove that he and his administration had the "balls" to win the Cold War, he just as often backed down from conflict with America's adversaries. His critics would claim that his greatest error during the Bay of Pigs—he would commit it later that Sunday—stemmed not from too much aggression, but too little.

There is really no good way to measure how Kennedy's health affected his performance as president in mid-April 1961. He does seem to have experienced some of the profound fatigue common among Addisonians in times of high stress, but the fatigue did not in any obvious way debilitate him. Perhaps the most remarkable fact of Kennedy's illness, physicians who have studied the matter agree, is how ably the man functioned in spite of it.

At the very least, though, it must have made a difficult few days all the harder to bear.

HISTORY RECORDS MORE about what was going on in Kennedy's bowels than in his head that Sunday morning, but his thoughts were surely fixed on the toughest decision of his young presidency, perhaps of his life so far. More than twenty-four hours had passed since the first air strikes on Cuba. In fewer than twenty-four more hours, the brigade would be fully landed on the beaches at the Bay of Pigs—if, that is, the president gave his final go-ahead. As Richard Bissell of the CIA had informed him, he had until noon to cancel the invasion and call back the ships.

Every move Kennedy had made regarding the Cuban invasion over the previous months bespoke a man deeply conflicted, even after his Easter weekend conversion. At each step where his approval had been required to go forward on plans for the invasion, he had delayed as long as possible, then assented only reluctantly, and usually contingent on changes intended to reduce the invasion's impact—to undo what he was doing, as if he could somehow have his cake and eat it, too. Or, better yet, eat it yet not eat it. Later that Sunday, this bulimic impulse would produce its inevitable result.

Kennedy did not leave the house until nearly noon, when he and his wife drove to Middleburg Community Center, a large assembly hall where local residents held dances, fund-raisers, and, on Sundays, a noon Catholic Mass. The president was disappointed if he hoped to use the Mass as a last chance for solemn reflection on Cuba. As if to remind Kennedy that presidents never have the luxury of confronting one serious issue at a time, the local pastor addressed himself—and Kennedy—to another unfolding drama in America that spring, the civil rights movement. The pastor delivered a prayer for desegregation. Half an hour later, Kennedy was back outside, ready to return home.

Havana, Early Afternoon

AS KENNEDY WAS leaving the Catholic Mass in Middleburg, Fidel Castro was concluding a two-and-a-half-hour funeral oration to a crowd of ten thousand at a Catholic cemetery in Havana. He stood at the gravesides of seven victims killed in Saturday's air strikes. The mood of the people turned agitated, then vengeful. "*¡Guerra!*" the people cried out. War!

Even as he fulminated, Castro was puzzled. Like the brigade pilots at Happy Valley, he did not understand the lull after Saturday's attacks. "Sunday went by," he later marveled, "and nothing happened." Not for a moment did he assume that the bombing raid was an isolated attack; there was more to come, he was sure. But why would the Americans stand down after the previous morning? Whatever the explanation, he used the lapse to his advantage. As combat units and militia mobilized, Castro's security forces rounded up suspected dissidents who might join an attempted coup, imposing, as *Time* would call it, "a reign of terror" over Cuba. Over the next twenty-four hours, thousands would be crammed into makeshift prisons—sports arenas, theaters, hotels, an old castle in Havana. And in the days to come, dozens of men deemed spies or traitors by Castro's regime would be executed, a warning to any Cuban who might be tempted to join a rebellion.

Even this funeral Castro was putting to good use, preparing his people for war. The old Havana cemetery, named for Christopher Columbus, was an ornate stage for a stirring tirade against the imperialists, and Fidel Castro, a student of military history and a gifted practitioner of the dramatic arts, did not fail to deliver. Condemning Saturday's attacks as "twice as treacherous and a thousand times more cowardly than Pearl Harbor," he demanded that President Kennedy present the so-called defectors to the United Nations, so their veracity could be tested. "If not, then the world had a right to call him a liar."

Histrionics notwithstanding, Castro demonstrated a good grasp of what had occurred—and of what was soon coming. He predicted that "the attack of yesterday was the prelude to the aggression of the mercenaries" and told the crowd that the aggressor's weapons were "Yankee planes, Yankee bombs, and Yankee weapons." The Americans' attempt to credit the attack to defecting FAR pilots was simply ridiculous, another far-fetched lie from the same folks who had lied about the U-2 a year earlier. "Hollywood would never have come up with something like this, ladies and gentlemen."

Castro threw one more oratorical punch before he was done. "The United States sponsored the attack because it cannot forgive us for achieving a socialist revolution under their noses." *A socialist revolution.* This marked the first time he publicly characterized the Cuban Revolution as socialist. Now he left it in no doubt, calling out in his raw, defiant voice, "we shall defend with these rifles this socialist revolution!"

The crowd chanted, "War! War! War!"

Washington, D.C., 1:45 P.M.

BEFORE THE CUBA operation overtook his life, Sunday afternoons had been Richard Bissell's time to take a breather from the demands of his work. When the weather was favorable, as it was turning out to be this afternoon after the gray morning, Sundays were his "expedition days," as his daughter recalled. He would take walks on the towpath of the C&O Canal with his family, the narrow, placid canal on one side, the broad, fast Potomac River on the other. Often he boated over to a small island that he and his friend (and CIA colleague) Sherman Kent co-owned in the Potomac, just off the Maryland shore. Later, back at his home in Cleveland Park, Bissell might unwind by listening to opera and thumbing through the thick railroad timetables he'd derived so much pleasure from since his boyhood.

This Sunday there would be no expeditions, no music, no musing over timetables. Richard Bissell sat restlessly at his desk at the CIA, waiting for the president to call. Noon had passed and the phone had not rung. Then it was 1:00 P.M. There was still time for the president to cancel—Bissell had padded the deadline a little—if cancel is what he intended to do. A single phrase, from Kennedy's lips to Bissell's ears, could undo everything or seal the deal.

Bissell waited alone for the call. Both of his superiors were absent. Charles Cabell, the deputy director of the CIA, was at the Chevy Chase Club playing golf. Allen Dulles was out of town. The director had left for San Juan, Puerto Rico, the previous day, making good on an invitation he'd accepted months earlier to speak before a group called the Young Presidents' Organization. Bissell had urged Dulles to keep the appointment despite the invasion—because of it, in fact. The director's absence would support the fiction that the CIA had no part in the activities in Cuba. Bissell preferred it this way in any case. He was a man who liked to captain his own ship, and this invasion was indisputably his own. "I was prepared to run it as a single-handed operation," he later admitted. "I was impatient if Dulles raised too many questions." Now it was just him in charge—and the president.

The phone finally rang on Bissell's desk shortly before two. The president was on the other end, at Glen Ora, back from church and another round of whacking golf balls into the pasture.

"Go ahead."

The words ended Bissell's wait. They also effectively ended, though he could not know it yet, the best years of his life.

New York, Afternoon

UNTIL THAT AFTERNOON of Sunday, April 16, it was still possible to believe the invasion might succeed. The bombing raid had gone about as well as could be expected. Two pilots had died, which served to remind everyone that this was, in fact, a real war. But no certifiable disaster had occurred yet.

The difficulty so far had surfaced not in the real war, but in the pretend war. Mario Zuniga's story was springing more leaks under pressure. Newspapers were continuing to scour over the "puzzling circumstances" attending Saturday's attack. Then, on Sunday afternoon, the wall between the pretend war and the real war collapsed.

Adlai Stevenson was inside his quarters on the forty-second floor of the Waldorf when an assistant, Richard Pedersen, called on him. Pedersen had spent the morning seeking data of his own about the previous morning's bombing raid on Cuba. After a number of phone calls to the State Department, he finally gleaned the truth: Mario Zuniga's defection had been, in fact, a fiction; the CIA had been behind the air attacks, just as Raúl Roa had charged; and everything Adlai Stevenson had said in the U.N.'s Political Committee the previous afternoon had been false.

The ambassador sat calmly as Pedersen broke the news. Perhaps, having read the *New York Times* that morning, he was prepared. Still, the revelation that his own government had knowingly allowed, even encouraged, him to lie in the United Nations—had "deliberately tricked" him, as he said—was hard to swallow. "I've got to resign," Stevenson would later confide in a friend. "There's nothing I can do but resign. My usefulness and credibility have been totally compromised."

Sometime that afternoon, Stevenson called Secretary Rusk. He did so not to resign, but to make clear how mortified and concerned he was. In the minds of some Bay of Pigs participants, this phone call would stand as the critical moment in the drama—when Stevenson's reaction set off a chain of events that led, ultimately, to disaster. Stevenson, an unintended victim of the Bay of Pigs, would now be cast as one of its villains.

Washington, D.C., Late Afternoon

ADLAI STEVENSON WAS absorbing Pedersen's news when a second unlikely villain of the day, Charles Cabell, still wearing golf attire from his afternoon outing at the Chevy Chase Club, dropped by Quarters Eye. Cabell had not played a significant role in planning or executing the Cuban operation, but he was second in command at the CIA and therefore technically in charge in Allen Dulles's absence from Washington. As Cabell saw it, he went to lend a helping hand in the director's absence. For others in the CIA, his arrival was about as useful to the operation as a gust of wind upon a house of cards. Howard Hunt, in a 1973 memoir of the Bay of Pigs, would portentously describe Cabell's visit to Quarters Eye that afternoon as "this chance decision that was to affect the destinies of men and nations from that moment on."

Before joining the CIA in 1953, Cabell had been a highly decorated four-star air force general. He had commanded a B-17 squadron during World War II and assisted Eisenhower in the planning for D-Day. After the war, he served as director of air force intelligence and later as director of the Joint Staff under General Omar Bradley, the first chairman of the Joint Chiefs. For all his past accomplishments and medals, though, Cabell was not greatly admired within the CIA. Some agency officials pegged him as a know-nothing meddler and first-class fussbudget—this even before April 16. Now, for the men of WH/4 who had been devoting their lives to this operation, he was about to become a major pain in the neck.

Cabell found his way to the war room and approached Colonel Stanley Beerli, the man in charge of air operations at headquarters. After looking over the U-2 photographs, Cabell asked Beerli for an update on air operations. Beerli told him they were preparing for the next morning's follow-up strikes.

"Do we have approval for the mission?"

Cabell's question hung in the air for a moment, teletype machines clacking in the background.

"Yes, we do," replied Beerli. The D-Day air attack had been included in the plans for weeks.

"Well," said Cabell, "I better check this out." Ignoring the protests of Beerli and the others, Cabell strode off to contact Dean Rusk.

To the men of WH/4, Cabell's presumption was galling. Raising questions at this late hour about the most essential thread in the fabric was asking for trouble. Even the normally proper Bissell would reportedly utter an epithet—"Fuck Cabell!"—when he learned how the general had inserted himself into the matter.

Adlai Stevenson and Charles Cabell. It is ironic and a little preposterous that these two men who would be blamed so often for precipitating the disaster at the Bay of Pigs had either very little (in Cabell's case) or nothing at all (in Stevenson's) to do with the planning and implementing of the invasion. Fueling the blame was the natural urge to find villains—villains, that is, other than oneself—but also a wistful notion that if only these two had stayed clear that afternoon, the rest would not have followed and the operation would have succeeded. If only Cabell had not dropped by the headquarters and started asking pesky questions. If only Adlai Stevenson had not felt a need to gripe.

At six that evening, Stevenson followed up on his phone call to Rusk with a cable to the State Department and the CIA:

> Priority
> Eyes Only
> For Secretary and Dulles from Stevenson
>
> 1. Greatly disturbed by clear indications received during day in process developing rebuttal material that bombing incidents in Cuba on Saturday were launched in part at least from outside Cuba.
>
> 2. I had definite impression from Barnes when he was here that no action would be taken which could give us political difficulty during current UN debate. This raid, if such it was, if exposed will gravely alter whole atmosphere in GA. If Cuba now proves any of planes and pilots came from outside we will face increasingly hostile atmosphere. No one will believe the bombing attacks on

Cuba from outside could have been organized without our complicity.

3. I do not understand how we could let such attack take place two days before debate on Cuban issue in GA. Nor can I understand if we could not prevent such outside attack from taking place at this time why I could not have been warned and provided pre-prepared material with which to defend us. Answers I made to Roa's statements about incident on Saturday were hastily concocted in Department, and revised by me at last minute on assumption this was clear case of attacks by defectors inside Cuba.

4. There is gravest risk of another U-2 disaster in such uncoordinated action.

Caribbean, Near Cuba, 6:00 P.M.

THE SIX SHIPS of the brigade's fleet, having traveled five hundred miles over separate routes from Central America, rendezvoused forty miles off the southern coast of Cuba. As dusk descended, the ships continued north to Cuba in a loose convoy, the command ship *Blagar* leading the way. This was the first time since leaving Puerto Cabezas two evenings earlier that the ships traveled together as a single armada. They may have been poorly armed rust buckets skippered by merchant mariners, but in their convergence they made an impressive and encouraging sight to the men aboard them. They made a navy.

On board, the brigade's leaders reviewed plans for the last time and spoke gravely of obstacles they would soon encounter. The men gathered solemnly on the decks. Pepe San Román, the military leader of the brigade, and Manuel Artime, the civilian representative of the provisional government that would assume leadership of Cuba, led the men on the *Blagar* in a moving ceremony. Artime spoke of the great and historical deed the men were about to perform in liberating their country. A Cuban flag was run up the mast. The ceremony ended with a salute.

On the decks of the hulking cargo ships trailing the *Blagar*, men came together to sing the Cuban national anthem and to pray. They checked their packs one last time—hunting knives, ponchos, folding plates, and stainless steel eating utensils. Most of this was American surplus from World War II or Korea. Each man carried an M1 Garand semiautomatic rifle, and some also carried .45-caliber pistols on their belts. New uniforms were issued—duck-hunting camouflage of splattered green and tan, complete with matching visor cap, all available from the Sears catalog as "Hunters Camo." They changed into their duck-hunting outfits as the last light left the sky.

Washington, D.C., Evening

JACK HAWKINS, the marine colonel on loan to the CIA, had not been home in days. That Sunday evening, knowing he was likely to be even busier in days ahead, he took advantage of the lull to go out to dinner with his wife. "Don't let them do anything to this operation," he called out to his colleagues on his way out the door of the war room at Quarters Eye. By the time he returned from dinner, the operation would be in tatters.

Just as the CIA men had feared, Cabell's meddling question—"Do we have approval for the mission?"—opened a can of worms. Cabell had taken it upon himself to phone Secretary Rusk; Rusk, in turn, had taken the inquiry as an opportunity to revisit the D-Day air strikes. The air strikes that had been in place for weeks. The air strikes the operation required to succeed.

When Cabell phoned the State Department, Dean Rusk had not yet received Adlai Stevenson's 6:00 P.M. cable from New York—this did not come into the State Department teletype until 7:33 P.M.—but the secretary and the ambassador had spoken on the phone at least once. Exactly what Stevenson had said to Rusk is uncertain. Some in the Kennedy administration would blame Stevenson for insisting that all additional strikes be called off, even threatening to make a scene and resign his post if they were not. Stevenson himself, until the end of his life, pointed out that he could not have done this for the very good reason that he did not know more air strikes were planned.

Whatever the specifics of the conversation between Stevenson and Rusk, there is no question that Cabell's request for confirmation, combined with the nearly simultaneous complaint from Adlai Stevenson, sparked a line of inquiry in Rusk's mind that led him to pick up the phone and call the president.

The time of Rusk's call to Glen Ora is difficult to place: in some accounts, it came in late afternoon on Sunday; in others, night had fallen. Most likely, if the president's official schedule for that day is accurate, the call occurred sometime after 6:20 P.M., when Kennedy returned to Glen Ora from playing nine holes of golf at the Fauquier Springs Country

Club in Middleburg. According to historian Michael Beschloss, Kennedy was in the master bedroom when he got the call. (Other accounts have him downstairs with company.) Over the phone, Rusk discussed the air strikes and his own concerns about them. Rusk would later state that when he "suddenly found out there were additional air strikes coming up," he was surprised. So, apparently, was the president. "I'm not signed on to this," said John Kennedy.

Not signed on, that is to say, to the D-Day air strikes.

In that single phrase—*I'm not signed on to this*—John Kennedy distilled several essential problems with the plan to invade Cuba. First, the president's apparent belief that he had not *already* signed off on the April 17 air strikes betrays either a stunning failure by the CIA to have effectively communicated its plan to the president or an equally stunning failure by the president (and Rusk, among others) to comprehend the plan. The D-Day air strikes had been included in preinvasion briefing papers, specifically in the papers for the final briefing on April 12. Possibly Richard Bissell failed to draw enough attention to these strikes in his oral briefing. In the minds of the CIA planners, though, there had never been any doubt that a necessary condition for the operation's success was the destruction of Castro's air fleet prior to the landing. Indeed, everyone involved with the operation seemed to take this condition for granted, with the exception, apparently, of the men whose opinion would matter most that Sunday evening: John Kennedy, Dean Rusk, and McGeorge Bundy.

A more fundamental problem revealed by Kennedy's late-hour reversal goes to the heart of the operation's irresolvable goals: to invade Cuba and oust Fidel Castro with an amphibious landing involving half a dozen ships, tanks, arms, and bombers, but to do so without attracting any notice of U.S. involvement. And the best way to achieve this, Kennedy believed, was to cut down on aerial bombardment. *Less like World War II*, Kennedy had told the CIA from the start. *Less noise.* By the evening of April 16, the first round of air strikes had already created a great deal of noise. The press was raising all sorts of questions about American involvement. The Cubans and the Soviets were causing a furor at the United Nations. Adlai Stevenson was upset. Around the world, groups of protesters were starting to demonstrate outside American embassies. All exactly what Kennedy had hoped to avoid.

So on Sunday evening, with the brigade just hours from landing in Cuba, the president told Rusk to halt the air strikes. *I'm not signed on to this.*

* * *

THE PRESIDENT'S BROTHER was throwing another party that evening, a casual Sunday barbecue at Hickory Hill. Until Richard Bissell's briefing a few days earlier, Robert Kennedy had known little about the operation to invade Cuba, too busy running the Justice Department to concern himself with foreign affairs. Now that the invasion was on, though, he seemed eager to talk about what was coming. He approached an old Kennedy family friend, Paul Fay, better known as Red. "Redhead, do you know that early tomorrow morning some Cuban patriots are landing in Cuba to try to overthrow Castro?" Fay was abashed to admit he knew nothing of it. Kennedy pulled aside another guest, *Time* writer Hugh Sidey, and quietly asked if the magazine had any correspondents in Havana. "There is going to be a big story there tomorrow," Kennedy said. "It is going to be dangerous. I can't tell you any more. Just be ready."

Washington, D.C., 9:30 P.M.

THE PHONE RANG inside Quarters Eye at nine-thirty. It was Mac Bundy calling for General Cabell. The deputy director took the call in Jacob Esterline's office. Bundy was in a hurry and got right to the point. "The President has directed that the air strikes scheduled for tomorrow morning be canceled." The air strikes were off, Bundy added, "until they could be conducted from a strip within the beachhead." There would be no more air strikes, in other words, until *after* the invasion—and after the brigade had succeeded in securing the beachhead and the landing strip nearby. Bundy could not discuss the decision himself, he told Cabell, as he was about to board a late plane to New York City "to hold the hand of Ambassador Adlai Stevenson." If Cabell wanted to pursue the matter, he should talk to the secretary of state.

As he hung up, Cabell was stunned. Although his own meddling would forever be blamed for triggering the president's decision, Cabell understood better than anyone how detrimental canceling the air strikes would be. He was an air force veteran who had participated in several invasions during World War II, including Normandy, and he grasped the fundamental importance of safe skies for amphibious landings. "This peremptory change of orders struck me like a falling bomb," he later wrote. "I, of all people, recognized that this was no simple amendment: this was drastic."

Cabell immediately called Richard Bissell, who was home in Cleveland Park, "freshening up" before returning to Quarters Eye. Bissell had already gotten his own call from Bundy and was as alarmed as Cabell. With no time to waste, the two men agreed to meet at once and plead their case to the secretary of state.

Half an hour later, Cabell and Bissell entered Rusk's office at the State Department. "The Secretary informed us that there were political considerations preventing the planned air strikes before the beachhead airfield was in our hands and usable," Cabell later wrote in a statement. Rusk told the men that Stevenson's anger was the primary cause for the cancellation. "Ambassador Stevenson had insisted essentially that the air strikes would make it absolutely impossible for the U.S. position to be sustained."

"At the present time," Rusk told Cabell and Bissell, "political requirements are over-riding."

Dean Rusk was not one to state his opinions emphatically. Nonetheless, he'd had some experience with amphibious landings while in Burma during World War II and had some thoughts on the matter. Forgetting that a little knowledge can be a dangerous thing, he told the CIA men that the air strikes were not really that important. Assuming the ships could unload under cover of darkness, as planned, they could be safely withdrawn to international waters by the time dawn—and Castro's planes—arrived. Once the men were landed on the beach, the B-26s could fly in from Nicaragua and claim the skies. This was the sound reasoning of an intelligent man unacquainted with Murphy's Law.

At about ten-fifteen, an outside call came into Rusk's office. On the line was Jack Hawkins. The marine colonel, back at Quarters Eye from dinner with his wife, had learned of the cancellation and was reeling. Bissell took the call in Rusk's office. Hawkins's tone was dire. He wanted Bissell to communicate to Rusk that the result would be disastrous if the cancellation was allowed. "I offered the prediction at this time that shipping, with the essential supplies on board, would be sunk, possibly to the last ship," Hawkins later wrote in a postmortem, "since it was known that Castro still possessed a dangerous fighter and bomber capacity." Had he been informed about the strike cancellation earlier, he added, he would have "strongly urged" diverting the whole operation. It was too late for that now. He begged Bissell to change the president's mind.

The time was closing in on eleven o'clock, one hour from the scheduled midnight launch for the invasion. Rusk reached for the telephone—"impulsively," thought Cabell—and asked the White House operator to connect him to the president. A few moments later, John Kennedy picked up at Glen Ora.

Rusk told Kennedy that Cabell and Bissell were with him in his office, then carefully, thoroughly, laid out their concerns about the cancellation. He also recapped his own opinion that the air strikes would be politically—diplomatically—intolerable. Cabell and Bissell could not hear the president's response, but it was a brief one and evidently not favorable. Before hanging up, Rusk put his hand over the mouthpiece and turned to the CIA men. "Do you wish to speak to the president?"

"I don't think there's any point," said Cabell. His commander in chief had spoken. As a former military man, he did not argue with an order.

"I think I agree with that," added Bissell. Years later, he would regret turning down the opportunity to change the president's mind as "a major mistake." At the time, he agreed with Cabell that it was useless.

Off the Southern Coast of Cuba, 11:00 P.M.

FIVE THOUSAND YARDS from shore the convoy of the Cuban Expeditionary Force drifted to a stop. Moments later, out of the darkness to the east, came the sound of another ship's engines, followed by the great mass of the vessel itself. Seen from its bow, the dark shape gave the appearance of a navy destroyer. Only as it turned and came abreast of the convoy did its most pertinent feature swing into view: a stern as flat and wide as a barn door. The USS *San Marcos* was a 460-foot U.S. Navy LSD (landing ship, dock) of World War II vintage. The ship had come from Vieques to meet the convoy with a special delivery.

In the quiet darkness, the *San Marcos* proceeded to engage in a series of peculiar maneuvers, as if it were a great cetacean giving birth. First, the LSD gulped in seawater through its backside, flooding its well deck. As the water rushed in, the ship's stern slowly sank. Then the stern gate dropped, and out from the *San Marcos*, one by one, like calves issuing from their mother, seven smaller vessels floated out into the sea. These were flat-bottomed landing craft, each carrying heavy equipment, including five M-41 tanks, two dozen trucks, one bulldozer, one crane, and nine tractors. Then the *San Marcos* turned away and went back wherever it had come from.

Landing craft in tow, the convoy now continued north, toward shore. It had gone off without a hitch. In fact, so far, the cruise of the brigade had proceeded just about perfectly.

Washington, D.C., 11:15 P.M.

"THERE'S BEEN A little change in our marching orders," announced Cabell to the men gathered in the war room in Quarters Eye.

Cabell and Bissell had hurried back from the State Department. They were now faced with an urgent errand: to warn the brigade of the altered plans and to improvise a response. First, though, they had the unpleasant task of informing the men of WH/4 that their visit to the State Department had been fruitless. They had failed to reinstate the air strikes.

"Probably out of cowardice, I allowed Cabell to be the one to deliver the message," Bissell later admitted, "and so he bore the brunt of everyone's anger." Bissell would still vividly recall years later the "shock and disbelief" in the men's expressions, followed immediately by shouting and cursing, as months of hard work and anxiety fused into rage. Jack Hawkins, the marine colonel, slammed his hand against a table. "Goddamn it, this is criminal negligence!" Jake Esterline, too, exploded. "This is the goddamndest thing I ever heard of!" Both men lit into Cabell with predictions of what this would mean for the brigade's landing—for the entire operation. Castro's planes would certainly attack. The brigade's ships, loaded with gasoline and arms, would explode. Everything would be lost.

Cabell tried to calm them. "I know that some of you have lived very close to this operation for a long time and feel very deeply about it, but when you get a change in the marching orders you have to react now and you have to take your orders and do what you are told." The comment endeared Cabell to no one. Or, as Cabell himself later put it, "Those thoughtful, responsible men did not like what they heard."

"I almost went to jail," Jacob Esterline said later, "for strangling that four-star general."

In the end, Cabell was right. The decision had been made, and now they had to deal with it. They had to send notice to Happy Valley to cancel the air strikes and they had to warn the brigade of what was coming. They had to do what they could to protect the men from Castro's planes. They had to do these things, and yet Jack Hawkins, for one, knew that no matter what they did now, the consequences of President Kennedy's last-minute decision to cancel the air strikes were already certain: "The Cuban Brigade was doomed."

17

"There Goes the War"

Monday, April 17: D-Day

Bay of Pigs, Midnight

THE BAY OF PIGS is a crooked finger probing Cuba's soft southern underbelly. From mouth to head, the bay is eighteen miles long, and narrower than four miles for most of its length. Despite its unbeguiling name—Bahía de Cochinos in Spanish—it is surpassingly beautiful. The water is turquoise, translucent, and warm. The shoreline alternates between rocky coral shoals and beaches of soft white sand lined with palm trees, thickets of mangrove, and feathery pines. Just inland of the bay, across the road that runs along the coast, is the Ciénaga de Zapata, a vast and dense swamp swarming with mosquitoes, crabs, and crocodiles, among other abundant wildlife. In 1961, the Zapata made a nearly impenetrable 1,850-square-mile barrier between the beaches along the bay and the interior of Cuba. It was a critical factor in the CIA plan at the Bay of Pigs.

Given all that occurred in the days after April 17, it's easy to forget that the plan to invade Cuba at the Bay of Pigs had merit to many reasonable and intelligent people who reviewed it beforehand. That it was risky was obvious enough, but it did not appear risible or impossible to most who reviewed it. In fact, until it failed, the plan made a kind of sense.

Operation Zapata started with the designation of three landing points within and adjacent to the Bay of Pigs. The first and most significant of the landing points was Playa Girón, christened by CIA planners as Blue Beach. Just to the east of the mouth of the bay, on its outside lip, Girón was a small coastal village. Fidel Castro, who often fished in the area, had high hopes for the Bay of Pigs as a tourist destination and had recently ordered construction of a resort at Playa Girón. This brought in a temporary population of construction workers, but the village remained remote and poor. The locals scraped out a living fishing or making charcoal from the wood of mangrove trees harvested from the swamp. Few roads led to town, and no telephones connected it to the outside world. Here at Girón the 4th and 6th battalions, about seven hundred men, would land with most of the big hardware—the tanks, the tractors, the trucks. Pepe San Román, the brigade's commander, would set up his headquarters on Blue Beach.

The secondary landing was to occur about twenty miles northwest of Girón/Blue Beach, at the very head of the bay, near the town of Playa Larga. Designated by the CIA as Red Beach, Playa Larga would take the 2nd and 5th battalions, about four hundred men under the leadership of deputy commander Erneido Oliva. The third landing would occur sometime later, about twenty miles east of Blue Beach, where a single battalion, the 3rd, comprising some two hundred men, would protect the eastern flank of the invading force. This final landing site was to be called Green Beach.

The only access to the beaches from the interior of Cuba was by way of three hard-packed roads that ran through the swamp atop beds of gravel. If these roads could be secured—so went the reasoning of the CIA planners—Cuban ground troops would be unable to reach the beaches. To hold the roads initially, 1st Battalion paratroopers would land several miles inland on the morning of the invasion and take up defensive positions. Tanks and mortars would later be deployed to seal the roads, turning them into lethal cataracts—"shooting galleries"—for all who tried to pass. Castro could amass all the troops he wanted, but if his columns could not get through the choke points, they had no chance of advancing. Successfully secured, the three invasion points—Red Beach, Blue Beach, and Green Beach—would form a contiguous beachhead, or "lodgment," more than forty miles in length.

Exactly what would happen after this sizable slice of Cuban real estate was skimmed off by the brigade had always been less clear than the invasion plan itself. At some point, approximately ten days to two weeks after the full beachhead was established, the provisional government—the coalition assembled by Droller and Hunt, cooling its heels at that moment at a safe house in Miami—would be flown into Girón and declare itself the rightful leadership of Cuba, and the U.S. government would offer aid and assistance in Cuba's "civil war." John Kennedy's speech on April 12, in which he specifically ruled out American intervention in Cuba "under any conditions," might seem to have precluded any sort of support from the U.S. military, but to judge from Secretary McNamara's discussion with the Joint Chiefs on Sunday morning (see the previous chapter) the navy was prepared, at the very least, to offload an extraordinary quantity of war supplies.

The end goal of the plan, in other words, was never a military takeover of Cuba by a fourteen-hundred-man force; the CIA planners may have been ambitious, but they were not mad. It was, rather, to hold a piece of Cuba long enough to allow events to develop. Richard Bissell had no clear picture of what to expect, but he was confident that *something* would happen. One hope that nearly everyone involved in the operation shared from the start was that mass uprisings would spontaneously materialize around the island. The foundation for this hope remained weak as the invasion began. CIA intelligence coming out of Cuba continued to suggest that most Cubans supported Castro, the opposition having either been crushed or, in many cases, having fled to Florida. Nonetheless, the U.S. Navy was waiting offshore not only with tanks and jeeps but also with thirty thousand rifles to distribute to presumed hordes of anti-Castro Cubans who might suddenly come out of the woodwork and flock to the side of the brigade, either in spirit or in some sort of armed rebellion, or even—here's where the plan became very vague—by somehow penetrating Castro's bottlenecked forces and joining the brigade on the beaches at the Bay of Pigs.

Of course, there was one other assumption, more critical than all the others, on which the plan depended: Fidel Castro would have no airplanes. The operation would work only if brigade planes knocked out Castro's air force in advance, eliminating the threat of attack from above and attaining dominion of the air. If Castro still had airplanes when the invasion began, it was going to be a whole different story.

Castro still had airplanes.

THE CONVOY OF brigade ships had divided shortly before midnight. Two of the ships, the *Barbara J* and the *Houston*, carrying the 2nd and 5th battalions of the brigade, had veered slightly west, heading into the bay. They still had almost twenty miles to go before reaching their destination of Playa Larga. The other four ships—the *Río Escondido, Blagar, Atlántico*, and *Caribe*—continued north. The *Río* stopped about five miles offshore, where it would hang back for the time being. The other three ships did not stop until they were within two thousand yards of Playa Girón. From here the invasion would begin.

The first brigademen to go into the beach were the five members of the underwater demolition team—the frogmen—to mark the landing channel. They had appeared on the deck of the *Blagar* in wet suits and flippers just before midnight, their faces blackened. They carried ammunition belts on their waists, machine guns, and BARs (Browning automatic rifles). After exchanging embraces with Pepe San Román and Manuel Artime, they climbed off the ship into an eighteen-foot outboard-powered launch. The invasion was supposed to be an entirely Cuban undertaking, but at the last moment Grayston Lynch, the CIA case officer, decided to join the frogmen. He believed he needed to get a firsthand appraisal of the beach before he could confidently give the signal for the landing to proceed.

The problem in those very first minutes of the landing was not military resistance; this turned out to be fairly minimal, as the CIA had predicted. Rather, the first troubling obstacle was a small aquatic anemone with a hard calcium shell classified by marine biologists as cnidarian and commonly known as coral. The coral cnidarian generally dwells in very large colonies—coral reefs—in shallow tropical waters, such as those off the shore of Playa Girón. To biologists and scuba divers, coral reefs are splendid natural phenomena. To anyone attempting an amphibious landing at night, they spell disaster. In the days before the invasion, a number of the brigade members had seen the aerial photographs of Playa Girón and were sure they detected coral in the shadows under the water. When they told their American advisers as much, they were assured that CIA analysts had studied the photographs and determined the shadows to be seaweed or the reflections of clouds. The brigademen, it turned out, were right.

Bad enough there was coral. More unnerving was the fact that the CIA had gotten this basic detail of preinvasion reconnaissance wrong.

Lynch and the five Cuban frogmen were about a hundred yards from shore when they hit the coral. They were no longer in the launch, having transferred to a smaller raft for the final approach. By this point they'd already come to realize that the CIA had misled them on a few other matters. They had been told, for instance, that the beach would be deserted and quiet. In fact, on this dark, moonless night, the beach was "lit up like Coney Island," in Lynch's words, by bright floodlights. As they slowly puttered over the black, undulating water, they saw a small crowd socializing outside a bodega at the eastern edge of the intended landing area. The sounds of salsa music drifted over the water. The construction workers building the new hotel at Girón were apparently having a fiesta. Under Lynch's direction, the raft had changed course toward a darker stretch of beach.

When the raft hit the coral, the frogmen, muttering curses, quietly slipped into the shallow water to coax it over the jagged outcroppings. Lynch remained in the raft, lying on his stomach with his BAR aimed at the shore. The water deepened again and the frogmen clambered back into the raft, taking up paddles to lily-dip their way to the beach.

Not until an hour later, when Lynch learned of the canceled D-Day air strikes, would the coral reveal its full import. For the moment, the men were confronted with another piece of bad luck demanding an urgent response. Halfway between the coral and the beach, one of the red marker lights—the signals they would place onshore to show the infantry where to land—flickered on for no apparent reason, a wire malfunction, maybe, or a message from the gods. Lynch told one of the frogmen to sit on the light to cover it, but it was too late. Almost at once, a military jeep came racing down a road running parallel to the beach. The frogmen could see the vehicle's headlights sweeping over the mangrove and sand. Then they heard the long squeal of brakes as the jeep slowed. Directly ahead of them, the jeep turned to face the sea, bathing them in its headlights.

Inside the jeep were two Cuban militiamen. Believing Lynch and the frogmen to be fishermen, they had come to warn them away from the coral. But Grayston Lynch did not know that. He opened fire. The frogmen followed his cue, blasting away with rifles and machine guns, until the headlights were extinguished.

So much for surprise. The entire town of Girón abruptly went dark, as if somebody had pulled a master switch to shut off the power. Lynch radioed Pepe San Román and urged him to order the *Blagar* in closer to the beach. They were going to need the support of its mounted guns.

Over the next half hour or so, as the *Blagar* moved in, the frogmen secured the beach and marked it with the lights. Grayston Lynch landed with them. He would be one of two Americans to step onto Cuban soil with the invasion force that day.

The frogmen were still preparing the beach when three trucks, headlights off, approached. Lynch and the others took cover. A couple of dozen militiamen jumped from the trucks. They were local residents, charcoal makers who earned their livings from the swamps. Like tens of thousands of Cubans, they had been called up to their militias to prepare for war—and war is what they now got. The frogmen opened fire; the militia returned it. The *Blagar*, just three or four hundred yards offshore, swung broadside to the beach and joined in with its .50-caliber guns. The air came alive with bullets passing in the night. Tracer fire flashed over the beach, visible to the men on the ships thousands of yards out at sea, where they were preparing for the landing. In ten minutes the blazing guns of the *Blagar* cleared the beach. The militia retreated into the darkness.

Once the shooting stopped, the brigade landing began in earnest: two landing craft, known as LCVPs (landing craft, vehicle, personnel), rushed in from the sea with men and matériel. Lynch had been too caught up in securing and defending the beach to find an opportunity to warn the incoming brigade of the coral, and now, as he watched, the LCVPs hit the reef hard and stopped abruptly. They tried to ride over the coral but failed. They could not budge.

The way the invasion was supposed to go was that each LCVP would ride up a gentle sand beach close to the shore, drop its front ramp, and the infantry would bound out into ankle-deep water and charge the shore—just like newsreels from World War II, just the way the LCVP crews had practiced it over their last few months of training in Vieques. Instead, the Bay of Pigs invasion began with the front ramps slapping down more than seventy-five yards from shore and the men, laden with heavy equipment, stepping mincingly over the biting coral, slowly wading through waist-deep water, arriving in Cuba with their uniforms and radios drenched.

The return to their native land was ungainly, but it did not lack emotion. Many of the men kneeled on the beach and kissed the sand.

While the frogmen went back into the water to search for a navigable channel through the coral or, if necessary, to hack or blast one out, Grayston Lynch returned to the *Blagar*. He'd been summoned on the radio: there was an important message waiting for him from CIA headquarters. This was handed to him when he climbed back onto the *Blagar*'s deck: "Castro still has operational aircraft. Expect you will be under attack at first light. Unload all men and supplies and take the ships to sea."

The time was just after 1:00 A.M., one hour into D-Day. The landing had to be complete by dawn or everything would be lost. Had there been no coral, this would have been a monumental challenge. The coral made it virtually impossible.

Washington, D.C., After Midnight

LONG BEFORE THE bad news began to pile up at Playa Girón and Playa Larga, the men in Quarters Eye were suffering the first convulsions of despair. Unlike the Cubans on the beach, they were dry and safe, but they grasped the odds against the mission's success far earlier. After their anger had spent itself, a thick funk settled over them. "All of us had to live with our feelings of responsibility for those brave men who were now going into battle against odds which we all felt were far too great and probably insurmountable," Charles Cabell later wrote. He was not alone, he surmised, in briefly entertaining the tempting thought that creative "foot-dragging" could delay the order to cancel the air strikes and thereby allow them, by default, to proceed. But as a military man who respected rank and the orders of a superior, he was "proud that not a single man suggested" it as an option.

At one point that night, Howard Hunt, exhausted by days of work and strain, went up to an improvised bunkroom to lie down and rest. David Phillips came in later. "I'm not asleep," said Hunt.

"I can't sleep either," said Phillips. "I'm thinking about tomorrow morning. Christ! If only Cabell hadn't come mousing around."

"I share your sentiments," said Hunt. "If the director were here it wouldn't have happened."

"You're damn right it wouldn't."

Inside his office, Jacob Esterline turned inward. He'd later remember little of the night. Howard Hunt recalled seeing him sitting at his desk with a bottle of whiskey, writing out his resignation.

Cabell, too, had fallen into anguished lassitude after delivering the bad news to the troops in headquarters and attending to the urgent business of notifying the troops in the field. He quietly puffed on a cigar, obscuring the glares of his colleagues behind a haze of smoke. In his description of that night in his memoir, he left out any mention of the anger he had stirred up in the others, but it must have magnified his anguish to know they blamed him. His own hard feelings were aimed at Kennedy and Rusk. Years later, he would still recall these men bitterly. In his opinion, the president and the secretary had not made their decision to cancel the strikes out of military ignorance of the likely consequences. Rather, by cynical calculation, they had knowingly sacrificed the brigade to other interests. "Success was no longer relevant," he wrote, understriking the words for emphasis. "The new relevancy had become the political acceptability of the action. . . . Our guns were spiked!"

Shortly after midnight, about the same time Lynch and the frogmen were setting their landing lights at Playa Girón, Cabell roused himself. He reached for a phone and called Major General David Gray, the staff man from the Joint Chiefs who had been acting as liaison between the CIA and the Department of Defense. Gray was asleep in his Georgetown home when the phone rang. Cabell urged Gray to get to Quarters Eye as soon as possible.

"I want you to think up things that your people can do to help us," Cabell implored when the general walked into Esterline's office at 1:00 A.M. In the absence of the second strike, might the navy's carrier *Essex* lend air support to protect the brigade as it landed? Gray agreed to propose this immediately to General Lyman Lemnitzer of the Joint Chiefs. Privately, Gray was not hopeful. As he left headquarters, he confided his concern to one of the CIA men. "Surely Cabell realizes that this means this operation is doomed to failure." Gray drove over the bridge to Fort Myer, just west of Arlington National Cemetery, to make the pitch to Lemnitzer in person.

Back at Quarters Eye, Colonel Jack Hawkins made his own attempt to change the outcome he, like General Gray, believed was all but certain. He placed a call to General David M. Shoup, commandant of the Marine Corps. It was Shoup who had volunteered Hawkins for the planning assignment at the CIA back in late summer. Now Hawkins was desperate for his help. When Shoup picked up the receiver at about 1:30 A.M., he thought he heard Hawkins crying on the other end.

"General, you've got to get ahold of the president," Hawkins pleaded. "We're going to fail. You've got to help."

"Has he already made his decision?" asked Shoup.

"Yes, they told us we're not going to do it," said Hawkins, referring to the canceled air strike.

"Well, Christ knows I can't do anything," said Shoup. "Maybe if I'd had a chance beforehand."

In retrospect, General Shoup is one of those who might have made a difference. If the commandant of the U.S. Marine Corps, the branch of the military that knew more about amphibious landings than any other, had called the president at one-thirty in the morning and told him in no uncertain terms that his decision would lead to disaster, the president was likely to have taken the advice under consideration. Kennedy may not have changed his mind, but he would have made his decision fully aware of its implications. But Shoup did not call.

Nor did General Lemnitzer. The chairman of the Joint Chiefs learned of the cancellation at about 2:00 A.M., when Major General Gray rang his doorbell at Fort Myer. Lemnitzer opened the door in his bathrobe. He did not seem startled to see Gray.

"How did things go?" he inquired sleepily.

"They canceled the air strike," Gray told Lemnitzer.

That jolted the chairman awake. He was stunned; it was "almost criminal." Gray explained the situation, then passed on Cabell's request for navy air cover. Lemnitzer consented. But, of course, the president would have to sign off first. Lemnitzer did not offer to call the president himself to press the case. He apparently closed the door and went back to sleep.

Happy Valley, 1:15 A.M. (2:15 A.M. EST)

GAR THORSRUD WAS in the air operations tent when the teletype began to chatter. The time was one-fifteen in the morning in Nicaragua, an hour earlier than in Washington. Out on the runway, a dozen B-26s, pilots already tucked into the cockpits, were within fifteen minutes of takeoff for the dawn strikes on Cuba. Thorsrud read the incoming cable in disbelief. It was from Colonel Stanley Beerli, the chief of air operations in Washington. Thorsrud slowly realized it was a complete list of cancellations. One by one, the cable named a target, then a new order: canceled. There would be no attacks on Castro's airfields. No air strikes at all. "Complete plan amended," read Beerli's cable. Instead of delivering air strikes, the B-26s were now to provide air cover for the brigade over the beaches.

Thorsrud spent some time with the list, checking to make sure it said what it seemed to say. When there was no doubt, he summoned Reid Doster, the commander of the Alabama Air National Guard who had come down to Puerto Cabezas with his volunteers. Thorsrud handed the cable to Doster. The Alabaman exploded, throwing down his cap. "There goes the whole fuckin' war!"

As Thorsrud dealt with Washington, Doster, who had developed a good rapport with both the American and Cuban pilots, took it upon himself to deliver the bad news. He drove out onto the airfield in a jeep, going from plane to plane. Moments from takeoff, the pilots were staggered by what he told them. Some teared up. Others blew up. "Goddamnit, they're crazy!" shouted Gustavo Ponzoa. "How can they do this?"

Back in the air operations tent, Gar Thorsrud was wondering the same thing. "Refs received and complied with," he wrote in a cable back to CIA headquarters. "Complete plan amended . . . with all pilots in cockpits ready to start engines. Needless to say this less than desirable operating procedure."

Evidently unaware that this cancellation came from the president, Thorsrud tried to explain the error of it. "The only real offensive danger to the Brigade is enemy fighters and bombers which are better hit on their home field—not repeat not over the beachhead."

Cuba, 2:30 A.M.

CASTRO WAS SPENDING the night at the apartment of his sometimes lover and full-time helpmate, Celia Sánchez, on Eleventh Street in downtown Havana. This put him about ten minutes by car from the military headquarters at Punto Uno. He had slept little over the past days, but he allowed himself a nap in the early hours of that Monday. The first word of the attack at Playa Girón reached him at about 2:30 A.M. The delay owed to rudimentary communications at the Bay of Pigs; the nearest telephone to Playa Girón was nearly an hour away by jeep, in the town of Jaguey Grande.

Castro immediately called Captain José Ramón Fernández. A thirty-seven-year-old army officer who ran several cadet schools, Fernández was sleeping in the commander's quarters at the school in Managua, just south of Havana. He was awoken by frantic knocking. "The Commander in Chief is calling you!" shouted a guard. Fernández bounded out of bed and pulled on his pants.

"They've already come," were Castro's first words over the telephone. It took a moment for Fernández to realize the prime minister was talking about an invasion. Castro ordered him to proceed at once to Matanzas, about sixty miles east of Havana, and rouse the nine hundred cadets of the Militia Leadership School. These were the crack troops of the Cuban militia, young men training to be officers. Fernández considered them the best troops in Cuba—motivated, bright, and strong. More than five hundred of them had recently completed their training regimen with a hike up the highest mountain in Cuba, the sixty-five-hundred-foot Turquino Peak. Now Fernández was being honored by the opportunity to lead these men against a force invading the homeland. He was still hurriedly pulling on his clothes when Castro called back. "What are you doing?"

"I just finished getting dressed, Commander."

As Fernández nervously raced around headquarters to prepare, alerting fellow officers who would accompany him, attempting to collect maps from the map room (nobody could find the key), and ordering his driver to fill up the jeep with gasoline, the phone kept ringing. "Why are you still there?" Castro barked into the phone. Ten minutes later: "Why haven't you left yet?" Fernández ordered the door to the map room broken down and grabbed what he needed.

AT BLUE BEACH (Playa Girón) the landing was progressing too slowly. Troops had been ordered to gain shore with all due speed, but the coral was a killer of speed and a slayer of boats. The landing craft kept getting hung up, forcing the men to wade and waddle in from a hundred yards out. Every attempt to surmount the coral only made matters worse. One of the landing craft sank after gutting its bottom. Another was beached. With fewer craft to bring in the men, the landing would move more slowly.

Grayston Lynch, aboard the *Blagar*, contacted Pepe San Román, who was onshore now with the landed units of infantry. Over the radio, Lynch recommended scrapping the Green Beach landing. According to plans, the *Blagar* was supposed to take the 3rd Battalion to Green Beach once Blue Beach had been achieved. As things were going, this meant the 3rd would be attempting to land at Green Beach in daylight and would therefore be exposed to Castro's still extant (though not yet seen) air force. It would also remove the *Blagar*—and the *Blagar*'s eleven mounted machine guns—from Blue Beach. They would need those guns when Castro's planes arrived. San Román agreed. Better to get the 3rd into Blue Beach before dawn. Later they could truck them to Green Beach.

San Román also consented to Lynch's recommendation to hold off bringing in the heavier equipment—tanks, mainly—until later in the morning, when the tide was up, at about 7:00 A.M. This obviously ran counter to the logic of completing the landing *before* dawn, but it was a concession to the coral. There was really no way to land the heavy equipment until the water rose and allowed the LCUs (landing craft, utilities) to pass over the reefs and get closer to the beach. With incoming aircraft on the one hand and coral reefs on the other, the leaders were caught between rockets and a hard place.

AS THE 4TH and 6th battalions struggled over the coral at Blue Beach, the 2nd and 5th battalions were encountering their own frustrations at Red Beach (Playa Larga). The landing there had begun shortly after the Blue Beach landing, and in similar fashion. The American CIA case officer aboard the *Barbara J*, Rip Robertson, accompanied three frogmen onto the beach to place marker lights. Like Gray Lynch, Robertson was among the first to fire a weapon at Red Beach and set foot on Cuban soil.

Red Beach was a smaller operation than Blue Beach, involving several hundred fewer men and a good deal less equipment, so it was, in theory, less challenging. Furthermore, the coral that delayed the men at Blue Beach was not as much of an impediment here. Still, from the moment the 2nd Battalion commenced its landing at about 3:00 A.M., its efforts to gain shore proceeded as gracefully as a drunken ballerina. The tone of the enterprise was heralded by the ear-splitting bray of rusty winches lowering the small landing craft from the *Houston*. For days, the brigade leaders had stressed the utter importance of stealth during the landing, but the moment the winches began to turn, all pretense of stealth was lost. "You could hear them in Havana," recalled Jorge Silveira, a radioman aboard the *Houston*. "It was totally absurd."

When the landing craft hit the water, it became apparent at once that they were entirely inadequate. For one thing, they were too light and began to flip over in the surf. "Landing craft" was, in fact, a fancy term for eight small open-hulled fiberglass boats, the sort a weekend sportsman might take out onto the local lake for a little trout fishing—the only difference being that the sportsman probably would have had better luck operating his outboard motor than the brigademen had operating theirs. The seventy-five-horsepower Evinrudes were plagued with ailments. According to one diagnosis, they had been fueled with an incorrect mixture of gas and oil. Many of the engines did not start, and those that did smoked and coughed—and died. On one boat, the motor simply fell off the stern and vanished into the water. Soon only two of the eight boats were serviceable. Each could hold about ten men. Four hundred men had to get to shore by dawn.

AT ABOUT 3:30 A.M. the phone rang at San Antonio de los Baños Airport, southwest of Havana. The central air base for the Cuban FAR, it was here most of the planes that had survived Saturday morning's attack were gathered. The pilots and crew had been on alert ever since. When Fidel Castro called, his chief pilot, Captain Enrique Carreras, was dozing in the cockpit of his Sea Fury, strapped in, ready to fly at a moment's notice. Startled awake by news that the commander in chief wanted to talk to him, Carreras jumped from his plane and ran across the tarmac to the phone. Castro told the breathless pilot to get ready to fly at dawn.

Castro seemed to understand instantly what the enemy was attempting to accomplish. He could not let the brigade establish a beachhead; a beachhead was a foot in the door—a door through which Americans would gladly enter. The key to stopping the invasion in its tracks was not the infantry—which could be dealt with later—but the ships. A student of military history, Castro understood that without ships, there could be no supplies, and without supplies, there could be no sustained beachhead.

To Captain Carreras, he gave explicit instructions: "Chico, you must sink those ships for me," he said. "Don't let those ships go." Carreras promised to do his best.

Swan Island, 3:44 A.M.

"TAKE UP STRATEGIC positions that control roads and railroads!" the CIA radio station blared across the Caribbean to Cuba. "All planes must stay on the ground. See that no Fidelist plane takes off. Destroy its radio. Destroy its tail."

One charge later leveled against the CIA was that it failed to give advance notice of the invasion to the anti-Castro underground, such as it was, thereby depriving the insurgents of a chance to mobilize and pitch in. The CIA, probably correctly, believed that any notice to the underground was also a warning to Castro, who had spies everywhere. Better to announce it as it was occurring.

Since the previous evening, Radio Swan had been broadcasting breathless and mystifying exhortations that sounded like code but were mainly senseless verbiage concocted by the CIA's David Phillips to stir up intrigue and excitement: "Alert! Alert! Look well at the rainbow. The fish will rise soon. Chico is in the house. Visit him. The sky is blue. . . . The fish will not take much time to rise. The fish is red." Now that the invasion had commenced, Radio Swan turned to issuing explicit instructions. Receiving these were presumably legions of bright-eyed Cubans, ears to the radio, ready to run onto the streets to join the rebellion. In fact, there does not seem to have been such an audience. Judging from the reaction it failed to stir, Radio Swan fell on deaf ears.

Washington, D.C., 4:30 A.M.

FOR ALL THE criticism Charles Cabell took from his colleagues for "mousing around" and unwittingly sabotaging the invasion, no one made a more valiant effort that night to save it than he did. At 4:00 A.M. he called Dean Rusk at the Sheraton Park Hotel, where the secretary kept a suite of rooms. He needed to speak to him at once, Cabell told Rusk—in person.

Normally, the number two man at the CIA would have a duty officer to drive him in such circumstances. But tonight, with all hands occupied, no one was available, so Cabell drove himself. The fastest route took him through the wooded darkness of Rock Creek Park, emerging onto Connecticut Avenue and continuing north toward the residential neighborhood of Woodley Park. When he arrived at the Sheraton Park a few minutes later, he faced a dilemma, yet another to add to the night's catalog of hard decisions: should he slip into the *No Parking* zone in front of the hotel and risk a ticket, or should he park legally a few blocks away and lose precious minutes walking? Always the good soldier, Cabell took the legal space and walked. It was 4:30 A.M. when he arrived at the Sheraton Park. The secretary of state, in a bathrobe, met him at the door of his suite.

Just minutes before Cabell entered Rusk's suite—at 4:22 A.M.—Major General Gray had sent a "warning order" from the Joint Chiefs to Admiral Dennison, commander of the Atlantic Fleet, in Norfolk, Virginia. This advised the navy to prepare its A-4 Skyhawk jets aboard the aircraft carrier *Essex* to lend air cover—known in military parlance as CAP (combat air patrol)—to the brigade's small fleet of ships. This was essentially the proposal Cabell had discussed earlier in the night with Gray, and that General Lemnitzer had endorsed in his home at Fort Myer. But for the order to go into effect, as Lemnitzer had indicated, a higher level of approval was required, which is what brought Cabell to the Sheraton at four-thirty in the morning.

In a heartfelt and personal appeal to Rusk, Cabell made his last-ditch pitch for limited CAP. This CAP would not be initiated to protect the troops on the beaches. It would apply only to shipping. Cabell reminded Rusk that ships were critical to the success of the invasion; if they went down, the brigade would be sunk.

Cabell and Rusk discussed the matter for more than half an hour. Then Rusk had a White House operator place a call to Glen Ora. The time was just after 5:00 A.M. Given how quickly President Kennedy picked up, Cabell guessed that Rusk had already phoned ahead. Now, as Cabell sat by, Rusk related the request for CAP. Then the secretary offered the phone to Cabell, as he had six hours earlier, so the general might make his own case. Cabell did not decline this time. He was desperate. And he was prepared. As Kennedy listened quietly on the other end of the line, Cabell ran through a menu of three possible courses of action, each an attenuated version of the one before it.

First, he proposed CAP from the deck of the *Essex* all the way to the beaches at the Bay of Pigs. If the president would not consider this liberal air cover—Cabell had to know he would not—another option was a modified CAP starting three miles from Cuba's shore, thus excluding Cuba's territorial waters. This would give the brigade's ships a fighting chance of getting to safety if they came under attack. Finally, if the president could not see his way to authorizing navy jets to provide CAP, Cabell hoped that he would at least consider authorizing them to fly routes beyond the three-mile line, so that they might intimidate Cuban pilots with their mere presence.

Cabell could not have entertained realistic hopes for any of his three requests. Why, if Rusk and the president had been set against letting B-26s with Cuban pilots bomb airfields, would they now allow U.S. Navy jets flown by U.S. pilots to enter the fray? They were seeking *less* American commitment, not more.

When Cabell was done, Kennedy asked him to put Rusk back on the line. "No," said the president to Rusk. No to all three requests. Moreover, he told Rusk, almost as an afterthought, he wanted the *Essex* and all other U.S. naval craft to move farther *away* from the Cuban shore, well beyond the horizon, to a distance of thirty miles.

In these final moments before dawn, after months of vacillating, the president had become utterly decisive: he intended to keep American involvement at an absolute minimum. U.S. Navy jets, for the moment at least, were to stay out of it.

Cabell reported back to Quarters Eye with the discouraging result. At 5:25 A.M. Richard Bissell put in a call to the Joint Chiefs operations center at the Pentagon to let Major General Gray know the president had been consulted and the decision had been made. There would be no American air cover.

Over the Caribbean, Dawn

EDWARD FERRER HAD flown in near silence since leaving Nicaragua with a planeload of paratroopers. Like the other men aboard the C-46, he was "wrapped in thoughts," he later wrote, "cloaked against the dangers to come." He did not know the full extent of those dangers: he and his thirty paratroopers had taken off before hearing of the canceled air strikes.

Ferrer and his copilot, Raúl Solís, spoke softly when they spoke at all, and then only to address practicalities of flight: a slight course adjustment due to the wind; a change of fuel tanks; a change of altitude. Night still lay over the ocean, but from thousands of feet above the earth the men inside the C-46 could see the horizon to the east, to the right of the airplane, widening with dawn. Ferrer began to descend for the approach into Cuba. They were still seventy-five miles off the coast when the gray contours of western Cuba came into view. A short while later, Ferrer saw three large, dark shapes on the water. "What the hell is this?" Ferrer asked aloud before realizing that he was looking at an American aircraft carrier and two U.S. Navy destroyers. Elated by the sight of the American ships below, Ferrer handed the controls over to Solís and went back into the cabin. *Look through the windows,* he told the paratroopers as the plane passed eight hundred feet over the *Essex,* Skyhawk jets neatly lining the flight deck, the carrier's wheelhouse towering from the vessel like a seaborne skyscraper. Hundreds of American sailors and officers were looking back up at them, waving. It was a grand and rousing sight. The C-46 rocked its wings as the paratroopers inside let out a great cheer. "Now we can't lose," said Ferrer. "Our friends are down there."

Approaching the Bay of Pigs from the east, Ferrer followed the line of the coast. He saw the brigade ships near the beach—another heartening sight—then banked inland to drop the paratroopers over the town of San Blas, about eight miles northeast of Playa Girón. Suddenly, they were over a war zone. They could see militia in jeeps, rifles pointing up at them, bullets tinging the body of the aircraft. Ferrer flew beyond the drop zone to escape ground fire, then turned back. He pressed the green button that signaled the paratroopers to prepare themselves. The time had come to jump. He wished them all well. "Don't worry," said Alejandro del Valle, the paratroopers' commander and Ferrer's friend. "We'll meet again soon in Havana and I'll buy you a couple of beers." Del Valle jumped, followed by the rest of the men. Fifteen seconds later, the plane was empty but for Ferrer and Solís. They never saw del Valle again.

Not until the plane turned back for Happy Valley did Captain Ferrer notice the B-26 out of the window. At first glance he mistook it for one of the brigade planes that had accompanied the transports. Then the wing-mounted .50-caliber machine guns opened fire. Ferrer had no guns on his C-46 to fire back. He raced for the beach, seeking protection from one of the brigade ships. This proved to be a life-saving move. As he passed over the *Blagar*, the ship's guns opened up on the B-26. The Castro plane turned tail and fled.

Ferrer had survived his first experience of air combat, and it sickened him. Later, after he managed to light a cigarette with trembling fingers, he looked down and realized his flight suit was wet where he'd pissed himself. He was already battlewise enough to know there was no shame in it.

Aboard the *Houston*, Dawn

DOWN THE COAST from the *Blagar* and Blue Beach, deep in the bay, the brigade ship *Houston* was still unloading the infantry onto Red Beach. The landing had been progressing at the pace of a funeral procession. This owed to the shortage of motorboats, but also to the peculiar reluctance of the commander of the 5th Battalion, a former Cuban Army officer named Ricardo Montero Duque, to order his men off the ship. Under Duque's command were some of the greenest recruits of the brigade, but it was Duque himself who seemed to have cold feet at the critical moment. Finally Rip Robertson, the CIA man supervising the Red Beach landing, could take no more excuses. "Look, mister, it's your war and your country, not mine," Robertson exploded. "If you're too scared to land and fight, then stay here and rot!"

In fact, staying and rotting was not an option, because moments later a B-26 appeared overhead, perhaps the same B-26 that had fired on Ferrer. When the brigademen first saw it, they assumed, like Ferrer, that it was one of their own. And when it opened fire, strafing the deck of the *Houston* with its machine guns, they were stunned. They had been told the only airplanes in the sky would be theirs.

"I was holding a coffee pot in one hand and was about to pour a cup for the quartermaster when we felt a tremendous impact and then machine gun bullets spat across the deck," the captain of the *Houston*, Luis Morse, later told *Life*. "I leaned over the port side and saw a gaping hole near the water line. I could see oil spreading out over the water. I poured myself more coffee and gulped it down—you never know when you can get another cup of coffee—then I went to check on the damage."

Rip Robertson grabbed a machine gun aboard the nearby *Barbara J*. "Everybody fire at the goddamn thing!" The ship's guns blasted away at the B-26 with the desired effect. The plane careened off, spewing smoke, and crashed into the swamp. There was no time to celebrate, though, because more planes arrived, and this time there was no mistaking them for the brigade's lumbering B-26s. One was a British-made Sea Fury, a small and agile prop plane that Castro had inherited from Batista's air force. At its controls was Enrique Carreras, the ace pilot whom Fidel Castro had ordered to sink some ships.

Carreras made good on his pledge to Castro. After raking the *Blagar* with machine-gun fire, he turned on the *Houston* with his rockets. The first few missed and exploded in the water. Then one hit. Water began gushing through a hole in the ship's hull as fires broke out in the hold. Another rocket split open the stern and knocked out the rudder. Two hundred and twenty men were still on board, including one unit of the 2nd Battalion, the entire 5th Battalion, and the ship's twenty-man crew of merchant mariners. The ship was ablaze, could no longer be steered, and was rapidly filling with water. The time was six-thirty in the morning. Castro's air force had already struck, and the sun had only just begun to rise.

New York/Washington, D.C., 7:00 A.M.

THE PHONE RANG in Adlai Stevenson's suite at the Waldorf. The ambassador's assistant, Richard Pedersen, was calling at 7:00 A.M. to tell him that an all-out invasion of Cuba was under way. "Yes, I know," replied Stevenson. "Bundy is here."

McGeorge Bundy, having flown in the previous night from Washington, was sitting across from the U.N. ambassador, finishing up breakfast. He had brought Stevenson up to speed, nothing but the truth this time. The breakfast gave Stevenson an opportunity to learn the details of the operation, and it gave Bundy the opportunity to observe the finer attributes of the man before him. "I told him all about it," recalled Bundy later. "It was most difficult for him. He was very decent about it. . . . All he wanted was more information so he would not dig deeper holes."

As Adlai Stevenson was breakfasting with Bundy and learning the truth of the invasion, many of the Pentagon's military leaders were getting their first reports of its progress, and learning, for the first time, of the canceled air strikes. Most of them understood at once what the cancellation meant for the brigade. Arriving at 7:00 A.M. for a scheduled 8:00 A.M. Joint Chiefs meeting, General Curtis LeMay, air force vice chief of staff, lost his temper. "Look, you just cut the throats of everybody on the beach down there," he scolded Roswell Gilpatric, an assistant secretary of defense and the nearest person in the Kennedy administration he could yell at. "It's bound to fail." Admiral Arleigh Burke was "horrified" to hear that the politicians had pulled "the strings out of an operation at the last minute."

Playa Larga (Red Beach), Early Morning

IN THE BEST of all possible worlds—the world Dean Rusk apparently conjured when he counseled the president to cancel the air strikes on the assumption that they were "not all that important"—the convoy of brigade ships would have been unloaded before first light. The men and their equipment would have been safely landed on the beaches and the ships would have retreated to international waters before Castro's planes appeared. There would have been no coral reef at Blue Beach, no malfunctioning outboard motors at Red Beach—nothing to hold up the landings and pin the ships to the shore.

The Bay of Pigs on the morning of April 17 was not the best of all possible worlds. Still, it could have been worse.

At Red Beach, the captain of the *Houston*, Luis Morse, had managed to run his stricken vessel aground on a sandbar about four hundred yards from shore. Morse thus saved the *Houston* from sinking and gave the nearly two hundred men still on board a reasonable chance of escape. These men were now frantically trying to get off the ship. Men who could swim jumped into the water. Those who could not waited for landing boats to rescue them. Castro's planes returned again and again, strafing them. Twenty men were killed by the bullets. Another ten drowned, a few of these probably victims of the sharks who patrolled the warm waters of the bay.

Many decades later, a seventy-nine-year-old man named Jorge Marquet sat in a small room in downtown Miami and reflected on his escape from the *Houston*. He remembered particularly his concern for the welfare of his younger cousin, who was with him in the 5th Battalion. A former lifeguard, Marquet was a strong swimmer, but his cousin was not. Marquet found a life jacket aboard the ship, but when he tossed it into the water to test its buoyancy, it sank. He rummaged around the ship for something else that might float. He found a large plank of wood, about the size of a door, that could serve as a raft for his cousin. The cousin lay down on the plank and Marquet, swimming behind, kicked him to shore.

Once his cousin was safe, Marquet looked back at the enfeebled hulk of the ship. Men were still hanging to it, unable or afraid to swim, some of them wounded from the air attack. Marquet got into a rowboat with another man and made several runs to and from the *Houston* until he was too exhausted to continue.

Incredibly, most of the men of the 5th Battalion had survived the bombing and strafing of the ship and the passage to shore. The problem now was that they were five or six miles from the intended landing site at Red Beach, marooned on a distant stretch of beach, and out of action—for good, as it would turn out. When they regrouped later in the morning under Montero Duque's command and attempted to march to Red Beach, they ran into a squadron of militia and retreated. They dug in near the spot they had come ashore from the *Houston*, and there they would remain, out of action, for three days.

MOST OF THE 2nd Battalion had made it ashore at Playa Larga either before the attack on the *Houston* or shortly thereafter. Erneido Oliva, the brigade's second in command and the man in charge at Red Beach, immediately began moving troops up the road, inland, to the north. Ahead of them, paratroopers were to have secured the road at a town called Pálpite, about three miles from Playa Larga. In fact, though Oliva did not know it yet, the paratroopers had failed to do so. Like so much else that would go wrong that morning, this misfortune owed indirectly to the canceled air strike and—more directly—to the arrival of Castro's airplanes. Just before reaching the drop zone, the brigade pilots transporting the paratroopers (not to be confused with the paratroopers Edward Ferrer successfully dropped over San Blas, twenty miles to the southeast) had seen two Castro planes in the distance and taken action to evade them. As a result, the pilots had approached the drop zone from the wrong direction and, in their confusion, dropped the men over the swamp rather than over the dry roadbed. Many of the paratroopers landed far from where they were supposed to be. Worse, their equipment—weapons, ammunition, radio equipment—fell into the muck and sank. The men were too disorganized and too lightly armed to be of much use after that.

Playa Girón (Blue Beach), 9:30 A.M.

BY SOME MEASURES, despite the early setbacks, these early hours of battle appeared to favor the brigade. There continued to be positive signs for those inclined to see them. Although the 1st Battalion paratroopers had missed their mark at Pálpite, the 2nd Battalion was in position to defend the road by midmorning and would soon prove a formidable obstacle to Castro's advance. "God is with us," remarked one of the men.

Over at Blue Beach, the landing had been dicey since the air attacks began at dawn, but nonetheless the 6th Battalion (armored) had managed to land most of its heavy equipment by 8:30 A.M. Only the *Río Escondido*, about three miles at sea and patiently awaiting its turn, had not unloaded. Meanwhile, up the road from Playa Girón at the town of San Blas, the thirty paratroopers whom Edward Ferrer dropped earlier in the morning had landed well and encountered little resistance. They had sealed the road to the beach by midmorning.

All of this was good. But none of it, tactically speaking, was going to amount to much in the end. Castro's planes would make sure of that.

From the moment of its sunrise debut, the Cuban FAR was at the least an irritant to the brigade and, on several instances, much worse. The best defense against the FAR planes were the antiaircraft guns aboard the *Blagar* (at Blue Beach) and *Barbara J* (at Red Beach). The brigade managed to bring down two FAR planes that morning, including the Castro B-26 that crashed into the swamp after the *Blagar* strafed it. When the brigade's own B-26s began to arrive over the beach that morning, brigade gunners, like everybody on the battlefield, found it nearly impossible to distinguish them from Castro's B-26s. Not until the planes were directly overhead could they detect the subtle difference in stripes. As a result of the confusion, a few of the brigade planes were mistakenly fired at from below.

The brigade B-26s, having been diverted from their original task of striking Castro's FAR on the ground, had been flying air cover over the beach in pairs since dawn. Predictably, they had been useless in fending off Castro's planes, a deficit that became increasingly evident as the day wore on. Maintaining constant air patrol was, in any case, a challenge. Shifts could last no more than forty-five minutes, the maximum allowed by the planes' fuel supply. The CIA's hope was that the brigade planes could soon begin using the small landing strip at Girón to refuel. Not only would this give the planes more time and greater range in the air, it also conformed to the White House's desire to have the brigade planes take off from Cuban soil. There was just one very important step that had to take place before the landing strip could be used and the wish come true: two hundred barrels of airplane fuel had to be offloaded from the decks of the *Río Escondido*.

THE TIME WAS just before 9:30 A.M. when the Cuban pilot Enrique Carreras returned over the Bay of Pigs. His Sea Fury had been refueled and rearmed and he was back to sink more ships. When he saw the *Río Escondido* offshore, low in the water, burdened with its freight, he dove for it. The *Río Escondido* was the main supply ship for the brigade. In addition to its human cargo of the 6th Battalion, and along with two hundred barrels of airplane fuel, the ship's decks held ten days' supply of ammunition, including twenty tons of explosives, as well as most of the brigade's food stocks and the radio van with the main communications equipment for the brigade. In retrospect, loading so much essential matériel onto one ship was a mistake. Then again, when the freight had been distributed among the brigade's ships, the operative assumption was that Castro's air force would be destroyed.

"Sea Fury!" somebody aboard the ship shouted out. "Sea Fury!"

Carreras came out of the sun from the east. He leveled to three hundred feet, firing all four of his wing-mounted rockets. The first three overshot and hit the sea. The fourth hit the forward deck, not far from where the barrels of aviation fuel were held—and where twenty tons of incendiaries were stacked. The captain ordered the crew to abandon ship. Men scrambled into boats, or they jumped into the water and swam.

And then, all at once, the *Río Escondido* exploded: a vast, fiery eruption sending debris hundreds of feet into the air and shock waves shuddering across the water. Sixteen miles away, at Red Beach, Rip Robertson heard the explosion, then saw the mushroom cloud rising. He radioed Grayston Lynch. "What the hell was that?" When Lynch told him the *Río Escondido* had just exploded, Robertson's first reaction was almost relief. "For a moment, I thought Fidel had the A-bomb."

San Juan, 9:30 A.M.

AS THE *RÍO ESCONDIDO* was exploding off the coast of Cuba, Allen Dulles stood at a podium in San Juan, Puerto Rico, concluding his remarks to the Young Presidents Organization. The Young Presidents were, according to a sassy brochure they sent to Dulles weeks earlier, "men (and women) who prior to age forty became presidents of corporations with annual sales volumes of at least $1,000,000 and full-time employees totaling at least fifty." They had come to San Juan for their annual "University of Presidents" convention, and Allen Dulles was the keynote speaker. Later, the Soviet news service would report that Allen Dulles, "the notorious American master spy," had gone to San Juan to direct the invasion of Cuba. Radio Moscow informed listeners that Dulles intended to "command in person the aggressive actions against Cuba." The truth was stranger. On the most important day in the history of the CIA, its director was delivering a speech to a trade organization.

The subject of Dulles's speech—"the Communist challenge in Latin America"—had been chosen long before this day, but it seemed tailor-made for the circumstances. "Revolutions are in progress and in the making," Dulles told the executives. "It is against this backdrop that I speak to you today."

For about forty-five minutes, Dulles had warned the Young Presidents of the threat of communism, finally winding down at about nine-thirty with a word of encouragement to his audience of capitalist prodigies: "Let us pledge our mutual cooperation to advancing the best interests of our country in an effort to strengthen and extend freedom in the world."

Washington, D.C., 9:40 A.M.

THE YOUNG PRESIDENTS were applauding Allen Dulles in Puerto Rico, the *Río Escondido* was burning off the coast of Cuba, and President Kennedy was touching down on the south lawn of the White House in a marine helicopter, back from his weekend at Glen Ora. Following a quick walk across the lawn to the Oval Office and a brief conference with Kenneth O'Donnell, his appointments secretary, Kennedy stepped into the cabinet room. Dean Rusk was waiting for him. Rusk still knew very little about the progress of the invasion—he would hear about the sinking of the ships in a phone call from Charles Cabell at ten-fifteen—but he knew enough to realize they had a problem on their hands.

Kennedy picked up a phone receiver and called his brother Robert, who was in Virginia giving a speech to a group of newspaper editors. Until this moment, the president had kept the attorney general mostly out of national security issues. That would no longer be the case. "I don't think it's going as well as it should," he told his brother. "Come back here."

Bay of Pigs, 10:00 A.M.

THE GROUND WAR began ten hours into the invasion. Before this moment, the brigade had come under small-arms fire from local militia, but nothing like an army had met it. The first significant contact occurred on the road to Pálpite, the town three miles north of Playa Larga, and it came as a surprise to the brigade. The military leaders had been expecting Castro's troops to attack first at Playa Girón, by way of San Blas, which was one reason the brigade concentrated its manpower and heavy arms there. But Castro had other ideas. First he would hit Playa Larga, which was twenty miles farther inland—and closer to Havana. Then he'd swing east to Girón.

Troops from the brigade's 2nd Battalion were dug in along the road to Pálpite when Castro's militia arrived at 10:00 A.M. The most forward position of the brigade was held by a few dozen men under the command of Máximo Cruz. At five feet five inches and 120 pounds with his boots on, Cruz was a slight man who seemed almost to vanish under his lieutenant's cap, but over the next sixteen hours he and his men would prove themselves among the most courageous and stalwart of the brigade.

The appearance of Castro's militia, approaching from the north in a convoy of trucks, was the first real indication to the 2nd Battalion that the paratroopers had missed Pálpite, for it was clear that the column had advanced unmolested. Cruz's men allowed the trucks to advance a little farther, then opened fire from covered positions. Though vastly outnumbered, they immediately brought the column to a halt. This was the first test of the theory that a few men could hold off Castro's army at choke points on the roads to the beaches. Cruz and his men passed with flying colors.

EVEN AS THE 2nd Battalion was achieving this early victory, a more tactically significant drama was occurring off the coast. The brigade's ships, under orders from headquarters, were turning away from the beaches and heading for open sea. Only a small portion of the cargo these ships carried had been delivered to the beach, but after the attacks on the *Houston* and the *Río Escondido*, the CIA commanders back in Washington—Esterline and Hawkins—decided they had to remove the *Caribe* and the *Atlántico* or lose them, too. "This seemed the only logical thing to do," wrote Grayston Lynch. "To remain off the beach would risk everything." Lynch was under the impression that when the ships reached international waters twelve miles from shore, they would come under protection of U.S. naval jets. They could spend the afternoon in their haven at sea, then return to the beaches to resume unloading as soon as dark fell. When Lynch explained the situation to Pepe San Román by radio, the brigade leader was concerned. Aboard those ships was all the ammunition, food, medical supplies—everything the brigade needed to fight. "Don't desert us," he said to Lynch.

"We're not going to desert you," the CIA man assured him.

The *Atlántico* and the *Caribe* led the way to the horizon, followed by the smaller LCIs (landing craft, infantry) and finally the *Barbara J* and the *Blagar*. It was a slow-motion getaway, since the smaller landing crafts' top speed was about six knots. As the boats fled, Castro's planes repeatedly harassed them. The ships finally reached the twelve-mile mark, but Castro's planes were still on them and there was no sign of American jets. Lynch got on the radio and contacted the USS *Eaton*, the flagship of the American fleet that had escorted the brigade's navy to Cuba. The American vessels were nearby, keeping a close watch.

"We are under air attack in international waters," said Lynch to the commander of the *Eaton*. "Can you help us?"

The response floored him. "My heart is with you, but I cannot help you," said the commander. "My orders are not to become engaged in any way."

Another Castro B-26 appeared. "Ask the bastards if they'll allow you to stand by and pick up survivors," Lynch yelled into the radio. "If someone doesn't get these damn planes off us, that's exactly what all that is left of us will be."

A combination of inexperience on the part of Castro's pilots and sure-handed shooting by Lynch and the other gunners aboard the *Blagar* kept the planes at bay. But not without consequence. After shooting down one attacking plane, Lynch looked up to see that the two cargo ships, the *Atlántico* and the *Caribe*, had separated from the convoy. Their captains, having apparently concluded that war was not for them, were steaming full speed for open sea. They told Lynch they would wait at Point Zulu, a preset rendezvous fifty miles south of the Bay of Pigs.

New York, 11:00 A.M.

"I MUST ANNOUNCE OFFICIALLY, on behalf of the government which I have the honor to represent," began Raúl Roa in the General Assembly of the United Nations, "that the Republic of Cuba was invaded this morning by a mercenary force which came from Guatemala and Florida and which was organized, financed, and armed by the government of the United States of America."

Roa went on to blast the United States in a sermon that, for all its fire and brimstone, never strayed far from fact.

"These crimes and depredations have been sanctified, paid for, and blessed by the State Department, the Pentagon, and the CIA in advance," he told his fellow delegates. "They have received the absolution of high ecclesiastical officials. In exchange for this absolution they are at the same time crucifying the mandates of man and God and the principle of nonintervention." A U.S.-backed attack on Cuba—an attempt to place the "imperial yoke" over the shoulders of a sovereign nation—was illegal not only under international law, Roa pointed out, but American law as well. (Thomas Mann, of course, had made the same point in his paper to the president two months earlier.)

When it came his turn to respond, Adlai Stevenson managed to sound nearly as indignant as Roa, but he chose his words carefully. "These charges are totally false and I deny them categorically," he began. "The

United States has committed no aggression against Cuba and no offensive has been launched from Florida or any other part of the United States." This was true in letter if not quite in spirit. Stevenson was a man walking the wire between national honor and personal integrity, attempting to preserve what secrecy remained of the invasion while simultaneously grasping at remnants of virtue—not an easy thing to do that Monday.

Stevenson was on firmer ground when he turned from defending America to deploying his dry wit on Raúl Roa. He dismissed Roa's "lurid oratory" and "colorful challenges," as if the Cuban were pathetically deluded. He went on to respond to a personal attack Roa had made on him earlier, in which the Cuban suggested that the Adlai Stevenson who flacked for the White House at the United Nations was a different man than the Adlai Stevenson whose writings Roa had once read and admired.

"Well, I confess that I am flattered that Dr. Roa has read some of my writings, but I am not sure that I equally appreciate his suggestion that I am so versatile that there are two of me," said Stevenson. "Dr. Roa will find that on the subject of tyranny . . . I have only one view—unalterable opposition."

It was a strong performance, but it left Stevenson depleted and pale. Later that day, a friend named Jane Dick would run into him coming out of an elevator at the Waldorf. The usually affable ambassador hardly returned her greeting. "I was shocked by his appearance. He looked dazedly right through me, apparently not seeing me."

Havana, 11:08 A.M.

"BY SEA AND AIR, invading troops are attacking various points of the nation's territory in southern Las Villas Province, backed by warplanes and warships," Fidel Castro informed his compatriots over Cuban National Radio. "The glorious soldiers of the rebel army are already locked in combat with the enemy at all landing points. They are fighting to defend the sacred homeland and revolution against the attack of the mercenaries organized by the imperialist government of the United States. . . . Forward Cubans!"

Shortly after his radio address, Castro got into a car and raced east, then south, toward the Bay of Pigs, where he intended to direct the war against the imperialists in person. At 3:15 P.M. he arrived at the town of Central Australia, about fifteen miles north of Playa Larga, where a sugar mill had been requisitioned as a military command post. José Ramón Fernández, the officer he'd placed in charge of the attack early that morning, was there to greet him. Castro wanted to continue down the road to lead the assault already under way south of Pálpite, but Fernández implored him not to risk going to the front. Castro remained at the sugar mill instead, giving orders and stalking around with a cigar between his lips and a rifle in his hand. Many photographs would be taken of Castro over the next several days, leaping out of tanks, gazing out over the bay, ministering to his troops, and admonishing the "mercenaries." The first of these soon-to-be famous images were taken of Castro that afternoon at the sugar mill and immediately sent by wire services around the world.

Playa Larga (Red Beach), 2:30 P.M.

THE SIXTY MEN under the command of Máximo Cruz were the first to see what was coming down the road from Pálpite that afternoon. The time was about 2:30 P.M. when one of Cruz's forward observers came back to report a column approaching. He handed the binoculars to Cruz. Five decades later, Cruz still vividly recalled what he saw through the glasses as he peered out from behind cover. "There were not a hundred. Not two hundred. There were not five hundred. Probably over a thousand people with weapons were coming down the road, on each side of the road. And I said, 'Uh-oh.'"

Having repulsed the earlier attack, it now fell to Cruz and his men to hold the front lines on this second and much larger advance. They were better fortified this time. After the morning skirmish, Pepe San Román had sent over one of the brigade's five M-41 tanks. The men of the 2nd Battalion had cheered when they saw it rumbling down the road from Blue Beach. A few kissed its side. "Maybe there will be a miracle and everything will turn out all right," one of the men had said to Erneido Oliva.

"Don't be foolish," Oliva had responded. "There are no miracles at a time like this."

The advancing troops were the cadets from the Militia Leadership School in Matanzas—the men Castro had ordered José Ramón Fernández to rouse early that morning. The cadets had come south to the Bay of Pigs in whatever transportation they could hastily requisition, including buses and freight vans, even the open trucks of farmers from which crates of fruit or chickens had been removed to make room for soldiers. Their caravan did not look formidable, but they were well armed and highly trained.

About fifteen minutes after Cruz's observer first spotted it, the advancing column halted, its front just a few hundred yards from where the brigade company was lying in wait. Castro's troops were setting mortars when Máximo Cruz gave his men the signal. "They had no idea where we were," he later recalled. "We opened fire with everything we had."

One of the best gunners in the battalion, a small man named Gilberto Hernández, had earned himself the nickname El Barberito (the little barber) by being skillful with a pair of hair shears at Base Trax. The same steady hands that won him tonsorial acclaim also made him an ace marksman. His first shot hit the trucks with an explosive shell, then a white phosphorus shell, which set the truck on fire. With nowhere to hide from the blistering onslaught, Castro's cadets dove off the side of the road into the swamp grass or retreated back down the road.

The fighting had been going on for about twenty minutes when two B-26s appeared in the sky. The Cubans read the planes' FAR markings and saw their salvation. They waved joyfully, realizing too late that the planes were not their own. The B-26s were the brigade's *Puma One* and *Puma Two*, the same planes that had attacked Libertad on Saturday morning, flown by the same pilots—José Crespo and Osvaldo Piedra. Unlike their ill-starred fellow Puma pilot Daniel Fernández-Mon, Crespo and Piedra had survived the barrage of Czechoslovakian artillery on Saturday to fly again this Monday.

Since the start of the invasion, five two-plane sorties—Linda, Lobo, Chico, Gorilla, and Paloma—had flown from Happy Valley to the Bay of Pigs to patrol the skies over the beaches. Of those ten brigade planes, two had been shot down. First, in midmorning, *Chico Two* had been downed over Playa Girón, killing the pilot. Later in the morning, *Paloma One* had been hit by a T-33 jet. Navigator Demetrio Pérez had parachuted from the falling plane to the sea. The pilot, Raúl Vianello, bailed, but his chute did not open.

The Puma planes dove on Castro's column, spewing bullets from their nose-mounted machine guns. They returned to release their missiles and bombs. Bunched on the road below, with nowhere to seek shelter, hundreds of men were felled as if cut down by a scythe. "It was awful," one brigade soldier later recalled. "First I saw a lot of caps flying through the air; then there were men screaming and running and gasoline tanks blowing up. . . . You could smell the burning flesh right away." Almost instantly, the redheaded buzzards roosting in the swamps smelled it too and flew over the road, where they remained for days to come. Castro's troops retreated, leaving piles of injured and dead men bleeding on the road.

The terrible efficacy of *Puma One* and *Puma Two* over the road to Pálpite was a testament to the power of air support, and a hint of what might have been achieved strategically if the brigade had dominated the air at the Bay of Pigs. But the brigade did not dominate the air, and it would now fall to *Puma One* and *Puma Two* to demonstrate the significance of this fact as well. As the planes turned to go, a T-33 suddenly appeared, followed by a Sea Fury. The B-26s, vulnerable in air-to-air combat under the best of circumstances, were out of bullets.

"I've got a T-33 on my tail," called out Osvaldo Piedra, the pilot of *Puma Two*, as he turned back to Happy Valley. "Shoot at him! Shoot at him!"

"I don't have any ammunition," replied *Puma One*'s pilot, José Crespo.

"They hit me!" shouted Piedra. "They hit me!" *Puma Two* plummeted and crashed in the water. Both Piedra and his navigator, José Fernández, were killed.

Puma One had been hit as well but remained airborne. Venting smoke from one engine and losing fuel, José Crespo barreled over the sea toward Puerto Cabezas. A Sea Fury pursued, closing in. There was little Crespo could do but pray for a miracle—and then one arrived. A pair of A-4 Skyhawks swooped out of the skies from high above. The jets were unmarked but their origin was obvious. The only fleet in the world that flew Skyhawks was the U.S. Navy.

The Skyhawks had been performing reconnaissance off the *Essex* when they happened upon the chase scene over the Caribbean. The American pilots were prohibited by the Rules of Engagement from taking offensive action against the Sea Fury, but their mere presence was intimidating enough. The Sea Fury turned tail and headed back to Cuba. One of the American pilots gave Crespo a thumbs-up, then soared away.

Miracles aside, the Skyhawks could not save *Puma One* in the end.

As pilot José Crespo limped back to Nicaragua, evening descended and the fuel gauge creeped ominously toward empty. The plane began to lose altitude, flying on one engine. Crespo came to realize he was too far from base to make it. "I'm only about six hundred feet above the water," he broadcast to his fellow pilots over the radio. "We're running the right engine almost at max, but it looks like we're going to have to ditch soon." Later that evening, the brigade's priest, Father Cavero, got on the radio to give Crespo and his navigator, Lorenzo Pérez-Lorenzo, last rites. Then *Puma One* vanished into the dark Caribbean. Neither the plane nor its crew were ever seen again.

New York City, 7:15 P.M.

IN NEW YORK CITY, a publicist named Lem Jones distributed a bulletin on behalf of the Revolutionary Council, the provisional government waiting in Florida to fly to a liberated Cuba. The bulletin declared that a "tremendous army of invisible soldier-patriots has now received its instructions" and predicted that "before dawn the island of Cuba will rise up en masse in a coordinated wave of sabotage and rebellion" that would sweep communism from Cuba. The main battle would commence within the next several hours, according to the release.

Jones, a former press secretary for Wendell Willkie, was a real and fairly reputable Madison Avenue publicist, but there was nothing authentic about this press release. It had, in fact, been composed by David Phillips at the CIA and was entirely a work of fiction.

Playa Larga (Red Beach), 7:45 P.M.

ERNEIDO OLIVA, THE man in charge at Red Beach, could take some satisfaction in the obliteration of Castro's troops on the road to Pálpite. But he knew that more, much more, was soon to come. Members of Castro's militia who had been taken prisoner spoke of troops and equipment, including artillery and forty tanks, amassing to the north for a night attack. In preparation, Oliva pulled his front lines back, including Máximo Cruz's brave company, and set the new line at a small traffic circle, or rotunda, less than a mile from Red Beach. Any troops of Castro's hoping to penetrate the coast near Playa Larga would have to pass through here. Pepe San Román sent a large segment of the 4th Battalion to reinforce Oliva. "I am very happy to have you," Oliva told the men of the 4th, many of whom he had personally trained. "This is going to be a strong fight." San Román also sent two more tanks, giving Oliva a total now of three M-41s. Máximo Cruz and his men were assigned the unenviable honor of holding the front.

The so-called Battle of the Rotunda began at seven forty-five that evening with an attack of artillery from four Cuban batteries of 122-millimeter howitzers. As the shells rained down, Oliva ordered his men to stay in their trenches. About two thousand shells fell over the next four hours, one of these just narrowly missing Oliva himself. Fortunately for the brigade, Castro's artillerymen were still new to their equipment and not very accurate. Brigade radiomen, too, had managed to tap into enemy communications, so they knew where to expect the shells to land. They even managed to issue a few target readings of their own to fool Castro's artillery. "Whenever we heard Fidel's mortar commander asking for the range and firing angle, we'd cut in and tell him, 'Compañero, up 15 and 10 to the right,'" a brigade radioman later told *Life*. "The barrage would miss us completely, and the fool would shout into his radio, 'You are nothing but a damned idiot, compañero!'"

Washington, D.C., 11:40 P.M.

ALLEN DULLES LANDED at Baltimore's Friendship Airport aboard a CIA agency plane shortly before midnight. Richard Drain was there to greet him, having been sent by Richard Bissell to brief the director upon his return from Puerto Rico. "Well, how is it going?" Dulles asked as the men shook hands on the tarmac.

"Not very well, sir."

"Oh, is that so?" Dulles proposed that they drive back to Georgetown in his Cadillac so Drain could fill him in. In the car, Drain told the director of the canceled air strikes, the first Dulles had apparently heard of this. He could not understand. "The president must be confused."

They arrived at Dulles's home on Q Street in Georgetown. Drain was intending to drop off the director, then return to Quarters Eye. Dulles asked him to come in for a drink. Drain tried to beg off, but Dulles insisted. "Do come in," he said. "We need a drink." Once inside and sipping scotch, Dulles seemed determined to change the subject from Cuba. They chatted about this and that, as if they were two old chums without a care in the world. It was, Drain later said, "unreal."

Bay of Pigs, Near Midnight

THE BRIGADE COMMANDER Pepe San Román knew his troops were confronting hard attacks on two fronts. So far, twenty-four hours into the invasion, the brigade had held its positions fairly well, but its ability to maintain these depended on the amount of ammunition the men had at their disposal. The problem was that they had spent most of it, and the resupply had either gone down with the two bombed ships or was somewhere out at sea aboard the *Caribe* and the *Atlántico*.

From his post at Blue Beach, San Román peered over the dark water. Grayston Lynch had assured him the ships would be back at nightfall to finish unloading, but there was no sign of them. San Román climbed into a boat with a radio operator and took off to hunt for ships. He motored more than five miles out to sea, all the while calling on the radio. He got no response. The ships were nowhere to be found.

At Red Beach, five minutes before midnight, the air suddenly went quiet. The shelling had stopped. Máximo Cruz and his company hunkered down at the rotunda and waited, listening for the tanks that would soon arrive. They had survived D-Day. Now the real battle would begin.

18

"Sour Like You Wouldn't Believe"

Tuesday, April 18: D+1

Bay of Pigs, 12:30 A.M.

THE FIRST MINUTES of April 18 passed in eerie quiet. This, like the calm at the eye of a hurricane, would not last, and every man there knew it. The artillery had been a prelude; its absence only meant that Castro's troops were on the move and would soon arrive.

The vanguard of the 2nd Battalion, including the small company under the command of Máximo Cruz that had performed so valiantly the previous afternoon, was entrenched just south of the rotunda. The rest of the battalion, combined with elements of the 4th (heavy weapons) Battalion, was positioned behind and along the flanks of the front. As they waited, the men could sense the approaching column even before they could hear it or see it. The spongy ground vibrated beneath them as if alive. It was alive, in fact. Millions of black and red land crabs, drawn out by the springtime mating season, scampered through the swamps and over the men's legs and feet. Mosquitoes swarmed, too, drawing the first blood of the night.

The men endured the crabs and the mosquitoes and tried to remain motionless behind their battlements. Most had not slept or eaten anything substantial in days, in some cases not since leaving Puerto Cabezas on April 14. They were exhausted, hungry, anxious, shell-shocked from the artillery barrage, and now facing (as they had been told) a vast army. And with the supply ships either sunk or gone at sea, they were low on ammunition. The tanks had only twelve rounds apiece of antitank charges, and limited antipersonnel rounds.

Máximo Cruz was among the first to see the enemy tanks. The time was about 12:30 A.M., just half an hour since the shelling ceased. The lead tank was a dark, rumbling shape filling the narrow road about a hundred yards distant. Behind it followed men, then more tanks, then more men.

Not until the lead tank entered the rotunda and was practically on top of them did Cruz give the order to fire. The three M-41s blasted the column with antitank and antipersonnel rounds. The battalion joined in with bazookas, mortars, and small arms, splintering the darkness with flashes of white fire. The first Castro tank stopped in its tracks. Two more came; they were knocked out as well. Castro's troops dove for cover into the swamp or fell to the ground where they stood.

The tanks and the men kept coming down the narrow road, directly into the shooting gallery at the rotunda; the brigade held fast and repelled them. The battle was shaping up as a late-night reprisal of the previous afternoon's rout. Unlike that attack, though, this one had no clear end. New tanks arrived to take the place of disabled or destroyed tanks, and new men followed. The more littered the road became with stalled and ravaged equipment, the more obstacles the new tanks met on approaching the rotunda. But they kept grinding forward. In some cases, because there was no other way to go, the Cuban tanks ran over their own wounded and dead, flattening the bodies under their treads.

For hours the combat at the rotunda raged, unrelenting and grotesque, lit by flashes of fire, punctuated by the splintering of steel and the screams of men. "It was scary as shit," said Rafael Montalvo of the brigade's 2nd Battalion; ". . . people moving in the shadows, shooting; you don't see shit, you just shoot and shoot and shoot, and every time you hear a noise, you shoot."

The brigade's M-41s engaged Castro's Soviet-made tanks from no more than twenty paces, blasting them at nearly point-blank range. When the brigade tanks ran out of ammunition, their drivers went at the enemy steel to steel, ramming them like giant "prehistoric monsters," in the words of José Alvarez, one of the brigade's tank drivers. At 3:00 A.M. the brigade's mortars began firing incendiary grenades of white phosphorus, throwing flickering light and shadow over the swamps, burning whatever the phosphorus touched. Erneido Oliva, the commander who ordered the mortars, thought the screams of burning men sounded "just like hell."

From the horror of the night arose acts of extreme courage. One of the bravest feats was performed by Gilberto Hernández—the one they called El Barberito—who had been so nimble and devastating in the afternoon. Several hours into the battle, after the brigade tanks ran out of ammunition, Hernández, already blinded in one eye from an encounter earlier in the night, jumped from cover and charged a tank, armed with a recoilless rifle. From yards away, dodging and feinting, he danced around the tank and fired at it. The shells did not penetrate the tank's thick hide, but the Cubans inside, overwhelmed by the relentless pounding, surrendered anyway. Later, the tank commander inquired after the fierce young man who had come at them with a recoilless rifle; he wanted to meet him. But by then it was too late. El Barberito was dead, felled by the guns of another Soviet-made tank.

A short while after El Barberito's death, Máximo Cruz was badly injured, pierced by shrapnel in his left arm and shoulder as he stood beneath a street sign firing at a tank with a bazooka. He continued to fight for another three hours, until he collapsed from blood loss.

Five hours had passed since the start of the battle. Dawn was breaking, and the first real cracks were starting to show in the brigade's defense. The spent tanks had retired from the rotunda; the soldiers were exhausted and nearly out of ammunition, and some had begun to retreat toward the beaches. Out of Máximo Cruz's company of sixty men, only a dozen or so remained unscathed. Had Castro's troops continued the assault, they might well have broken through the rotunda at last. Instead, much to the brigade's relief, they began to withdraw.

One last enemy tank approached the rotunda just after dawn. Erneido Oliva lifted a bazooka and stood in the middle of the rotunda, prepared to fire. The tank halted, the hatch opened, and the driver appeared. He called to Oliva through smoke and morning fog. "Are you the commander of these men?"

"Yes," replied Oliva.

"I congratulate you because these men are heroes. I would like to fight with you."

The tank driver told Oliva that the brigademen at the rotunda, numbering fewer than 370, had stymied a force of more than 2,100 men and more than 20 tanks. While the brigade had lost 20 dead and 50 wounded, Castro's forces had taken extremely heavy casualties: 500 dead, 1,000 wounded.* But the tank commander also told Oliva that more men were coming, gathering at the sugar mill down the road. And more behind that, and more beyond.

---

* The Cuban government reported much lower casualty figures.

The Battle of the Rotunda ended as it had begun, with eerie quiet. Occasionally a man would call out. "*Lieutenant, don't leave me,*" one voice kept shouting. "*You son of a bitch, Lieutenant, come get me.*" The light seeping into the sky revealed a battlefield smeared by fog, and through the fog a phantom tableau of carnage: blasted tanks and abandoned weapons; burned bodies and crushed bodies; buzzards pecking at the ground and circling in the air.

The battle had been a victory for the brigade, but it would be the last. Despite his fatigue, Oliva was clearheaded enough to understand this. His men had held, but they were wrecked. No amount of ability or pluck—or luck—could substitute for bullets. Barring a miracle, the gig was up. He gave orders to retreat to Blue Beach.

THE *CARIBE* AND the *Atlántico* remained AWOL. After vanishing over the horizon the previous morning, they had stayed out of sight and out of touch. Neither had stopped at Point Zulu, as their captains had assured Grayston Lynch they would. Instead, both freighters, loaded with everything the brigade needed to survive, put as much distance between themselves and Cuba as possible.

For several hours, the *Blagar* and the *Barbara J* had searched the shipping lanes south of Cuba for sign of the missing freighters, but they had come up empty-handed. A message arrived over the wireless from Washington: forget the cargo ships; return to shore as soon as possible and complete unloading. Both the *Blagar* and the *Barbara J* carried small amounts of ammunition, hardly sufficient for the increasingly urgent needs of the brigade, but better than none. Because the *Barbara J* had suffered damage in the previous morning's air raids, Lynch and Robertson ordered the crews to transfer the ship's cargo to the faster *Blagar*, which had a better chance of making it back to Playa Girón before daylight.

That chance was soon lost. Aboard the *Blagar* were most of the men who had been rescued from the sinking *Río Escondido* the previous morning. Long after the rescue they remained badly shaken, huddling in a corner of the ship in their life vests. When these men realized they were about to be sent back into harm's way, they balked. A handful of them, armed with .45s, took over the engine room and shut off the *Blagar*'s propellers. The mutiny did not last long—the troublemakers were soon subdued and taken into custody—but by the time order was restored, the opportunity for the *Blagar* to make landfall and unload before daylight had been lost. Washington told Lynch to cancel the order. The *Blagar* would stay put at Point Zulu and wait for the *Caribe* and the *Atlántico* to return.

Happy Valley, Predawn

THE AIRFIELD AT Happy Valley was busy through the night. Among the planes taking off from Nicaragua were four C-54s and two C-46s. They flew to Cuba to deliver supplies, including ammunition, to the strapped brigade. The air drops were for the most part successful, but inconsequential—drops, as it were, into a leaky bucket.

A squadron of six B-26s also took off in the direction of Castro's airfield at Santiago de Cuba that night. These planes were sent to perform essentially the same mission President Kennedy had retracted late Sunday evening—to knock out Castro's airplanes on the ground before they could take off the following morning. The hastily arranged air strikes were a flop. Two of the planes had to abort on takeoff. The pilots who made it to Cuba found themselves blinded by the same fog that enshrouded the battlefield at the rotunda. They could not destroy Castro's planes because they could not see them. They turned around and flew back to Happy Valley.

The fact that the White House approved this air strike suggested that the president and his men were starting to grasp the consequences of the earlier decision to cancel. "Of course we did not ask for an explanation for their 'after-after-thought' and none was given," Charles Cabell later wrote. "To me, it appeared that we were now dealing with a thoroughly scared bunch of national leaders."

Washington, D.C., 7:00 A.M.

RADIO SWAN, the CIA frequency under David Phillips's propaganda outfit, continued to churn out exhortations to rally Cuban audiences. At 7:00 A.M., Radio Swan encouraged its listeners to turn on all electrical switches and appliances in an attempt to overload the country's power grid. It also falsely reported that five thousand more troops had landed in the east. "Nothing and no one will be able to stop the advance of the Cuban liberation forces."

Inside Quarters Eye, where David Phillips was busily composing the scripts for Swan Radio, the mood remained gloomy. Some reports of victorious battles had been momentarily encouraging, but these were no antidote to the steady poison of bad news from air and sea: two ships bombed out of commission; two other ships AWOL; the brigade nearly out of ammo and in retreat.

That "horrible morning," as Richard Bissell referred to the early hours of April 18, found President Kennedy in his office by 7:00 A.M. for an update by Bissell, Dulles, and Cabell. Also present were McGeorge Bundy and Major General Chester Clifton, the president's senior military aide. At the last minute, Bundy invited Walt Rostow, his deputy national security adviser, to join them. Rostow had until this moment been out of the loop on Cuba, focusing mainly on issues in the Far East. He was another of the brilliant young men of the New Frontier—Yale graduate at nineteen, Rhodes scholar, MIT professor—who had been taught by Bissell, and the two men had stayed close. The enchanted snowy night before the inauguration, when Rostow and his wife, Elspeth, had driven straight through from Boston to Washington to be present for Kennedy's swearing in, it had been at the Bissells' house in Cleveland Park they first stopped, before the ceremony, to refresh and warm themselves in the company of old friends. Now Rostow sat among that despondent bunch in the Oval Office and watched Bissell and Dulles deliver the bad news. "Here they were telling our President their plan had failed and, three months into his administration, he was about to confront unmitigated disaster," Rostow recalled. "They were wholly professional, Kennedy completely calm. But all were evidently shaken."

After the meeting, Rostow approached Bundy and offered his services. He still had little idea of how the administration had landed in this disaster, but he thought a "fresh man" might be useful. "Mac, if you and the President want me to help you mop up this mess, I'll be glad to do so." Bundy asked him to go over to CIA headquarters and keep an eye on things.

Rostow drove with Bissell to Quarters Eye. There was not much for Rostow to do there. His role that day would be to bear witness to men in despair. "It was terrible," Rostow later recalled. "They all turned to Dickie. . . . They were pulling at Dickie's coat, begging him to send in the army." The CIA men assumed that Bissell, with his ties to Kennedy and his powers of persuasion, could convince the president to save the operation with a show of overt American force. They overestimated Bissell's persuasiveness. Or underestimated the president's resolve.

"I'd rather be called an aggressor than a bum," Kennedy told his brother at one point that day, but that was not really true. Certainly if he wanted to be an aggressor, he had the means to enter—and perhaps end—the fray. A word from Kennedy could alter the course of events at the Bay of Pigs by lunchtime. But if Kennedy's comment to his brother made him sound like he intended to send in the cavalry, that was a false impression.

Really, the last thing Kennedy wanted to do that morning was fan the flames. News agencies were reporting protests against the United States around the world. American embassies were being marched upon and stoned in Tokyo, New Delhi, and Cairo. In Mexico City, student protesters were shouting anti-American slogans: "*¡Castro sí, Kennedy no!*" The same was true in Bogotá and Buenos Aires, where protesters threw tar balls at the American offices. The government of Venezuela passed a resolution condemning the United States. Embassy windows were shattered in Belgrade and Warsaw. Even America's strongest allies were emitting murmurs of disquiet.

Most alarming, if least surprising, was the reaction from Moscow, where thousands of demonstrators had gathered to protest—"*Cuba da, Yankee nyet*"—while throwing bottles of green and purple ink at the yellow walls and smashing the windows of the U.S. embassy. Privately, Khrushchev must have enjoyed watching the United States, which had given him so much grief for invading Hungary in 1956, stew in its own juices; publicly, the Kremlin was outraged.

At 2:00 P.M. local time—6:00 A.M. EST—the chargé d'affaires of the U.S. embassy in Moscow had begun transmitting to the State Department a letter just delivered to him by the Soviet Foreign Ministry. Addressed to President Kennedy from Premier Khrushchev, the message was not exactly a private communiqué. By the time it arrived in Washington at 8:53 A.M., its contents had already been broadcast over Radio Moscow. Kennedy received the letter just as he was about to sit down to his weekly Tuesday breakfast with congressional leaders. It was enough to ruin the heartiest of appetites.

"Mr. President, I send you this message in an hour of alarm, fraught with danger for the peace of the whole world," Khrushchev began. He informed Kennedy that it was no secret the United States was fully behind the invasion of Cuba and expressed indignation that the United States would engage in such a reckless pursuit. Then the premier got to the point of the matter:

"As far as the Soviet Union is concerned, there should be no mistake about our position: we will render the Cuban people and their government all necessary help to repel armed attack on Cuba," Khrushchev wrote. The United States was risking a "military catastrophe" with its actions—an "incomparable conflagration." If the allusion to nuclear war went over the heads of some Americans, the Soviet government issued a public statement declaring that the invasion of Cuba could "endanger the peaceful life of the population of the United States."

Kennedy's breakfast with the congressional leaders, in the family dining room on the first floor of the White House, was a glum affair. Though Kennedy did not believe Khrushchev actually meant to start a nuclear war over Cuba—the Soviets would probably retaliate by moving on West Berlin, thought Kennedy—this was little solace, because anything Khrushchev did could send both nations sliding down a slippery slope headfirst. When one of the legislators asked Kennedy to estimate the chance of the Cuba operation's success, he put it at 40 percent.

After the breakfast, Sam Rayburn, the seventy-nine-year-old Speaker of the House, came out onto the White House lawn with his fellow legislators to talk to the press. "It's a serious situation down there," Rayburn grimly told reporters, "and I don't know whether it will work out or not."

Bay of Pigs, Morning

DOWN THERE, MEANWHILE, Erneido Oliva and his men of the 2nd Battalion had completed their withdrawal from Playa Larga, marching to Playa Girón along the road that ran beside the bay. Arriving at Playa Girón at eight forty-five that morning, they learned that the eastern front had been under constant attack through the night, including by artillery fire. While none of the attacks had the force of the one at the rotunda, they had taken a toll. Men had been lost and units had retreated under pressure, shrinking the beachhead that the brigade had claimed the previous day. As at Red Beach, ammunition was running short.

Oliva conferred with Pepe San Román and Manuel Artime inside the beachside bungalow that served as brigade headquarters. The walls were covered with maps. The radio that Pepe used to stay in contact with the *Blagar* was in there, too, silent now since the *Blagar* had vanished out of range. Oliva, although fresh off victory, was the first among the leaders to see that the situation was untenable. Not only were they almost out of ammunition, they also had little food and medical supplies. He made a bold suggestion: while they were still able, they should make a break to the east, along the shore, and head for the Escambray Mountains. Retreat to the Escambrays had been an emergency option back when the landing site was in Trinidad, at the very foot of the mountains; now the Escambrays were eighty miles away. Nonetheless, Oliva thought it was worth the try. "It's better than to be killed," he told San Román and Artime.

San Román did not like the proposal. The road east, heading into the more populated province of Cienfuegos, would be lousy with enemy troops, and when they met the enemy they would not have enough ammunition to fight. More important, Pepe wanted to stay where they were because he was convinced the brigade ships would return to resupply them. Along with his faith in the ships, he had faith in the Americans. "I was sure they were coming today with help," he later told the writer Haynes Johnson. "I was sure of that, so we were not going."

San Román was expressing his conviction to Oliva when—as if on cue—a runner arrived breathlessly at the headquarters. He carried an urgent message: radio operators had just restored contact with the missing *Blagar*. San Román hurried to the radio and snatched the microphone. "Where have you been, you son of a bitch?"

The captain of the *Blagar* briefly filled San Román in on the tribulations the *Blagar* had encountered at sea, then handed the radio to Grayston Lynch. "Hello, Pepe," said Lynch. "I want you to know that we will never abandon you." Lynch told San Román that if worse came to worst, the brigade could be evacuated.

"I will not be evacuated," San Román replied. "We will fight to the end here if we have to."

He liked better what Lynch told him next: the ships would return that night with supplies. San Román reminded Lynch that exactly the same promise had been made the previous night—so why should he believe it this time? Because, said Lynch, this time it was for real. Then the American delivered another piece of good news. He'd just been informed by Washington that unmarked American fighter jets would soon be flying over the beach to give air support to the brigade. American air cover! Exactly what San Román had been hoping for—the deliverance for which he had told Oliva they must wait. "Now we will hit them!"

Oliva felt ashamed. How could he have suggested a retreat to the Escambrays? How could he have abandoned hope in Americans? For a moment, even he, who had chided one of his men the previous day for expecting miracles, became a believer.

Washington, D.C., Noon

"I THINK YOU will find at noon that the situation in Cuba is not a bit good," McGeorge Bundy wrote to the president shortly before the two men stepped into the cabinet room for an emergency meeting. "The Cuban armed forces are stronger, the popular response is weaker, and our tactical position is feebler that we had hoped. Tanks have done in one beachhead, and the position is precarious at the others."

Outside, another fine day was bathing Washington in springtime sunshine. Inside, a funereal miasma wafted through the rooms of the White House. Following his breakfast with the congressional leaders, President Kennedy attempted to carry on with business as usual, meeting the foreign minister of Ecuador, sending a housing bill to Congress, and consulting with speechwriter Ted Sorensen about his tax message, among other matters. By noon, all pretense of normalcy was gone. The cabinet room had been transformed into a crisis center, cluttered with maps of Cuba and boldly headlined newspapers. Staffers came and went bearing more bad news. In the pressroom, reporters nagged Press Secretary Pierre Salinger with a growing list of questions about the invasion. Adlai Stevenson's aides phoned in from the United Nations, seeking guidance.

In late morning, the White House sent out an urgent summons to the top brass of the Pentagon. Carloads of uniformed generals and gray-suited civilian staffers piled into sedans and cruised over Memorial Bridge into the city. By the time the generals walked into the cabinet room at noon, the president was already conferring with Bissell and Dulles from the CIA and Dean Rusk's team from the State Department. Robert Kennedy was there, too, and would remain at his brother's side for the next several days—would, in a sense, never really leave it.

Bundy had told the president to expect the CIA men to request air support, and they did. Bissell and Dulles wanted U.S. Navy jets to give air cover to the brigade's B-26s. Bundy, who had been frequently oblique in his opinions about the invasion over the past several months, stated a clear opinion in favor of the CIA's request: he thought the president should permit unmarked jets to eliminate the Cuban Air Force "because it cannot easily be proven against us and because men are in need."

Richard Bissell's behavior during these days of the invasion generally supported his reputation as cool, even aloof, under pressure. But as Bissell tried to make the case for air support to the president, at least one witness, General Earle Wheeler from the staff of the Joint Chiefs, noted that he seemed "tremendously upset" and "could hardly talk coherently."

President Kennedy addressed the group for nearly half an hour. He may have been dying inside but he appeared composed. He was already coming to terms with the fact that the operation was going to fail, and he was moving on to the next step. According to Fred Dutton, serving as cabinet secretary, Kennedy did not try to cover himself by giving the others in the room "a public line they were to take."

Kennedy stood and walked over to a metallic map of Cuba that had been set up in the cabinet room. Miniature magnetic boats representing the U.S. fleet near Cuba adhered to the surface of the map. As Admiral Burke described for the president how the destroyers were deployed, Kennedy picked up one of the little magnetic boats. "Well, don't you think we ought to get our forces out over the horizon?" He set the boat down farther from the coast of Cuba. Admiral Burke was visibly stunned that Kennedy would take it upon himself to redeploy vessels of the U.S. Navy. This deviation from standard operating procedure exemplified what was, in Burke's opinion, the total lack of professionalism of the operation.

"Nobody knew what to do," Burke told a colleague later that day. The CIA officials were as clueless as the rest of them, even though, Burke stressed tartly, they "were wholly responsible for the operation" and for everything that had gone wrong. "They are in a real bad hole because they had the hell cut out of them."

Burke seemed to view the CIA's fiasco, "a military operation which was conducted by amateurs," as a well-earned comeuppance not only for the agency but also for the administration. After enjoying Kennedy's "wonderful" inaugural address, he had quickly become disillusioned with the New Frontiersmen. He found them arrogant, for one thing. It bothered him greatly that in their headlong rush to do things their way, they lacked respect for the chain of command and the established lines of communication. They were personally ill-mannered, too. When he invited them into his home—this stuck in his craw for years—they behaved "as if they were slumming." He recalled one evening when he invited one of the bright young men to dinner. The admiral came home to find that the man and his wife had already arrived and were snooping around his private quarters. The familiarity of the act galled him and spoke volumes about the contempt Kennedy's men had for military officers. "He wouldn't have done that to anybody that he had any regard for; he just wouldn't have done it."

Now trouble had hit and the tables had turned. In Burke's version—which is really the only version we have—it was to him in particular that the president came in his hour of need. Robert Kennedy told Burke that the president was "putting me [Burke] in charge of the operation," is how Burke later described matters. Burke warned the attorney general that President Kennedy would be "bypassing" the normal chain of command—Lemnitzer, as well as Secretary McNamara—in dealing directly with him, but Robert Kennedy did not care. "The president is going to rely on you to advise him in this situation."

"It is late!" Burke responded.

Caribbean, Near Cuba, Early Afternoon

DURING THE HOUR and a half the president and his advisers met in the cabinet room, U.S. Navy vessels patrolling the Caribbean off the coast of Cuba intercepted increasingly urgent requests from Pepe San Román:

12:03 P.M.: "Blue Beach under attack. . . . Request jet support or cannot hold."

12:15 P.M.: "Blue Beach must have jet air support in next few hours or will be wiped out. Under heavy attacks by MiG jets and heavy tanks."*

12:28 P.M.: "Without jet air support cannot hold. Have no ammo left for tanks and very little left for troops. Enemy just launched heavy land attack supported by tanks. Cannot hold for long."

1:25 P.M.: "Under heavy attack supported by twelve tanks. Need air support immediately. Red Beach wiped out. Request air strikes. Need ammo of all types immediately."

Washington, D.C., Early Afternoon

THE WHITE HOUSE meeting ended at 1:26 P.M. No clear plan of action emerged from the discussion, but President Kennedy made clear he would not budge from his earlier position: no navy planes would be permitted to fly in combat; no American military combat assistance of any kind would be offered. He was willing, however, to authorize reconnaissance flights by navy jets. The White House was short of real-time

---

* There were, in fact, MiGs in Cuba in April 1961, but they were still in crates, unassembled, with no pilots trained to fly them. Possibly San Román mistook Castro's T-33s or American A-4s for the Soviet-made fighter jets.

information from the beaches, and good intelligence was desperately needed.

After the cabinet meeting, Kennedy walked outside onto the White House lawn. This was the first of at least three times he would retreat to the lawn over the next fifteen hours, as if fleeing the stifling confines of the White House. His brother Robert followed. The two men conferred quietly, then the president turned back to the private residence for lunch. Robert Kennedy later remarked that his brother "kept shaking his head, rubbing his hands over his eyes." He had never seen Jack so distraught.

Five minutes later, the president sat down to eat in the residence with Arthur Schlesinger and *New York Times* columnist James "Scotty" Reston. Schlesinger and Reston made odd luncheon companions under the circumstances—one an aide who had tried to warn him against the Cuban operation, the other a powerful journalist who could with a few sharp words carve him to pieces. It was just like Kennedy, though, to embrace those who might question him, pulling them into sympathy, even complicity. Minutes earlier, he may have been shaking his head in front of his brother, but now Kennedy was "in superb form," Schlesinger observed. "I had rarely seen him more effectively in control." For Schlesinger and other advisers, the Bay of Pigs disaster betrayed some of the president's limitations as a leader—his grab-bag style of administration, mainly—but also demonstrated his remarkable capacity for pulling himself together in trying circumstances.

"I probably made a mistake in keeping Allen Dulles on," the president confided to his guests. "I can't estimate his meaning when he tells me things." Part of the problem was that Allen Dulles was "a legendary figure, and it's hard to operate with legendary figures." Kennedy was looking to the future, already testing the administration's line on the failure. That future would begin, Kennedy made clear, with Dulles's departure. Perhaps he would move his brother from Justice to take over the job of CIA director. "It's a hell of a way to learn things," he said between bites, "but I have learned one thing from this business—that is, that we have to deal with CIA."

Reston asked the president if he thought defeat in Cuba would hurt American prestige. "No doubt we will be kicked in the ass for the next couple of weeks," said Kennedy, "but that won't affect the main business." This episode would count as "an incident, not a disaster." Kennedy was clearly trying to put the best face on the facts. Or perhaps the truth had not quite sunk in yet. In any case, he now told his guests—repeating more or less what he said to Richard Bissell and others in the cabinet room—he would not throw American military muscle into Cuba to change the outcome down there, no matter how much pressure he got to do it, no matter how much he grieved for those dying on the beaches.

As the men ate in the White House, another message was received by navy vessels from San Román:

1:45 P.M.: "We are under attack by two Sea Fury aircraft and heavy artillery. Do not see any friendly air cover as you promised. Need jet support immediately. Pepe."

Cuba, Afternoon

STILL, THE JETS did not come. That morning, over the radio, Grayston Lynch had told San Román to expect American air cover. But either Lynch or somebody up the chain of command was confused. It is true that Kennedy had authorized reconnaissance flights, but he had not said a word in favor of CAP. Wherever the information originated, it was false, and it had set up cruel expectations for the brigade. For hours, San Román and his men waited, listening, looking hopefully to the clear skies above Playa Girón. But the only planes to appear were Castro's Sea Furies and T-33s bolting out of the sun to strafe them and send them for cover.

Through the day, Castro's troops advanced down the road to San Blas in the north. Others were pursuing the route of Oliva's morning retreat from the west, on the coastal road from Red Beach/Larga, and still others were amassing in the east. Castro was no longer directing troop movement from the area. He had returned to Havana, drawn back to Punto Uno by reports of landings west of Havana. (These reports turned out to be false.) He was still very much in command of the troops, though, issuing orders by telephone to the sugar mill at Central Australia. From the sugar mill his messages were run by jeep to the front lines. Reports back to Castro were mostly good. He had the enemy where he wanted them, closed in on all sides, with the sea to their backs and no supply lines behind them.

Somewhere out at sea was the brigade's life support. The *Blagar* and the *Barbara J* had arrived back at Point Zulu earlier in the day and were waiting there now for the cargo ships to return, so they could offload them and take critical supplies to shore as soon as darkness fell. The

Atlántico and the *Caribe* were still miles away, in fact, but they had at last been located by U.S. jets flying off the *Essex*. The *Atlántico* was discovered early that morning about 100 miles south of Cuba. Its captain had agreed to turn back for Point Zulu; the ship would arrive late in the afternoon. The *Caribe* had been harder to track down. The ship was 218 miles south of the Bay of Pigs and still steaming toward Central America. Later, the owner of the García shipping line, who was aboard the *Caribe*, defended his ships' retreat by insisting that he and his crew had been misled by the CIA. They had been told there would be no enemy planes. When they saw two sister ships destroyed, then found themselves under air attack, they lost faith in their protector and took matters into their own hands.

After some strong encouragement that afternoon—threats may have been issued; money may have been exchanged—the *Caribe* turned back. By the time it got to Zulu, though, it would be too late to do any good.

Washington, D.C., Midafternoon

IN THE WHITE HOUSE, Admiral Burke, via the command center at the Pentagon, was sending out a steady stream of orders to Admiral Dennison, commander of the Atlantic Fleet. "Prepare unmarked Navy planes for possible combat use," Burke directed at 2:49 P.M. "This instruction in addition to earlier message regarding recce [reconnaissance] mission." The last line of the order dispelled any implication that the United States was about to enter the fray: "FYI. There is no intention of intervening with U.S. forces."

At 3:23 P.M., Burke contacted Dennison directly, through back-channel communications. His message gave a sense of the confusion inside the cabinet room. "What is urgently needed here is information on which to make an assessment of the situation or a judgment on what to do at high levels." Could the brigade go into the bush as guerrillas? Could they be evacuated by unmarked navy vessels? Could they break through Castro's lines? Answers to all of these were needed at the White House.

"Nobody here wants to commit United States forces to bail out this affair," Burke added, "but if the situation is as bad as reported something may have to be done."

Bay of Pigs, 3:30 P.M.

FINALLY, THE AMERICAN jets arrived over Playa Girón. There were two, possibly three of them, unmarked, silver with swept-back wings. They flew in tight formation, coming from the sea and soaring over the beach, blazing toward the interior. The men saw them first at Girón, then seconds later up the road at San Blas, where they dipped their wings but did not slow. All along the front, the fighting stopped as men looked up at the gleaming metal roaring across the clear blue sky. The brigademen whooped with joy, leaping from their foxholes and waving guns in the air. They stopped shouting to listen, waiting for the concussion of the bombs that would announce the beginning of the end of Castro.

The sound never came.

The planes reappeared, flying now in the direction from which they had arrived. They shot out over the sea and disappeared beyond the horizon, and then they were gone. "Watch for them," one of the brigademen called out. "They'll be back."

"They were beautiful," another soldier later recalled. "We never saw them again."

ACCORDING TO THE CIA plan, the landing strip at Playa Girón was supposed to have been secured and functioning as the brigade's air base by the afternoon of April 18. The brigade's fleet of B-26s should have been taking off and landing inside of Cuba, refueling and rearming, flying continuous sorties over the battlefield and beyond. As matters stood that afternoon, though, brigade planes were still flying from Puerto Cabezas, Nicaragua, more than five hundred miles away. The distance had taken a serious toll on the pilots, their exhaustion exacerbated by the emotional strains and rigors of combat. A few of the pilots had been going almost nonstop since early on the seventeenth and seemed indomitable, notably Gustavo Ponzoa, Gonzálo Herrera, and Mario Zuniga—the same Mario Zuniga who had flown to Miami on April 15 and done his bit of playacting. Since returning to Happy Valley, Zuniga had distinguished himself as a brave and durable pilot. Others, though, were unable or unwilling to go back for more. It was for this reason, on the afternoon of April 18, that American pilots began to fly for the brigade.

The first Americans were known to the Cubans only as "Seig" and "Doug"; their full names were Connie Seigrist and Doug Price. They were CIA contract pilots who had been working with the brigade from the start as trainers (not to be confused with the men from the Alabama Air National Guard, whose chance to fly would come later). Seigrist and Price were not the first Americans to enter combat at the Bay of Pigs—that honor belonged to Grayston Lynch and Rip Robertson—but they were the first officially authorized to participate.

The use of the American pilots had long been a possibility considered by the CIA. The agency never made any secret of its intentions within the administration. "It is very questionable that the limited number of Cuban B-26 pilots available to us can produce the desired results unless augmented by highly skilled American contract pilots," the agency had briefed Dean Rusk as far back as January. Not until April 18, though, did the CIA give Gar Thorsrud the authorization to put Americans in the air. The cable from headquarters to Happy Valley set strict guidelines to keep the Americans' role secret:

> American contract crews can be used B-26 strikes beachhead area and approaches only. Emphasize beachhead area only. Can not attach sufficient importance to fact American crews must not fall into hands enemy. In event this happens despite all precautions crews must state hired mercenaries, fighting communism, etc.; U.S. will deny any knowledge.

Sieg and Doug piloted two of six B-26s that took off from Happy Valley at about 2:00 P.M. that Tuesday. The other four pilots were Cubans—Gus Ponzoa, Mario Zuniga, Rene García, and Antonio Soto. Each of the planes was armed with napalm, eight rockets, and machine-gun rounds.

At 4:20 P.M., Admiral Clark, standing aboard the *Essex*, saw the six B-26s pass over, flying north toward Cuba.

Dusk was near as the planes arrived over the beaches. From the air, the narrow road that ran along the edge of the bay from Playa Larga to Playa Girón—the same road over which Oliva's troops had retreated that morning—looked like a dark snake: a seven-mile-long convoy of trucks, buses, and tanks writhing slowly eastward toward Girón. These troops were under orders from Castro to advance about halfway down the twenty-mile road by motor, then get out of the vehicles and continue on foot. Castro expected them to make contact with the "mercenaries" and seize Playa Girón by 6:00 P.M.

When Castro's militia first saw the planes, they made the mistake, as they had the previous afternoon, of greeting them as their own. When the bullets began to pelt them, joy turned to panic. The first B-26 took out the lead vehicle in the convoy; the second plane took out the tail. Now the entire convoy was trapped between the two burning heaps, and between the sea and the swamp. On the first pass, the planes strafed the convoy, shattering the windows of the buses. On the second pass, they dropped drums of napalm onto the road. When the napalm exploded, the incendiary gel ignited everything it touched, sucking the oxygen from the air. Men ran from the buses and trucks, flinging themselves onto the ground or jumping into the sea in the vain hope that the dirt or water would douse the flames. By the time the planes withdrew, they had destroyed seven tanks, countless trucks and buses, and caused untold casualties. Smoke rose two miles into the sky.

Washington, D.C., Late Afternoon

IT WAS CLEAR to everyone in the White House that the brigade was marooned on a narrowing beachhead near Playa Girón. Administration officials were operating at a serious intelligence deficit, hours behind real-time action on the beach, but the news trickling in was uniformly bad. As the day went on, the pressure on John Kennedy to respond with military force only intensified. Men were dying on the beach. Just offshore their guardian angels lay in wait. A word from Kennedy could save the brigade in an instant. Failure to act committed the brigade to certain defeat. "It was a long and grim day," Arthur Schlesinger wrote of April 18.

Kennedy's detractors would later attribute his refusal to send in U.S. forces at this critical hour to lack of spine. The fact is, whatever faults he displayed in the crisis, weak resolve was not one of them. He said he would not send in U.S. military support, and he kept his word throughout the terrible day of April 18.

As advisers scrambled for information and prepared for contingencies, Kennedy came and went from the cabinet room. At 4:00 P.M. he sat down with his advisers to draft a response to Khrushchev's blistering letter of the morning. In addition to the usual crew, a few new men were called in for consultation, including the State Department's Soviet experts Charles Bohlen and Foy Kohler. Also from the State Department came Assistant Secretary Harlan Cleveland, the man who served as liaison to Adlai Stevenson at the United Nations.

Cleveland was impressed with Kennedy's calm, as were others that day, but he also observed an air of distraction in the president. Kennedy's questions were not penetrating; they skirted the main point. He struck Cleveland as a man with fragments of a picture in his head but not the full view. Still, Kennedy focused well enough to do what had to be done, which at the moment was getting a letter back to Khrushchev. The State Department had already prepared a draft, but Kennedy was not satisfied. He called in two secretaries and began to dictate. At four forty-five, leaving his advisers to fine-tune the letter, Kennedy stood and went outside on the south lawn with Vice President Johnson to briefly stretch his legs—his second time out for air—then stepped into the Oval Office. He approved the letter at 6:00 P.M. As a secretary typed up the final draft on White House stationery, the State Department contacted the Soviet ambassador, Mikhail Menshikov, and summoned him to the State Department to receive the letter.

"Mr. Chairman," the letter began, "you are under a serious misapprehension in regard to events in Cuba." Without flatly stating so, Kennedy implied that the invasion in Cuba was the work of Cuban exiles, supported by Cuban citizens, interested in unburdening the country from Castro's rule. "Where people are denied the right of choice, recourse to such struggle is the only means of achieving their liberties." He chastised Khrushchev for the tone of his own letter.

> I have taken careful note of your statement that the events in Cuba might affect peace in all parts of the world. I trust that this does not mean that the Soviet Government, using the situation in Cuba as a pretext, is planning to inflame other areas of the world. I would like to think that your government has too great a sense of responsibility to embark upon any enterprise so dangerous to general peace.

Ambassador Menshikov arrived at the State Department shortly before 7:00 P.M. and remained in Rusk's office to read the letter. The Soviets needed "to understand the importance to the United States of peace and well-being in this hemisphere," Rusk told Menshikov. To which the Soviet ambassador, neglecting to recall his nation's own invasive tendencies, responded that "the Soviet government will never recognize intervention in the affairs of other countries as indicating a desire to have peace."

Playa Girón (Blue Beach), Evening

ON THE BEACH they waited to be rescued or destroyed. Castro's troops had been momentarily slowed by the brigade bombers in the afternoon, but the column was moving again, pressing in from the west. Erneido Oliva was in charge of the defense of the road from Playa Larga, but he and his men lacked ammunition. Earlier in the evening, a brigade C-54 had flown over the beach with an air drop from Happy Valley, but wind had blown the supplies away into the swamp and the sea.

In the infirmary at Playa Girón, Máximo Cruz, recovering from the serious wounds he received at the rotunda, was seen getting out of bed and stumbling off to join the 2nd Battalion on the western front. Manuel Artime ordered him to return to the infirmary; a cargo plane was scheduled to land later in the day to evacuate casualties, and Cruz needed to be on it. Cruz begged Artime not to issue such an order, for he would have no choice but to disobey. "I was not going to leave my men," Cruz later explained. Before he could get far, he passed out and was carried back to the infirmary.

Washington, D.C., Evening

JUST BEFORE 8:00 P.M., Admiral Burke, acting on behalf of the Joint Chiefs and under the authority of the White House, sent a cable to Admiral Dennison requesting "[a]s feasible and without violating current restrictions" intelligence regarding the location of airfields from which Castro's aircraft were operating. Somebody in high authority was evidently considering the use of U.S. naval aircraft to destroy Castro's planes.

At 8:37 P.M., Burke cabled Dennison again to inquire about the possibility of the brigade going guerrilla. "Anything you can do to get answer to that question would be appreciated." Burke raised the possibility of evacuating wounded men from the beaches at the Bay of Pigs. His own thought was that the brigade ships could remove casualties from the beaches, then "later could ask *Essex* to take them as a humanitarian move . . . until suitable hospital arrangements could be made on beach in some place inaccessible to news hawks." Forty minutes later, at 9:17 P.M., Burke sent another cable:

> I was asked once again if it were possible to land an experienced Marine (or Naval officer who has amphibious knowledge) on beach with CEF without danger of him being killed or captured

> or it becoming known U.S. was involved. The urgency stems from lack of knowledge here of true situation on beach and what should be done now without overtly involving United States.

"Please advise," Burke concluded, "on this one along with any further information on situation or comments on how to get dope."

AS BURKE HUSTLED to get the "dope," Kennedy left the Oval Office, where he'd been conferring with McGeorge Bundy and Robert Kennedy, among others, and retreated to the private residence upstairs. He remained there for nearly two hours, eating dinner then dressing in formal attire. A little after 10:00 P.M., fulfilling what must rank among the most unwelcome social obligations in presidential history, John and Jacqueline Kennedy floated down the crimson-carpeted grand staircase into the front entrance hall of the White House as the Marine Band played "Hail to the Chief." The president wore white tie and tails. The First Lady, in the words of the *Washington Post*'s society writer, was "radiant . . . in a gown of pink and white straw lace." She wore matching pink slippers on her feet and a diamond clip in her hair.

The occasion was the traditional congressional reception. Nearly every U.S. congressman and senator, along with spouses, had come to the White House to meet the president. Also among the twelve hundred guests were cabinet members and the Joint Chiefs, resplendent in their medal-spangled dress uniforms. This was the first gala event of the new administration, and the White House staff had gone to every effort to make it spectacular. In the rooms beyond the entrance hall, buffet tables of hot and cold dishes and bowls of spiked punch glimmered under the great crystal chandeliers. A dance floor had been installed in the East Room.

In keeping with the looser style of the Kennedy administration, the president and First Lady eschewed a formal receiving line in favor of more democratic mingling. Sometimes together, sometimes apart, they swam through the crowd in the direction of the East Room, the First Lady lovely and ethereal, the president witty and warm. Senate chaplain Frederick Brown Harris—the same who had presided over the CIA cornerstone ceremony eighteen months earlier—buttonholed Kennedy. "What we need now," he told the president, "is more firmness." When the band struck up "Mr. Wonderful," the president took the First Lady's hand and together they glided around the dance floor in the East Room.

For a few moments, it was possible to forget Cuba. *"It's a strange and tender magic you do, Mister Wonderful, that's you."*

John Kennedy was never so wonderful as in such circumstances as these. There had been talk of canceling the reception at the last minute, but Kennedy had overruled it, for he understood the importance of appearances, and he possessed an uncanny ability to look relaxed, to seem even to be enjoying himself, when, almost certainly, he was not.

The president's more tightly wound younger brother was less skilled at concealing his emotions. Robert Kennedy grabbed the president's old friend Senator George Smathers by the arm and pulled him aside. "The shit has hit the fan," he murmured to the senator. "This thing has turned sour like you wouldn't believe."

WALT ROSTOW SKIPPED the reception. He was back at the CIA that evening, after shuttling to the White House for meetings on Cuba in the afternoon, then stopping off for a quick shower and change of clothes at home. He watched over his old friend Bissell, who was unshaven and haggard but maintaining his composure. CIA colleagues, grasping for straws, shouted around Bissell and continued to press him to go back to the president and request support. That evening, Bissell decided to give it one more try. He asked Rostow to arrange a meeting. Rostow put in a call to the White House and got ahold of Kenneth O'Donnell, Kennedy's thirty-seven-year-old appointments secretary, who had left the reception and was sitting at the president's desk to field incoming calls. Word was sent to Kennedy and his advisers at the reception. The meeting was set for midnight.

Bissell and Rostow got into Rostow's Volkswagen. As the men drove across the darkened Mall, Rostow glanced over at his old mentor, amazed that Bissell was keeping it together as well as he was. A time would come when Rostow, as one of the architects of the Vietnam War, would face his own dark nights, but that April he was just beginning his career in Washington, and Richard Bissell was just ending his.

Cuba, 11:52 P.M.

REAR ADMIRAL CLARK sent a cable to Admiral Dennison. It was eight minutes before midnight. The *Essex* had intercepted another cry of help from Pepe San Román:

> Do you people realize how desperate the situation is? Do you back us up or quit? All we want is low jet cover and jet close support. Enemy has this support. I need it badly or cannot survive. Please don't desert us. Am out of tank and bazooka ammo. Tanks will hit me at dawn. I will not be evacuated. Will fight to the end if we have to. Need medical supplies urgently.

Washington, D.C., 11:58 P.M.

THE PARTY WAS winding down in the state rooms. As the congressmen and their wives danced their last steps and swallowed their last sips of punch, the president's advisers said their good-byes and peeled away, the waft of perfume and music falling behind. President Kennedy left the reception at eleven fifty-five. He walked from the Mansion to the West Wing under the portico, through the head-clearing chill of the night. When he arrived, two minutes before midnight, the others were already there, waiting to begin what Walt Rostow later described as "a session in the Oval Office no one present is likely to forget."

Many of those present—the president and vice president, McNamara, Rusk, Bundy, among others—still wore white tie and tails. General Lemnitzer and Admiral Burke were in dress uniform. Richard Bissell and Walt Rostow were more informally attired in work suits, having come directly from the CIA. In Bissell's case, the suit was probably the same one he had been wearing in the Oval Office seventeen hours earlier, when he'd met Kennedy at 7:00 A.M. As the night wore on, others would arrive, summoned by urgent phone calls, dressed in whatever they could quickly find.

Richard Bissell had called for the meeting, but it was Admiral Burke who got right to the point.

"Let me take two jets and shoot down those enemy aircraft," he proposed to the president.

"No," said Kennedy. "I don't want to get the United States involved in this."

"Hell, Mr. President," Burke erupted, "we *are* involved!"

19

"The Loneliest Man"

Wednesday, April 19: D+2

Washington, D.C., After Midnight

"ADMIRAL," PRESIDENT KENNEDY repeated, "I don't want the United States involved in this."

"Can I not send in an air strike?"

"No."

"Can we send in a few planes?"

"No, because they could be identified as United States."

"Can we paint out their numbers?"

"No."

It was after midnight now in the Oval Office. Admiral Burke persisted: if Kennedy refused to allow jets, how about ships? Two American destroyers could easily wipe out Castro's tank units, then quickly retreat to open seas. The president remained adamant. There would be no naval interference.

"One destroyer, Mr. President?"

"No."

Admiral Burke continued to press hard for military intervention at the white-tie meeting in the Oval Office. Richard Bissell, visibly shaken but nonetheless coherent, quietly echoed Burke, methodically reviewing options open to the president. Outside the Oval Office, aides of the president milled about, on call. At one point, Kennedy's secretary, Evelyn Lincoln, in a ball gown, stopped by the West Wing with her husband. She had come to fetch her coat after the reception, but seeing the president there, she waited in case she was needed. When the door to the Oval Office swung open briefly, she glimpsed Kennedy sitting at his desk, deep in thought. A few moments later, the door opened again and she saw him standing, pacing the floor, an utterly different figure than the man who had been trading pleasantries in the East Room minutes earlier. One of the president's aides came through the door muttering something about Cuba. Kennedy noticed Mrs. Lincoln and sent word for her to go home; there was nothing she could do.

Kennedy's dilemma, as April 18 slid into April 19, was a variation of the same jawbreaker he had been gnawing over since he entered office. It came down, at last, to this: should he save the brigade and risk a larger conflagration, or cut his losses and accept disaster? Kennedy was concerned with the fate of the men on the beaches, but was he concerned enough to bail them out? Was he willing to contradict his own stated ban on American military power in aid of the brigade? Was he willing to risk greater American humiliation? Because if he *did* commit U.S. forces to the operation, they *had* to succeed. (It was one thing for Castro to declare victory over fourteen hundred Cuban exiles, but quite another for him to declare victory over the U.S. military.) And if he did make such a commitment, would the Soviets then have no choice but to respond in kind? And would not the United States then have no choice but to respond—and where would it end? The greater the effort Kennedy put into saving the operation and the men on the beach, the greater the risk he took of sparking something truly catastrophic. "For had the U.S. Navy and Air Force been openly committed," he later explained (as paraphrased by his aide Theodore Sorensen), "no defeat would have been permitted, a full-scale U.S. attack would ultimately have been required, and—assuming a general war with the Soviets could have been avoided—there was no point in beginning with a Cuban brigade in the first place."

"Obviously," Kennedy told Sorensen, "if you are going to have United States air cover, you might as well have a complete United States commitment."

From the start of this Cuban ordeal he had been faced with bad choices, but never worse than at this moment. "The limits and dilemmas of power—the relationship of power to the fate of human beings—was never more clear or poignant," wrote Walt Rostow of that night.

Even as Kennedy grappled with the brigade's fate in Cuba, he faced an affiliated crisis in Florida. This one concerned not the exiled Cuban soldiers but the exiled Cuban politicians. The Cuban Revolutionary Council had been sequestered since Saturday in a safe house at Opa Locka air base near Miami. The members of the council were being held there until the moment they could be airlifted to the Bay of Pigs and declare themselves the rightful leaders of a free Cuba. Of course, that moment would never come. But the council did not know that yet.

The council was nominally in charge of the operation but almost wholly ignorant of its details and progress. Nobody told them anything, certainly not their CIA minders, who included the dependably unhelpful "Frank Bender." What they knew came from the transistor radio around which they huddled in the safe house. From the radio they first learned that the invasion had been launched; and from the radio they monitored the steady stream of communiqués issued in their name, none of which they had ever read, much less written. As they waited to be flown to Cuba, they were kept in the dark and under virtual house arrest. Armed U.S. soldiers patrolled the perimeter. The guards were there to keep intruders away—or was it to keep the council in? In either case, the situation was intolerable. The men had been growing increasingly agitated as the hours passed. Some of them, such as Dr. José Miró Cardona, had sons in the invasion force and were desperate to join them. They were ready to blow.

"Where is Berle? Find Berle," the president called out. Somebody went to wake up Adolph Berle, the State Department adviser on Latin America. In the meantime, McGeorge Bundy placed a call to Arthur Schlesinger. The Harvard historian was at his Georgetown home, having skipped the White House reception in favor of a restful night. The phone awoke him at 1:00 A.M. "I am in the President's office," Bundy told him, "and he would like to have you come down here as soon as possible."

Schlesinger threw on some clothes and hurried to the White House. When he arrived in the West Wing, he found the president and others scanning dispatches from the battlefield. "We have no real news," Bundy told him, "but we fear that things are going badly." The men resumed the debate over air support, Schlesinger listening in. The tempers that had flared earlier in the night were now smothered under a "general sense of gloom," Schlesinger recorded. They spoke in a "desultory, rather distraught way." Some were still in denial. Others were in shock.

It was nearly 2:00 A.M. when President Kennedy at last yielded—a little—to Burke's and Bissell's entreaties. He would allow U.S. Navy jet cover, he told them, but it would be *very* limited. For exactly one hour, six unmarked jets from the *Essex* could fly over the beaches to provide an "umbrella" of support for an already scheduled squadron of B-26 bombers from Happy Valley. The navy jets were to give mainly moral support—Kennedy did not want them looking for a fight—but they would be permitted to defend the brigade planes should these come under attack from Castro's fighters.

This was the first explicit executive authorization of American military force over the beaches of Cuba. Limited as it was, it contravened Kennedy's earlier policy. Dean Rusk did not like it. "That's a deeper commitment, Mr. President," grumbled the secretary. "The President shouldn't appear in the light of being a liar." Rusk seldom spoke so plainly in front of others, but circumstances did not allow for private consultation.

Kennedy raised his hand to his nose. "We're already in it up to here."

The air cover was set from 6:30 A.M. to 7:30 A.M., a single but potentially invaluable window of daylight. For that one hour, the brigade planes would own the skies over the beaches. They would have free rein to bomb Castro's forces on the ground. Every bit as important, the air umbrella would allow brigade ships to return to Blue Beach and unload materials and evacuate the wounded.

Richard Bissell stood. He needed to hurry back to CIA headquarters to relay the order to Happy Valley. "Keep your chin up," Kennedy called to him as he was leaving the room. Kennedy turned to Adolph Berle, who had finally arrived at the White House. "One member is threatening suicide," Kennedy said of the Revolutionary Council. "All are furious with CIA. They do not know how dismal things are. You must go down and talk to them."

"I can think of happier missions," Berle responded drily.

"You ought to go with Berle," Kennedy said to Schlesinger.

Bissell was already gone. Now Berle and Schlesinger left, and Bundy soon departed for the airport, too, dispatched by the president to New York, back to "hold the hand" of Adlai Stevenson. The time was nearly three in the morning. There was nothing left to do now but wait, yet some of the president's advisers were slow to leave. "Somehow," Walt Rostow wrote, "it was difficult to go home that night."

As Rostow loitered in Ken O'Donnell's office, O'Donnell talked quietly with Kennedy and Pierre Salinger in the Oval Office. Kennedy had kept his composure through the long day and night, at least publicly, but all at once the full impact of the disaster seemed to hit him. In the middle of a sentence, he abruptly stopped talking and turned to the French doors that gave onto the Rose Garden. "He must be the loneliest man in the world," said Ken O'Donnell as John Kennedy stepped out into the dark.

Happy Valley, Predawn

THE CABLE FROM CIA headquarters arrived at Happy Valley shortly after 2:00 A.M. local time. A squadron of B-26s was already rumbling on the runway, their pilots preparing for morning runs over the beaches, just as they had been two nights earlier when news arrived of the canceled air strikes. This time the news was better: U.S. Navy jets, according to the cable, would give one hour of support to the B-26 pilots. Word of the impending air cover was communicated at once to the pilots inside the cockpits, where it was greeted with joy. "Now we'll smash them!" shouted Major Riley Shamburger, one of the B-26 pilots. The Americans would be there, if only briefly, to lend a hand.

Actually, as Major Shamburger's presence in the B-26 cockpit suggested, a few Americans were already there to lend a hand. Of the six planes on the tarmac at Happy Valley, four had Americans in the cockpits. In addition to Shamburger, the pilots were Joe Shannon, Billy Goodwin, and Thomas "Pete" Ray. Each was accompanied by an American crew member, bringing the total number of U.S. airmen to eight. They were among those who had been recruited months earlier from the 117th Tactical Reconnaissance Wing of the Alabama Air National Guard.

Until this moment, the Alabamans had been responsible for training the Cuban pilots and crews. That had been their exclusive role: to support the brigade's air force, not to fly with it. But the previous evening the rules of the game had changed. Gar Thorsrud, while attempting to fill out the flight crews, had come up short. Only two of the Cuban pilots, Gonzálo Herrera and Mario Zuniga, were able and willing to fly. To round out the roster, Thorsrud asked for volunteers from among the Americans. Nearly every man available stepped forward. They did so knowing the invasion was in all likelihood coming to an inglorious end. They also knew the mission was extremely dangerous; not only did Castro still have his T-33s and Sea Furies, but now his troops swarmed the ground with state-of-the-art antiaircraft artillery. "We did it for the Cubans," explained Joe Shannon later. Many of the Americans had become close to the brigade pilots over the previous months and had taken up the battle against Castro as their own. They could not now forfeit the opportunity to come to their fellow pilots' aid and possibly turn the tide.

The role of the Alabama pilots in the Bay of Pigs was a secret that would be closely held by the American government for years. In fact, the CIA did not publicly admit American pilots flew in the operation until nearly two decades later, and then only after journalists and private citizens—notably Janet Ray, daughter of American pilot Thomas "Pete" Ray—turned up enough evidence to make the admission unavoidable. The way the pilots were handled by the U.S. government ranks as one of the sorriest episodes in the history of the Bay of Pigs operation, indeed in the whole history of American covert operations.

The Alabama pilots were a well-bonded group. Many of them had grown up near one another and attended Tarrant High School, within sight of the Birmingham airport. They were fathers and husbands with young families. Some were veterans of World War II or Korea but had not flown combat for many years. A number of them earned their livings as pilots and inspectors for the local Hayes Aircraft Corporation, a company that maintained and repaired planes for the U.S. Air Force.

Pete Ray was a fairly typical recruit. A thirty-year-old Hayes pilot, raised in Birmingham and educated at Tarrant, he had been a member of the Air National Guard since age sixteen. Flying, family, and church—these had been the pillars of his life until the winter of 1961. On February 5, Ray said good-bye to his pretty wife, Margaret, and to his six-year-old daughter, Janet, and eight-year-old son, Thomas, and left his brick home in suburban Birmingham. Like the other fliers, he had prepared a cover story, with the help of the CIA. Not even his wife was permitted to know the truth. He gave her an address in Chicago, where he would be attending a special training school, he told her. For the next two months, she sent her letters to Chicago, care of "Joseph Greenland," and he, sooner or later, wrote back.

Once, in early April—shortly before the operation—Pete came back to visit in person. He had a dark tan, odd for a man who had just spent a winter in Chicago, but Margaret knew better than to ask. Their six-year-old daughter had no such compunctions. "We were sitting eating banana sandwiches with mayonnaise," Janet Ray vividly recalled fifty years later of her father's brief homecoming. "My mother was washing dishes and him and I were sitting at the table. He had on sandals and shorts. And I looked down, and he was fair like me, and I saw the tan lines, and I said, 'Daddy, where have you been, you've been to the beach without me. Why would you go to the beach without me?' My mother broke a glass and kind of gasped. My father got up, he put his napkin down. He walked out of the room, he put on a pair of long pants, and came back and sat and ate the sandwich. And I was so sick. Right then and there I knew something was wrong." The next day her father kissed them all good-bye again. That was the last she ever saw of him alive.

Norfolk, 3:37 A.M.

HALF AN HOUR after Happy Valley learned of the navy air cover, the Joint Chiefs sent the order to the aircraft carrier *Essex* to provide it. Telegram JCS 994369, outgoing from the JCS command center at 3:37 A.M., instructed the navy to "furnish air cover of 6 unmarked aircraft over CEF forces during period 0630 to 0730 local time 19 April to defend CEF against air attack from Castro forces." Beyond this fairly straightforward directive, the cable's message was decidedly mixed. "Do not seek air combat but defend CEF forces from air attack. Do not attack ground targets." The pilots were further instructed to carry "as little identification as practicable" and to ditch at sea if in danger of crashing. This was to be done in the interest of preserving the by now absurd fiction that the Americans were not behind the invasion.

For Admiral Dennison, working through the night at his desk at the navy base in Norfolk, the cable just added more fuel to his smoldering outrage. The Joint Chiefs were asking his men to do the impossible—to fly with one arm tied behind their backs. It was "ridiculous," thought Dennison. He could hardly contain his fury, even at the risk of insubordination. At 2:01 A.M., responding to an earlier telegram from Admiral Burke regarding evacuation of wounded, Dennison had written that evacuation was "completely out of the question" and "a fantastically unrealistic project." Ten minutes later, responding to Burke's query about the possibility of putting a U.S. military observer on the beach, Dennison had written, "The proposal is completely unrealistic and I will have no part of it."

At 3:41 A.M., Admiral Burke told Dennison that his comments were "not very helpful" and reproached him:

> God knows this operation is as difficult as possible and we are trying to do all we can without much info and without having been in on all initial stages. I too am irked and tired and I realize many

of these suggestions are most difficult. Yet we will have to do all we can to help even if it is not the way we would like to do it.

Off the Coast of Cuba, Predawn

AT ABOUT THE time the Joint Chiefs were authorizing early-morning air cover, presumably making it safe for the brigade ships to land, one of the ships, the *Blagar*, was steaming *away* from the Cuban coast, back to the distant refuge of Point Zulu. This is one of the many mixups of the night difficult to explain, even accounting for the fog of war.

According to Grayston Lynch, the *Blagar* and several accompanying LCUs were making their way to Blue Beach at about 2:30 A.M. when an order from the CIA instructed them to turn back. The *Blagar* and LCUs had been on a much-delayed mission to deliver ammunition and supplies that had been offloaded several hours earlier from the *Atlántico*. This was to be a last-chance run to the beaches to resupply the brigade. Because the loaded LCUs could not attain more than six knots, it became obvious to Lynch and the men at CIA headquarters that the landing party would not be able to make the beach and unload before dawn—meaning that if they tried, they would be subjected, again, to aerial bombardment.

"If jet cover is not furnished beginning at first light, expect to lose all ships," Lynch cabled to Washington. Headquarters apparently agreed with his prognosis. Forget delivering the supplies, came the response. Turn back to the safety of the open sea. Lynch later claimed he was never informed of the president's decision to allow naval jet cover. As events turned out, that was probably for the best.

Washington, D.C., 4:00 A.M.

JOHN KENNEDY WAS still on the south lawn, where he had been strolling alone for nearly an hour in his long dress coat and white bow tie. The temperature had dropped to a crisp forty degrees in the city; a spring frost threatened the suburbs. The south lawn rolled gently down to the Ellipse and gave a clear view beyond to the Washington Monument and the dome of the Jefferson Memorial. What went through Kennedy's mind as he walked over the damp grass? Perhaps he worried over his decision to allow air cover. Or revisited his decision to cancel air strikes two days earlier. Most likely, his thoughts circulated around the question that would nag him for months to come: *How could I have been so stupid?* At last he crossed back to the White House and went upstairs to bed.

Bay of Pigs, Early Morning

SOMETIME AFTER DAWN—the precise time is uncertain—the brigade B-26s came in low from the south. Navy A-4s were supposedly waiting for them: six Skyhawks from the *Essex*, scheduled to provide air cover from 6:30 A.M. to 7:30 A.M., per the president's orders. But something in the plan went awry. Instead of Skyhawks, the B-26 pilots found themselves in the company of Castro's jets, the insidious T-33s that had already caused so much harm. The B-26s were defenseless. One was badly damaged. Two others were shot down, their crews killed. The dead were all Americans.

Of the many enduring mysteries of the Bay of Pigs, none is more perplexing than the case of the missing air cover over the skies of Cuba on the early morning of April 19. Where were the promised Skyhawks that Burke and Bissell had wrested from the president? Numerous attempts have been made to explain the air cover that never was. The most common explanation is the one first recited, twelve days after the fact, by Rear Admiral Clark, task force commander aboard the *Essex*. "We were ordered to fly cover for the CEF bombers from 0630 to 0730 Romeo," Clark would testify to an investigative committee on May 1. (Romeo is the military designation for the time zone into which both Cuba and Washington, D.C., fall when Daylight Savings is not in effect, as was the case in mid-April 1961.) "I decided to play this one safe and ordered my people to be on station one-half hour early in the event that the CEF aircraft made the trip quicker than they had anticipated. However, they came over our ship an hour early and consequently we launched our aircraft immediately."

According to Clark, in other words, the B-26s from Nicaragua arrived over Cuba at 5:30 A.M., rather than 6:30 A.M. Clark went on to testify that as soon as he saw the B-26s, he ordered the navy jets into the skies, but by the time the jets made it over the beaches, at 5:50 A.M., they were too late. The bombers had already completed their missions and were gone. Clark neglected to add that two of the B-26s were shot out of the sky by Castro's jets. His point was that the timing blunder belonged to the brigade—the CIA, that is—and not to the navy.

How the blunder occurred has never been adequately explained because no one has ever confessed to screwing up. "The mistake, made in Washington, is not the kind men readily admit to, since it cost the lives of four Americans," Grayston Lynch wrote. Lynch's own investigation led him to believe that the person responsible for the mixup was Jake Esterline, the CIA's task force chief—that Esterline wrote the order to Puerto Cabezas and, in doing so, failed to take into account the fact that Nicaragua was one hour behind Cuba. (To further confuse the confusion, Lynch incorrectly believed the president's order provided air cover from 5:30 to 6:30, not 6:30 to 7:30.) More recently, a professor of history at the University of Alabama, Howard Jones, came to Esterline's defense, pointing out that Esterline would certainly not have written the order because Esterline was outside the chain of command for air operations. Jones fingers Richard Bissell as the true perpetrator. "It stands to reason that Bissell set the rendezvous time," Jones writes. "Bissell doubtless called for the 6:30 rendezvous so they arrived shortly after daylight in Cuba; but he did not remember that Nicaragua was a different time zone."

In the long view of history, this timing mishap may not merit more attention than it has already received; nobody is arguing that it changed the outcome of the invasion. The truth of what happened matters, though, for the simple reason that four men died and several other men have been accused of contributing to their deaths. If nothing else, the charge that top men in the CIA—whether Esterline or Bissell—made a mistake of such gross incompetence adds to the impression that the CIA was run by feckless bunglers.

In this one case at least, a small sheet of paper vindicates the CIA. This is the telegram that communicated the orders from CIA headquarters to Air Operations at Puerto Cabezas. Somehow this telegram, Cable 4834, has managed to fly under the radar for nearly fifty years.

The telegram was sent from the CIA to Puerto Cabezas on April 19 at 3:04 A.M. EST and contained the following message: "*POSITIVE AGGRESSIVE NAVY AIR SUPPORT AND COVER GRANTED FOR ONE HOUR 11:30Z TO 12:30Z 19 APRIL.*" The Z after the hour stands for Zulu time, the military equivalent of Greenwich Mean Time, generally used in military orders to prevent time zone confusion. (Strangely, it was the navy, not the CIA, that posted in local, or Romeo, time.) In April 1961, Cuba, like the eastern United States, was five hours off Zulu time. In other words, 11:30Z to 12:30Z was 6:30 to 7:30 local time in Cuba. So the time given on the CIA order was exactly right. As for the matter of authorship, the cable was signed by Stanley Beerli, not by Esterline or Bissell.

The cable proves the CIA was blameless for the timing error, but it does not reveal what really happened. For that we have to consult other sources as well as common sense. Most likely, the brigade planes *did* arrive too early, as Rear Admiral Clark testified. Possibly they did so for the simple reason that they had already taken off from Puerto Cabezas before the order arrived. Although some reliable sources—including Edward Ferrer, the C-54 pilot who later wrote a book about the air wing of the brigade—record that the first takeoff that night was at 2:30 A.M. in Nicaragua (which, factoring in the time difference and three-plus hours of flying time, would have put the planes over the beaches shortly after 6:30 A.M., right on schedule), others set the takeoff earlier. Notably, author Peter Wyden has the planes leaving Puerto Cabezas as early as 1:30 A.M. Nicaragua time, which would have put them over Cuba at 5:30—exactly as Admiral Clark reported. Since the order cable from the CIA was not sent until 3:04 EST—2:04 A.M. in Puerto Cabezas—it may have come too late to do any good.

But there is another possibility suggested by Wyden's reporting: the order arrived too late at the *Essex*. According to Wyden, the cable from Admiral Dennison to supply air cover was not decoded on the *Essex* until 6:30 A.M. And once it was decoded, another hour was required to prepare and launch the planes from the deck, meaning that the Skyhawks would not have been airborne until 7:30.

A cable from Admiral Clark to Admiral Dennison, in reference to the cable sent by the Joint Chiefs at 3:37 A.M., gives credence to this scenario: "Will devote my entire resources to execution of JCS 190837Z." That sounds like a response written upon the receipt of an order—as if Clark is referring to an action he is *about to take*, not one already taken. Since Clark's cable was transmitted at 6:30 A.M., it suggests that the Skyhawks were scrambled well *after* 6:30. Which suggests, in turn, that when Clark testified to the Taylor Committee eleven days later, he was either misremembering the sequence of events after all, or he was intentionally dissembling so as to shift blame for the screwup away from the navy (which apparently required nearly three hours to decode an order cable) and onto the CIA. The fact that the commanding officer of the *Essex*, Captain S. S. "Pete" Searcy, was later ordered to burn the ship's logs adds to the impression that the navy had something to hide.

* * *

HOWEVER THE EVENTS of that morning unfolded, the first brigade planes arrived over Cuba to find no Skyhawks, no protection of any kind. Instead, very quickly, Castro's T-33s appeared, and the sound of a distressed American voice could be heard over the radio. It belonged to Riley Shamburger. His plane had been attacked by a T-33. The other pilots heard him but there was nothing they could do. "I'm hit," called Shamburger. "I'm hit and on fire!" Moments later, issuing black smoke and flame, the plane slashed into the water a few hundred yards offshore. Shamburger and his navigator, Wade Gray, were killed.

Meanwhile, Pete Ray's B-26 had arrived over the beaches. Flying with another American, Leo Baker, in the navigator's seat, Ray banked in low over the thick swamps. He headed inland toward the sugar mill at Central Australia, the field headquarters for Castro's forces, where Castro himself had taken command earlier in the battle. Ray was hit before he made it near the mill, apparently by a T-33. According to witnesses, Ray and Baker were still alive when they crash-landed on a sugarcane field. What happened then only the militiamen who killed them know for sure. Photographs later released by the Cuban government would show bullet holes in their heads, evidence to some that the men were executed. The Cuban government contended the Americans were shot only after they shot first. As in the case of other events that morning—of the entire five-day drama—the truth will probably never be known.

Playa Girón (Blue Beach), 7:50 A.M.

THROUGHOUT THE NIGHT, the fighting had been light at Girón, limited mainly to small skirmishes where Castro's militia attempted to break through the lines. The brigade still held a beachhead reaching as far north as San Blas and including the landing strip in Girón. But at first light, the attack resumed. By 7:50 A.M., the war room at the Pentagon received notice that Blue Beach was under heavy assault by air and artillery, as a truck convoy of enemy troops advanced from the north. These last hours saw the brigade in its death throes, gasping but also lashing out with astounding fury. There were valiant efforts to delay the inevitable as Castro's troops pushed the brigade to the edge of the sea. Early that morning, shortly after the B-26s passed over, the twenty-two-year-old paratrooper commander Alejandro del Valle leaped onto a brigade tank and led his men in a rash, swashbuckling run on Castro's forces near San Blas, driving them back before running low on ammunition and collapsing into retreat. To the west, where enemy forces were fewer than two miles from Blue Beach, Erneido Oliva dug in stoically with the 6th and 2nd battalions to hold the line. Over the next several hours the road to Larga would see as fierce and bloody a battle as had yet been waged.

Pepe San Román saw what he took to be U.S. jets pass overhead at one point that morning. But the planes were fleeting specks in the sky, many thousands of feet over the beach, useless. They might as well have been orbiting the Earth with Yuri Gagarin. "Have you quit?" San Román radioed to anyone who was listening. "Aren't you going to support me anymore?" He could not hold on, but hold on he would.

"Regardless of whether you help or not, I will fight on regardless."

Opa Locka, 8:15 A.M.

AFTER FLYING THROUGH the night aboard a military transport, Arthur Schlesinger and Adolph Berle landed in Miami at 7:00 A.M. They were met there by Gerry Droller, aka Frank Bender ("The famous Bender," Schlesinger called him), and James Noel, the former CIA Havana station chief. The car ride to Opa Locka air base was long and undertaken with "conspicuous stealth." For security reasons—did he think he was being tailed by Cuban spies, or was he only trying to confuse Berle and Schlesinger?—Droller took them on a meandering route, stopping at a hamburger stand to switch automobiles, then continuing on through "mile after mile of hot, vulgar, sterile Miami landscape," Schlesinger recorded. It was 8:15 A.M. by the time they finally arrived at Opa Locka.

At the air base they came to a "nondescript" barracks-type structure guarded by pistol-toting GIs. Inside, the members of the Revolutionary Council were asleep on cots. After rousing the men, Schlesinger and Berle sat with them at a wooden table. The six Cubans were a bleary-eyed, woeful-looking group. Schlesinger and Berle had seen José Miró Cardona just the previous weekend, when they had taken him to lunch at the exclusive Century Club in New York City to discuss the invasion. Schlesinger was struck by the toll the week had taken on the chairman. He appeared years older, his eyes hollow with fatigue.

Cardona's eyes teared up as he spoke. He was clearly on the verge of breaking down. They all were. Despite the information vacuum surrounding them, the council was aware by now that the invasion had faltered. They were anxious and inconsolable—"as unhappy as men might be," Adolph Berle recalled.

"We don't know whether we are your allies or your prisoners," said Tony Varona, the angriest of them. If the United States did not come to the brigade's aid, he threatened, he would leave Opa Locka at noon and go to Miami to hold a press conference. The council wanted the United States to do something, anything, to save the invasion. If nothing else, José Miró Cardona insisted, the council must be flown at once to the landing site to be with the brigade in its hour of need. Cardona wanted the chance to fight alongside his son and fellow exiles. "It is this which I request," he implored of the president's men. "This which I beg."

Schlesinger and Berle did their best to soothe the council and explain the government's position, but they realized there was little they could offer in the way of hope or consolation. "What could be done?" wondered Schlesinger. "How to break the news that the CIA had shattered their hopes and sent their sons to death or captivity? How to do so and at the same time dissuade them from calling a press conference, telling all they knew, and issuing public denunciations of the CIA and the Kennedy administration?"

Schlesinger and Berle excused themselves and stepped out into the dazzling Florida sunlight to confer. Berle suggested they contact President Kennedy. "It seemed to me only the president could deal with that kind of situation," said Berle later. "Who else could?" Schlesinger agreed. They went into the shade of an airplane hangar, where a telephone hung on the wall.

Washington, D.C., 10:00 A.M.

PRESIDENT KENNEDY ARRIVED in his office at 9:28 that morning. He had slept little and poorly. His usually neatly combed hair was mussed, his tie askew. He spent seven minutes alone with Ken O'Donnell, whom he had last seen in the Oval Office six hours earlier—before abruptly stepping out into the Rose Garden—then undertook a schedule of meetings not so different, according to his public appointment log, than the usual: the former prime minister of Costa Rica at 9:35; the current prime minister of Greece at 10:30; a Rose Garden ceremony at noon to present Jacques Cousteau a medal from the National Geographic Society.

But through the morning, between the cracks of the official schedule, Kennedy returned again and again to the crisis in Cuba. At about 10:00 A.M., Arthur Schlesinger's call came from the hangar at Opa Locka.

Schlesinger had already spoken to Dean Rusk about bringing the council to Washington; now he was calling to get Kennedy's approval. "We can't do any more here," Schlesinger told the president.

Kennedy did not hesitate. "Bring them up here."

Bay of Pigs, Morning

SAN BLAS FELL shortly after 10:00 A.M., opening the enemy's way to Blue Beach from the north. Rear Admiral Clark, aboard the *Essex*, had been receiving urgent requests from Pepe San Román all morning. At 9:14: "Blue Beach is under attack by 2 T-33 and artillery. Where the hell is jet cover?" At 9:25: "2000 militia attacking Blue Beach from east and west. Need close air support immediately." At 9:55: "Can you throw something into this vital point in the battle? Anything. Just let the pilots loose."

Clark relayed the messages to Admiral Dennison. His own brief comments reflected the frustration felt by the officers on the U.S. Navy vessels off Cuba. They were in a position to save the Cuban Expeditionary Force from disaster, but without authorization from Washington they could only watch it happen from a safe distance.

Those farther down the chain of command, though less informed of events on the beach, understood enough to share the distress of their superiors. "It don't look good," Don Roberts had written in his journal on April 18. Then, on April 19, "Situation is bad. No sleep—3 days." On both the carrier and the seven destroyers, the men had been on general quarters since April 16. They had not participated in any fighting, but they had been kept on edge, manning combat positions around the clock. The men aboard the USS *Murray* had gotten a serious scare late on the morning of April 17 when a B-26 appeared over the ship and dove at them "like a kamikaze," recalled Billy Houston, the gunner's mate on the *Murray*. "We were locked on the plane. We were loaded and waiting for 'commence fire.'" Just then, two objects tumbled out of the plane. For a moment, some of the men on the *Murray* mistook these for air-to-surface torpedoes. When they saw a parachute flare open, they realized they were looking at crewmen bailing from a stricken plane. The plane, in fact, was the brigade's own *Paloma One*. (See page 255.) The *Murray* rescued the survivor, navigator Demetrio Pérez.

That was the closest any of the American destroyers had come to combat. But some of the men on the destroyers believed that might soon change. According to Jim Padgett, gunner's mate on the USS *Eaton*, on the night of the eighteenth the captain of the destroyer ordered up "a full battle meal" for the men and assured them that "we were going to go in the next morning and we were going to liberate the rebels."

Now the next morning had come. The navy ships remained dozens of miles out at sea, liberating no one.

At 11:09 A.M. Rear Admiral Clark reported that two of Castro's planes were circling near one of the destroyers. This might be a fitting pretext, he suggested to Dennison, for an air strike from the *Essex*. Nine minutes later, Clark passed along a plea from Pepe San Román: "We are out of ammo and fighting on the beach. Please send help. We cannot hold."

Thirteen minutes after that, at 11:31 A.M., came another message from Pepe: "Out of ammunition. Men fighting in water. If no help given Blue Beach lost."

Admiral Dennison could not approve an air strike. Instead, he instructed Clark to begin exploring ways to evacuate the troops. The CIA and the Joint Chiefs had come to believe that evacuation by sea was the only possible way to save the brigade from capture or death. Dennison ordered Clark to send two destroyers in close to Blue Beach to determine the chances for evacuation. "Final instructions on evacuation will follow."

New York, Noon

ADLAI STEVENSON CABLED President Kennedy and Secretary Rusk at noon. His fellow delegates' reaction to the invasion was exactly as Stevenson had feared.

> Atmosphere in U.N., among both our friends and neutrals, is highly unsatisfactory and extremely dangerous to U.S. position throughout world. Sovs and Castro Cubans have been able capture and so far hold moral initiative. This is at least partly due to lack of advance planning on how to defend ourselves politically.

Stevenson had been a good soldier so far, but this was pointed criticism, just a few shades shy of *I told you so*. "So far we have received virtually no support in speeches of others," he continued in his cable. "Everyone, of course, friend or foe, believes we have engineered this revolution and no amount of denials will change their minds. . . . Whatever happens now we are in for period of very serious political trouble."

Aboard the *Essex*, 1:12 P.M.

SHORTLY PAST NOON, Rear Admiral Clark cabled Admiral Dennison again to update him on the rapidly deteriorating conditions at Playa Girón. The beachhead held by the brigade, reported Clark, was now less than half a mile in length along the shoreline and penetrated no deeper than a quarter mile into Cuba, a mere fingernail clipping compared to the great "lodgment" the CIA had hoped to hold by this point. Clark confirmed that two navy destroyers—the *Murray* and the *Eaton*—were heading to shore to evaluate the possibilities for evacuating the troops, but he wanted Dennison to know where he stood. "Believe evacuation impossible without active engagement with Castro forces."

Clark reiterated this point forty minutes later, pressing for a change in the Rules of Engagement: "I must point out that they [the destroyers] will be subjected to air attack and surface artillery fire and in my opinion will not be able to make any contribution to decision as to feasibility of evacuation which is feasible if we stand ready to support by air cover and counter battery fire and start at once."

Ignoring Clark's warning, the Joint Chiefs sent new orders at 1:12 P.M. The destroyers were to begin evacuating the brigade as soon as they arrived at the beach. But they were to do so without stirring up trouble:

> Direct DD to take personnel off the beach and from water to limit of their capability. We are anxious to save people as long as you can do so. We are extremely reluctant to become engaged but as long as we have some prospects of saving significant number of people to make hazards worthwhile, save the people.

The order gave the American ships permission to engage in self-defense if necessary. "If DD fired on they are authorized to return the fire to protect themselves while on this humanitarian mission. . . . God be with you."

Bay of Pigs, 2:32 P.M.

THE BRIGADE'S NORTHERN front had given way after the fall of San Blas in the morning. This was followed by the gradual buckling of secondary defenses in the early afternoon. As of midafternoon, though, the western front still held. Along the road between Playa Larga and Playa Girón the brigade waged the last true battle of the Bay of Pigs.

Ever since Erneido Oliva and the 2nd Battalion retreated from the rotunda the previous morning, Castro's troops had been flooding into Playa Larga—formerly Red Beach—then moving eastward along the coastal road to Playa Girón. Now Oliva was in command again, with the 6th and 2nd battalions under him. The men were dug in at a bend in the road between Larga and Girón, the bay to the left and the endless swamp to the right. Sea grape trees and palms grew along the road. Brigademen with bazookas hid among the trees and took aim at Castro's tanks as the enemy rumbled down the road. "The trees were good cover," said one of the bazooka gunners, "and our camouflage suits were wonderful. They blended right in with the foliage." Oliva also had positioned three tanks along the road. For hours they blasted anything that came along, tanks or trucks, steel or flesh.

By 2:00 P.M. Castro's artillery was close enough to heave its shells accurately onto brigade positions. Cuban militia swarmed down along the beaches and through the trees at the side of the road, seeking to breach the brigade's line. Oliva threw everything he had left at them, including the incendiary white phosphorus that had been so devastating the night of the rotunda. If the brigade was to go down in flames, Oliva would take some of Castro's army down with it. The fight was brutal, bloody, "Danteesque," to use Oliva's own word. In bush so thick they could not see in front of them, the men on both sides shot blindly, or, suddenly coming upon one another, fought hand to hand. The day was very hot. Between torrents of gunfire men gasped for water.

The Last Stand, as the brigademen would come to call this battle, was a moment of valor but also of senseless suffering. Every man who died there on the road to Girón, either brigade or Cuban army, died in vain. This fight only postponed what was inevitable. And yet it was impossible to give up. The men who fought, including Oliva, did not know that San Blas had already fallen and Castro's troops were flooding the outskirts of Girón. They knew only that they fought well and held their ground. Later, some would point to the Last Stand as further evidence of what might have been. They had the will, they had the strength. All they lacked was ammunition. It ran out in midafternoon. The mortars were spent. Oliva ordered a retreat and retrenchment.

A MILE DOWN the road from Oliva and his men, Playa Girón was under ceaseless bombardment. Earlier in the afternoon, Fidel Castro, now returned to the field and directing his troops from San Blas, had ordered the artillery batteries to open up on Girón. Shells hailed in from eight miles inland. Some overshot the beach and landed in the water, sending up plumes of water, but others pitted the sand and sliced leaves off of palm trees and slammed into houses. Castro's planes flew overhead, apparently spotting where the artillery shells were landing. The shells fell truer to their targets after that. Men came straggling into Girón, retreating from the north, looking for safety where none was to be found.

Pepe San Román stood on the beach near the water, talking calmly into his radio. He told Grayston Lynch the situation had become untenable.

"Hold on," Lynch urged. "We're coming with everything." They could get there in another three or four hours, he told San Román.

"That's not enough time," said San Román. "You won't be here on time. Farewell, friends. I am breaking this radio right now." The time was 2:32 P.M. This was San Román's last message. "Am destroying all equipment and communications. I have nothing left to fight with. Am taking to the woods. I can't wait for you."

They smashed the radios and weapons they could not take with them. An orderly retreat was impossible—it was every man for himself. There were two ways off the beach. One was to find a boat and paddle or sail out of range of Castro's guns, then hope to be rescued by an American ship. The other was to head into the swamp. As the shells fell, men ran for the sea, then back to the road beyond the beach, then back to the sea—a wave of panicked indecision ebbing and flowing.

Pepe San Román chose the swamp. Before fleeing with a group of his men, he sent Erneido Oliva a message by runner. The runner never made it to Oliva. When Oliva tried to reach San Román by radio to consult with him, the radio was dead. So Oliva started back to Girón on foot during a lull in the shelling. A jeep came by on the road and stopped for him. Somebody ran up to the jeep and yelled out that Playa Girón had fallen. "That's impossible," barked Oliva.

The moment he arrived at Girón, though, he could see that it was true. San Román and Artime were gone—without a word, as far as Oliva knew. Men were running frantically about. Empty tanks and guns littered the beach, along with spent artillery shells. Out on the water, boats and rafts of men bobbed on the waves. Farther out, two unmarked gray navy destroyers were plowing toward the beach.

Oliva went into the operations headquarters, looking for San Román. Shattered radios and other gear littered the floor. There was no sign of the brigade leader. Oliva asked somebody where San Román had gone. The man pointed to the sea, indicating that he had fled by boat. In fact, there was a San Román on a boat, but a different San Román—Pepe's younger brother, Roberto. Oliva did not know that yet. He felt angry and abandoned. He turned toward the water and shook his fist in disgust at the boats of brigademen paddling toward the gray ships in the distance.

"Here are the Americans!" a man shouted, stumbling out of the infirmary. "They have come to save us!" It was Máximo Cruz. The badly wounded company commander had seen the two destroyers off the coast. No sooner did Cruz declare the brigade's salvation than the destroyers, miragelikc, began to turn away from shore.

CASTRO'S COMMANDER, JOSÉ Ramón Fernández, had seen the American ships, too, of course, and thought they meant to attack. "Seeing them come directly toward us, I issued the order to halt offensive action and position all cannons, tanks, and other weapons toward the sea." Later the Cuban commander would claim he never ordered his tanks to fire at the American ships, that they were only aiming for the small boats of brigademen trying to escape from the beaches.

Aboard the *Eaton*, Captain Robert Crutchfield saw it differently. He believed his ships were being fired upon by the tanks, just two thousand yards away. Others aboard had the distinct impression that they were being bracketed by the tanks onshore—first a shell would land in front of the ship, then a shell would land behind the ship, as if Castro's tank gunners were setting target ranges on the American destroyers. Gunners aboard the *Eaton* and the *Murray* were ordered to lock and load. They were now just a finger's squeeze from opening fire on the tanks.

"They weren't hitting us but they were firing all around us," recalls Jim Padgett, gunner's mate on the *Eaton*. "And I can remember we lost fire control—the radar that automatically adjusts the sights on the guns—we lost that going in, and so they had to relay the range to our targets. We'd switched to armor-piercing ammunition to blow up targets. And they kept giving us the sight—the distance to change the sight on our gun manually—and the gun boss kept saying, *'Hold your fire, hold your fire, hold your fire.'* We were taking on fire and we were getting ready to get rid of this thing. . . . We were hoping they would hit us. If they hit us, we could blow them away."

Every student of Cold War history knows how close the United States came to war over Cuba during the missile crisis in October 1962. Less well known is that on the afternoon of April 19, 1961, the U.S. Navy came within a word—*Fire!*—of opening its guns on Cuban forces in an overt act of war. Captain Crutchfield later stated that if the shells had fallen any closer to the destroyers, he would have given the order. There is little doubt that the guns of the *Murray* and the *Eaton* could have obliterated Fernández's tank corps and nearly everything else related to Fidel Castro on the beach that afternoon. "Oh, it would have been so easy to solve the problem," Jim Padgett recalled years later. But it might also have started a war. A real war that would have been much harder to stop than to start.

Crutchfield decided the risk was not worth the satisfaction. He also determined there was nothing the U.S. Navy could do to help the brigade people. At about 3:15 P.M., the destroyers turned around and steamed out to sea at full speed, leaving a foam wake behind.

"We turned our tails and left," said Jim Padgett bitterly. This would still be hard to swallow fifty years later. "The feeling's not for me," explained Padgett, choking up. "It's for the people we disappointed."

The men of Brigade 2506 who were still on the beach forgot their fear for a moment. They stood and watched the American ships go. A few of the men lifted their guns, pointed them at the sterns of the departing ships, and pulled the triggers to register their displeasure. The ships, of course, were too far away. The bullets, like most at the Bay of Pigs, were fired in vain.

Washington, D.C., 3:40 P.M.

JOHN KENNEDY SPENT much of Wednesday afternoon in the private residence of the White House with his wife. At one point he went into her room and lay on her bed, close to tears. Jacqueline tried to comfort him. Kennedy also called his father several times that afternoon. The proud family patriarch found the effort of buoying Jack's morale exasperating. He lost his patience and snapped at his son, "Oh, hell, if that's the way you feel, give the job to Lyndon."

At 3:40 P.M. Kennedy returned to his office, again exhibiting a singular ability to mask his emotions. "You suddenly know why these guys are born to command," reflected John Plank, a Harvard professor who spent time with Kennedy later that day. The Pulitzer Prize–winning journalist Marguerite Higgins also happened to see Kennedy for a few minutes on April 19 and "marveled at the composure of the man." But she also noted a less noble attribute peeking out from beneath the veil of composure. "It was the first time in nearly a decade of knowing President Kennedy that I detected a note of resentment, muted as it was, toward the people around him."

In the cabinet room that afternoon, the resentment was less muted. The president's counselors had been gathered there much of the day, trying to come to terms with the disaster. Robert Kennedy made no effort to soft-pedal his bitter feelings. He spoke "in anguish," according to Walt Rostow. He was angry at Castro, but he saved much of his fury for the other men in the room. "We've got to do something," he said, pacing. "All you bright fellows have gotten the President into this, and if you don't do something now, my brother will be regarded as a paper tiger by the Russians."

Walt Rostow did not know Robert Kennedy well, having never spoken to him before the inauguration, but he was concerned enough about the attorney general's outbursts that afternoon to approach him and request a private word. They stepped out of the cabinet room onto the portico near the Rose Garden. "I told him that if you're in a fight and get knocked off your feet, the most dangerous thing to do was come out swinging. Then you could really get hurt," Rostow wrote. "Now was a time to dance around until our heads cleared." Robert Kennedy was silent for a moment, then responded. "That's constructive," he said.

Still, Robert Kennedy seemed resolved to punch back when he sat to write a memo to his brother that day. He opened with a review of the president's reasons for going into Cuba in the first place, as if to reassure John Kennedy that the decision was not unfounded. "The present situation in Cuba was precipitated by the deterioration of events inside that state. The news that 100 Cuban pilots were being trained in Czechoslovakia, the information that MiGs and other jet planes had already been shipped to Cuba and that these shipments were expected to continue, that thousands of tons of military equipment had arrived each month in Havana, were all matters of consternation."

Having recapitulated the case for the intervention, Robert Kennedy argued for *more* intervention, the sooner the better. This was no time for licking wounds, he warned his brother. Castro would only be better armed, more vocal, and more threatening in the future. "Our long-range foreign policy objectives in Cuba are tied to survival far more than what is happening in Laos or the Congo or any other place in the world," wrote Robert. "The time has come for a showdown for in a year or two years the situation will be vastly worse. If we don't want Russia to set up missile bases in Cuba, we had better decide now what we are willing to do to stop it."

Washington, D.C., Late Afternoon and Evening

THE FLIGHT BACK to Washington with the Revolutionary Council was "funereal," wrote Arthur Schlesinger. He, Adolph Berle, and the six members of the council landed at National Airport, then went directly to the White House. At about 4:00 P.M. they entered through the East Wing entrance to avoid the cluster of press snooping about the West Wing. The Cubans were ushered up to the second floor, where they ate sandwiches and sipped coffee and waited. As they munched away, Schlesinger excused himself briefly to type a note to the president. "Our visitors are in a somewhat composed and constructive mood. At present they are talking with Berle about the future relationship." He added, as a postscript, "They are now devoting their attention to the question of a rescue program."

The council finally entered the Oval Office at 5:00 P.M. Arthur Schlesinger's old friend Harvard professor John Plank, who specialized in Latin American studies and spoke fluent Spanish, had been hastily summoned from a class in Cambridge earlier in the day to do the translating—so hastily, in fact, that he had arrived in Washington without money or an overcoat. Also in the Oval Office were McGeorge Bundy, Walt Rostow, and Dean Rusk. The president sat in a rocking chair. The six men of the council were offered the two couches near the fireplace.

Schlesinger was initially struck by how drawn Kennedy looked as he greeted the council, a toll surely of poor sleep but also probably of Kennedy's Addison's disease; the lack of natural adrenaline production makes stress particularly exhausting to Addison's sufferers. (Kennedy took extra doses of cortisone and other synthetic hormones during times of high stress, and probably did so during the Bay of Pigs.) But Schlesinger was almost immediately struck by something else: how impressively Kennedy handled these distraught men. Telling them how much he regretted the outcome of the invasion, Kennedy showed a photograph of his older brother, Joseph P. Kennedy Jr., who had been killed while piloting a fighter plane over the English Channel during World War II. "I know something of how you feel," said Kennedy. He tried to explain his actions to them—why he had not sent in the U.S. military to help, and why he initially supposed the brigade might succeed. To make his point, he reached for a paper and read from it to the council. It was Jack Hawkins's memo, the glowing review the colonel had written on April 13 from Nicaragua.

"You have been taken for a ride, Mr. President," Tony Varona told him. Kennedy did not disagree.

WHILE THE PRESIDENT was attempting to comfort the Cubans, the men of the CIA's WH/4 task force were beyond comfort. They had predicted this outcome from the moment Kennedy canceled the second air strike on the evening of April 16, and now their worst fears had been realized. "Never before had I seen a room filled with men in tears," wrote Howard Hunt.

Jack Hawkins kept a hand over his face, as if shielding himself from a glare. Jake Esterline was pale with exhaustion and guilt; later he would remember little of these days—"like when you were in a bad accident . . . and your memory, from the time the thing happened and for quite a period of time after that, isn't very good." Esterline's assistant Dick Drain left the room to vomit into a wastebasket. David Phillips, the chief of propaganda, fought his own nausea as he sent cables to the radio station at Swan Island for broadcast, mostly gibberish. "But something, however desperate, had to be said," he later wrote. Tracy Barnes, ever sociable and upbeat, tried to cheer the men up, but his smiles were thin.

Richard Bissell remained stoical. "We've done all we can," he told the others when he came into the war room at about 6:00 P.M. "Why don't we all get some sleep?" With that, he said good-bye and went home. When an assistant called him from the office later that night, the man was surprised to hear the sound of music over the telephone. Richard Bissell was sitting in his living room with his family, listening to his wife play the piano.

ALLEN DULLES STOOD at Richard Nixon's front door. Nixon had flown into Washington that afternoon from California, where he had been living since January. He still kept a home in Washington, and he had asked Dulles to stop by to say hello. "The minute I saw him I realized he was under great emotional stress," Nixon later wrote. Nixon asked Dulles if he would like a drink. "I certainly would," the CIA director responded. "I really need one. This is the worst day of my life."

"What's wrong?"

"Everything is lost."

As they sat over drinks, Dulles told Nixon of Kennedy's decision to cancel the air strikes. "I should have told him that we must not fail. And I came very close to doing so, but I didn't," said Dulles. "It was the greatest mistake of my life."

LEM JONES, THE public relations man, released a final notice from the Revolutionary Council at 9:00 P.M. Of course, Jones did not compose the notice—Howard Hunt at the CIA dictated it to him—and the council had nothing to do with it. "The recent landings in Cuba have been constantly although inaccurately described as an invasion. It was, in fact, a landing of supplies and support for our patriots who have been fighting in Cuba for months." The brigade, the press release claimed, had gone into the mountains. Every word was a lie.

After dictating the release to Jones, Howard Hunt went home: "I was sick of lying and deception, heartsick over political compromise and military defeat." In retrospect, this was a remarkable statement—the first part, anyway—coming from Howard Hunt. Unlike many of those involved, Hunt's life would not be forever defined by his involvement in the Bay of Pigs. A decade later, he would define it all over again with his involvement in Watergate.

PRESIDENT KENNEDY WAS back in the cabinet room with his advisers at 11:00 P.M., having spent the evening dining at the Greek embassy. The mood in the White House remained grim, as it would for months to come. Following the inauguration, the administration had been living in a "golden interlude," as Arthur Schlesinger put it. Now it was as if the men of the New Frontier had all fallen into a backward fairy tale—the sweet elixir had turned into a witches' brew and the prince was revealed as a frog. "We should pick ourselves up," said Robert Kennedy, "and figure out what we are going to do that would be best for the country and the President over the next six to twelve months." The others could nod in agreement, but nobody had any solutions. "What worries me most," said the attorney general, "is now nobody in the government will be willing to stick his neck out, to take a chance, to plan bold and aggressive action against the Communists."

The immediate question before John Kennedy was how to handle the fiasco in public. He was scheduled to give a speech the following afternoon to the American Society of Newspaper Editors, the same organization Fidel Castro had stood before two Aprils earlier in Washington. The speech would have been widely covered in any case; now it was sure to be scrutinized intensely, for it would be the president's first forum to address the invasion. Every important newspaper in the country would be represented there, and they would all be looking to lead their front pages with Kennedy's comments.

At about midnight, Kennedy left the cabinet room to consult with Theodore Sorensen, his thirty-three-year-old speechwriter. Sorensen had been working on a draft of the speech for several days. He had started, as usual, with a list of topics. Most of these were broad musings on the first three months of the administration. "The education of John Kennedy—the lessons learned with interest, pain or amusement in the first hundred days." That had been one of the suggested topics.

By the evening of April 19, it was clear that such boilerplate was out of the question. Sorensen discarded his earlier drafts and started from scratch. He was a remarkably empathic writer, able to channel the president's thoughts into ringing syllables, and to do it quickly. For this one, Kennedy gave him a tall order. The speech had to reassure American allies that the nation had good intentions—appearances to the contrary—and was not about to trigger a war. At the same time, Kennedy had to signal to both allies and adversaries that he would not allow the United States to be pushed around. He had to show the world—and Americans—that he was neither rash nor weak.

Kennedy spilled out his feelings and thoughts to Sorensen, then left to go upstairs while Sorensen stayed through the night to complete the speech. Utterly drained, Kennedy knew tomorrow would in some ways be even more difficult than today. As he walked out, he picked up a magazine from a table in Sorensen's office and took it with him, a bit of light reading to take his mind off his troubles. The time was after 1:30 A.M. when Sorensen stepped into the corridor and found the president slumped in an armchair, still awake, the magazine open on his lap.

PART V

AFTERMATH

April 20–December 31, 1962

20

"The Way Things Are Going"

April 20, 1961

Washington, D.C., April 20

NEWSPAPERS ACROSS THE country met readers that first morning after with the kind of page-spanning, ink-drenched headlines usually reserved for presidential elections and natural disasters. It was the same story everywhere: the *Detroit News* (INVASION CRUSHED); the *San Francisco Chronicle* (CASTRO REPORTS EXILES WIPED OUT); the *Dallas Morning News* (WELL-ARMED CASTRO ARMIES APPARENTLY CRUSH INVASION); and the *Miami Herald* (INVADERS ADMIT "TRAGIC LOSSES"). The *Herald* naturally gave the invasion the most exhaustive and plangent coverage. One moving article in that morning's edition described an anti-Castro rally in Miami's Bayfront Park, where fifteen thousand Cuban exiles chanted the three-syllable Spanish word for "help"—"*¡Ayuda! ¡Ayuda! ¡Ayuda!*"—which soon turned into a three-syllable word for "please"—"Kennedy! Kennedy! Kennedy!"

Americans had never woken up to a day quite like this. Certainly the nation had suffered grievous blows in its past—assassinations and attacks; hurricanes and floods and earthquakes—and would suffer others in years to come. What made this one singularly painful was, first, that it had been self-inflicted, and second, that it was mortifying. With few exceptions (such as the *Los Angeles Times* columnist who insisted on calling it a "strictly intramural Cuban struggle"), the world fully understood by now that the invasion, for all the pretense, had been an American effort and an American failure. As C. L. Sulzberger would put it in the

New York Times a couple of days later, "We look like fools to our friends, rascals to our enemies, and incompetents to the rest." General Lauris Norstad, supreme commander of Allied Forces in Europe, spoke for many when he told a friend that the Bay of Pigs was the worst defeat the United States had suffered since the War of 1812. "Everybody had been so delighted by Kennedy," Arthur Schlesinger wrote in his journal while traveling in Europe immediately after the invasion. "Now Kennedy is revealed as if no more than a continuation of the Eisenhower-Dulles past. . . . We not only look like imperialists; we look like ineffectual imperialists, which is worse; and we look like stupid, ineffectual imperialists, which is worst of all."

Nobody found all of this harder to comprehend than Kennedy himself. "How could I have been so far off base?" he asked Ted Sorensen during a despondent stroll on the south lawn that Thursday morning. "All my life I've known better than to depend on the experts. How could I have been so stupid to let them go ahead?"

"For the first time in his life, John F. Kennedy has taken a public licking," James Reston wrote in the *New York Times*. "He has faced illness and even death in his 43 years, but defeat is something new to him, and Cuba was a clumsy and humiliating one, which makes it worse."

By cruel coincidence, this first day after the invasion happened to fall on President Kennedy's ninetieth day in office—the day by which he had promised to accomplish so much, a day that had been circled on the calendars of the New Frontiersmen as one meant for celebrating the administration's early achievements. "There would be no special significance in this milestone if Mr. Kennedy had not himself prophesied during last year's campaign that the first three months would be the touchstone to his accomplishments," an editorial noted in the *Chicago Tribune* that morning; now these prophesies amounted to nothing more than "the vanity of words." The *Dallas Morning News* offered the president support, but also a veiled warning: "The President is our leader, our spokesman. Destiny knocks now at his door. It is his door; but it is our house."

Inside the house on Pennsylvania Avenue, the president and his advisers spent the morning struggling to come to terms with the failure. Undersecretary of State Chester Bowles, sitting in for an absent Dean Rusk at an 11:00 A.M. cabinet meeting, found the discussion to be overwrought and vengeful. "Reactions around the table were almost savage, as everyone appeared to be jumping on everyone else," Bowles recalled.

Altogether, it was "about as grim as any meeting I can remember in all my experience in government, which is saying a good deal."

No one was more savage than Robert Kennedy. The becalming effects of Walt Rostow's advice the previous afternoon had been temporary. As President Kennedy, looking "quite shattered," sat quietly, his brother excoriated the men around the table. In Richard Goodwin's opinion, "Bobby's harsh polemic reflected the president's own concealed emotions."

After forty-five minutes, President Kennedy stood and walked out of the cabinet room without a word. Bowles followed, distressed by the "dangerous mood," and asked to talk privately. In the Oval Office, he told Kennedy that profound setbacks were to be expected in a modern American presidency; time would heal such wounds. "What history would primarily be concerned with would be how the President reacted to such setbacks." Bowles hoped Kennedy would resist the reflexive militant fury of some of his advisers, but he could not read the president's intentions. "The President appeared the most calm, yet it was clear to see that he had been suffering an acute shock and it was an open question in my mind as to what his reaction would be."

As Bowles pressed his case for prudence, he and the president were joined in the Oval Office by Lyndon Johnson, Robert McNamara, and Robert Kennedy. The younger Kennedy instantly spoiled the mood Bowles was trying to set. He seemed to have it in for Bowles—"rather a weeper," the attorney general later tagged him. Robert Kennedy was probably already aware that Bowles had disapproved of the invasion. He was no doubt aware, too, that Bowles, or someone close to him, was letting the press know of his stand. This constituted an unforgivable act of disloyalty in Robert Kennedy's view and would, soon enough, get Bowles booted from his position in the State Department. For the moment, the attorney general was in a rage, and Chet Bowles was in his line of fire. "When I took exception to some of the more extreme things he said by suggesting that the way to get out of our present jam was not to simply double up on everything we had done," Bowles later wrote, "he turned on me savagely."

THE FIRST TRUE indication of John Kennedy's reaction to the failure came early that afternoon, when he went to the Statler-Hilton Hotel, a few blocks from the White House, to deliver his long-scheduled speech to the American Society of Newspaper Editors. The setting was the same hotel—same hall, same rostrum—where Fidel Castro had addressed the ASNE two years earlier on a visit to America. Castro had been long-winded, rambling, and mostly conciliatory in April 1959. By contrast, Kennedy was terse and confrontational. After assuring the editors that the United States would never engage in unilateral intervention, he sounded a call to arms. "But let the record show that our restraint is not inexhaustible," he told the editors, his voice rising in pitch, his throat tightened around his words:

> First, it is clear that the forces of communism are not to be underestimated, in Cuba or anywhere else in the world. . . . The complacent, the self-indulgent, the soft societies are about to be swept away with the debris of history. Only the strong, only the industrious, only the determined, only the courageous, only the visionary who determine the real nature of our struggle can possibly survive.

Kennedy's voice regained some of its resonance near the end as he turned from ringing tocsins to blaring trumpets:

> We intend to profit from this lesson. We intend to reexamine and reorient our forces of all kinds. . . . We intend to intensify our efforts for a struggle in many ways more difficult than war, where disappointment will often accompany us.
>
> For I am convinced that we in this country and in the free world possess the necessary resource, and the skill, and the added strength that comes from a belief in the freedom of man. And I am equally convinced that history will record the fact that this bitter struggle reached its climax in the late 1950s and the early 1960s. Let me then make clear as the president of the United States that I am determined upon our system's survival and success, regardless of the cost and regardless of the peril!

Putting teeth into the words he spoke at the Statler-Hilton, Kennedy issued two significant orders that same day to Secretary of Defense McNamara. Both would do much to define American foreign policy in the decade to come.

The first of these instructed the Department of Defense to develop a plan to overthrow Castro with overt U.S. military force. Just one day after the invasion, Kennedy had evidently decided that his brother was right: Castro must be taken care of immediately, and by any means necessary. This effort would become one of the primary fixations of both Kennedy brothers over the next two years.

Kennedy's second order would have even more significant long-term consequences. He directed the Pentagon to create a Presidential Task Force on Vietnam, to be headed by Deputy Secretary of Defense Roswell L. Gilpatric. The president gave Gilpatric a week to prepare a report regarding—as McNamara described it in a memo that afternoon—"A program of action to prevent Communist domination of South Viet-Nam." Until this moment, Vietnam had been a back-burner concern of American foreign policy. As of April 20, 1961, that would no longer be the case.

DESPITE A HECTIC crisis schedule, President Kennedy set aside time that afternoon for a hastily arranged meeting with Richard Nixon. The former vice president had been having a full day of his own. That morning, Nixon had met with Republican leaders on his first visit back to the Capitol since Kennedy's inauguration, then had joined the party leadership for its weekly morning press conference. When a reporter asked him to rate Kennedy's performance, Nixon said that it was too early to pass judgment. "I want to be fair. In the campaign Mr. Kennedy said he intended to do a great deal in 90 days. I don't think it's proper to hold him to 90 days. He ought to be given ten more days." As for the Cuban situation, Nixon refrained from comment. It was "obviously a very grave crisis" and he knew better than to "pop off."

After the press conference, Nixon stopped by the home he kept in Washington. There he found a message written by his fifteen-year-old daughter, Julie. "President Kennedy has tried to reach you several times in the last hour. Please call the White House operator." (In a more effusive version, the note read: "JFK called! I knew it! It wouldn't be long before he would get into trouble and have to call on you for help.")

Nixon slipped in through a side gate of the White House at 4:00 P.M. The men spoke in the Oval Office for an hour and fifteen minutes. Pierre Salinger declined to release details of their conversation, but the White House did allow an Associated Press photographer to snap pictures of the men conferring—this, after all, was part of the reason Kennedy had asked Nixon to the White House. He *wanted* the public to know that his old rival, the man still presumed to be leader of the Republican Party, had come calling.

The fullest record of this meeting issued several years later from the pen of Richard Nixon. In a 1964 article for *Reader's Digest*, Nixon recounted his conversation with Kennedy in detail. As Nixon described the scene, Kennedy sat in his rocking chair at first, then stood and paced the room, speaking of the past few days in "his down-to-earth Irish," as Nixon put it. "It was the worst experience of my life," Kennedy told Nixon (according to Nixon). "What would you do?"

"I would find a proper legal cover and I would go in."

Kennedy shook his head. If he moved on Cuba, Khrushchev might move on Berlin. "I just don't think we can take the risk."

When the subject turned to another front in the war against communism, Laos, Nixon again suggested "affirmative action." Again, Kennedy demurred. "I don't see how we can make any move in Laos, which is five thousand miles away, if we don't make a move in Cuba, which is only ninety miles away." Nixon assured Kennedy that if he did take action in either Cuba or Laos, he could count on Nixon's support, even if they faced each other again in 1964. "I am one who will never make that a political issue if such action becomes necessary."

"The way things are going and with all the problems we have," responded Kennedy, "if I do the right kind of a job, I don't know whether I am going to be here in four years." Later, after Kennedy's death, this comment would strike Nixon as prophetic.

It was five-fifteen when Kennedy escorted Nixon to his car. Under the evening shadows on the White House lawn they shook hands and parted. Kennedy turned back for the White House, his head bowed. Through the car window, the former vice president peered at the man who had beaten him. "As I watched this weary, stooped figure, usually so erect and buoyant, disappear into the terrible loneliness of the White House office, I had an overwhelming sense of how depressed and discouraged he must have felt." Nixon's observation would turn out to be prophetic in its own right. He would know that lonely feeling himself someday.

21

"Defeat Is an Orphan"

April 21, 1961

Washington, D.C.

"THERE'S AN OLD saying that victory has a hundred fathers and defeat is an orphan," John Kennedy told reporters at a press conference on the morning of Friday, April 21, two days after the invasion's collapse. "I am the responsible officer of this government." This admission sounded the theme the White House was quick to attach to the narrative of what went wrong in Cuba. "In the first place, he is not looking for scapegoats," James Reston wrote of Kennedy in the *New York Times* that morning. "He is taking full personal responsibility for the Government's part in the adventure."

The truth was more complicated. Even as he continued to blame himself for being "stupid," the president made clear, at least privately, that his stupidity resided mainly in the faith he'd placed in his advisers. "There is only one person in the clear—that's Bill Fulbright," he announced in the cabinet room that morning. "And he probably would have converted if he had attended more meetings. If he had received the same treatment we received." McGeorge Bundy reminded the president that Arthur Schlesinger had also gone on record against the invasion. "Oh, sure," said Kennedy. "Arthur wrote me a memorandum that will look pretty good when he gets around to writing his book on my administration." Kennedy wryly suggested a title: *Kennedy: The Only Years.*

Kennedy's self-deprecation only barely masked his resentment against those he believed had led him astray. And as James Reston rehearsed the message of presidential responsibility, the columnist also managed to convey a subtext of presidential finger-pointing. Kennedy was determined to "learn" from the experience, Reston explained in the *Times*; and the chief way he was going to learn was to "reevaluate" the CIA. "The question naturally arises," wrote Reston, "how it could be that this apparatus, with all its access to Cuba and to friendly nations within the hemisphere, could be so sure that the Cubans would revolt, and be so wrong on the critical point of judgment." Nobody could miss the point. Yes, Kennedy was man enough to shoulder the blame, but the real screwups were the folks at the CIA.

When Arthur Schlesinger dropped by the Oval Office to say goodbye to the president that Friday afternoon—he was departing for a previously scheduled trip to Europe—he found Kennedy sitting with Vice President Johnson, looking exhausted but cogently discussing the problem of the CIA. "The President said that he could not understand how men like Dulles and Bissell, so intelligent and so experienced, could have been so wrong."

Had he been a less loyal acolyte, Schlesinger might have reminded Kennedy that—*ahem*—he had been given plenty of warning about the invasion from sources *outside* the CIA. But now that the deed was done, Schlesinger, best recalling his last preinvasion memo—the one in which he recommended identifying "someone whose head can later be placed on the block if things go terribly wrong"—joined Kennedy in excoriating the CIA. "Allen Dulles and Dick Bissell brought down in a day," he would write, "what Kennedy had been laboring patiently and successfully to build up in three months."

Already anonymous sources in the White House were feeding the press stories of how the CIA "sold" them on the plan; how the Joint Chiefs had signed off on it; how the president had been ill-advised, duped. "Many key pieces of Washington's share in the Cuban fiasco are now beginning to fall into place," a front-page article in the next day's *Washington Post* would begin. "What emerges is a picture of President Kennedy accepting the advice of the Joint Chiefs of Staff and the Central Intelligence Agency—advice which events proved to be faulty."

The Joint Chiefs fought hard to squelch any insinuation that they deserved blame for the fiasco. As General George H. Decker, chief of staff of the army, put it, the CIA had held the operation close to the vest and the chiefs had merely been "on the sideline as observers and advisers." Kennedy knew this description downplayed the chiefs' advisory role, and he was nearly as angry at the Pentagon as he was at the

CIA. But going after generals was a politically risky business for a new president who had just failed his first military test. The CIA was easier to blame because it had no real constituency and no good way to defend itself.

That Friday, Kennedy appointed a committee to investigate what went wrong. At 10:45 A.M. he met with General Maxwell D. Taylor, former army chief of staff, and asked him to lead the inquiry. Since leaving the army, Taylor had written a book, *The Uncertain Trumpet*, which Kennedy had read and admired. (The book argued for an American military less reliant on nuclear "massive retaliation" and better able to flexibly respond with conventional and unconventional forces.) In mid-April 1961, Taylor was living in New York City, where he had just undertaken a new job as the president of Lincoln Center for the Performing Arts and where, on Thursday afternoon, a White House operator had tracked him down at a business luncheon. Now, fewer than twenty-four hours later, he was sitting in the Oval Office with the president, agreeing to chair the committee.

Looking around the West Wing that morning, Taylor was reminded of a military command post that had been badly overrun. "There were the same glazed eyes, subdued voices, and slow speech that I remembered observing in commanders routed at the Battle of the Bulge or recovering from the shock of their first action," Taylor wrote. "The latter is a more accurate analogy because this new administration had, indeed, engaged in its first bloody action and was learning the sting of defeat."

Cuba

PAINFUL AS THE sting of defeat may have been in Washington, it was far worse on the beaches of Cuba. In some ways, the defeat had been mercifully quick. Just over a hundred brigademen had lost their lives to Castro's forces. But this was little consolation to the men clinging to life and hope after the invasion failed. Since Wednesday afternoon, hundreds had been hiding in the swamps under ever more desperate conditions, hunted by Castro's troops even as they foraged for food. Many had already been captured. Others had perished from wounds. Still others were adrift on rafts and other vessels somewhere off the coast of Cuba, praying to be picked up by an American ship. In some cases their prayers were soon answered; in others, not.

On land, the brigadistas had fled to the swamps in large groups with some semblance of military order, but they soon broke up into smaller ad hoc units to avoid detection in the bush. By that first weekend they were scattered across the vast wilderness in parties of two or three. Some dug into hiding places and stayed put; others kept walking, with vague and half-delirious intentions of reaching the mountains eighty miles away. They assumed that if they were captured, they would be killed, either on the spot or later by firing squad. In the meantime, they starved. They had eaten little food since leaving Puerto Cabezas, and now they had only what they could find. One group killed a chicken and consumed it raw, not daring to make a fire to cook it. Others chewed on snakes and insects. The hunger was terrible, but the thirst was even worse. The swamp was damp, but the water was brackish and sludgy. When they could bear the thirst no longer, they drank it anyway, or swallowed their own urine.

Survival was hardest for the injured men, of course. They could do little but lie on the ground and wait for help, capture, or death. One of the injured, Máximo Cruz, was hardly able to stand. He had taken to the swamp on crutches, then collapsed and passed out. Waking up with a start on the first morning out, he looked down to see crabs, with black shells and livid red claws, crawling over his body. They were chewing his wounded flesh where it had rotted. Unfortunately, Cruz and the others could not return the favor and eat the crabs. Their meat was poisonous.

A lucky few men were rescued by the U.S. Navy. President Kennedy had authorized some of the destroyers to stay behind and "evacuate" the brigade. For several days, the destroyers put small motorboat crews into the bay to search for survivors. The sailors puttered over the reefs and through the reeds, calling for the men to show themselves. Sometimes they were met by bullets from brigadistas who mistook them for Castro's militia, until a Spanish-speaking member of the crew called out for them to hold fire—they were Americans, they had come in peace, they had come to help.

One of the Americans aboard a small motorboat from the USS *Murray* was Billy Houston, the gunner's mate. He joined the rescue operation as a rifleman. Fifty years later, he would recall how the rescuers were forced to practice a grim triage mandated by the size of the boat. "We could only take those who could sit up, because if you laid somebody down in the boat that took up room for a lot of guys. We had to try to get as many of them as we could. We could handle six or eight guys sitting, and maybe just one or two lying down. Some of them were injured pretty bad, and that was kind of tough. Sometimes we'd just have to leave them."

Those not rescued—the great majority—were sooner or later flushed from the swamps and captured. They were marched back to Playa Girón, where they found themselves in the middle of a prison camp qua media circus. Fidel Castro spent a lot of time in Girón after the invasion, always surrounded by scores of sympathetic reporters and photographers—Russians, Czechs, Chinese—there to record the hour of victory over imperialism. Castro himself interrogated a few of the "mercenaries," as he referred to the brigade, suddenly appearing before a prisoner and demanding to know how he could have brought himself to commit such "treason."

These were very good days for Fidel Castro. He was the toast of the Communist world, the dragon-slayer of American imperialism, the Maximum Leader of Cuba, and a hero to his people. The fact that he had beaten an army of fewer than fifteen hundred men with a force of at least twenty thousand and had taken heavy casualties in doing so was lost beneath the more compelling David and Goliath narrative: Castro had beaten America itself.* He was a busy man in the post-invasion fervor, everywhere at once, shuttling between Havana and Girón, giving tours of the battlefield to foreign journalists, and finding time—lots of time—to go on television and speak of how the Cuban people had defeated the imperialists and their mercenary stooges. Over time, this narrative would help Castro solidify his power in Cuba, for his leadership at Girón turned him from a mere revolutionary into a savior. More ominously, it would help him complete the transformation of his country into a police state by justifying all and any measures against threats to the homeland. What remained of the ideals to which Castro had at least paid lip service during his trip to the United States two years earlier, such as freedom of the press and open elections, fell by the wayside under the necessities of self-defense. Cuba would become, just as the United States had feared, a ruthless, full-fledged Communist dictatorship.

For the moment, though, Castro put ruthlessness on hold and decided he did not want the invaders executed. They were worth more to him alive than dead, in both propaganda and monetary value. Perhaps he feared American retaliation, too, should he start killing the brigade.

---

* The official death toll recorded by the Cuban government was 176, but American estimates put it significantly higher, from two thousand to five thousand.

Cuba's prisons were already overflowing with suspected counterrevolutionaries arrested in the days preceding and during the invasion, so little space remained for an additional thousand men. Castro had them sent to the Palacio de Esportes (Sports Palace) in Havana. There they would begin a twenty-month ordeal as his prisoners and puppets.

First, though, they had to survive the ordeal of the journey from the Bay of Pigs to Havana. In at least one case, this turned out to be the most harrowing experience of the entire invasion and its long aftermath. The nightmare began at Girón after Castro returned to Havana. A Cuban commander charged with transporting the prisoners, Osmany Cienfuegos*—a name brigade soldiers still utter today as if spitting out something vile—ordered the brigademen into the back of a paneled truck. When 100 prisoners were packed in, already gasping for breath, one of Castro's soldiers approached Cienfuegos. "Sir, we can't put any more in. They will die."

"Let them die," responded Cienfuegos, according to prisoners who were there. "It will save us from shooting them." Apparently he had not gotten word that Castro did not intend to execute the prisoners.

Cienfuegos ordered another 50 men into the truck. The last to board was the badly injured Máximo Cruz. "I hope you keep the door open," Cruz warned Cienfuegos. "Otherwise, we're going to die."

"You are going to be shot when you get to Havana, so what's the difference—dying now or dying tomorrow?" Cienfuegos turned to his men. "Get the son of a bitch and throw him into the truck."

The doors shut on 149 men, locking them into total darkness and unbearable heat. As the truck rumbled north under the beating sun, the air became hotter and more stifling. A journey that could have been made in three or four hours was stretched (intentionally, in the opinion of those inside) by frequent stops to eight or nine hours. Men shouted out for help. The devout prayed with rosary beads. Others desperately began to claw and scrape the walls, some using belt buckles to gouge small but precious air holes. "At one point, we felt rain inside," recalled Jorge Silveira, who served as a radioman for the brigade. "It was the condensation of our sweat falling from the ceiling. People drank it." A paratrooper named Juan Jesús Gonzáles passed out and had a vision of his own death. "I saw me go outside the truck," he vividly recalled nearly

---

* The older brother of the late Camilo Cienfuegos, Osmany went on to become a powerful figure in the Cuban government.

fifty years later. "Underneath of my feet, I see the truck, the roof of the truck. I saw it. I was smiling and said 'bye-bye, everybody.' Then my friend hit me in the face twice and say, 'J.J., what's happening to you? You smiled and said *bye-bye*.'" The friend lifted Gonzáles's mouth to one of the holes and revived him with a taste of fresh air.

By the time the truck reached Havana that evening and the doors finally opened to the fresh air, nine more men were dead. This brought the total number of fatalities in the brigade to 114.

22

"No One Knows How Tough"

Spring 1961

Camp David/Gettysburg, April 22

PRESIDENT KENNEDY BOARDED a helicopter on the south lawn just after noon on Saturday, April 22, and lifted off for a thirty-minute flight to Camp David, in rural Maryland. He landed at the presidential retreat just a few minutes before Dwight Eisenhower arrived in a separate helicopter from his farm in Gettysburg, Pennsylvania.

In private, Kennedy was furious at Eisenhower, not only for the plan the former president had dropped in his lap, but also for the men who came with it. "My God, the bunch of advisers we inherited," Kennedy complained to his wife. "Can you imagine being President and leaving behind someone like all those people there?" Despite his resentment, Kennedy was eager to meet with the former president. He needed Ike in his corner.

The men shook hands on the helipad, then strolled to the terrace of Aspen Cottage, where they talked until lunch. The day was cloudy but warm. The trees in the Maryland woods were showing their first wisps of green, and early buds colored the azaleas and dogwoods. For Eisenhower, this meeting was a return to the national spotlight, and to a place he had loved as president (and had christened with the name of his grandson, David Eisenhower). For Kennedy, the encounter was like a trip to the woodshed.

"No one knows how tough this job is until after he has been in it a few months," Kennedy confided to Eisenhower as they reached Aspen Cottage.

If John Kennedy was hoping for presidential camaraderie or a fatherly pat on the back, he was in for a rude awakening. "Mr. President," responded Eisenhower tartly, "if you will forgive me, I think I mentioned that to you three months ago." According to Eisenhower's own recollection of the conversation, as shared with his biographer Stephen Ambrose, the former president went on to pepper Kennedy with hard questions, as if young Kennedy were a none too bright pupil falling behind in his studies. Had Kennedy made sure to air all opposing views in his meetings? Well, yes, Kennedy sputtered; he had meetings, but really he just took the advice of the CIA and Joint Chiefs—

"Mr. President, were there any changes to the plan that the Joint Chiefs of Staff had approved?"

"Yes, there were," acknowledged Kennedy. "We did want to call off one bombing sally."

"Why was that called off? Why did they change plans after the troops were already at sea?" By which he meant, of course, why did *you* change the plans?

"Well, we felt it necessary that we keep our hand concealed in this affair; we thought that if it was learned that we were really doing this and not these rebels themselves, the Soviets would be very apt to cause trouble in Berlin."

"Mr. President, that is exactly the opposite of what would really happen," chided Eisenhower. "The Soviets follow their own plans, and if they see us show any weakness then is when they press us the hardest."

"Well, my advice was that we must try to keep our hands from showing in this affair."

"Mr. President, how could you expect the world to believe that we had nothing to do with it?"

Each time Eisenhower repeated "Mr. President" it sounded less like an honorific and more like a dig. "I believe there is only one thing to do when you go into this kind of thing, it must be a success," he added. (And *you*, he did not have to add, allowed it to *fail*.)

Eisenhower had little advice to offer Kennedy. With every word and gesture, he let it be known that this was Kennedy's problem to solve, not his. After lunch, the two men walked for fifteen minutes on the lawn and through the woods. Before boarding the helicopter, Eisenhower spoke to a group of reporters. They asked him if he supported Kennedy. Eisenhower offered a tepid endorsement. "I say I am all in favor of the United States supporting the man who has to carry the responsibility for our foreign affairs."

At two-thirty, fewer than two hours after arriving, Eisenhower lifted off for the quick hop back to Gettysburg. He was unimpressed by the "bewildered" man who had succeeded him. The story of the invasion was "a very dreary account of mismanagement, indecision, and timidity at the wrong time," he wrote in his journal. Making a play on the title of Kennedy's Pulitzer Prize–winning book, *Profiles in Courage*, Eisenhower suggested a title for the Bay of Pigs story: *Profile in Timidity and Indecision.*

Clearly, Eisenhower had a right to lay the blame on his successor. It was on Kennedy's desk, not his, that the buck stopped, to borrow Harry Truman's phrase. Nonetheless, given his role in developing the operation—launching it, enlarging it, encouraging his successor to pursue it—his attitude in the wake of its failure was uncharitable. The former president went out of his way to wash his hands of the fiasco. The operation "could not have happened in my administration," he told friends, who in turn spread the message: Eisenhower would not have approved an operation in the form it took under Kennedy. This was fair and perhaps true. But Eisenhower went further. Until his death, he would claim that he never approved a "plan" to invade Cuba. What he had approved was merely a "program." The distinction was more semantic than practical, but Eisenhower insisted on it.

Shortly after the invasion, Eisenhower contacted several men who had served as his aides in the White House. He wanted to affirm his memory of meetings on Cuba—and to confirm his assumption that no notes survived those meetings. Since the practice of plausible denial discouraged aides from writing anything down regarding covert activities, Eisenhower believed there would be little record of his decisions regarding the CIA's Cuba operation. It came as a surprise, then, when Gordon Gray, his former national security adviser, told him otherwise.

According to Gray, he called Eisenhower on the telephone in June 1961. "Would you like to see a record of all your conversations about Cuba?"

"I think I'd give my right arm to have such. But of course there isn't anything."

"There is," Gray corrected him.

Gray went to Gettysburg to review his notes with Eisenhower. When they got to the March 17, 1960, meeting at which Eisenhower approved the CIA's four-point "Program of Covert Action," Eisenhower studied it. "This is wrong," he said.

"Well, all right, sir," said Gray. "What is it?"

Eisenhower did not like the word "planning" that Gray had used in the memo. "We did no military planning," said Eisenhower. "With your permission, I'm going to have this page rewritten to reflect the facts." The memorandum was rewritten, Eisenhower signed it, and the new draft, thus modified, became the historical record.

Washington, D.C., Late April

THE ABRUPT AND humiliating culmination of months of intense work left the men of CIA's WH/4 reeling. Those most responsible had not only to cope with the fact that they had ordered men to their deaths and imprisonment, but also come to terms with the price they were likely to pay personally.

A few days after the operation, Jacob Esterline took a leave of absence from the agency and traveled down to Miami on a kind of pilgrimage. He visited families of brigade members and expressed how sorry he was—and how angry. "We were screwed by Kennedy," he told people he met. "They made me send these men to their slaughter. I will never forget this as long as I live."

As for his career at the CIA, Esterline was philosophical. "I guess that kind of put an end to it for all practical purposes," he told an interviewer some years later. "But that is the name of the game—if you let yourself get involved in one of these things, and it doesn't work out, that's it."

Tracy Barnes, the once abundantly cheerful man who had acted as Richard Bissell's chief lieutenant throughout the operation, was never quite the same after the Bay of Pigs, according to those who knew him well. He lost the bounce in his step, the easy smile. Barnes took especially hard the charge that he misled Adlai Stevenson in the pre-invasion briefing in New York. Stevenson was a hero of his. He could not stomach the idea that he had been the cause of the ambassador's distress.

As for Richard Bissell, that first Sunday after the invasion found him sitting in the garden behind his house in Cleveland Park, listening to opera on the record player. A week had passed since the go-ahead phone call from President Kennedy. Along with everything else that had happened during that week, Bissell, the genius with the golden briefcase, had publicly morphed into a dunce with a ball and chain. Sometime that Sunday he received a caller. It was the ubiquitous James Reston of the *New York Times*, a man who seemed to know the mind of the White

House better than most of those who worked there. "You know, don't you, that you've got to go?"

"No," said Bissell. "But I do now."

Mac Bundy confirmed it later: "The president thinks you should swing your axe elsewhere for a while."

Bissell would, in fact, linger at the CIA for many months to come, in part because the president did not want to fire anyone abruptly and in part because there was still much work for him to do. But after the Bay of Pigs there was never any doubt that Bissell would go. In private, Kennedy put it this way to Bissell: "If this were a parliamentary government, I would have to resign and you, a civil servant, would stay on. But being the system of government it is, a presidential government, you will have to resign." There must be heads for the chopping block, as Arthur Schlesinger had put it prior to the invasion.

Schlesinger suggested that the president find Bissell another position. "Dick Bissell presents a particular problem. He is a man of exceptional abilities who has been tragically miscast in his present assignment. I believe it would be a mistake to continue him in any job having to do with clandestine activities. On the other hand, I think it would be a mistake to lose his services to the government."

Some old friends were mystified and disappointed by Bissell. Certain "capital gangsters," according to the *New York Times*, cracked wise about the "Bissell gap" that had led to the disaster. Adolph Berle was one of the precious few who stepped forward to admit he had actively favored the invasion. He called Bissell to tell him as much. "I voted for this operation," he told Bissell. "I still believe we should have tried. . . . I think what you did was the best that could be done." Bissell would never forget the kindness of that call.

In the end, Bissell consoled himself with the conviction, as he had expressed to his children before things went south, that his line of work offered only two likely outcomes: total success or total failure. And the latter was always more likely than the former. "The risks are very high, but people must have the courage to take chances. History deserves that it be tried."

In the same memo in which Schlesinger recommended finding another spot for Bissell, he suggested putting Dulles out to pasture. "Mr. Dulles," wrote Schlesinger, "has told everybody that he wants to write his memoirs. By June 1 he should be given this opportunity."

The Bay of Pigs did not change Dulles's career much as a practical matter; this was nearing its culmination anyway for the sixty-eight-year-old director. What it affected was his legacy. Everything Dulles had done with his life, especially over the last decade of it, was cast in shadow, as was the agency with which his name had become synonymous. As Dulles and Bissell fell on their swords, the press and the politicians drew out their knives and began carving. The CIA had too little congressional oversight; the CIA should concern itself only with intelligence-gathering and leave military ops to the Pentagon; the CIA had gotten too big, too uppity, too "public" and indiscreet; the CIA needed to be overhauled from the top down.

BEFORE FIRING ALLEN DULLES, the president asked the director to perform one last task. He wanted Dulles to sit on Maxwell Taylor's investigative committee.

In addition to General Taylor and Dulles, the members of this group, to be known as the Cuba Study Group, or simply the Taylor Committee, would be Admiral Burke from the Joint Chiefs and Robert Kennedy from—well, whom Robert Kennedy represented could pretty easily be guessed. It was a peculiarly partisan panel, since three of its principal members had a strong personal interest in the outcome of the investigation. General Taylor would presumably steer this triumvirate to a unified and objective conclusion. The *New York Times* opined that the selection of the highly admired General Taylor "suggests the seriousness of President Kennedy's determination to find out what went wrong."

Taylor, fifty-nine, attired in civilian clothes, returned to his old haunts at the Pentagon, where offices were set aside for him and a small staff. The committee began taking testimony that Saturday after the invasion, April 22, while Kennedy was at Camp David with Eisenhower. Taylor launched his inquiry by calling in the CIA men—Bissell, Cabell, Esterline, Hawkins, and J. C. King—to discuss the evolution of the operation. After a few days of CIA testimony, the committee turned to the Pentagon staffers who had reviewed the invasion under the Joint Chiefs, then to the field staff of the invasion—men freshly arrived from Nicaragua and Cuba and Guatemala, heads still spinning behind sunburned faces and bloodshot eyes.

On April 27, Grayston Lynch and Rip Robertson arrived in Washington from the deck of the *Essex*, by way of Guantánamo and Jacksonville. Stepping off a plane at Anacostia Naval Station, they still wore the boots they had on their feet during the invasion. Lynch and Robertson spent the first night in Washington holed up in a hotel room with a bottle of Jack Daniel's. Conferring with other CIA men, they learned for the first time why the air strikes had been canceled on the night of April 16. In the newspapers, the agency was bearing the brunt of criticism for the failure, but it was clear to Grayston Lynch, as it was to his fellow CIA officers, who really deserved the blame: John F. Kennedy.

GIVEN HIS OWN bitter feelings, it probably would not have troubled Lynch to know that John Kennedy's friends and family had never seen the president so dejected. "You know, we'd been through a lot of things together," Robert Kennedy later said. "And he was just more upset this time than he was any other." Kennedy's old pal from boarding school Lem Billings, who spent several weekends at Glen Ora in the aftermath of the invasion, noted in a journal that Kennedy was ready to give up being president. "All during the weekend, he said he certainly wasn't interested in a second term—that this was the most unpleasant job existent." As far as he was concerned, Kennedy told Billings, "Lyndon can have it in 1964." Another longtime Kennedy friend, Red Fay, recounted a similar comment by Kennedy. They were in the president's limousine, driving out through the gates of the White House, passing through a crowd of tourists. "By God, if they think they are going to get me to run for a second term," muttered Kennedy as he waved back at the crowd, "they're out of their minds."

The adjective "bewildered" came up frequently in discussions of Kennedy. Eisenhower had applied it after their Camp David meeting; others followed. Dean Acheson compared Kennedy to "the fellow who knew little about boomerangs; throwing one around, was knocked out cold by the one he himself has thrown. Kennedy can't yet believe that he has been hit in the head by his own boomerang."

The pain was slightly reduced by the fact that the American public rallied around the president. On a Tuesday afternoon at the start of May, Evelyn Lincoln stepped into the Oval Office with the results of a new Gallup poll. Kennedy had an astonishing 82 percent approval rating, a 10 percent lift from the last poll. "It's just like Eisenhower," Kennedy said after he looked at the poll. "The worse I do, the more popular I get."

23

"Success Is What Succeeds"

Late Spring 1961

Washington, D.C., April–May

MANY OF THE effects of the Bay of Pigs that seemed dire in the days immediately after the invasion proved fleeting. America's allies, despite their initial dismay, forgave Kennedy quickly, apparently willing to chalk up the invasion to a youthful indiscretion. Other consequences were more enduring, and in some cases more costly. These included several set in motion by Kennedy himself in reaction to the failure.

As the history of the Kennedy administration is usually written, John Kennedy learned valuable lessons from the Bay of Pigs that allowed him to become a better president. Mainly, he learned not to depend on the advice of his military and intelligence advisers—the Joint Chiefs and the CIA. He turned instead to men he knew and trusted implicitly, above all his brother Robert. Expertise having failed him, he put his faith in loyalty. "When the crunch came," said Lem Billings, "Bobby was the only person he could rely on to be absolutely dedicated. Jack would never have admitted it, but from that moment on the Kennedy presidency became a sort of collaboration between them."

Jack Kennedy also learned to trust his own instincts. Despite pressure from Burke and Bissell, he had refused to commit American military strength in Cuba, and he never seriously doubted that this was the right decision. As McGeorge Bundy would later put it, "the lesson was burned into his mind: the Commander-in-Chief had better be careful to ensure his own control over the use of American combat forces. *He* is the one who will inevitably be held accountable for their success or failure."

Altogether, the Bay of Pigs was a valuable lesson that benefitted Kennedy (and the world) eighteen months later, when John Kennedy, trusting his closest advisers and his own best judgment, steered the world from the brink of nuclear war in the Cuban Missile Crisis—or at least this is how the story is usually told. As Arthur Schlesinger wrote, "no one can doubt that failure in Cuba in 1961 contributed to success in Cuba in 1962."

On a purely administrative level, Kennedy realized that he needed to make significant changes. McGeorge Bundy was designated foreman of the overhaul, and he undertook the task with a penitent's relish. "You know I wish I had served you better in the Cuban episode," Bundy wrote to the president shortly after the Bay of Pigs. "If my departure can assist you in any way, I hope you will send me off—and if you choose differently, you will still have this letter for use when you may need it." Bundy was not expressing false modesty; he really had served the president poorly. Wishy-washy in articulating his views, he also had been negligent in preparing Kennedy. The job of national security adviser was like that of a triage nurse: to make sure the critical cases got the attention they needed and that the physician had the relevant facts. Bundy should have insisted that Kennedy know exactly what the plan was before he approved it. And he should have highlighted for the president the critical elements, such as air strikes.

One might have expected Kennedy to be disappointed in his aide of such vaunted brilliance. But Kennedy refused Bundy's letter of resignation. Instead, he ordered Bundy to move closer to him—"get your ass into the White House"—and effectively promoted him. Within weeks of the Bay of Pigs, Bundy vacated his spacious, elegant rooms in the Executive Office Building and settled into quarters in the cramped but precious real estate of the West Wing.

Even before the Bay of Pigs, Bundy had come to worry about inefficiencies in the White House's handling of national security issues, and he welcomed an opportunity to get serious about improvements. A memorandum he composed on April 24 contained the kind of hard-hitting, clear-eyed advice his pre-invasion work had lacked, starting with the proposition that White House aides such as himself owed it to the president to be more forthright in opinions. "The President's advisers must speak up in council," Bundy wrote. "The President and his advisers must second-guess even military plans. . . . What is and is not implied in any specific partial decision must always be thought through." He ended with a tautology: "Success is what succeeds."

Several weeks later, with stories swirling in the press regarding chaos in the postfiasco White House, Bundy followed up with a remarkably blunt memo to Kennedy. Between the lines, the memo acknowledged that poor administrative practices inside the West Wing had contributed to the mess in Cuba; if they did not want to find themselves in similar messes, they had better change—meaning *you* must change, Mr. President.

"I hope you'll be in a good mood," Bundy began his memorandum, a dollop of humor before a dose of honesty. "We need some help from you so that we can serve you better."

> Cuba was a bad mistake. But it was not a disgrace and there were reasons for it. . . . But we do have a problem of management; centrally it is a problem of your use of time and your use of staff. You have revived the government, which is an enormous gain, but in the process you have overstrained your own calendar, limited your chances for thought, and used your staff incompletely. You are altogether too valuable to go on this way.

Bundy asked Kennedy to commit to regular time slots for daily national security meetings. He gently scolded the president for his habit of calling and canceling meetings at the last minute, or wasting time in meetings to vent about some story he had read in the newspapers. "But of course you must not stop reading the papers, and maybe another time of day would be better for daily business," wrote Bundy a little cheekily. "After lunch? Tea? You name it. But you have to mean it, and it really has to be every day. . . . Will you try it? Perhaps the best place for it would be the new Situation Room which we have just set up in the basement of the West Wing."

The Situation Room, a space created in the White House that May as a direct result of the Bay of Pigs, would be one of the crisis's more enduring legacies. Bundy had taken over and remodeled, with the help of navy Seabees, a neglected bowling alley in an underground section of the West Wing. Construction began within days of the Bay of Pigs and was completed by the middle of May. The new space was meant to address what Kennedy's aides took to be a serious problem during the invasion.

The White House had been hours behind the real-time flow of orders, field reports, and other cables. Had the president seen more and known more of the raw data, so the thinking went, he could have made more informed and better decisions. Actually, this is an arguable premise—Kennedy would have benefited from *better* information, not *more* information—but in keeping with the president's resolution after the Bay of Pigs "never to rely on the experts," as Schlesinger put it, the Situation Room was to function as sort of a Cold War command center, plugged into communication networks of State, CIA, and Defense, putting the White House at the nexus of the information flow. Thousands of electronic bulletins a day would now flow directly into the West Wing. At its simplest level, this was an office renovation. At a deeper level, it remade the presidency itself, asserting and expanding the command and control of the chief executive.

MORE IMPORTANT THAN administrative or architectural alterations was the shift in White House policies following the invasion. Kennedy had entered office determined to cool tensions with the Soviet Union. The Bay of Pigs made this impossible. His overriding imperative now was to appear resolute. In the Cold War, where the antagonists dared not fire a shot for fear of triggering Armageddon, the perception of strength was at least as important as strength itself. America looked vulnerable, and that could not be sustained.

One move Kennedy made in the wake of the Bay of Pigs was symbolic but had a lasting impact. On April 20, the day after the defeat at Girón, when administration officials were grasping for ways to strike back against the Communists, Kennedy had sent a memo to Vice President Johnson directing him to lead "an overall survey of where we stand in space" and report "at the earliest possible moment." Johnson got back to Kennedy a week later with the unsurprising news that the Soviet Union, having just sent Yuri Gagarin into orbit, was well ahead of the United States in the space race. "This country should be realistic and recognize that other nations, regardless of their appreciation of our idealistic values, will tend to align themselves with the country which they believe will be the world leader—the winner in the long run," wrote Johnson. "Dramatic accomplishments in space are being increasingly identified as a major indicator of world leadership." On May 25, in a special message to Congress regarding "urgent national needs," President Kennedy announced the goal of putting an American astronaut on the moon by the end of the decade. Kennedy's ambition paid off. Eight years later, Neil Armstrong would be the first human to set foot on the moon.

Kennedy's descent into Vietnam would arrive at a far less happy conclusion. Indeed, Vietnam would make the Bay of Pigs look like a canapé beside its gluttonous feast of disaster.

On April 27, the Presidential Task Force on Vietnam—the one Kennedy had ordered into existence on April 20—came back with a twenty-three-page top-secret draft of a "Program of Action to Prevent Communist Domination of South Vietnam." Two days later, at a National Security Council meeting, Kennedy committed four hundred Special Forces antiguerrilla troops to Vietnam, adding to several hundred already there. Though the number was still very small, Kennedy had crossed a bridge of sorts—a bridge that would end in a quagmire.

Entire books could be (and have been) devoted to America's gradual submersion into Vietnam, and there remains much to be debated regarding Kennedy's commitment, intentions, and culpability. But certainly any study of Kennedy's role in that war must begin in the moments after the Bay of Pigs, inside the minds of the defeated president and his ashen advisers. Walt Rostow, the deputy national security adviser, made the link between the Bay of Pigs and Vietnam explicit in a memo titled "Notes on Cuba Policy" that he wrote to Secretary McNamara on April 24, just five days after the defeat at Playa Girón. "There is building up a sense of frustration and a perception that we are up against a game we can't handle," wrote Rostow. "There is one area where success against Communist techniques is conceivable and where success is desperately required in the Free World interest. That area is Viet-Nam." Rostow went on to argue that "a clean-cut success in Viet-Nam would do much to hold the line in Asia while permitting us—and the world—to learn how to deal with indirect aggression." John Kennedy agreed. His back against the wall, he believed he needed to draw a "line in the sand" against communism. He needed a place where he could strike back—and win. With the nudge of advisers such as Rostow, Kennedy came to believe that the conflict between the Communists in the North and the Diem government in the South was just the place to make a stand.

Until the day he died in the fall of 1963, Kennedy would remain conflicted about America's involvement in Vietnam. He was, as his biographer Robert Dallek has described him, a "reluctant warrior." There are those who argue that had Kennedy stayed in office, the United States would have avoided the war that ultimately claimed the lives of tens of thousands of Americans. But anyone who wants to portray him as a president who knew better than to get trapped in Vietnam has to reckon with the math: fewer than seven hundred American personnel were there when he was elected president; more than sixteen thousand were there by the time he died three years later.

On May 9, three weeks after the Bay of Pigs, Kennedy sent Vice President Johnson to Saigon. Johnson's assignment was to deliver a message to Diem that the United States intended to fully support the South Vietnamese effort to beat the Communists and that the United States, as the Gilpatric report put it, "intends to *win* this battle." Johnson had been less than eager to go to Vietnam, worried that he might get shot there ("Don't worry, Lyndon," Kennedy assured him. "If anything happens to you, Sam Rayburn and I will give you the biggest funeral Austin, Texas, ever saw") but he returned an enthusiast. He recommended that the fight against the Communists "be joined in Southeast Asia with strength and determination." This trip not only pulled Kennedy more deeply into the vortex of Southeast Asia, it also marked the beginning of Johnson's own tortured odyssey in Vietnam, a protracted calamity that would rend the nation and ultimately destroy Lyndon Johnson's presidency.

THE FAILURE IN Cuba had prompted Kennedy to summon Maxwell Taylor back into government service to conduct the postmortem. After performing this task, Taylor would remain in the administration, first as Kennedy's chief military adviser, then as chairman of the Joint Chiefs (replacing Lyman Lemnitzer). It would be Maxwell Taylor as much as any other man in government in the early 1960s who pressed Kennedy to increase America's presence in Vietnam. That the man charged with gleaning the lessons of one of the greatest foreign policy embarrassments in American history should go on to help foster an even greater debacle is an irony that tells a great deal about the Kennedy administration's response to the Bay of Pigs.

But such ironies were for the future. For the moment, Taylor devoted his complete attention to Cuba. The Taylor Committee completed its investigation on May 11, and presented its findings to President Kennedy on June 13. To General Taylor's credit, the report he oversaw was credible and comprehensive, and it remains revelatory fifty years later.

Among the more illuminating—and diverting—bits of testimony was that provided by the Joint Chiefs, who continued to deny any responsibility for the failed invasion. The most compelling performance was turned in on May 8 by General David Shoup, commandant of the Marine Corps. Moments after stating that he had believed the operation could and should have succeeded, he told the panel that "if this kind of an operation can be done with this kind of force with this much training and knowledge about it, then we are wasting our time in our divisions, we ought to go on leave for three months out of four."

"General Shoup," an unidentified member of the committee wondered, "isn't that statement of yours somewhat in contradiction with your overall optimism that this plan would work?"

"No, sir, it is not."

Shoup was questioned about his understanding of the Joint Chiefs' responsibility for the plan. He believed that the chiefs had virtually none. "Did you understand that the president and his advisers were looking to you for your military evaluation of this plan?"

"The thing that we were asked to do," responded Shoup, "was to determine which of the three alternatives was the best."

"But then after that, did you understand that during that period of time that the president was looking to you, the JCS, for the military evaluation of the operation?"

"I would have to presume that in accordance with his title as commander in chief he would be thinking about the military part."

"But you understand," pressed Shoup's baffled interrogator, "that he wanted to get your advice and ideas also?"

"That was never stated."

Shoup was at least more straightforward than Admiral Burke, who later told at least two interviewers that he knew nothing of the invasion plan until Kennedy came into office. In a 1967 interview for the John F. Kennedy Memorial Library, Burke claimed that the invasion "didn't come up until after the election. . . . There was no consideration of that landing before." In a narrow sense, this was true—the actual landing site came later—but the plan to use the brigade offensively in Cuba was old, and Burke had been personally briefed on it. Indeed, he had been in the room when President Eisenhower first approved the "program" against Castro on March 17, 1960. Yet he repeated his claim in a 1973 interview for the U.S. Naval Institute:

Q: How much in advance did the chiefs know about this?

A: The operation? Not until after Kennedy was president, the planning—

Q: The planning had been under way for a long time?

A: No, the planning had not been under way for a long time. This is one of the sad things about it, the planning—the first time I knew about that was when our navy intelligence people uncovered some operation in Guatemala. So I knew that something was cooking. And then it was either just before the inauguration in January that we were informed that there was going to be an operation, or just after.

Given the role he and the navy had played in the operation from the start, Burke's faulty recollection was puzzling at best.

SOME OF THOSE who appeared before the Taylor Committee, such as Grayston Lynch, later charged that the final report edited and skewed testimony to the point of deceit—a whitewash, Lynch thought, to cover up the failures of the administration. The truth, though, is that Taylor's report spread guilt evenly and spared no one—not the CIA, not the Joint Chiefs, not the men of the brigade, and certainly not the Kennedy administration. "The proximate cause of the failure of the ZAPATA Operation was a shortage of ammunition," the report concluded. This shortage was partially attributable to a tendency common among troops for "poor ammunition discipline"—they shot too many bullets and shells too early—but the primary reason for the shortage was the sinking of the *Houston* and the *Río Escondido*, which could be traced back to "restraints put on the anti-Castro air force in planning and executing its strikes, primarily for the purpose of protecting the covert character of the operation." These restraints, of course, had been placed on the air operations by none other than President Kennedy.

Kennedy came in for some fairly serious additional criticism despite the presence of his brother on the Taylor Committee. The last paragraph in the "Immediate Causes" section, for instance, emphasized the problem of administrative weakness in the Kennedy White House. "The Executive Branch of the government was not organizationally prepared to cope with this kind of paramilitary operation. . . . Top level direction was given through ad hoc meetings of senior officials without consideration of operational plans in writing and with no arrangement for recording conclusions and decisions reached." The loosey-goosey structure of Kennedy administrative practices, in other words, let details slip through the cracks.

Given the harsh verdict history would come to render on the CIA, it's notable how mildly this first investigation censured the agency. The CIA's mistake, according to the report, chiefly lay in its failure to articulate the details of the operation to the White House. The agency had overestimated and oversold the possibility of strong indigenous support for the invaders. Moreover, "leaders of the operation did not always present their case with sufficient force and clarity to the senior officials of the government to allow the latter to appreciate the consequence of some of their decisions."

This relatively benign assessment did little good for the CIA men whose reputations were ruined by the operation, for after the report was presented to the president, it was classified and locked away for years to come. By the time it was released in the 1970s, the history of CIA malfeasance was carved in stone, as indelible as Allen Dulles's name on the corner of the CIA headquarters in Langley.

Cuba, Spring 1961

AS WASHINGTON ASSESSED and assigned blame for the fiasco, the men who had put their lives on the line for it suffered their imprisonment in Havana. They were forced to sit for endless hours on the hard benches of the amphitheater of the Sports Palace. Standing and stretching were forbidden; lying down was permitted just several hours a day. Sleep was difficult, hygiene impossible. With nowhere to bathe, the men still wore the dirt, sweat, and dried blood they had brought with them from the battlefield and swamps. Bathroom breaks were infrequent and begrudgingly granted. They were also increasingly, urgently needed due to an outbreak of dysentery that ran through the men. (Some of the prisoners suspected Castro's guards of sprinkling their food with laxative.) Then, to make matters worse, on April 26, Fidel Castro showed up, cameras in tow, to harangue and interrogate them for hours on live television. The prisoners had no choice but to sit in their hard seats and listen, the very definition of a captive audience.

The same day Castro went to the Sports Palace—April 26—the U.S. Navy gave up looking for survivors on the coast of the Bahía de Cochinos. The fleet turned back to port at Norfolk, Virginia, having managed to rescue just a few dozen men. For many of the American seamen, the return voyage was accompanied by mixed feelings, the anticipation of going home soured by the conviction that they had let the Cubans down. "All hands are strongly reminded that *everything* connected with this at sea period is highly classified and not for disclosure to *anyone*," read an order from the executive officer aboard the USS *Murray* on Friday, April 28, two days before the ship pulled into port. "All hands must accept the responsibility in not confirming anything of what may appear in newspapers or magazines, what may be seen or heard on television, or what your wife, neighbors, or best friend in or out of the Navy may have heard or guessed. This is important to your Navy, your country, and yourself."

Brigademen remained hidden in the swamps, struggling for life. There were men on open seas, too, such as the twenty-two who had clambered onto a twenty-foot sailboat to flee Playa Girón on the afternoon of April 19. A week later, they were adrift somewhere in the Gulf of Mexico, with nothing to eat but the occasional raw fish or seagull, nothing to drink but salt water and urine. Three of the men were already dead; the rest were slowly succumbing to hunger and thirst. By the time they were finally spotted by a freighter and picked up in the gulf, they had spent more than two weeks at sea. Just twelve of them would still be alive, including Robert San Román, brother of the brigade leader.

Pepe San Román was captured in the swamp on April 25, after walking into a militia patrol. When his captors realized who he was, they let him know he would be executed by firing squad. They also searched him for pills, lest he try to kill himself first. "I am not that kind of man," said Pepe as he was dragged into the Sports Palace to join the other prisoners.

He may not have been suicidal but he was, in fact, extraordinarily disheartened. The humiliation of the loss and surrender to Castro were bad enough. But the depth of resentment he felt toward the United States was worse. "I was discouraged with everything," he later told author Haynes Johnson. "I hated the United States, and I felt that I had been betrayed. Every day it became worse and then I was getting madder and madder and I wanted to get a rifle and come and fight against the U.S. Sometimes the feeling came very strong to me that they had thrown us there knowing that they were not going to help us." As brigade commander, Pepe perhaps experienced his anger more wrenchingly than his fellow fighters, but he was not alone in believing that he—that all of them—had been knowingly sacrificed by the U.S. government.

After several weeks of detention, the prisoners were transferred to a naval hospital under construction in Havana. The new facility offered better conditions and better treatment. The men had cots to sleep on, were allowed to clean themselves and shave, and the food improved as well. Even better, rumors of freedom circulated among the men. Castro was going to make a deal for their release, it was said. Any day now.

Washington, D.C., Late Spring 1961

IN FACT, CASTRO *was* trying to make a deal. He first floated the possibility in public on May 17, in a speech to a group of Cuban farmers, declaring that he would gladly exchange the brigade prisoners for five hundred tractors, which could be used to "clear brush and jungle."

Kennedy was in Canada, his first foreign trip as president, when Castro made his speech. Castro was dreaming of clearing brush and jungle; Kennedy was joining the Canadian prime minister in a tree-planting ceremony. He was under a great deal of strain. The failure of Cuba still weighed on him, of course. Meanwhile, closer to home, the civil rights movement was heating up, as Freedom Riders marched in the South and met attacks by angry white mobs. Kennedy regretted that the nation was divided right after the Bay of Pigs failure, at a time when it should appear strong and solid. He had a summit coming up in Vienna with Khrushchev. The last thing he wanted was to project national or personal vulnerability.

All in all, this was a bad time for a man with a bad back to wield a spade. Digging into the dirt for the tree planting, Kennedy experienced a stab of pain in his lower back. He could barely walk by the time he got back to *Air Force One*. Using crutches to support himself, he had become the hobbling embodiment of his own crippled presidency.

Kennedy needed something good to happen. Getting the prisoners out of Cuba could put a happy end on a sordid saga and assuage some of the guilt he felt. "I put those men in there," he told his aide Richard Goodwin. "They trusted me. And they're in prison now because I fucked up. I have to get them out."

As soon as he returned to the White House, he began pursuing Castro's offer. He knew the administration itself could not enter into any sort of bargain with Castro. This would be political suicide. Moreover, the United States no longer recognized the government of Cuba, so could not very well negotiate with it. Kennedy would need a body outside of government to handle the deal, preferably a nonpartisan group of distinguished Americans.

Milton Eisenhower was sitting in his living room in Baltimore entertaining guests on the evening of May 19 when the phone rang. He was startled to hear the voice of President Kennedy on the other end. "I want to ask you for some help," said Kennedy.

"I'll do whatever I can," Milton Eisenhower replied before he knew what he was getting into.

Milton Eisenhower was the younger brother of Dwight Eisenhower, but he was also—naturally, in that age of remarkable brothers (the Dulleses; the Kennedys; the Bundys)—an accomplished man in his own right, president of Johns Hopkins University and an expert on Latin American affairs. Of course, it did not hurt that he was closely related to the former president and known to be a loyal Republican. As Kennedy had shown numerous times in the past, the best way to dilute criticism from the opposition was to invite the opposition to share your problem.

Kennedy asked Milton Eisenhower if he would agree to serve on a committee with former First Lady Eleanor Roosevelt and Walter Reuther, president of the United Auto Workers. As the president presented it, the task of the committee would be to raise the funds to send the tractors to Castro. Eisenhower agreed to join the effort, then spent the next six weeks regretting his response.

He initially grew uneasy when he realized Kennedy had no intention of publicly acknowledging the committee as his own creation. Rather, Kennedy allowed the fiction to persist that Mrs. Roosevelt, Mr. Reuther, and Mr. Eisenhower were acting entirely on their own. Kennedy really had no choice but to try to distance the White House from the committee, but Eisenhower felt sandbagged. Lacking explicit government approval, the committee was potentially violating the Logan Act, which prohibited unauthorized American citizens from negotiating with foreign governments. Furthermore, the committee was left to absorb the political heat in what became a seriously controversial undertaking.

Almost at once the committee came under "vitriolic and unrelenting criticism," as Eisenhower put it. Republicans and Democrats alike joined in the attack, senators as far apart on the political spectrum as Barry Goldwater and William Fulbright suggesting the committee was giving in to Castro's "blackmail." Goldwater declared that America would be lucky "if he doesn't wind up demanding five hundred hydrogen bombs rather than five hundred tractors." This sort of rhetoric had an effect on public opinion. A Gallup poll conducted in June found that just 19 percent of Americans were in favor of the deal, with 57 percent opposed. Milton Eisenhower was personally "bombarded" by "viciously critical" letters and phone calls lambasting him for capitulating to Communists. And when Castro made clear that by "tractors" what he really had in mind were Caterpillar bulldozers, some began to suggest that the Cubans might use the machines to build sites for missiles that could be launched against Americans. As one letter writer put it to his New Jersey congressman, "When Nikita remarked that he would bury us, I didn't think that we would have to supply the equipment." Eisenhower had joined the committee for humanitarian reasons, only to find himself accused of enabling mass murder.

Fidel Castro paroled ten of the brigademen and sent them to America to negotiate on behalf of themselves and their fellow prisoners. The delegation arrived in Washington on May 22. The deal was dead on arrival. The sticking point was the meaning of the word "tractor." Although Castro had stipulated five hundred Caterpillar-type "tractors," a value of $28 million, the committee chose to interpret his demand as five hundred *farm* tractors, a value of $17 million. The argument over the tractors dragged on for weeks. Castro would not accept the committee's offer, which he considered insulting, and the committee would not consider his, which it considered outrageous. On June 23, the committee sent a "last chance" cable to Castro. He could either take the five hundred farm tractors—or nothing. Castro cabled back his angry answer: there would be no deal.

With this, the committee disbanded. All contributions that had been mailed in from citizens were returned unopened. The controversy died. And the men of the brigade remained imprisoned inside Cuba.

24

"It Will Be a Cold Winter"

Summer 1961–Winter 1962

Vienna, June 1961

THE FAILURE TO get the brigade out of Cuba was another in a seemingly endless series of blows to hit President Kennedy after the Bay of Pigs. Later, Robert Kennedy would look back on 1961 as "a very mean year," when his brother's administration could not seem to catch a break. That June, the year just halfway done, John Kennedy went to meet Nikita Khrushchev in Vienna, and 1961 suddenly got a whole lot meaner.

The summit had been in the works almost from the day Kennedy entered office. Brokering an arms agreement and a general de-escalation of tensions with the Soviet Union had been high among his ambitions. After the Bay of Pigs, Kennedy considered withdrawing from the summit but decided to go ahead anyway; if he could not find peace with Khrushchev, he at least wanted a chance to meet the man one on one and show himself to the premier as a formidable adversary. Kennedy had been using crutches since the back-wrenching tree-planting ceremony in Canada, but he tossed these aside before leaving for Europe so as not to arrive at the summit "as a cripple." Instead, he wore a back brace and brought along his personal physician to administer regular shots of painkiller.

The summit got off to a fine start. When Kennedy greeted Khrushchev on the steps of the U.S. embassy in Vienna on June 3, he looked fit and confident, towering over the Soviet premier as the heads of state posed for photographs. At public events during the next two days,

Kennedy appeared similarly comfortable and in command. It was only when they were away from the crowds that Khrushchev took the upper hand.

Kennedy had worried that Khrushchev might think him foolish and irresolute after the Bay of Pigs, and he was right. When they sat to talk, Khrushchev belittled the United States for attempting to halt the spread of communism—it was inevitable, unstoppable—and for fearing Fidel Castro. "Can six million people really be a threat to the mighty U.S.?"

Kennedy admitted the invasion had been a mistake, but insisted America could not tolerate a Communist Cuba. Khrushchev made this into a debate on the respective merits of communism and capitalism. This was an argument Kennedy was not going to win against the patronizing premier. "He treated me like a little boy," Kennedy told aides at the end of the first day. The aides did not disagree.

The next day was worse. Kennedy and Khrushchev addressed the vexed subject of Berlin. The city had been a headache for Khrushchev for years, largely because refugees kept fleeing Communist East Germany for democratic West Berlin, a situation that angered the East German government and did nothing to support the case for the inevitability of communism. Khrushchev told Kennedy he intended to sign a treaty with East Germany that would effectively block access by the West to Berlin, isolating West Berlin and subjecting it to the rule of East Germany. The United States could never accept such conditions, responded Kennedy. To this Chairman Khrushchev gave a chilling rhetorical shrug. "If the U.S. wants to start a war over Germany let it be so," said the premier. "It is up to the U.S. to decide whether there will be war or peace. The decision to sign a peace treaty is firm and irrevocable and the Soviet Union will sign it in December if the U.S. refuses an interim agreement."

"Then, Mr. Chairman, there will be war," said Kennedy. "It will be a cold winter."

Ten minutes after the meeting ended, Kennedy walked into a gloomy room to be interviewed by James Reston. "How was it?" asked Reston.

"Roughest thing in my life. He savaged me," said Kennedy, slumping on a couch. "I think I know why he treated me like this. He thinks because of the Bay of Pigs that I'm inexperienced. Probably thinks I'm stupid. Maybe most important, he thinks that I had no guts."

Washington, D.C., Summer 1961

KENNEDY CAME BACK from Vienna more chastened and disconsolate than ever. He had lost in Cuba, Laos was slipping away, and now Khrushchev was more or less promising to snatch West Berlin, damn the consequences. "There are limits to the number of defeats I can defend in one twelve-month period," Kennedy told advisers. Meanwhile, he instructed them to find out how many Americans would die in the event of a nuclear attack by the Soviets. The answer came back: seventy million, or about 40 percent of the population. It was an impossible number to contemplate, of course, but if Khrushchev really intended to take West Berlin, the president had to consider all possibilities. As the columnist and Kennedy confidant Joe Alsop wrote, the issue came down to whether "the United States should risk something close to national suicide in order to avoid national surrender." Kennedy instructed McGeorge Bundy to step up civil defense preparations. This reflected a genuine concern about Americans' safety, but also sent a message to Khrushchev: America was willing to fight.

That summer brought "a time of sustained and draining anxiety," as Bundy put it. Americans got busy digging underground bunkers, stocking them with canned food and weapons. Shovel and gun sales were brisk. The possibility that two of the largest nations on earth might destroy each other for the sake of one-upmanship seemed not only within the bounds of possibility but, to many Americans, acceptable. A public opinion researcher named Samuel Lubell found that four of five Americans believed the United States should stand its ground in Berlin "even if it means war." A young Seattle woman wrote to *Time*: "I hope the President knows that even mothers of small children are losing sleep over the dread situation. But I can say that this mother would rather lose all than raise her children under less than freedom. Courage, JFK!"

Then in August came news from Germany that the Communists were constructing a great wall along the border between West Berlin and East Germany. The Berlin Wall was potentially a provocation, but Kennedy understood that it was also a solution—a barbed-wire olive branch from Khrushchev. The wall would stop the flow of East Germans into West Berlin, ending the population drain that so distressed Khrushchev, letting him achieve what he desired without closing off West Berlin to the United States. A giant concrete wall was hardly an ideal solution, but Kennedy could live with it.

Montevideo, August

BERLIN PUSHED CUBA to the back burner, but the Kennedy administration remained committed to ousting Fidel Castro. Over the summer the Central Intelligence Agency, under orders from the White House and with the oversight of the attorney general, sorted through plans of action while working toward a comprehensive plan to remove the Cuban prime minister.

For his part, Castro seemed more open to resolving tensions. The most compelling evidence of this came in mid-August, when Kennedy aide Richard Goodwin attended an Alliance for Progress conference in Montevideo, Uruguay. Also in attendance was Che Guevara. When Guevara noted from afar that Goodwin enjoyed cigars, he sent over a mahogany box filled with fine Havanas. A few nights later, Goodwin was attending a birthday party in an apartment in Montevideo when, at about 2:00 A.M., Guevara showed up, accompanied by two bodyguards and attired in olive combat fatigues and his usual black beret. "Had I been wiser and more experienced, I probably would have left," Goodwin later wrote. "But what the hell, I told myself in the highest tradition of Kennedy-style machismo, an American didn't have to run away just because Che Guevara had arrived." The men were introduced. When Guevara indicated that he wanted to speak in private, Goodwin stipulated that he had no authority to confer on behalf of the U.S. government but said he was happy to listen. The two men, accompanied by two others who could translate, retired to a small sitting room.

The Che Guevara of 1961 was not the world-famous icon of T-shirts and silk screen prints he would become after his death in Bolivia in 1967, but he was already a renowned and beloved revolutionary. An Argentinean by birth and a physician by training, Guevara had the soulful aspect of a poet, although he was reputed to be capable of ruthless behavior when the revolution called for it. He seemed initially ill at ease with Goodwin when they sat to talk in the little room in Montevideo. He broke the ice by playfully thanking the American for the Bay of Pigs—it had done wonders for Castro and the revolution. Goodwin told Che he was welcome, then suggested the Cubans might repay the favor by attacking Guantánamo Bay Naval Base. "Oh, no," responded Guevara cheerfully. "We would never be so foolish as that."

As the two men began to talk in earnest, Goodwin found Guevara to be disarmingly straightforward—a true believer, clearly, but free from cant. Guevara wanted Goodwin to understand that the Cuban revolution was irreversible and there was no sense in Americans trying to undo it. That said, he proposed a "modus vivendi" for future relations between Cuba and the United States. It was clear to Goodwin that Guevara had been thinking seriously about this and was speaking with Castro's blessing.

Guevara told Goodwin that Cuba could not return American-owned properties expropriated during the revolution but was willing to provide compensation for them. Cuba could also agree not to forge any military or political alliances with the Eastern bloc and to refrain from fomenting revolution in other corners of Latin America, a long-standing concern of the U.S. government. In return for these concessions, the United States would lift its trade embargo and pledge to stop trying to overthrow the regime.

This was, in retrospect, a pretty reasonable deal, and apparently sincerely offered. It is tempting to speculate how future relations between the two countries might have developed had the proposal gotten any traction. But, of course, it was not to be. Goodwin may have been young but he was not so naive as to believe he could fly back to Washington after a late-night meeting with Che Guevara and bring the United States around to reversing its policy on Cuba. In fact, shortly after returning to Washington, Dick Goodwin would be appointed by the president to a task force of which the express objective would be Fidel Castro's overthrow.

Before the two men finally said good-bye at 6:00 A.M. that August day in Montevideo, Goodwin had grown to admire Guevara. "We were both trapped in the contending forces of the world we had not made; passionate adversaries in the struggle to control the future," Goodwin wrote. "Yet just the same, as we sat together in the small sitting room of a shabby Montevideo apartment, I could sense shared passions fruitlessly struggling to cross the barrier of irreconcilable loyalties and beliefs."

Washington, D.C., Autumn 1961

THERE ARE MANY reasons why working out a deal with Castro's government was nearly impossible after the Bay of Pigs, but the two greatest impediments were John and Robert Kennedy. Following the invasion, the brothers came together as never before in their shared mission to destroy Castro. Robert, especially, undertook the project with zeal; he seemed to think it his personal obligation to successfully complete the job his brother had started. "My God, these Kennedys keep the pressure on about Castro," said Richard Helms, the man who would soon succeed Richard Bissell at the CIA and who came to experience the Kennedys' obsession firsthand. Oddly, the same inadequacies that Kennedy insiders would blame on the CIA for the Bay of Pigs—dubious planning; unfounded assumptions of internal resistance—were repeated and compounded in the activities approved by JFK and overseen by RFK. As Richard Bissell observed of the president, "his attitude toward Cuba changed remarkably little, if at all, after the debacle."

A number of old hands well experienced in mischief and mayhem were brought in to assist the Kennedys in their attempt to take down Castro over the late spring and summer of 1961. Among these was the legendary Colonel Edward G. Lansdale, a supposed expert on guerrilla warfare techniques who had been stationed in the Philippines and Vietnam. At the CIA, a renowned agent named William Harvey, former station chief of Berlin and mastermind of the extraordinary Berlin tunnel operation (in which Americans bored from West Berlin into East Berlin to tap Soviet communications), was assigned to the case by special request of the Kennedys. Both men were larger-than-life characters. Lansdale was reputed to be the model for the protagonist in Graham Greene's *The Quiet American* and owned a reputation for creative approaches to undermining foes. Some who knew Lansdale considered him a lightweight, more impressive on paper than in practice. Harvey was a different story, highly regarded by peers within the agency but a man undermined by his prodigious appetites for food, alcohol, and sex. Though hardly a looker—he had the physique of a pear and the eyes of a cocker spaniel—he claimed to have slept with a woman every day of his life since his adolescence. He was also known to carry a gun at all times, an accoutrement most CIA men considered unnecessary. President Kennedy knew of Harvey by reputation and insisted on meeting him. After handing over no fewer than two handguns to the Secret Service outside the Oval Office (he later claimed he had a third hidden on his body), Harvey was introduced to the president. "So," said Kennedy, "you're our James Bond?"

Neither Lansdale nor Harvey were prudent men, but both had enough sense to realize that what the Kennedys wanted them to do was ludicrous. Much of the criticism coming out of the White House after the Bay of Pigs had been directed at the CIA for issuing false assurances about the likelihood of popular uprisings against Castro; now that there was even less reason to hope for such uprisings, the Kennedys were pushing for operations that relied on them to an even greater extent. Just weeks into the assignment, Lansdale turned to Richard Goodwin, who was representing the White House on the new Cuban Task Force. "You know, Dick, it's impossible."

"What's impossible?"

"There is no way you can overthrow Castro without a strong, indigenous political opposition. And there is no such opposition, either in Cuba or outside of it." Lansdale went ahead anyway, evidently never sharing his reservations with the Kennedys.

In early November 1961, President Kennedy signed off on Operation Mongoose. In concert with the CIA's Project ZR/RIFLE, a new unit approved by the Kennedy administration to undertake "executive action" on Castro and other enemies of state, Mongoose grew into a vast and protracted venture. Mongoose would further tarnish the CIA's reputation, already shaky after the Bay of Pigs, as a "rogue" outfit specializing in nefarious misdeeds. In fact, Mongoose was entirely a creation of the Kennedy administration. "Everyone involved in Mongoose knew it was a Kennedy operation," said CIA veteran Sam Halpern. "This did not have anything to do with the United States of America; it had to do with the Kennedy name, the Kennedy escutcheon. That reputation was blemished in the Bay of Pigs, and, goddamn it, they were going to get even." Robert Kennedy told the CIA that Mongoose was to be "the top priority in the United States government—all else is secondary—no time, money, effort, or manpower is to be spared."

When results were not immediate, Robert Kennedy railed at those responsible for failing to achieve more. Richard Bissell was among those who found himself on the receiving end of Kennedy ire. Bissell, still serving as director of operations, was called into the White House to be "chewed out." He was in constant contact with the Kennedys that fall, updating both brothers on CIA progress, even calling Robert at Hyannis Port a number of times over Thanksgiving weekend of 1961 to let him know where efforts stood. "I never lost sight of the irony that the same president who had canceled the air strikes and ruled out open intervention was now having his brother put tremendous pressure on the agency to accomplish even more."

* * *

THE DAY AFTER Thanksgiving, November 24, the CIA's inspector general, Lyman Kirkpatrick, delivered a 170-page internal report on the Bay of Pigs disaster to Allen Dulles and Richard Bissell, who read it with dismay. The inspector general's report was briefer than the Taylor Report, but far more eviscerating. Where Taylor's main criticism of the CIA pointed to the agency's failure to communicate effectively to the president, Kirkpatrick ripped into virtually every aspect of the operation, from flaws in the brigade's military training ("A worse training site could hardly have been chosen than the one in Guatemala") to missteps in recruiting the political leadership of the Revolutionary Council. The project was marked by bad planning surpassed only by worse execution, claimed Kirkpatrick. In response to the excuse that Kennedy's cancellation of the D-Day strike caused the failure, Kirkpatrick offered the back of his hand. The whole operation was so riddled with incompetence, nothing short of a miracle could have saved it.

Many of his CIA colleagues suspected the tone of Kirkpatrick's report—a "hatchet job," Allen Dulles called it—reflected its author's bitterness about events that had nothing to do with the Bay of Pigs. An ambitious career CIA officer, Kirkpatrick had once been in line for a high position in the agency, perhaps Bissell's job of deputy director of operations, possibly even Dulles's as director. But in 1952, while on assignment in Bangkok, he had contracted polio and was confined ever after to a wheelchair. Without use of his legs he also lost his chance to reach the top. "I think he never forgave himself or the rest of the community for that," said Sam Halpern. "He was no longer a key player, although they kept him in senior jobs."

FOUR DAYS AFTER receiving the blistering inspector general's report—which he himself had directed Kirkpatrick to undertake—Allen Dulles returned to the new CIA campus in Langley, Virginia. Two years had passed since the November day he and President Eisenhower laid the cornerstone for the building. The headquarters was nearly complete now, and CIA staff had begun to move into its vast acreage. Dulles had devoted much of his time over the previous months to the final touches on the building, right down to details of office decor, though he knew he would never occupy the director's office himself. In fact, this day, Tuesday, November 28, was to be his last as director of the Central Intelligence Agency.

Just before 11:00 A.M., the presidential helicopter came fluttering up the river from Washington and landed near the new building. Dulles waited for Kennedy in the lobby, seven hundred CIA employees fanning out behind him. Despite all that had occurred between Kennedy and Dulles, the two men remained on friendly terms. Kennedy blamed the CIA for the Bay of Pigs, but he was unfailingly civil to the director in person. "I talked to him a great deal about it afterwards," Dulles later recalled in an interview, "and while I did have a feeling that maybe he thought I had let him down, there never was one harsh or unkind word said to me by him at any time thereafter." Dulles himself never spoke badly of Kennedy, either, though he believed the failure of the invasion was largely the president's doing.

"Your successes are unheralded—your failures trumpeted," Kennedy told Dulles in front of the crowd as he presented the outgoing director with the National Security Medal. "I sometimes have that feeling myself." A few minutes later, the president was back in the helicopter, rising over the new building, and Allen Dulles was out of a job. "Allen Dulles has left the political arena," reported Moscow News Service, "and no honest man is likely to regret it." The following day at the White House, with Dulles standing nearby, Kennedy swore in John A. McCone, a Republican businessman and former Eisenhower appointee from Los Angeles, as Dulles's replacement.

In his speech at the CIA, Kennedy had flattered Dulles by assuring him that his work would be viewed kindly "in the long sweep of history," but, in fact, this would not be so. The long sweep of history, much like the short sweep, would value success over failure, and a failure of the magnitude of the Bay of Pigs overshadowed all that Dulles had accomplished before or anything he might do after.

RICHARD BISSELL WAS next on the chopping block. He was supposed to have departed before the end of 1961, but John McCone asked him to stay on a while longer to tie up loose ends. McCone even offered Bissell several other positions in the CIA, including deputy director of science and technology, but Bissell declined; he preferred a dignified exit to an obvious demotion. In any event, the CIA had lost its glow to Bissell, and he had lost his glow to Washington. He resigned in February 1962.

McCone, in the best CIA tradition, held a farewell dinner for him at the Alibi Club.

On February 28, Dulles wrote to Bissell, thanking him for "many unique contributions you have made to the development of intelligence collection." Bissell, perhaps recalling the letter he had written from the *Sea Witch* in the summer of 1954 to accept Dulles's offer of employment, wrote back to assure Dulles "that these have been among the best years of my life."

Leaving the CIA was difficult for Bissell, but as usual he kept his feelings buried. It was his wife who took it hardest. "I think that whole period was very hard for my mom," Bissell's daughter, Ann, later recalled. "She knew more than we did obviously, and she was very supportive. She kept him busy with people coming for dinner to take the pressure off, and made weekends nice." As for her own feelings as a girl, Ann Bissell says, "I just remember being very, very sad."

Some of the sadness was lifted on March 1, when Bissell went to the White House one last time to see the president. As Bissell's family looked on, President Kennedy presented him, as he had Dulles, with the National Security Medal. Ann Bissell would never forget Kennedy's graciousness. He spoke to her directly, asking whether things had been difficult for her at school after the Bay of Pigs. "Your father is truly brilliant," Kennedy assured her. "A great contributor to history."

25

"A Man Who Knows"

Spring–Autumn 1962

Havana, Spring 1962

AT THE END of March 1962, Fidel Castro put the imprisoned men of Brigade 2506 on trial. For three days, they were marched into the sun-baked courtyard of Principe Castle to face a five-man tribunal. Nearly a year had passed since the invasion. Castro hoped to use the trial to remind the world of America's perfidy and score propaganda points against the imperialists. For the accused, the trial would be a test of courage and will. The men had no idea what Castro meant to do with them. They knew only what he wanted them to do for him—stand and denounce America. That each man's fate might be tied to how well he fulfilled Castro's wishes could be assumed. Certainly Castro was not above executing men he deemed uncooperative. Five brigadistas, in fact, had already been shot after Castro identified them as criminal consorts of Batista.

Living conditions for the brigademen had deteriorated following a brief window of comfort the previous June. Over the summer, most of the men had been transferred from the new hospital to Principe Castle, a grim prison that loomed on a hill over Havana. Originally built as a fortress by the Spanish, Principe was nearly two hundred years old, and appeared even older—more Inquisition than Colonial: stone dungeons with thick, damp walls, snarling guard dogs, scurrying rats. The toilet was a hole in the ground. The food was tasteless gruel. Infectious diseases were rampant.

The men of the brigade could not expect the trial to be anything close to fair, certainly not after the attorney supposedly representing them referred to his clients as cowards and traitors. A parade of witnesses for the prosecution approached the microphone in front of the tribunal and disparaged them in even worse language. The brigade sat in rows of chairs in the courtyard under a beating sun, erect, unflinching. One by one, they refused to testify. Pepe San Román set the tone when he was called up. *Me abstengo*, he told the tribunal. *I abstain*.

One man did raise his hand to speak. The tribunal called on him. "Request permission to pee," said the man.

On April 7, 1962, the imprisoned men of Brigade 2506 were sentenced by the tribunal to thirty years of hard labor. The sentence could be overturned only by payment of an "indemnification." The price on each man's head depended on his rank and position. San Román, Artime, and Oliva were valued at $500,000 apiece. Another 211 men were put at $100,000. From there it stepped down to $50,000, then $25,000. The total price tag came to about $62 million, to be delivered in cash—Yankee dollars.

A week after the verdict, Castro released 60 injured men as a goodwill gesture, making clear he expected their indemnities to be paid before he released any more. Another 4 men were released when their families privately paid Castro's price. This left 1,113 men.

In late May, all whose ransom had been set at $100,000, as well as the three whose price was $500,000, were flown to the Isle of Pines, a sandy and desolate twelve-hundred-square-mile island fifty miles off the coast of Cuba. The Isle of Pines was the site of Modelo Prison, a place even more forbidding than Principe. For the next eight months, the men would remain there, surrounded by cement walls, guarded by high, gray towers, receiving few visitors, no mail, little contact of any sort with the outside world. As far as they knew, they had been forgotten.

Washington, D.C./New York/Havana, Summer 1962

AT LEAST ONE group, the Cuban Families Committee, did not forget. Founded in the summer of 1961, shortly after the collapse of the Tractors for Freedom negotiations, the committee represented loved ones of the brigademen still imprisoned by Castro. The committee was chaired by Álvaro Sánchez Jr., father of a brigade soldier. Berta Barreto, a citizen of Havana and mother of a prisoner, served as the group's de facto representative inside Cuba. A former prisoner named Harry Williams joined the committee when he arrived in Miami with the group of sixty injured men released by Castro.

In mid-June 1962, Harry Williams took a trip to Washington and found himself sitting in the office of the attorney general. Williams explained the difficulty the committee was encountering in raising the necessary funds. Robert Kennedy listened sympathetically. He and his brother wanted the prisoners out almost as much as the committee did, but the fact remained that the U.S. government could not directly involve itself in securing their release. Certainly America could not pay a ransom to Fidel Castro.

Nothing prevented the attorney general from offering some free legal advice, though. "What you need is a man who knows how to deal with Castro," Robert Kennedy told Williams. "You need someone who can represent you. I think I know of a lawyer who might help."

Robert Kennedy had never met James B. Donovan when he recommended him. But he knew him by reputation as a savvy negotiator comfortable in the gray world of secret operations, and the sort of man willing to take on difficult cases. Six months earlier, in January, Donovan had distinguished himself as a first-class Cold War brinksman by arranging a dramatic prisoner exchange between the United States and the Soviet Union. Donovan managed to trade a Soviet spy named Rudolph Abel, whom he was representing, for Francis Gary Powers, the U-2 pilot shot down in 1960, and a Yale student named Frederic Pryor, who had been accused of spying by the Soviets. The dramatic exchange had occurred on a cold January morning in Berlin, with Powers and Abel walking past each other on the Glienicke Bridge.

Donovan had worked as legal counsel for the OSS (a wartime predecessor of the CIA) as a young man, but he had long since entered private practice in New York. Though a graduate of Harvard Law School, he was no white-shoe lawyer. He had been born into the middle-class Roman Catholic Bronx neighborhood of Mott Haven and lived with his wife and four children in Brooklyn. He was short and stocky, with receding white hair that made him look older than his forty-six years. "He is a cigarette smoker and a moderate drinker" is how the *New York Times* described him in an article some months later. "He plays golf in the 90's and collects rare books and illuminated manuscripts." Most important for the task at hand, he was endowed with a strong will and a shrewd mind.

On the afternoon of June 20, several members of the Cuban Families Committee met Donovan at his law offices in Manhattan and explained their $62 million problem. They needed his help, they told him, but they had no money to pay for his services. Donovan heard them out, asked a few questions, and told them he would represent them pro bono, assuming he could personally get assurances he would not be violating U.S. law (such as the Logan Act) or otherwise acting against the interest of the government.

On the morning of July 2, Donovan traveled to Washington to meet the attorney general. Robert Kennedy bluntly warned Donovan to expect failure. But he also assured him that the president was in favor of the effort and would support it. The negotiations could proceed, in Donovan's words, as "a private humanitarian effort" with which the U.S. government expressed "sympathy." That was enough for Donovan. He was in.

Jim Donovan never entered a trial or a negotiation without intense preparation. In this case he began by studying everything about Castro he could get his hands on. He read articles about the Bay of Pigs, books about Castro, speeches of Castro. He studied, too, the record of the failed Tractors for Freedom negotiations, marking in his mind where they had gone wrong.

While preparing for negotiations with Castro, and in addition to his other duties as an attorney, Donovan took on one more heavy load in the middle of August. He announced that he intended to run as New York's Democratic candidate for the U.S. Senate, pitting himself against the formidable Republican incumbent, Jacob Javits. With a late start and little money in his campaign coffers, Donovan's chances were poor. But he was a man, evidently, who liked his odds long and interesting.

AT THE END of August, Jim Donovan flew to Cuba to meet Fidel Castro. He was accompanied by Álvaro Sánchez Jr., president of the Cuban Families Committee. Though this visit was officially a private affair between the Cuban Families Committee and the government of Cuba, the CIA gave Donovan money for expenses and promised communications support. Donovan was put up in Havana by Berta Barreto. It was she who had arranged the meeting between Donovan and Castro.

During the course of Donovan's stay, armed guards were stationed outside the stone wall of Berta Barreto's villa, perhaps to keep Donovan safe or, more likely, to keep an eye on him. Havana was awash that summer in rumors of another American-sponsored invasion. Donovan learned by watching the news on Havana television that he himself had been implicated as a possible "decoy" of anti-Castro forces, whatever that meant.

The Cubans were not far off base in anticipating new attacks from America. Operation Mongoose, with Lansdale and Harvey at the helm, was engaged in dozens of plots and devices that summer to overthrow Castro, by force or by farce. Some of these efforts deployed the usual methods of industrial sabotage—blowing up infrastructure, burning down sugar crops, eroding Fidel Castro's support by lowering the standard of living in Cuba. Others were of the nuttier, LSD-laced-cigar variety; indeed, some of the plots seem to have been hatched on a hallucinogen-fueled bender. One idea was to surface a submarine in Havana Harbor in the middle of the night. The sub would shoot exploding shells over the water to paint the sky with fire and give the appearance of the Second Coming. Meanwhile, the CIA's propaganda machine would have spread a rumor around town that Castro was the Antichrist. One CIA wag memorably tagged this scheme as "elimination by illumination."

Donovan and Castro met in the Presidential Palace for four hours on August 31. Donovan came with a list of discussion points, starting with icebreaking small talk. "Hospitality and honor by the visit" was the first item on his list. He also made a note to mention his Irish heritage, a subject he apparently believed would interest Castro. From here, he moved on to more serious matters.

"Private Citizen—sincere—no motives," Donovan had scribbled on his paper, followed a few lines later by "No 62 million. . . . Best no sell humans."

This was the heart of his message to Castro: $62 million in cash was out of the question. Not only was it financially impossible to raise that kind of money, but also it was politically unviable for any group in the United States to attempt to do so. A more practical and palatable means of payment, offered Donovan, would be in products such as foodstuffs that equaled the total indemnity in fair market value but could pass as humanitarian aid. This would make the deal easier for the American public to stomach and would win Castro admiration among his people. The products Donovan had in mind included skim milk, lard, canned fruit, soybean and corn seed oil, even chickens. "Now, this permits a certain flexibility," he told Castro. "If you choose to use this for propaganda purposes, I will remain silent. Also, the Cuban government can use these products commercially, if it so chooses."

Donovan finished and waited for Castro's response. The prime minister lit a cigar and drew in smoke. "I am aware that the mission you have undertaken is filled with difficulties," Castro said. "But there are also difficulties from our point of view." The damage the invasion had caused Cuba was incalculable, he told Donovan, and "all the money in the United States" would not be just compensation. Puffing on his cigar, Castro began to rant against U.S. leaders and journalists who were "poisoning" Americans against Cuba. Donovan wisely declined to engage Castro in a debate about the evils of America's press or politicians. They were here, he reminded Castro, to discuss a distinct and practical issue. "Two peoples can work together to solve a problem, you know."

Donovan was betting Castro wanted to play ball—and he was right. Castro came around to making a very important concession: he would agree to accept products, mainly food and medicine. He would be satisfied with products totaling a fair market price of $53 million. He would only require cash, in the amount of $2.9 million, to compensate him for the sixty injured men already released.

WHEN NEGOTIATIONS THAT first day concluded after four hours, Álvaro Sánchez, having sat through them white-knuckled, could hardly believe what Donovan had already accomplished. The attorney had gone into the meeting with nothing and had come out with a favorable arrangement. "He's the greatest poker player in the world," enthused Sánchez.

Donovan and Castro met again the next day for two hours to iron out details before Donovan returned to New York. "Remember, don't say anything good about me in public," Donovan joked to Castro after revealing his intention to run for the Senate. "A couple of friends like you and I won't need enemies."

"Don't worry," said Castro. "We men in public life understand these things."

Donovan returned to New York on September 2 and got to work. A few days later, he received a wish list from Cuba containing products Castro deemed acceptable for the indemnity package. Despite occasional snags, negotiations moved forward over the following weeks as

Donovan shuttled to Cuba between Senate campaign appearances in New York.

Suddenly, late in October, everything came to a standstill. Not just in Donovan's negotiations with the Cubans, but in the world at large. The human race held its collective breath.

26

"Abyss of Destruction"

October 14–November 24, 1962

Washington, D.C., October 14–16

IT WAS RICHARD BISSELL'S spy plane that saw the missiles first. On the morning of October 14, 1962, a U-2 passing 70,000 feet over Cuba captured nearly a thousand images with its telephoto lens. Two days later, the CIA's National Photographic Interpretation Center completed its analysis of the photographs. The results were staggering. There were Soviet missiles in Cuba. At least two 70-foot medium-range ballistic missiles were visible in the U-2 photographs, one with a range of 630 miles, the other with a range of 1,100, both capable of hitting and destroying large patches of America east of the Mississippi. And there was evidence, including launch pads and missile trailers, of many more to come.

The president was in his pajamas when McGeorge Bundy alerted him to the NPIC's findings on the morning of October 16. Kennedy picked up the phone receiver and called his brother Robert. "We have some big trouble. I want you over here." He told Bundy to call an emergency meeting of his National Security team later that morning, assembling what would come to be known over the coming days as Ex Comm (Executive Committee of the National Security Council).

Thus began two weeks during which the United States and Russia came to the brink of nuclear war. For several days that October, Americans went to bed at night unsure that the world would still be there when they woke up.

History recalls the Cuban Missile Crisis as John Kennedy's finest moment, and for good reason. With the fate of hundreds of millions of people (Americans, Russians, Cubans) in his hands, he charted a course that led, after many twists and turns, to the Soviets pulling their missiles out of Cuba. No doubt Kennedy's firm and measured performance during the crisis owed something—as Arthur Schlesinger pointed out—to the valuable lessons he had learned during the Bay of Pigs. When the Joint Chiefs, eager to avenge the Bay of Pigs and destroy Castro, advised an all-out aerial bombardment of Cuba, to be followed by a ground attack, Kennedy knew to weigh their advice skeptically. The chiefs' solution would likely have triggered a nuclear war. Kennedy steered his advisers to a far less antagonistic "quarantine" and saved humanity more grief than it had ever known.

What history sometimes overlooks, though, is the role John Kennedy played in creating the missile crisis in the first place. Starting with the Bay of Pigs and continuing through a succession of covert (but none too secret) actions against Castro's government, Kennedy successfully convinced Castro that the U.S. government intended to destroy him—which, of course, it did. Before the Bay of Pigs, one might have reasonably dismissed Castro's concerns about American aggression as paranoid; afterward, to deny them was absurd. Fear of American attack was the prime motive to both the Soviets and the Cubans for installing missiles in Cuba. "It was clear to me," Nikita Khrushchev would later write, "that we might very well lose Cuba if we didn't take some decisive steps in her defense." Castro accepted the obvious risk of provoking the United States by taking the missiles. But if they drew an American attack, figured Castro, such an attack was probably coming anyway. And how sweet the day—just weeks away—when the little island of Cuba could enjoy the protection of dozens of nuclear missiles pointing at the United States of America.

New York, October 22

JIM DONOVAN HAD begun campaigning full-time as a candidate for U.S. Senate the same morning the U-2 first photographed the missiles in Cuba. With a tiny staff and just $25,000 in his coffers—mostly provided by himself—his chances of beating the well-funded Senator Javits were slim. His role in the prisoner exchange had raised his national profile, but it was also a distraction. Cuba was all anybody wanted to talk about with him.

Like the rest of America, Donovan first learned of the missile crisis on Monday, October 22. He was touring upstate New York, battling rain squalls, snow flurries, and laryngitis. That evening, at seven o'clock, he was in Otsego County about to give a speech at Oneonta State Teachers College when the television networks interrupted their usual broadcasts to carry the president live. Donovan stood alongside faculty and students to watch what may be the most frightening presidential address in history.

Kennedy began by delivering the ominous news that Soviet missile bases had been discovered in Cuba. "The purpose of these bases can be none other than to provide a nuclear strike capability against the Western Hemisphere." Warning that America would "regard any nuclear missile launched from Cuba against any nation in the Western Hemisphere as an attack by the Soviet Union on the United States, requiring full retaliatory response," Kennedy called upon Khrushchev to remove the missiles promptly and "move the world back from the abyss of destruction." In the meantime, the United States would impose a naval quarantine to prevent any new military equipment from entering Cuba. Failure to heed the quarantine or to remove the missiles would provoke war, for there was "one path we shall never choose, and that is the path of surrender or submission."

Three days later, Donovan was campaigning in the Finger Lakes region of New York when another highly dramatic moment was broadcast on television. The pictures showed Adlai Stevenson in the Security Council at the United Nations. The ambassador was reprising his role as defender of American integrity. He even came equipped with photographic props, just as he had at the start of the Bay of Pigs operation. His exchange with Ambassador Zorin of the Soviet Union nearly erased the humiliation of 1961.

"Do you, Ambassador Zorin, deny that the USSR has placed, and is placing, medium- and intermediate-range missiles and sites in Cuba—yes or no?"

Zorin, snidely: "I am not in an American courtroom, sir, and I do not wish to answer a question put to me in the manner in which a prosecutor does."

"You are in the courtroom of world opinion right now," responded Stevenson, "and you can answer yes or no."

"You will receive your answer in due course. Do not worry."

"I am prepared to wait for my answer until hell freezes over, if that is your decision."

John Kennedy, watching Stevenson on television in the Oval Office, was impressed. "I never knew Adlai had it in him."

When Stevenson brought out the U-2 photographs and set them on wooden easels for all the chamber to see, Zorin insinuated that they were fakes. He reminded his fellow members of Stevenson's performance during the Bay of Pigs. "He who has lied once will not be believed a second time," said Zorin. "Accordingly, Mr. Stevenson, we shall not look at your photographs." But others did look, and this time the pictures told only the truth.

The resolution of the missile crisis began on Sunday, October 28, when an announcer on Radio Moscow read a letter written by Premier Khrushchev to President Kennedy. As translations of the letter began arriving at the White House that Sunday morning, a fine autumn day was beginning in Washington, and it quickly became spectacular. The Soviets had agreed to dismantle the missiles. "I felt like laughing or yelling or dancing," said Don Wilson of the USIA, echoing the jubilance of millions of Americans. The sun was shining, the leaves were turning, and the world, having teetered on the brink of catastrophe, had somehow survived.

NOBODY WAS HAPPIER to see the crisis resolved than the families of the brigade. They knew the prisoners were likely to be among the first to die the moment a shooting war began. (In fact, though the families did not know it, Castro had planted explosives around Principe and intended to detonate them at the first sign of American aggression.) The families watched anxiously, wondering if the crisis spelled the end of their hopes. By the time it was over, they were more determined than ever to get the men out.

A week after the end of the missile crisis, on November 6, Jim Donovan lost his bid for the New York Senate seat. The good news was that he was now free to rededicate himself to bringing home the prisoners. Incredibly, he managed to pick up more or less where he had left off. Regardless of the several weeks that had just passed, much of which Castro spent in an underground bunker prepared to see his country blown off the face of the earth, Castro was still interested in making a deal.

So was the U.S. government. Robert Kennedy initially believed the missile crisis was a deterrent, but after talking to representatives of the Cuban Families Committee he came around. On Saturday, November

24, Kennedy met with Álvaro Sánchez at the Waldorf-Astoria in New York. Sánchez had recently had an opportunity to visit the brigade in prison and he tried to impress upon the attorney general a sense of urgency. The men were poorly nourished, and many were ill. They went weeks at a time without exposure to sunlight. "I'm a cattleman, Mr. Attorney General, and these men look like animals who are going to die. If you are going to rescue these men, this is the time because if you wait you will be liberating corpses." There would never be a better time to act. President Kennedy was riding high in the polls after the missile crisis; if ever he could afford to spend a little political capital to bring the prisoners out of Cuba, it was *now*. "Bring them home to their families by Christmas," pleaded Sánchez.

By Christmas: one month away. Given the details still to be hammered out in Donovan's negotiations with Castro, and the indemnity to be raised, a month was hardly enough time. And, of course, everything depended on Castro's cooperation—and who could guarantee that?

Robert Kennedy ran a serious risk in making a promise he could not keep. Failure would leave many thousands of Cubans more disappointed and heartbroken than they already were, and cause political havoc for his brother. But Robert was moved by Sánchez's appeal. Getting the men to their families by Christmas would be a gesture of goodwill from the Kennedys to the men who had suffered on America's behalf.

"You are right," said Robert Kennedy. "I think this is the moment." An assistant to the attorney general, Edwin Guthman, reminded the boss they could not possibly bring the men home in one month. But Kennedy had made up his mind. "We will."

From that moment, the clock began to tick on the final chapter of the Bay of Pigs story, racing toward a finale nearly as dramatic as the invasion itself.

27

"There Are No Obstacles"

Christmas 1962

Washington, D.C., December

UNTIL THAT DAY in late November when Robert Kennedy promised to bring the brigade home by Christmas, the U.S. government had assiduously avoided playing a direct role in the prisoner exchange deal with Castro. Even after the attorney general's meeting with the Cuban Families Committee at the Waldorf-Astoria, the administration remained officially aloof—an enthusiastically interested party, rooting from the sidelines but hands-off. Suddenly that pretense was all but dropped. Donovan was still the front man. Behind him now, though, was a team of amped-up New Frontier hotshots hustling to support his effort. It was as if, overnight, Donovan's horse and buggy had been traded for a race car, complete with crack pit crew and sponsorship.

After getting the go-ahead from President Kennedy on Monday, December 3, the attorney general called together several of his top assistants at the Justice Department. They were an exceptional group of lawyers. Many of them had been involved in the administration's attempts to enforce civil rights laws in the South and had been steeled for action by the bloody violence in Birmingham, Alabama, and Oxford, Mississippi. Louis Oberdorfer, assistant attorney general in charge of Justice's tax division, would be chief of the prisoner exchange operation. He would work under the guidance of Deputy Attorney General Nicholas Katzenbach and with the assistance of Joseph F. Dolan and John B. Jones. These men and a number of others would virtually live at the Justice Department over the next month, sleeping on couches, sometimes working straight through the night. They were joined by a roster of talent from other government agencies, including Mitchell Rogovin from the IRS, Stanley Surrey from the Treasury Department, and Mike Miskovsky, an attorney from the CIA. Assistance also would be lent by representatives of the State Department, the Civil Aeronautics Board, the Interstate Commerce Commission, the Department of Agriculture, the Immigration and Naturalization Service, the Department of Commerce, and the U.S. Coast Guard as the Justice Department sought permits and statutory exemptions to allow vast quantities of baby food and drugs to travel across the country and end up in Cuba.

By the time the attorney general got directly involved, Jim Donovan had changed the terms of the deal slightly. He convinced the Cubans that for shipping purposes, it made more sense to concentrate on pharmaceuticals than on food products. Cuba was a country deprived of basic medicines, as Donovan himself had discovered when he suffered an attack of bursitis while in Cuba and could not find the pain reliever he needed, so Castro's people would benefit greatly.

None of the men at Justice knew anything about the pharmaceutical industry, much less of the logistics required to ship tons of product across the country and overseas. They learned on the go, just as they had learned earlier that autumn how to command National Guard units after the president ordered the University of Mississippi to admit a young black student named James Meredith. This time no bullets were flying through the air, but there was the same kind of urgency, the same need for quick decisions that had to be acted upon immediately.

The urgency was dictated by the Christmas deadline. Christmas was in some sense arbitrary, since it was self-imposed, but once established, it became absolute and inviolable. This owed something to the concern the men shared with the prisoners' families following the missile crisis—getting the brigade out of Cuba was a now-or-never proposition. But the attitude also was a function of temperament, the no-excuse, must-do attitude that came from the top down. "It wasn't a question of whether or not we were going to do it; we were going to do it," recalled John E. Nolan Jr., an attorney who played a significant role in the effort to bring the men home. "It was a question of how the hell we could get through on the time schedule, which would seem to any reasonable observer to be completely impossible." In fact, said Nolan, the deadline is probably what made the effort succeed. "This was the sort of thing you'd have a better chance of doing in three weeks than two years, if you can get everybody revved up—if you can get a tempo established where there are no obstacles that cannot be overcome."

John Nolan would later join the Department of Justice as a close assistant to Robert Kennedy, but at the start of the prisoner exchange operation he was in private practice at the Washington law firm of Steptoe & Johnson. A former Marine who fought in Korea, he had worked with the Kennedys on the 1960 election, running the team of advance men. On Friday, December 7, Robert Kennedy called Nolan and asked him to come over to the Justice Department to meet with Lou Oberdorfer and the others. Would he be willing to devote the rest of the month to bringing home the prisoners? Nolan did not think twice.

In addition to Nolan, three other Washington lawyers were enlisted pro bono. These were E. Barrett Prettyman Jr., John Douglas, and, last but not least (in this author's opinion), Raymond J. Rasenberger. All were politically active young men in their midthirties; all were the sort of men who were demonstrably, in the words of Assistant Deputy Attorney General Joe Dolan, "our kind of guy—which around here means a fellow who is a utility infielder, that is, someone who will do anything that he is asked to and will take care of any problem that comes up whether it is emptying the ashtrays or going to see the president."

In the case of this author's father, the assignment came at the end of a busy few months. Ray Rasenberger had done some advance work for John Kennedy during the 1960 campaign, then again in 1962, prior to the midterm elections. His last assignment had been in October 1962 in Seattle, where Kennedy was scheduled to stump for local Democrats. Just before the president was due to arrive, my father realized that he had gotten himself into a terrific jam. In an effort to spread sunshine across the local Democratic machinery, he had promised too many politicians the much-coveted chance to ride in the presidential limousine with Kennedy. He was still trying to figure out how to revoke tactfully some of the invitations when the president suddenly canceled his trip. Instead of flying from Chicago to Milwaukee and Seattle, as planned, the president flew back to Washington, offering the excuse that he'd caught a cold. In fact, Kennedy had gone back to the White House to deal with the Cuban Missile Crisis. Those missiles may have brought the world to the brink of apocalypse, but they were my father's salvation in Seattle.

* * *

EVERYONE WHO WORKED on the project put his life on hold the month before Christmas; days ran from early morning until late night. Ray Rasenberger left his wife to care for five children, ages eight and under (including this newly born author). For John Nolan, the effort meant missing the birth of his fifth child, a daughter born on December 16. No one doubted the importance of the cause. It offered the chance to return more than a thousand men to their families for Christmas, and to restore some of the honor America lost when it had left them on the shores of Cuba.

"My brother made a mistake," Robert Kennedy told a group of representatives from the American Pharmaceutical Association on December 7. "These men fought well; the disaster was no fault of theirs. They are our responsibility." The Kennedys were both applauded and decried for being hard-boiled politicians, but there was in both men, and in those who worked for them, a frankly sentimental streak that fueled their efforts to bring the brigade out of Cuba. "Wait until you see the men get off the plane on Christmas Eve," Robert told the pharmaceutical executives. "Then you'll know it was worth it."

The attorney general provided the inspiration, but the grunt work of raising millions of dollars in contributions was taken up mainly by the private attorneys. These four men not only put more hands on deck, but also allowed Justice to maintain the pretense that the operation was a private enterprise—a pretense strained by the fact that all moved temporarily into the fourth floor of the Department of Justice, where a dozen new lines were installed to accommodate the increase in telephonic traffic.

Armed with a whopping copy of *Poor's Directory of Business Leaders*, the attorneys were given standard-issue government offices—green paint, desk and chair, and, most important, telephone. *Poor's* listed both work numbers and home numbers for the presidents of every major pharmaceutical or baby food manufacturer in the country. The attorneys cold-called executives, reaching them at work during the day, at home in the evening. If they could not find a number they needed, they contacted the FBI, and the bureau found it for them.

The pitch became routine. They were calling, they told the executives, from the office of the attorney general regarding a matter very close to both the president and his brother. Although Katzenbach repeatedly emphasized that the contributors could expect nothing in the way of special favors, mentioning the president's personal interest usually got the executive's attention, even in cases where the executive was not a particular fan of John Kennedy. "Some of the CEOs were obviously strong Republicans so initially hostile, others were sympathetic from the start," recalled Ray Rasenberger. "You got all kinds of reactions, but in the end most of them came around." The attorneys appealed, first, to the executive's humanitarian impulse—how good it would feel to see those brave young men out of Cuba—then to his appreciation for good public relations. In 1961, as now, American pharmaceutical companies were under a great deal of public scrutiny for exorbitant drug pricing, and much in need of good publicity.

If none of this was sufficient to inspire the executive's charity, there was the extra incentive of a very good tax break. The IRS was allowing the companies to write off contributions at retail market prices. Since pharmaceutical companies sold their products at huge markups, this amounted to a potential windfall, especially in the case of duds gathering dust in warehouses. What better use for these than to send them to Fidel Castro?

"We were taking everything as fast as we could get it," said John Nolan. It did not much matter to them what it was. Nolan recalled reaching one chief executive of a food company at home as the man was throwing a dinner party; over the phone, the executive offered millions of dollars' worth of a soluble starch, used for baking, that had evidently failed to catch on in the American marketplace. "This was a product that did not work," Nolan said. "Nobody was interested in a product you could make bread out of by putting water in it, or whatever the hell it was." There was no entry for soluble starch on Castro's wish list, "but of course Listerine wasn't on the wish list, either," said Nolan. "We took $500,000 of Listerine. We took $75,000 of Ex-Lax. We took fifty-seven different kinds of menstrual remedies. We took Guild's Green Mountain Asthmatic Cigarettes." And they took the soluble starch.

Many companies were very generous. Warner-Lambert donated nearly $3.4 million of supplies, Merck about $2.5 million. On the other side of the spectrum, Empire State Thermometer Company offered $26,000 worth of merchandise, and Crown Surgical Manufacturing Corporation gave $144. Altogether, nearly 200 corporations gave something. A large chart on the wall in Oberdorfer's office tracked drug and food contributions in blue and red crayon as they came in. Before the merchandise drive was complete, the chart would record pledges of $23 million in pharmaceuticals, $7 million in surgical and dental equipment, $9 million in powdered milk, and $14 million in baby food.

In addition to gathering products to send to Cuba to pay the indemnity, the men at Justice faced two other challenges. One was arranging transportation of the products to Cuba. As Barrett Prettyman prevailed upon trucking companies, railroad companies, and airlines to help move the freight without charge—and with great speed—during the height of the Christmas season, the American Red Cross agreed to oversee the effort. Its experience in disaster relief made the organization uniquely suited to navigating through a fast-moving logistical storm.

The Red Cross was a lifesaver on another critical matter: securing a letter of credit to give to the Cuban government. Fidel Castro had agreed to release the hostages once he received 20 percent of the shipment, which was about the most the Americans could realistically get to him before Christmas, no matter how fast the men at Justice worked. In return, Castro wanted the letter of credit guaranteeing cash for any shortfall in the final shipment. Lining up a financial institution willing to issue a $53 million letter of credit on short notice was no small feat, and it was further complicated by U.S. trade embargoes against Cuba. The bank issuing the letter of credit to Castro would have to be foreign. On December 14, Nicholas Katzenbach flew to Montreal to negotiate with the Royal Bank of Canada. After some reluctance, the Royal Bank agreed to issue the letter, provided that a U.S. bank agreed to cover the risk. In short order, following emergency meetings of their boards of directors, the Bank of America and Morgan Guaranty Trust issued their own letters of credit for $26.5 million each—but only after the American Red Cross, in turn, guaranteed the delivery with an insurance bond.

Throughout these negotiations, Robert Kennedy was a constant presence, cajoling and mollifying contributors as necessary. He regularly called Oberdorfer for an update on where matters stood and weighed in on the countless questions and hypotheticals. Was it necessary to hit 20 percent on the nose? Would Castro accept Desenex? What would they do with all the product if the deal fell through? "The Attorney General called Katzenbach about substituting something else for peanut oil," read Lou Oberdorfer's phone log for December 20, at 6:41 P.M. "Mr. Katzenbach said it could be done."

Later, some news reports would suggest that Robert Kennedy himself brokered the deal with Castro. But that was not so. For all the effort the U.S. government put into making the deal happen, the release of the prisoners depended on the relationship between two men: Fidel Castro and Jim Donovan.

GOODS WERE ALREADY starting to arrive in Florida when Jim Donovan returned to Cuba on December 18 to iron out the details of the deal with Castro. Essentially, it was the same deal he and Castro had brokered before the missile crisis, but the time had come to finalize it.

Before he left, Donovan learned that one of Castro's right-hand men had a child who needed a medicine not available in Cuba. Donovan arranged to have ten vials of the medicine sent to him from Bethesda Naval Hospital. He hand-delivered these when he arrived in Havana. The medicine said more than his words ever could: *this is what we can do for you.*

Castro was in good spirits and welcomed Donovan back with a humidor of fine Cuban cigars. Nonetheless, the Cuban prime minister expressed skepticism about some of the items the Americans intended to give him. He was wary the Americans would try to put one over on him. Donovan suggested Castro send some of his own men to look over the products that were awaiting shipment from Florida. He hoped to quiet Castro's concerns, but the offer was risky. If Castro's representatives should come back with a negative report, the whole deal could collapse. Even riskier was the chance the Cuban officials would be discovered in Miami by Cuban exiles. Emotions were running high in the Little Havana section of the city. There was no telling what the exiles might do if they found Castro's men in their midst. They might attempt to kill them. They could certainly kill the deal. Castro accepted the offer. He told Donovan he would send a team from the Cuban Red Cross to examine the merchandise.

On the morning of Friday, December 21, four days before Christmas, the letter of credit was formally issued by the Royal Bank of Canada and delivered to Castro. Later that day, Castro and Donovan signed the Memorandum of Agreement.

Three men dressed in the olive uniforms of the Cuban Red Cross flew out of Havana that night, arriving at Miami International Airport at about one o'clock in the morning of December 22. They were met by John Nolan, Barrett Prettyman, and Dr. Leonard Scheele, a former surgeon general of the United States who could speak authoritatively on the merchandise. The Cubans immediately began inspecting the goods, first at the Opa Locka air base, where commercial aircraft had been loaded with some of the products, then at Port Everglades, where a ship called the *African Pilot* carried the rest in its holds. As they watched the three Cubans sniff around the crates and boxes, Nolan and the others suspected the men were not really Red Cross employees but agents of the Cuban government. (In fact, at least one of them, Gilberto Cervantes, was with the Red Cross in Cuba; he was the organization's president.) A few of the items gave the Cubans pause. They failed to see how Alka-Seltzer or Listerine or aspirin, for that matter, solved any medical or nutritional needs in Cuba. John Nolan, a man of measured speech and cool persuasion, managed to make a case for each questionable product to the Cubans' satisfaction. By dawn, the Cubans were ready to pronounce the shipment satisfactory. They would call and deliver the news to Castro at the earliest opportunity, they told Nolan and Prettyman. First, though, they hoped to get some rest. If the Americans did not object, they would check in for a while at the nearby Howard Johnson motel. "We thought we'd go back when you start sending the stuff in," they told Nolan.

This was not what Nolan or the other Americans wanted to hear. "We could not have them in Miami. Think Cuban refugees. Think what they would do if they knew there were three agents of Castro's Cuba in the bosom of our operation." Nolan tried to gently dissuade the men from staying. "We've been with you all night and we've gotten to like you," he told the three Cubans. "And if you've decided you *really* want to stay here, I *think* we can protect you. But I'm not sure of that." The Cubans got the message. They flew home later that morning.

A few hours after their departure, the *African Pilot*, loaded with the first batch of merchandise, set off for Cuba. In Havana that night, Castro and Donovan stayed up late, drinking champagne and smoking. The deal was done. Almost.

THE NEXT DAY, Sunday, December 23, it nearly fell apart.

The day began well enough. Early in the morning, the brigade prisoners on the Isle of Pines were roused from their cells and informed they were leaving. For days they had been hearing rumors from the guards that Castro intended to free them, but they had dismissed these as a cruel joke, at least at first. It was a good sign when they were permitted to go outside to get sun, the first opportunity to do so in weeks. Prison officials were apparently shaping them up before releasing them. Even better, the food began to dramatically improve in the latter days of December, following months of paltry and tasteless rations of macaroni. ("The plate of slop they call food used to be our crystal ball," a prisoner later explained. "When the food would get better, we would say they must be making progress with the negotiations.")

And then, Sunday morning, they found themselves being marched to airplanes, and a short while later they were stepping onto the airfield at San Antonio de los Baños, where they were given new shoes and clothes, freshly made cots to rest in, and a meal of chicken and beef and pork—delicacies the likes of which they had not tasted in months. Armed Cuban soldiers were everywhere, but so were American officials, representatives from the Immigration and Naturalization Service, there to process them for their journey to America. The men walked around in a daze, hardly believing this was happening, hardly trusting their happiness.

John Nolan also landed in San Antonio de Los Baños that morning. He came to assist Donovan with last-minute details. This gave Nolan his first opportunity to meet the brigademen. It also brought his first meeting with Fidel Castro. Nolan and others were eating lunch at the officers' mess when the word went around that Castro was near. "Fidel is coming, Fidel is coming, come, we must meet Fidel!"

Nolan found Castro standing next to Jim Donovan in the middle of an airfield, surrounded by a crowd. No sooner did Donovan introduce him to Castro than four fighter jets—newly acquired Soviet MiGs—swept down over the field. Apparently the Cuban pilots wished to impress the Maximum Leader with their flying prowess. One of the jets swooped down as low as two hundred feet, directly over the heads of the crowd. Everybody, including Castro, hit the ground. "It's the invasion!" Jim Donovan called out loudly enough for most of the crowd to hear when the plane had passed. Not until Castro laughed did anyone else realize it was funny and dare to laugh, too.

The first plane of the airlift, a Pan Am DC-3, left late that afternoon with 107 men aboard. The plane arrived at Homestead Air Force Base in Florida just as the sun was falling below the horizon, burnishing the plane orange. "My God," a woman said with a gasp, "they are really coming now." Only a small crowd had been permitted to wait at Homestead. As floodlights bathed the plane in the falling darkness, the door swung open and the men poured out, hurrying down into the embraces of loved ones, separating from them only to eat again—a hearty American meal of roast beef, mashed potatoes, and ice cream—and change yet again into new wardrobes (khaki trousers and shirts). After handing the men $100 each to start their new lives in America, officials loaded them onto buses that transported them to Dinner Key, an auditorium where thousands of family members and friends had been waiting since early morning.

THAT EVENING, back in Havana, Castro suddenly seemed to have second thoughts. He reminded Donovan that he still had not been paid $2.9 million outstanding for the 60 wounded prisoners released on debit back in April.

Four planes and 426 men had gone. Another 623 prisoners remained in Cuba. Castro gave Donovan an ultimatum: get me what I am owed or the prisoner release will halt.

Now began an extraordinary effort to raise $2.9 million in twelve hours. At 2:00 A.M. John Nolan boarded a plane back to Homestead. Lou Oberdorfer drove onto the tarmac in a jeep to greet him when he landed. Together, Nolan and Oberdorfer went to a safe phone and called Nick Katzenbach to discuss what to do. Katzenbach then placed a call to Robert Kennedy. The time was now 5:00 A.M. on the morning of Christmas Eve. Nolan explained the situation to Kennedy. They needed $2.9 million or the deal was off. "John, what are you going to do now?" the attorney general asked him.

"Well, I'm going to go back."

"Don't you think you ought to wait until you see whether we can get the money or not?"

"No, I think I'll rely on you to do that. . . . I'll just assume that you're going to get it. And I think, really, that's the only way to play it."

"Okay."

Nolan went back to the house at Homestead where Oberdorfer was staying. Nolan shaved, put on a clean shirt, and then flew back to Cuba. "How did it go?" Donovan asked him when he returned to Berta Barreto's house a few hours later, as if Nolan had gone down the street to get a pint of milk.

"Well, I think it's going to be okay."

Donovan did not ask any more questions, clearly deciding to proceed as if everything was going to work out as Nolan said. And it did. That morning, Robert Kennedy raised $1 million with a single phone call to Cardinal Cushing, the Boston archbishop who had delivered the invocation at John Kennedy's inauguration. The rest was gathered within hours. Early that afternoon, just before the banks closed for Christmas Eve, the Royal Bank of Canada issued a check for $2.9 million to its branch in Havana. The check was in Castro's hands by 3:00 P.M.

The planes began to fly again late on the afternoon of Christmas Eve. These landed at Miami International Airport, arriving with blinking lights from the dark sky, like Santa's sleigh, to deliver the balance of the prisoners into the arms of wives and parents and children. That evening there was celebrating all over—in Miami, where the Cuban exiles cried for joy; in Palm Beach, where the president was spending Christmas with his family; in the corridors of the Justice Department, where the men who worked for the attorney general were getting ready to call it a night.

After all the planes had landed, Nick Katzenbach called Hickory Hill, where Robert Kennedy and his family were celebrating Christmas Eve. "Bob, they are all in," Katzenbach said. "It's over."

"That is fine."

"Bob, I don't think I will come in tomorrow."

"Why not?"

"No reason at all, Bob. I'm just not coming in."

Everybody laughed. "All right, you guys," said Kennedy over the phone. "What about Jimmy Hoffa?"

LATE ON CHRISTMAS EVE, John Nolan flew back to Washington with Jim Donovan. The plane dropped Nolan off at Andrews Air Force Base before continuing on to New York with Donovan. A government car was waiting to drive Nolan home to Chevy Chase.

It was nearly three o'clock on Christmas morning when he walked through his front door. The dark house was decorated, the presents under the tree. Everyone was asleep. After checking in on his newborn daughter, he climbed into bed next to his wife for his first real sleep in days.

Three hours later, his wife shook him awake. There was a phone call for him. Still dazed and half asleep, Nolan took the receiver and said Merry Christmas to the president of the United States. "My brother told me you did good work," said John Kennedy. "Thank you."

Miami, December 29

FOR THE LARGER force of government officials and private attorneys who had devoted themselves to the prisoner relief effort that December, the best thanks came a few days after Christmas, on December 29. President Kennedy went to Miami that morning to address the brigade and celebrate the homecoming with the released prisoners. Around Washington, phones began ringing in the middle of the night, summoning men to National Airport by 5:00 A.M. to fly down to join the president at the Orange Bowl Stadium in Miami. No one missed the plane. "Most of us had not seen any prisoners or had any direct contact with the fruit of the labors," recalled John Jones. "I had the feeling it was a very great thing and that it seemed even more important to some of us who had worked on it."

The newspapers were filled with praise for the "wholly extraordinary three-week campaign," as the *New York Times* called it, that these men had pulled off. The operation had yielded the release of 1,113 men, but it had done something else, too, which was demonstrate the American capacity for doing the right thing, and doing it right. Not a bad antidote to the fiasco at the Bay of Pigs.

The men flew as a group aboard the *Caroline*, the family plane Kennedy had used during his campaign. The plane ran into a headwind, and the ride was slow and bumpy. "It was very uncomfortable," Ray Rasenberger recalled fifty years later. "It made you appreciate what Kennedy had to go through campaigning, flying around on that. But it was fine, because it was an extraordinary group of men."

The men were late landing in Miami, but they found a fleet of cars awaiting them, complete with police motorcycle escort. President Kennedy had already begun his address when they arrived at the Orange Bowl. The president stood on a platform on the fifty-yard line, surrounded by the leaders of the brigade—San Román, Oliva, and Artime. Forty thousand men, women, and children watched from the stadium bleachers.

Kennedy delivered a fiery speech under a hazy sky as storm clouds threatened from the south. Rather than take the prisoner exchange as an opportunity to broker peace between Cuba and the United States, he piled on more or less the same rhetoric he had been using since the failed invasion. The audience in the Orange Bowl loved it. "*¡Guerra! ¡Guerra!*" the crowd was chanting by the time Kennedy finished talking.

Jackie Kennedy took a brief turn at the microphone. She had wowed the French in Paris by addressing them in fluent French, and now she demonstrated her linguistic facility again by addressing the brigade—"a group of the bravest men in the world"—in fluent Spanish. She told the men that when her baby son, John John, grew up, she would tell him the story of their feats. "It is my wish and my hope that someday he may be a man at least half as brave as the members of Brigade 2506."

Before the ceremony ended, Pepe San Román presented President Kennedy with the flag of the brigade. "I can assure you," said Kennedy, "this flag will be returned to this brigade in a free Havana." Later, many of the men of Brigade 2506 would look back on these words as one more broken promise. For the moment, though, the president's speech put a hopeful ending on a troubled story.

"The great forces moving mankind at the end of 1962 seem to be running a little more in our favor," wrote James Reston in an end-of-year reflection in the *New York Times* on the last day of 1962. "Enormous problems and dangers remain, ruffling the surface of the water, but the deeper tides are reassuring."

EPILOGUE

"It Could Have Been Worse"

The great enemy of the truth is very often not the lie—deliberate, contrived, and dishonest—but the myth—persistent, persuasive, and unrealistic.

—John F. Kennedy

Winter 1963–Spring 1965

WHAT JAMES RESTON did not—could not—know when he wrote his column at the end of 1962 was that a year later the deeper tides would be as reassuring as a rip current. President Kennedy would be dead, killed by Lee Harvey Oswald in Dallas, Texas, and the nation would be careening into the bloody 1960s. The assassination of John Kennedy unveiled a frightening new world of possibilities, even as it ended an extraordinarily tumultuous thirty-two months of American history.

A few years after Kennedy's death, Richard Nixon, with a touch, perhaps, of Schadenfreude, wrote that Fidel Castro was "the most momentous figure in John F. Kennedy's life." Castro had delivered Kennedy his victory in the election of 1960, Nixon believed; Castro had nearly destroyed Kennedy's presidency with the Bay of Pigs in 1961; Castro (and his Soviet friends) had lifted Kennedy to his greatest moment in the Cuban Missile Crisis of 1962; and finally, Castro was "an indirect cause for the tragic snuffing out of John Kennedy's life" in 1963.

In Nixon's construction, the road to Dallas began at the Bay of Pigs. Nixon was hardly alone in believing this. At least two persistent theories of Kennedy's assassination would draw the same connection. The more preposterous of these held that the CIA—or certain "rouge" elements within it—arranged the assassination as payback for Kennedy's cancellation of the D-Day air strikes. If nothing else, such conjecture was a testament to the fact that a segment of the public was willing to believe pretty much anything about the CIA after the Bay of Pigs.

Harder to dismiss is the theory apparently held by Richard Nixon: that Lee Harvey Oswald was acting on behalf of Fidel Castro—or at least *thought* he was—when he killed Kennedy. Two months before the assassination, in September 1963, Oswald was seen entering the Cuban embassy in Mexico City, ostensibly to obtain a visa to Cuba. Might he have discussed Kennedy's assassination with Cuban agents? Feeding speculation is the fact that Castro almost certainly knew Kennedy was trying to kill *him*. Among those who believed Castro sought preemptive retaliation was Lyndon Johnson. "Kennedy was trying to get to Castro," Johnson explained, "but Castro got to him first."

Fidel Castro himself ridiculed the notion that he or his government supported Oswald, but there is little doubt (as the author Gus Russo, among others, has established) that Oswald believed he was doing the Cubans a favor. He had been personally intent on avenging American misdeeds since the Bay of Pigs, when he was living in the Soviet Union and accumulating grievances against Kennedy. Later, when he returned to America and became an organizer for the Fair Play for Cuba Committee in New Orleans, he saw himself as Castro's anointed protector. Oswald knew of the Kennedy administration's attempts to oust Castro during the Bay of Pigs, and of its "terrorist bandit" measures (as he called them) against Castro after the invasion, and he announced his intention to do something about it.

In his memoir of the Bay of Pigs, Howard Hunt wrote, "Let this not be forgotten, Lee Harvey Oswald was a partisan of Fidel Castro, and an admitted Marxist who made desperate efforts to join the Red Revolution in Havana." Howard Hunt was a man of fervid imagination and a narrator of limited reliability, but his take on Oswald may be close to the truth. "In the end, he was an activist for the Fair Play for Cuba Committee," Hunt reminded readers of Oswald. "But for Castro and the Bay of Pigs disaster there would have been no such 'committee.' And perhaps no assassin named Lee Harvey Oswald."

* * *

LONG BEFORE HIS death, John Kennedy's presidency was transformed by the Bay of Pigs. There were the tactical changes mentioned earlier in these pages—the tightening of the inner circle; the increasing reliance on his brother Robert; the skepticism regarding the advice of military and intelligence advisers—and broader policy changes that escalated the Cold War. Kennedy felt compelled to make a strong stand against the Communists after the failure in Cuba, and he did. Most significantly, as we have seen, he put the country on a path into the Vietnam War, the disaster that eventually would overwhelm the lives and careers of his closest advisers. McNamara, Bundy, Rusk, Rostow, Taylor—these were the men Kennedy turned to after the Bay of Pigs, and these were the men who oversaw, under President Johnson, the perpetuation and escalation of a tragedy far worse than the fiasco in Cuba.

The American people were more deeply changed by the Bay of Pigs than were the men who oversaw it. The immediate popular reaction may have been to rally around the president, but over the long term the invasion, bearing its twin sins of deceit and incompetence, left many Americans profoundly disillusioned. Like Don Roberts, the young seaman who served aboard the *Essex*: he went to sea that April with a faith in his government that admitted little doubt; he returned a different man. "I was a boy from Indiana. I believed that when my government told me something, it was true. But it wasn't."

The disillusionment registered most obviously and immediately in the press, particularly the big-city East Coast press, and most emphatically in the *New York Times*. Before the Bay of Pigs, the press had been respectful of the White House, approaching its relationship to power as collaborative rather than adversarial. The "Gentlemen's Agreement," as David Halberstam called it, still applied. In the name of good citizenship, journalists treated delicate subjects (state secrets; presidential indiscretions) with kid gloves. A handful of publications had reported the lead-up to the invasion—the *Nation*, notably—but newspapers generally had held their fire, observing the rules of "demented patriotism," defined by the authors of a 1967 *Columbia University Forum* article on the Bay of Pigs as "the urge to play along with government at whatever cost to truth."

Even this had not been enough to satisfy Kennedy. In a speech to the American Newspaper Publishers Association a week after the invasion (not to be confused with his speech to the ASNE the day after the failure), Kennedy chided the press:

> The newspapers which printed these stories were loyal, patriotic, responsible and well meaning. Had we been engaged in open warfare they undoubtedly would not have published such items. But in the absence of open warfare they recognized only the tests of journalism and not the test of national security. And my question tonight is whether additional tests should now be adopted.

Privately, Kennedy seemed to recognize that he was urging newspapers to take steps that might not be in anybody's interest. "Maybe if you had printed more about the operation," he confided in Turner Catledge of the *New York Times* shortly after his speech to the publishers, "you would have saved us from a colossal mistake." He reiterated the sentiment to *Times* publisher Orvil Dryfoos. "I wish you had run everything on Cuba. . . . I am just sorry you didn't tell it at the time."

How sincerely Kennedy meant this is difficult to gauge; he was a man, as the Bay of Pigs demonstrated, who often disagreed with himself. But whatever the president felt, the press, or at least certain members of it, experienced its own regrets after the invasion. Kennedy would continue to enjoy cozy relationships with some of the press royalty—lunches with Scotty Reston; dinners at the Joe Alsops; weekends with the Ben Bradlees—but boots-on-the-ground journalists such as Halberstam saw corruption in fidelity. The "genteel chumminess," in Halberstam's phrase, began to turn icy.

"That era was beginning to end: the President of the United States had, with one phone call, made the publisher of the *New York Times* a partner to a clandestine operation," Halberstam later wrote. "It was a decision that was to be very troubling to a generation of senior journalists in the years to come, no matter how much they loved their country."

Later, they would not be so readily brought to heel. Reporters such as Halberstam and Neil Sheehan of UPI and Malcolm Browne of AP, and many others to come, would be less credulous, less acquiescent to government. The Vietnam War would be the proving ground for a more forceful and querulous journalism. As government officials insisted the war effort was proceeding smoothly, reporters "could see what was really going on," Halberstam wrote, "and they refused, in their reporting, to fake it." Halberstam would become so despised a figure in the White

House that President Kennedy would personally urge the *Times* to recall him from Saigon. But the *Times*, this time, refused.

Summer and Autumn 1965

IN THE YEARS following the Bay of Pigs, the failure waxed and waned in public discourse. On one hand, there was little fun to be had in rehashing an ignominious episode; on the other hand, it had left open wounds, some still suppurating. Reviving the subject were regular doses of revelation and controversy, generally delivered by the publication of an article or a book. When Richard Nixon's 1962 book *Six Crises* made the charge that Allen Dulles had revealed the Bay of Pigs plan in his Hyannis Port briefing to John Kennedy, Dulles returned to the public eye to politely dispute Nixon's version. In 1964, Haynes Johnson's book about the invasion brought a new flurry of interest.

The summer and early autumn of 1965, four years after the invasion—and two years after Kennedy's death—were the heyday of second-guessing and revisionism. Journalist Marguerite Higgins called those months the "season of memoirs." First came two book excerpts, one from Theodore Sorensen in *Look*, the next from Arthur Schlesinger in *Life*. These were followed by Sorensen's full book, *Kennedy*, published in October 1965, and Schlesinger's *A Thousand Days*, published in November. Both gave substantial attention to the Bay of Pigs.

Sorensen's *Look* excerpt began with an interesting and telling exchange he had with the president. In late 1962, Sorensen went to Kennedy with a request from a "distinguished author" for files on the Bay of Pigs. "This isn't the time," the president told Sorensen. "Besides, we want to tell that story ourselves." Now, Sorensen announced in 1965, "This is the time to tell that story." Sorensen's story was the one Kennedy would have wanted him to tell. Indeed, both Sorensen and Schlesinger gave accounts of the Bay of Pigs that favored the man they had faithfully served. In both memoirs, Kennedy is pictured as a victim of an inherited plan (from Eisenhower), bad advice (mainly from the CIA but also from the Joint Chiefs), and a hard sell (from the CIA). Pressured to make a fast decision by a CIA-imposed deadline and fed a steady diet of false assurances by the agency, Kennedy finally went ahead, against his better judgment and with "heavy misgiving." As for Kennedy's decision to cancel the second air strike, Schlesinger downgraded its significance. "There is certainly nothing to suggest that [a second strike] could possibly have led to the overthrow of the regime on the terms which Kennedy laid down from the start—that is, without United States armed intervention."

The same autumn that Sorensen and Schlesinger published their White House memoirs, Dwight Eisenhower came out with his: *Waging Peace: The White House Years, 1956–1961*. Eisenhower's book dealt briefly with the Cuban invasion. More important, its publication provided the former president an opportunity and a platform to address the memoirs of the Kennedy men, specifically the insinuation that he had handed Kennedy a "plan" to invade Cuba. A New York *Newsday* interview devoted entirely to the question of Eisenhower's role in the Bay of Pigs ran under the banner headline, IKE SPEAKS OUT: BAY OF PIGS WAS ALL JFK'S. After the invasion, noted *Newsday*, the former president had called for bipartisan unity. "Now, however, he feels it would be well to set the record straight on at least a couple items in recent intimate histories" that were propagating a "perversion of history and a disservice to the late President Kennedy, who never sought to duck responsibility for his executive decisions."

Eisenhower insisted that Kennedy did not "inherit" a plan to attack Cuba. "At no time did I put before anybody anything that could be called a plan," the former president told *Newsday*. Although a covert "military instruction program" was indeed developed for the Cuban exiles, this was done more as an effort to keep the restless Cubans occupied than as part of a specific plan to overthrow Castro. There was "no mandate, no commitment by me or anyone in my administration" to send the brigade to Cuba. According to Ike, what he told Kennedy in their White House meeting before the inauguration was, "You people will have to decide what to do." (Others present that day, as noted earlier, recalled Eisenhower urging Kennedy to support the operation "to the utmost" and telling him, "We cannot have the present government there go on.") If Eisenhower himself had decided on an invasion, he would have made sure it succeeded. "Force is a naked, brutal thing in this world," he told *Newsday*. "If you are going to use it, you have got to be prepared to go all the way."

RICHARD BISSELL WAS interviewed about the Bay of Pigs several times that summer and fall of 1965, most notably in a long article for the *Washington Evening Star* on July 20. Back home in Connecticut after his long sojourn in Washington, Bissell was working as an executive at United

Aircraft Corporation (forerunner to United Technologies), comfortably ensconced in a bright white-paneled office at company headquarters near Stamford. His interviewer noted that his hands toyed with a miniature rubber tire as he spoke.

"No one can deny that it was a disaster and that a lot of people were wrong," Bissell acknowledged. "But to say it was irresponsible is false on the record." According to Bissell, the problem was not in the conception or in the original plan but in the "progressive modifications" of the plan for political reasons. The CIA's fault lay in not advising the president to cancel the plan in light of his changes. Whatever other flaws in planning or execution, "It did in fact fail because of lack of control of the air."

Bissell had gone through the ringer after the Bay of Pigs, but his tone was more elegiac than bitter. It was obvious he would have liked to flee from the quiet industrial park in Connecticut back to the fray of Washington. For a man who had once led armies and advised presidents, the eight-to-five routine was stultifying. Being on the sidelines during the Cuban Missile Crisis, for instance, left him feeling "very much an outsider," as he wrote to one of his sons at the time.

"My ten years at United Aircraft were, on the whole, unfulfilling," Bissell later acknowledged in his memoir. "I was used to a faster pace and a much closer relationship to and participation in active decision making. It was not easy to play a less active, more peripheral role." Gazing out through the slits in the venetian blind over his window at the placid summery lawn in 1965, he told his interviewer, "I think anyone who has been down there in Washington, right in the thick of things, misses it when he leaves."

ALLEN DULLES WAS still down there in Washington, if no longer quite as in the thick as he once was. Racked by gout that gnarled his feet and made shoes uncomfortable—he wore slippers—he maintained his usual circuit of cocktail and dinner parties. He was past seventy now. He had never made much money in government—his final salary at the CIA was $21,000, with a government annual pension of about $8,000—and in retirement he turned to lecturing and writing to make ends meet. When asked about the Bay of Pigs in interviews, he defended the agency politely, circumspectly. Of Kennedy he had only kind words. Or did, at least, until that summer of 1965.

The memoirs by Schlesinger and Sorensen put him in a dark mood.

Their accounts of the Bay of Pigs were sketchy and defamatory, he believed. "This story is being written while much of the background is still held as classified and unavailable," he wrote that summer. "I deplore the way this is being done. In effect, an attempt is now being made to write history and only part of the story is available. . . . I feel one has a duty to speak out before the repetition of myth becomes history."

For the first and the last time, Dulles sat down and composed an extended response to the charges against the CIA and himself. He arranged to publish his work in *Harper's* after conferring with the magazine's associate editor, Willie Morris, who was eager to have it. "Let me reiterate our feeling that *Harper's* would be the perfect forum for you," Morris wrote to Dulles at the end of that July. "It also strikes me that the timing could not be more perfect."

Morris sent Dulles page proofs of Schlesinger's *Life* excerpt. Dulles read these with pen in hand, carving *X*'s and question marks into the margins, along with running commentary—*No* or *This was later* or *Pure coincidence*. Handwritten notes taken by Dulles in preparation for his article hint at the depth of his anger. Schlesinger and Sorensen ("S&S," he called them) had written nothing more than "alibis" and "apologia" for Kennedy's mistakes. So caustic was an early draft of his article that Jack Fischer, editor in chief of *Harper's*, sent a note to Dulles suggesting "it might help the tone of the whole article if you were to add a few words of praise" for Schlesinger and Sorensen to "forestall any suspicion of personal animus."

Dulles was offended by the implication in Schlesinger's book (in a passage recounting the April 18 lunch Schlesinger ate with Kennedy and James Reston) that Kennedy regretted keeping him on as director of the CIA. "Were these offhand comments given in moments of great tension and stress, or were they President Kennedy's carefully considered opinions?" More irksome to Dulles were comments attributed by Sorensen to Kennedy regarding assurances Dulles had supposedly made prior to the invasion. Here is Sorensen quoting Kennedy quoting Dulles: "I stood right here at Ike's desk and told him I was certain our Guatemalan operation would succeed. And Mr. President, the prospects for this plan are even better than they were for that one." Dulles denied that he ever did, or ever would, utter such assurances.

Beyond defending himself personally, Dulles stood up for the agency. The CIA never "misled and misinformed" the president regarding the possibility of civilian uprisings or need for air control or the capacity of the brigade to go guerrilla in the event of failure. "The crucial point is that the use of the Brigade for guerrilla operations, or the alternative of dispersing into the countryside if a beachhead could not be held, was wholly dependent upon establishing at least a temporary firm foothold in Cuba" [Dulles's underlining]. The same went for the mass uprisings; no one ever told the president that the uprisings would be spontaneous or immediate. "We will never know whether significant uprisings would have taken place in Cuba," wrote Dulles, because there was not sufficient opportunity to test the hypothesis after Kennedy canceled the air strikes and doomed the operation before it began. As for the charge that the CIA had not adequately warned Kennedy of the need for air control—nonsense. The utter importance of dominion of the air "was stressed in the briefings" and was "obvious to everyone involved in the final decisions." If the president or some of his advisers missed the point, in other words, that was *their* fault.

In the end, Dulles posited, the biggest problem with the invasion may have been that Kennedy lacked the heart to see the job through—"a willingness to risk some unpleasant political repercussions, and a willingness to provide the basic military necessities." This was as close as Allen Dulles ever came to blaming John Kennedy directly for the Bay of Pigs fiasco.

Dulles's article went through multiple drafts over the summer and early fall. Then, in the middle of October, Dulles abruptly withdrew it. His reason for doing so must have been important; he could have used the money, and he had devoted significant time to it, not to mention the time and effort required of the *Harper's* staff. "I have decided, for reasons which I shall tell you when we next get together, not to publish an article at this particular moment," he wrote to John Fischer. "I have reached this decision after a good deal of thought, and, also, a certain amount of consultation, and I do not foreclose the possibility of publication a bit later."

Allen Dulles never did end up publishing *My Answer to the Bay of Pigs* before his death in 1969. Later, in donating drafts of the article, along with the rest of Dulles's papers, to the Seeley G. Mudd Manuscript Library at Dulles's beloved alma mater, Princeton University, his wife, Clover, enclosed a note in the file: "Mrs. Allen W. Dulles wishes to state that her husband decided not to publish this article, because there was so much more in his favor he could have said, if he had been at liberty to do so, that the material herein was inadequate."

Dulles's decision was unfortunate for the agency he had loved and cultivated. Perhaps his version of events would not have been able to compete with the S&S versions in 1965, but it would have circulated a timely alternative. As it was, the CIA never recovered from its real and perceived misdeeds at the Bay of Pigs. In fact, these became the prism through which every action of the agency was viewed and magnified, including many supposed actions it never took. In the spring of 1966, five years after the invasion, the *New York Times* ran a five-part series on the CIA in which the newspaper examined the "rising tide of dark suspicion that many people throughout the world, including many in this country, harbor about the agency and its activities"—a tide that had been lifted by the Bay of Pigs and drew strength from "spurious reports, gossip, misunderstandings, deep-seated fears and forgeries and falsifications." The *Times* pointed out that many commonly held assumptions about the CIA—that it operated without oversight, for example, as a kind of "invisible government"—were unfounded, but this seemed not to matter. Plenty of people had harbored dark suspicions about the agency before the Bay of Pigs; afterward, almost no one did not. Later there would be other versions of the Bay of Pigs story, but none would have the clout or reach of those written by Kennedy's men, and over time, just as Dulles feared, the repetition of myth became history.

WHAT, THEN, lies beyond the myth? I have tried in these pages to show the Bay of Pigs in a more nuanced and, I hope, truer light than conventional wisdom usually casts it. To damn the operation as an act of idiocy or evil perpetrated by fools and sinners is to miss the point; worse, doing so puts more distance between ourselves and those who undertook it than either we or they deserve.

The operation was, in fact, undertaken by well-intentioned people attempting to achieve the best solution to what they perceived to be a serious problem. Castro's ouster, most Americans believed at the time, was a requirement of national security. Given the risks of overt action, a covert operation was judged to be a safer method. Eisenhower set the "Program" in motion based on this assumption, and once that snowball began to roll and grow, it was nearly unstoppable. Coming into office in the winter of 1961, Kennedy found himself instantly in a bind. On the one hand, he could not easily halt the operation; on the other hand, he grasped the potential for serious repercussions if he went ahead; and on the third hand—you needed more than two to grapple with this mess—nobody had any better ideas for getting rid of Castro.

Kennedy had made matters worse for himself by raising Castro again and again as a political issue during the election. Once in office, he brought himself additional trouble by instituting an administrative philosophy that hampered the task of vetting and analyzing the CIA's operation. "Kennedy wanted the facts—not conclusions, but the details that had led to the conclusion," his assistant Richard Goodwin wrote. "He wanted opinions directly, not as mediated and homogenized through a hierarchy of committees and subordinate chieftains." The flaw in this method was that it placed an enormous burden on the president himself to wade through great volumes of information. Unless Kennedy could read every piece of paper—difficult even with his vaunted thousand-words-a-minute speed—and attend every meeting, then commit what he learned to memory and keep it all in perfect mental order, he was liable to get an incomplete picture. "[I]f he was not looking," Kennedy biographer Richard Reeves wrote, "there was no system and no guarantee that anyone was checking for him." He would have benefited from a staff that could boil it down for him, highlighting pros and cons, making sure he heard the important arguments, that he grasped the necessary and sufficient conditions for the operation's success. As it was, his knowledge was not comprehensive, and he seems to have comprehended the operation poorly. The most egregious consequence of this was the president's ill-considered abridgment of the air strikes on April 15, followed by his cancellation of the April 17 strikes altogether.

I am inclined to agree with Richard Bissell that the failure of the operation, as preordained as it may have been for other reasons, has to be attributed first and foremost to those canceled air strikes; while the rest is speculation, it is a near certainty (as most people involved grasped instantly) that canceling the strikes doomed the invasion. Of course, there is no guarantee that the second round of strikes would have accomplished what the first round did not. Castro later claimed that he dispersed his planes, and perhaps he did, which would have made the total destruction of his remaining fleet unlikely. Nonetheless, at least some planes were still on the runways and the CIA knew where these were.

The greater number of Castro's planes destroyed on the ground, the better the brigade's chances would have been on the beach. It is true that before the cancellation there had been snafus—all those screwups the

CIA's inspector general detailed—but as Bissell wrote in his response to the inspector general's report, "In any large and rapidly organized undertaking there are certain to be errors of organization and of execution." Bissell pointed out that the invasion did in fact achieve its military goals in the early hours. The landing was undertaken with surprise and met by little resistance. Most of the men managed to attain the beachhead. Early skirmishes tended to go in favor of the brigade. Had the brigade had the opportunity to land all personnel and supplies on the beach before coming under attack, there is reason to believe it could have held the beachhead for a sustained period of time. The air attacks from Castro's surviving fleet made this impossible.

But what would have happened had the beachhead been sustained? Could the invasion ever have achieved its ultimate goal of overthrowing Fidel Castro? Probably not.

As the CIA understood from the very beginning, there were only two ways an operation that pitted fourteen hundred men against a national army made sense over the long term. The first was for the brigade to somehow spark an internal reaction against Castro by serving as "a rallying point for the thousands who are estimated to be ready for overt resistance," as described in an early briefing paper for Secretary Rusk. The second was for an American military presence to sooner or later make itself known in Cuba. "If matters do not eventuate as predicted above," the CIA informed Rusk, "the lodgment established by our force can be used as the site for establishment of a provisional government which can be recognized by the United States, and hopefully by other American States."

After the invasion, the CIA was accused of misrepresenting its expectations for both of these eventualities. But if there was confusion, it may have been as much in Kennedy's comprehension as in the CIA's presentation. Both Dulles and Bissell correctly pointed out that the CIA never promised that civilian uprisings would be spontaneous or immediate. Indeed, uprisings were predicated on the brigade's ability to hold the beachhead for a protracted period of time—a week to ten days. In his *Harper's* draft article, Dulles argued that the plan was never given a chance to prove itself because any chance of the brigade holding territory ended with the canceled air strikes.

In all likelihood, though, such uprisings as the CIA anticipated would *not* have occurred, no matter how long the brigade held the beachhead. Certainly there was no evidence in the agency's own research to suppose the existence of a restive populace champing at the bit to overthrow the Maximum Leader. Castro himself had made the likelihood of this even smaller by incarcerating everyone who might have joined such an uprising. As for Plan B—overt military intervention—CIA critics have long assumed that the real plan of the CIA was to trick or cajole the president into using U.S. force to defeat Castro—to send in the marines, in other words. "With hindsight," McGeorge Bundy later told author Piero Gleijeses, "it is clear that both Dulles and Bissell thought that when Kennedy really had to choose between failure or putting U.S. troops ashore, he would do the latter." Evidence to support alleged trickery includes the memo written months before the invasion by the CIA's Richard Drain. For reasons discussed earlier in this book, I believe that memo is a red herring. There is no doubt that once the invasion began to falter, Dulles and Bissell, among others, desperately hoped Kennedy would rescue it with U.S. force, but evidence that the CIA planned the operation *in advance* with the expectation that the president would *have* to bail it out is scant.

Did the CIA go in expecting the president to eventually make U.S. military support available to the brigade? Almost certainly. It was no secret within the administration that the original CIA plan for the invasion supposed the United States would step in overtly after the provisional government was installed—that the provisional government was to provide, in fact, a pretext for overt intervention. Although on April 12, five days before D-Day, Kennedy specifically ruled out use of American force, Bissell and Dulles may have believed that he was prohibiting force only *during* the invasion. Did he really mean he would allow no U.S. intervention—*ever*? A note from McGeorge Bundy to Dean Rusk on the morning of Thursday, April 13, suggests that Kennedy's no may not have necessarily meant no. "There will be no employment of U.S. armed forces against Cuba unless quite new circumstances develop," wrote Bundy. Which closed the door—then opened it a crack. And whatever the president said, there were physical facts that seemed to contradict his pledge. Those American warships in the Caribbean, for instance—the seven destroyers and the aircraft carrier loaded with A-4 Skyhawks. What exactly were they doing there, numbers painted over, flags cut down, if military action was completely out of the question?

One charge against the CIA sticks. This was the agency's tendency to oversell the operation to Kennedy. Both Bissell and Dulles became invested in the operation—Bissell himself acknowledged this in later years—and did not want to see it canceled. Nor did Bissell's right-hand man, Tracy Barnes, as his memos written in March 1961 indicate. The CIA's sins were generally those of omission—certain inconvenient details the agency neglected to illuminate for the president's consideration. When William Bundy later defended Bissell and Dulles as essentially honest in their briefings to Kennedy, he also made an important observation about the obligations of presidential advisers: "I'll go back to a very basic tenet of staff work in government—that you're responsible for the impression created in the head of the man you are advising and it doesn't matter how much you put in the fine print because people skim that." If John Kennedy failed to understand, for example, that air strikes were planned and absolutely required on the morning of April 17, even though the briefing papers said so, part of the blame for his misapprehension belongs to the CIA.

But it cannot be concluded that John Kennedy was fooled or cajoled into proceeding. If the CIA presented too rosy a view, as it may have, the president did not lack Cassandras to paint him a darker picture of the outcome. No fewer than four highly placed aides in the administration, including two—Bowles and Fulbright—whom Kennedy had considered for secretary of state, wrote him long, urgent memos that alerted him to the invasion's pitfalls, but in the end he ignored them. And his apparent failure to grasp certain key components of the operation, such as the distance of the new landing site at the Bay of Pigs from the Escambray Mountains, seems almost willful. Anyone with a simple map of Cuba could have seen that the once-plausible option of the brigade fading into the mountains was closed.

Perhaps John Kennedy failed to understand the risks of the operation because he did not want to understand them. Canceling the operation would have exposed him to enormous political risks. At the same time, approving the use of military force to bail it out would have exposed him and the country to unacceptable diplomatic risks, and possibly worse.

Walt Rostow later recounted a conversation he had with Swedish economist and future Nobel Laureate Gunnar Myrdal, who happened to be in Washington the spring after the Bay of Pigs. Myrdal told Rostow he worked for a "great president." When Rostow asked him why, he responded, "If Kennedy had called it off, he would have been ruined politically at home. . . . But if he had engaged American forces to salvage a failing covert operation, he would have been ruined abroad."

A similar point was made to the president by Clayton Fritchey, director of public affairs on the staff of Adlai Stevenson. "Mr. President, it could have been worse."

"How?"

"It might have succeeded."

The United States would have become an occupying force in Cuba. The administration would have been faced not only with the prospect of fighting "house to house in Havana," as Richard Goodwin predicted, but also contending with resentment from countries throughout Latin America. And the Soviet Union—what would Khrushchev have done? The consequences can only be imagined, but they were potentially catastrophic. "An invasion force that succeeded in overthrowing Castro without a demonstrative show of popular support," wrote the historian Theodore Draper in 1962, "could have ruled Cuba only in a state of perpetual civil war or as a thinly disguised American occupation."

The peculiar truth may be that the result Kennedy got was the very best he could have desired, despite the obvious distress the failure caused him. If he achieved this result accidentally, then he was lucky. If he achieved it intentionally—if, that is, he sent the brigade into Cuba expecting, even wanting, it to fail—then he deserves a place as one of the most coldly calculating presidents in history. Whichever is true—and there is really no way to know for sure—John Kennedy, in the end, managed to have his cake and eat it, too.

1965–1974

THE FLURRY OF memoirs produced in 1965 seemed to close the book on the Bay of Pigs. More than four years had passed. Fidel Castro was clearly going nowhere soon, and the urgency to replace him had declined. Much as Senator Fulbright predicted to Kennedy before the invasion, Castro had turned out to be a "thorn in the side" but not a "dagger in the heart." The truth of this was self-evident: America had survived despite him.

The country had bigger concerns now. Vietnam, a small field fire when Kennedy came to power, had blown up into a full-fledged conflagration, with America adding the fuel—more equipment, more money, more lives. In 1965 President Johnson began sending combat units in earnest to Vietnam. The American presence there was overt, but it followed some of the lines rehearsed in Cuba—overconfidence, deceit, a bad idea gone wrong. In time, a large percentage of the American people understood the war to be immoral and unwinnable, and the government to be untrustworthy. For Lyndon Johnson, whose engagement with Vietnam had begun in the weeks after the Bay of Pigs when he traveled at Kennedy's request to South Vietnam, the war would bring only grief and, in the end, derail his presidency.

THE BAY OF PIGS was the poison that kept on giving to American presidents. Johnson's successor, Richard Nixon, came to office appealing to the "silent majority," as he referred to his constituency—those Americans who were weary of the antigovernment cynicism that had washed over the country during the 1960s and who wished to see their faith in America respected and restored. Matters did not work out quite the way either Nixon or his voters hoped. And before he resigned in disgrace, he found his own fate linked to the "Bay of Pigs thing." The failed invasion was not a direct cause of Watergate, of course, but residual elements of it surfaced in all phases of the scandal. Nixon was perceptive enough to grasp the role Fidel Castro played in Kennedy's rise and subsequent end, but apparently he never considered how Castro affected his own fate.

One of the central lessons Nixon drew from the Cuban escapade of the early 1960s was the one taught to him by John Kennedy before their fourth debate, when Nixon came to believe that his rival intentionally sandbagged him by recommending U.S. support for Cuban exile forces. Nixon pledged never to be caught off guard again. From such bitter seeds grew a culture of dirty tricks that came to flourish around Nixon and followed him into the White House. He wanted to catch his enemies in the act, to reveal the full perfidy of the Kennedys and their fellow travelers, including the liberal East Coast press. Nixon adopted the morality of the Cold War—the end justifies the means, even if the law must sometimes be broken in pursuit of higher causes—and applied it to domestic politics. The enemy was not communism this time; it was liberals. But Nixon, in his own injured righteousness, did not draw a firm distinction between the two.

Under Nixon, albeit at a distance from him—he had learned the tactics of plausible denial from Eisenhower—a dirty tricks task force was assembled. The group was called the "plumbers," in reference to its mission to fix "leaks" coming out of the government, a prime example being the secret Pentagon Papers printed in the *New York Times*. The head plumber, as Americans would soon come to learn, was an ex–CIA agent named Howard Hunt. Of course, Hunt had been a "plumber" once before, when he and Gerry Droller struggled to put together the Cuban exile coalition in advance of the Bay of Pigs. The term had a very different meaning in 1961 than it did in 1972. Then, the job of plumber had been to lay down the pipe for a political opposition to Fidel Castro. In 1972, it was to destroy the political opposition to Richard Nixon.

Hunt joined the White House staff at the start of 1971, a year after retiring from the CIA. Still operating under the alias "Eduardo" that he had acquired during the Bay of Pigs, Hunt began devoting his spying expertise—such as it was—to Nixon's effort to destroy all enemies, especially those named Kennedy. Hunt was sent to Massachusetts to dig up information on Edward Kennedy and the young senator's role in Chappaquiddick. He later attempted to find evidence that John Kennedy had ordered the assassination of Ngo Dinh Diem, the president of South Vietnam, in November 1963 (just weeks before Kennedy's own assassination). Anything embarrassing about John Kennedy, Nixon wanted. In his investigations, Hunt sometimes received the assistance of old colleagues at the CIA, much to the agency's later mortification. He also brought in a group of hired hands to carry out covert missions. Several of Hunt's henchmen were Cuban exiles whom he had come to know during the Bay of Pigs. Hunt convinced them that their actions on Nixon's behalf would ultimately serve the cause that still burned in their hearts—getting rid of Castro.

In June 1972, Hunt, with the help of G. Gordon Liddy, planned and executed an operation to break into the offices of the Democratic National Committee in the Watergate office complex in Washington. The five intruders were caught, including three Cubans, and the great constitutional crisis of Watergate began.

Richard Nixon did not know the details of the break-in at first, but the gap between the bungled crime and the defensive president closed quickly over the next weeks as Nixon sought to head off an investigation that might link the break-in to the White House. First, he approved hush-money payments to the five men who had been arrested. Then, on the morning of June 23, 1972, in an Oval Office conversation with his assistant H. R. Haldeman, he laid the groundwork for a conspiracy to obstruct justice. The conversation was captured on a tape-recording device Nixon had installed in his office. The recording made that morning came to be known as the "smoking-gun tape."

As the tape began rolling, Nixon wanted to halt the FBI's investigation into Watergate, and he hoped to use the CIA to do this. Go to the agency, he told Haldeman, and tell them the president needs them to run interference. His strategy really had two parts. First, he wanted the CIA to claim responsibility for the break-in and take the heat off the White House. Then he wanted the CIA to demand that the FBI, in the name of national security, back off from its investigation.

> When you get in [unintelligible] people, say: Look, the problem is that this will open the whole, the whole Bay of Pigs thing, and the President just feels that ah, without going into the details—don't lie to them to the extent to say no involvement, but just say this is sort of a comedy of errors, without getting into it—the President believes that it is going to open the whole Bay of Pigs thing up again. And, ah, because these people are plugging for [unintelligible] and that they should call the FBI in and say that we wish for the good of the country don't go any further into this case, period!

Later that afternoon, Nixon repeated the plan: "Tell them that if it gets out, it's going to make the CIA look bad, it's going to make Hunt look bad, and it's likely to blow the whole Bay of Pigs which we think would be very unfortunate for the CIA." Exactly what Nixon meant by the "Bay of Pigs thing" is not clear. Haldeman thought Nixon probably meant the Kennedy plots to kill Castro *after* the Bay of Pigs—Operation Mongoose, that is. Possibly he only meant to suggest some indefinite embarrassment that would befall the CIA and had nothing particular in mind. Clearly he knew, though, that the mere utterance of those words, eleven years after the fact, could make the agency jump.

Haldeman met with the director of the CIA, Richard Helms, the man who had once worked under Richard Bissell (and had since taken the route to the top that Bissell had hoped would be his). When Haldeman passed on Nixon's warning—"The President asked me to tell you this entire affair may be connected to the Bay of Pigs"—Helms exploded. "The Bay of Pigs had nothing to do with this!" Despite his anger, Helms came around. The CIA did Nixon's bidding and asked the FBI to lay off Watergate, for reasons of national security. The FBI complied, if only briefly.

The truth came out, thanks in part to the FBI, and thanks to intrepid reporting by journalists such as Bob Woodward and Carl Bernstein. Nixon held on for a while, but when the smoking-gun tape surfaced—the "Bay of Pigs thing"—he was finished and he knew it. He resigned the presidency on August 9, 1974.

1975–Present

IN SOME WAYS, the days after Watergate were darker for the CIA than those after the Bay of Pigs. Though the agency's role in the scandal was minor and undertaken only on direction of the president, Watergate gave Congress an excuse to do what many had been itching to do for years, which was to pry the CIA from executive control. Over the next several years, a series of congressional investigations opened up the closed vault of the agency. In 1975, the Senate Select Committee on Intelligence, under the chairmanship of Senator Frank Church, conducted an inquiry into the CIA's history of assassination—or, rather, of assassination plots, since none of them seemed to have amounted to anything.

Among those summoned to testify in the summer of 1975 was Richard Bissell. He returned to Washington after thirteen years away to sit before a panel of unfriendly and frankly contemptuous senators. "How many murders did you contemplate?" one senator asked. While under interrogation, Bissell tried patiently to explain his actions, but the senators were not interested in hearing explanations. His appearance before the committee was, wrote Bissell, "a most unwelcome and unrewarding task."

It is ironic, given that he would spend the latter part of his life explaining a venture that most people came to consider sheer folly, that Richard Bissell was an intensely rational man. Bissell's daughter recalls him as warm and compassionate, but he sometimes struck colleagues as aloof—the epitome of a cold-blooded blue blood. Arguably, it was precisely his intellectual detachment that allowed him to consider assassinations and other measures without serious pangs of conscience. But it also allowed him, in the long epilogue of his life, to look back on his actions dispassionately and objectively. He did not apologize for the Bay of Pigs, but he came to recognize and admit its flaws, and his flaws, and he was willing to answer for them. Contrary to the claim of one recent Kennedy biographer that Bissell "would remain silent about the disaster until shortly before his death"—which suggests he was hiding something—Bissell granted numerous interviews to scholars, journalists, and students over the three decades between his time at the CIA and his death. The same patrician worldview that came off as arrogance to some instilled in him an attitude of noblesse oblige, and he took seriously his responsibility to history. It could not have been easy to sit through rounds of questions about the most painful episode of his life, but, as he wrote in his memoir, "I feel an obligation to respond to such requests and almost always comply."

As for the memoir, undertaken when Bissell was in his eighties, the book makes for a fairly dry recitation of his eventful life, but its virtues are fair-mindedness and lack of vanity. Here were the facts of my life, Bissell seems to tell the reader; make of them what you will.

For all Bissell's efforts to serve history, history has not been kind to him since his death in 1994. When Bissell's name comes up in discussions of the Bay of Pigs, an unpleasant adjective usually lurks somewhere nearby. Some of his own former colleagues have been among his toughest critics. In 1996, Jacob Esterline and Jack Hawkins came together, for the first time since the invasion, to give a joint interview with Peter Kornbluh of the National Security Archive in Washington. Though the two men were largely responsible for the details of the operation at the Bay of Pigs, both laid blame squarely on Bissell for its failure. They believed he betrayed them personally when he permitted President Kennedy to cut the preinvasion air strikes, after promising them otherwise. Given what followed, Hawkins never got over the fact that his April 13 cable from Happy Valley may have influenced Kennedy's decision to proceed. "Had I known before setting off for Central America that the President, in concert with Bissell, would at the last minute cut by half the number of aircraft to participate in the first strike, and then, when the troops were actually nearing the beaches, the President would suddenly and unexpectedly cancel the second air strike altogether, I would not have made the trip." Hawkins never forgave Kennedy for his decision, nor Bissell for failing to change the president's mind. "I was really disgusted," he told journalist Don Bohning in 1997. "I just sort of washed my hands of it and put it behind me, went on with my life and tried not to think about it. It was one of the most disappointing things that I ever had to do with in my life, professionally."

Esterline was even less forgiving of Bissell: "I am forced to a very unhappy conclusion and that is that he was lying down and lying up for reasons that I don't yet totally understand." While participating in a

1996 conference that brought together many Bay of Pigs participants and commentators, Esterline told the panel that he never spoke to Bissell again after the invasion. "And he knew why to the day he died."

Arthur Schlesinger also attended the conference. He made the point several times that Bissell's slick sales job was the reason Kennedy went ahead with the operation. "It is clear in retrospect that Kennedy was seduced by Dick Bissell's smoothly persuasive estimation," said Schlesinger. "All of us—Kennedy and Bundy and the rest—were hypnotized by Dick Bissell to some degree."

The scheming, two-faced Machiavelli who haunted the conference in Bissell's name bore little resemblance to the well-mannered man most people knew during his lifetime. At one point, one of the conference's organizers, James Blight, suggested that Bissell was "the deus ex machina of this conference." Certainly he was the scapegoat.

THE BAY OF PIGS recedes into our past, but it is far from dead history. It is preserved, for instance, in the weirdly timeless relationship between the United States and Cuba, severed in the winter of 1961 and unrepaired since. Fidel Castro is now an old man in poor health and no longer officially in charge of Cuba, but his reign lasted through ten U.S. presidents—eleven, if we include President Obama, which would bring the count to *one-quarter* of all U.S. presidents.

In Cuba, the *Victoria de Girón* continues to be fervently observed each April, as if it were only yesterday that Fidel leaped off a tank and strode onto the beach in all his glory. In Miami, too, there is a quality of bottled time in certain precincts of Little Havana, where many of the old Cuban exiles have lived since 1961. Inside the Bay of Pigs Museum on Ninth Street, a small white house devoted to the memory of the brigade's feats of April 1961, photographs and uniforms and relics from the battle are displayed in glass cases. When the brigademen gather there, as many do every April 17 on the anniversary of the invasion, they bring arthritic joints and creased faces, but also memories that are sharp and vivid. They grow animated and loud as they talk of the battle, the anticipation, the excitement and confusion, the grief and anger that came later. The anger is still remarkably raw, against Castro, but also against John Kennedy, whose unfilled promise at the Orange Bowl to return the brigade flag to a liberated Cuba still rankles. (In 1977, the brigade demanded the return of the flag it gave to Kennedy; it is now among the exhibits in the Bay of Pigs Museum.) From the museum the men migrate to Calle Ocho in Little Havana to stand at a memorial to the men who died in the invasion. They salute the brigade flag and sing brigade anthems in a salty breeze, and for a moment they could be back on the decks of the rusty freighters, steaming toward Cuba to rescue the homeland, the battle still to be fought and won.

Of course, many of them understand that it is a changed world and the battle is long behind. Their children and grandchildren are Americans and do not care much about Fidel Castro or Cuba. As for themselves, none has set foot in Cuba since they flew out in the days before Christmas 1962. One man admitted to me, a little amazed, that he no longer knows a single person living on the island. Everyone he once knew is either dead or gone.

Many of the brigademen, too, are dead, perhaps half who landed in Cuba in 1961. Among the first to die after the battle was José San Román—Pepe, as they called him—the leader of the brigade. San Román never got over the disaster. When author Peter Wyden contacted him in the late 1970s, he refused to talk. The event, he said, had "ruined his life." In 1989, San Román committed suicide.

Sometimes Janet Ray visits the museum and talks with the old pilots who knew her father, Pete Ray, before he was shot from the sky on the morning of April 19 and killed. Ms. Ray was six at the time. Her father's body was put in a morgue and frozen by Castro, who wanted it on hand as proof of the Americans' presence at the Bay of Pigs. (He once threatened to bring Ray's body to the United Nations and put it on display for all to see.) The U.S. government never claimed Ray's body, and indeed denied its existence. Janet spent the better part of her childhood trying to unravel the mystery of her father's death, riding her bike to the local library to do research, secretly tape-recording whispered conversations of her widowed mother. She devoted years of her adult life to pressing the CIA to admit the truth of her father's death—that he was not a mercenary who drowned at sea, but an American pilot flying for his country who died in battle. The Cuban government returned the body to Ms. Ray for burial in 1979, and the CIA finally acknowledged his role in the invasion. In 2004, Ms. Ray was awarded $24 million following a lawsuit against Cuba for the wrongful death of her father. The money came from Cuban assets frozen in American banks since 1961.

The American sailors who were there at the Bay of Pigs, aboard the carrier *Essex* and the fleet of destroyers, are usually left out of the story, but they were also deeply affected, and some remain so today. After returning to Norfolk, they put the event behind them and did their best to forget, as instructed by their commanders. But some never got over the fact that they, sailors for the U.S. Navy, turned their backs on allies. The U.S. government finally recognized their role, too, and eventually awarded all sailors aboard the American fleet Navy Expedition Medals.

Nearly all the men who planned and organized the operation for the U.S. government fifty years ago are gone now. Kennedy, of course, and Bissell and Dulles and Barnes. Rusk and McNamara, even Schlesinger, who held on until just a few years ago. Jacob Esterline died in 1999. Grayston Lynch passed away in 2008, after writing a scathing memoir about the invasion. To recall these men in the spring of 1961 is to recall America at a moment before a very great change, when certain myths of American power and honor were disrupted, perhaps forever. Later, the Kennedy administration would be nostalgically recalled as Camelot, as if it were a fairy tale. In fact, those five days in April 1961 were the beginning of the end of a fairy tale, when the curtain fell on one story of America and began to rise on quite another.

ACKNOWLEDGMENTS

My thanks to Colin Harrison, my editor at Scribner, who first breathed life into this project and then nourished it with his spot-on suggestions and illuminating queries, every one of which made this a better book. He also saved the book from landing, unbrilliantly, in a structural swamp, and for that the book's author will be forever grateful. Colin's assistant at Scribner, the extremely able Kelsey Smith, steered the manuscript through the editing gauntlet with total ease—or at least she made it look easy, though it could not have been. A big thanks, too, to Kathleen Rizzo, who oversaw the book's production. Even before the first word had been typed, Kris Dahl, my agent, played a very important role in this book's creation. Kris's encouragement and wisdom have been invaluable to me over the past decade.

While researching and writing *The Brilliant Disaster*, I incurred more debts than I can possibly repay in words. I am grateful to Deborah Hellman, Peter Kuper, Jay and Fleur Chandler, Jim and Ruth Varney, James Varney, Andrew Meier, and Nancy Kopans. My four wonderful sisters—Mary, Jean, Cathy, and Ann—lent me their support and smarts. Constance Rosenblum kindly offered to read the book in galleys, then gave me the gift of her usual superb advice. Patricia O'Toole has been helpful to me in many ways; not least, she put me in touch with Julie Limbaugh, who gathered research for me as part of an internship at Columbia University's graduate writing program. Professor David M. Barrett of Villanova University was generous with his time and knowledge, as was Richard Valcourt of the *International Journal of Intelligence and Counter-Intelligence*. Mike Rubino gave me a good deal of insight into the CIA, an agency he served for many years.

I am grateful to the staffs of the Lawrenceville School Library, the John F. Kennedy Memorial Library, the National Archives, the New York Public Library, and the Bay of Pigs Museum in Miami. While at the museum, I was honored to meet members of Brigade 2506, who gave me their time to recollect events that remain exquisitely painful many years later. My thanks in particular to Jorge Silveira, Jorge Gutiérrez Izaguirre, Máximo Cruz Gonzáles, Raul Martínez, Jorge Marquet, Esteban Bovo, and Juan Jesús Gonzáles.

It was my honor, too, to interview some of the American sailors who accompanied the brigade to the Bay of Pigs and who opened up to me about their experiences. This includes Billy Houston, Jim Padgett, Bob Ziegman, Bruce King (who shared a useful PowerPoint presentation with me), and Don Roberts (who shared his journal).

Others who took the time and effort to enlighten me with their personal knowledge of the Bay of Pigs were Don Wilson, Ann Bissell, and Janet Ray. Ms. Ray probably knows more about the invasion than anyone on earth. Her efforts to recover her father's body from Fidel Castro changed the way the story of the Bay of Pigs is told—and make a pretty compelling story in their own right.

A special word of gratitude is owed to John Nolan, who brought my father into the Bay of Pigs drama in the first place and who has been a steady friend—and loyal tennis partner—of my father's since the Kennedy administration. John's memories and wisdom were invaluable to me.

And of course, my thanks to my parents, Raymond and Nancy Rasenberger, to whom I dedicate this book. To say these pages would not exist without them puts it mildly. They are the finest parents any writer—or any son—could wish for.

Last but not least, to my wife, Ann, and to my sons, Jackson and William, let me here repeat the words I don't, and can't, say often enough: thank you.

NOTES

PUBLISHED SOURCES ARE identified by author's last name and, if necessary, title. Unpublished sources are followed by brackets containing the specific origin of the material (listed in the Unpublished Sources section of the Bibliography). If the source is an interview, see the Oral Histories and Interviews section for specifics.

Commonly Used Abbreviations

Dulles Papers	Allen W. Dulles Papers, Public Policy Papers, Department of Rare Books and Special Collections, Princeton University Library.
FRUS I	*Foreign Relations of the United States, 1961–1963, Volume I, Vietnam.*
FRUS VI	*Foreign Relations of the United States, 1958–1960, Volume VI, Cuba.*
FRUS X	*Foreign Relations of the United States, 1961–1963, Volume X, Cuba.*
FRUS SUP	*Foreign Relations of the United States, 1961–1963, Volumes X/XI/XII. Microfiche supplement.*
JFKL	John F. Kennedy Memorial Library.
OH	Oral history.

Introduction: "The Bay of Pigs Thing"

xiv By one count: See Michael Sullivan; see also William Blum.

Prologue: *"Balls Were in the Air"*

1 "By one of those curious": *New York Times*, April 16, 1961.
1 John Kennedy's approval rating: Richard Reeves, 88; Dallek, 335.
1 "The air had been stale": Schlesinger, *Thousand Days*, 206.
2 The previous afternoon: *Washington Evening Star*, April 15, 1961.
2 "is the day before yesterday": Grossman, *Let Us Begin*, 9.
3 Never had Americans: Hine, *Populuxe*.
3 "lifestyle": Farber, 55.
3 "Let the capitalist countries": *Washington Evening Star*, April 12, 1961.
4 "What can we do?": Richard Reeves, 85.
4 "[A] President's first 90 days": *Chicago Tribune*, April 20, 1961.
4 Happy Valley: See Lynch, 58–59; Ferrer, 130; Persons, 56–77; Triay, 100.
5 Puerto Cabezas . . . as a launchpad: Wyden, 176; Hawkins, 32 [CIA/FOIA].
6 The men left behind: Beerli [CIA/FOIA]; Persons, 79.

1: *"Viva Castro!"*

11 Such a moment arrived: Castro's visit to the United States is drawn largely from contemporaneous newspaper coverage in the *New York Times*, *Washington Post*, *New York Daily News*, and *New York Post*, as well as magazine coverage in *Time*, *Life*, *Newsweek*, and *U.S. News & World Report*.
13 The general outlines of his biography: See Quirk's and Szulc's *Fidel*.
13 And so the world believed: *New York Times*, December 3, 1956, and February 24, 1957.
14 "I have come here to speak": *New York Times*, April 16, 1959.
14 "He must be crazy": *Time*, April 27, 1959.
15 "gone haywire": *FRUS VI*, doc. 260; Quirk, 224–25.
15 Eisenhower was not pleased: *FRUS VI*, doc. 266.
15 The morning after: Franqui, 31; *New York Times*, April 17, 1959; *Washington Post*, April 17, 1959.
16 After the lunch: *FRUS VI*, docs. 286, 292; Quirk, 236.
16 popular novelty: *Life*, April 13, 1959.
16 "What is your connection": *Washington Post*, April 18, 1959; see also Barrett, 427.
17 His first known contact: Quirk, 239.
18 "If the intercontinental": *Newsweek*, January 12, 1959.
18 HOW READY IS U.S.: *U.S. News & World Report*, March 23, 1959.
19 "Yours is a great country": Safford, quoting Nixon memo of April 25, 1959.
19 Operation Alert: See coverage in *Chicago Daily Tribune*, April 16–18, 1959; *Los Angeles Times*, April 18, 1959; *New York Daily News*, April 18, 1959; *New York Times*, April 18, 1959; *Washington Post*, April 17–18, 1959.
20 "I have said very clearly": *New York Times*, April 18, 1959.
20 "such kind eyes": *Washington Post*, April 22, 1959.
20 "younger Jimmy Stewart": *Time*, May 4, 1959.
20 "Go get me a tent": *New York Times*, April 17, 1959.
21 According to Nixon's memo: Safford, quoting Nixon memo of April 25, 1959.
21 "This man has spent": López-Fresquet, 169.
21 Nixon's depiction: Nixon, *Six Crises*, 352. See also Safford.
22 "I feel something sad": "Fidel Castro Speech," transcription courtesy of the Bunn Library at the Lawrenceville School. Castro's visit was described in an

article in the school's student newspaper, the *Lawrence*, also courtesy of the Bunn Library.
22 It was in New York City: *New York Times*, April 22, 1959; *New York Daily News*, April 22, 1959; *Newark Evening News*, April 21, 1959.
23 *Life* even caught: *Life*, May 4, 1959.
23 "We shall bestow": López-Fresquet, 110; see also Szulc, *Fidel*, 490.
23 "The hell of it is": *New York Post*, April 24, 1959.
24 5 HUNTED: *New York Post*, April 23, 1959.
24 The five brothers: *New York Times*, April 24, 1959; *New York Post*, April 24, 1959.
24 "This is like prison": *New York Times*, April 25, 1959.
24 By four-thirty, the area: *New York Times*, April 25, 1959; *Newsweek*, May 4, 1959.
25 "Thank God that's over": *New York Times*, April 26, 1959.
25 "He made it quite clear": *New York Times*, April 25, 1959.

2: *"Point of No Return"*

26 "Do you have information": *New York Times*, July 15, 1959.
27 most Latin American experts . . . agreed: See Bonsal, 72.
27 "I am not Communist": Quirk, 251.
28 "convinced Marxist-Leninist": Castro and Ramonet, 103.
28 "Castro has delighted": Bonsal, 56; see also Gjelten, 244.
28 Eighty percent . . . Forty percent: Beschloss, 91; see also Russo's *Live by the Sword*, 4.
29 The question: Welch, 110–11.
30 In the long run: López-Fresquet, 167–73.
30 "a direct interference": Bonsal, 80.
31 A dapper fifty-six-year-old: See Bonsal's *Cuba, Castro, and the United States*; see also Bonsal's obituary in *New York Times*, July 1, 1995.
31 "I was encouraged to believe": Bonsal, 53; see also Szulc, *Fidel*, 481.
31 "I strongly recommend": *FRUS VI*, doc. 330.
31 "In many respects": *FRUS VI*, doc. 349.
32 The Castro who showed up: *FRUS VI*, doc. 359; Bonsal, 89.
32 He spoke enchantingly: Bonsal, 101; *New York Times*, October 20, 1959.
33 The second development: Fursenko and Naftali, 25–28.
33 a letter from Huber Matos: Matos's arrest is covered in many sources; see especially treatments in Quirk and Szulc; also, *New York Times*, October 22, 1959.
34 Later that same Wednesday: Quirk, 268; *New York Times*, October 22, 1959, and October 24, 1959.
34 Castro mounted a platform: Quirk, 269; *FRUS VI*, doc. 379; *New York Times*, October 27, 1959.
35 "Castro's performance": Bonsal, 108.
35 "real point of no return": Draper, 65.

3: *"It's a Secret"*

39 a few cursory remarks: *New York Times*, November 4, 1959.
39 president's popularity: "Presidential Approval Ratings." Gallup Historical Statistics and Trends.
39 At a press conference: Eisenhower, news conference, October 28, 1959, American Presidency Project.
40 "The Current Basic United States Policy": *FRUS VI*, doc. 376.
40 The general idea: *FRUS VI*, doc. 423.
41 Already rising: *Washington Post*, November 1, 1959.
41 A crowd of five thousand: For a description of the cornerstone ceremony, see *Washington Post*, November 3, 1959, and November 4, 1959; and *New York*

Times, October 25, 1959, and November 4, 1959. See also "Transmittal Slip," dated 2 November 1959, guest list for "DCI PARTY," and "Invocation Offered by the Rev. Dr. Frederick Brown Harris" [Dulles Papers]. See also "The CIA Campus: The Story of Original Headquarters Building," at cia.gov.

41 switchboard operators still: *New York Times*, October 25, 1959.

41 The data were impressive: Ibid.

42 James Woodbury: *Washington Post*, October 25, 1959, and November 8, 1959.

42 magazines portrayed him: See, for example, *Cavalier*, April 1954 [Dulles Papers], and *Time*, August 3, 1953.

43 the Reverend Frederick Brown Harris: Harris's invocation [Dulles Papers].

43 Dulles would be here in name: Grose, 468.

45 Allen saw McCarthy: Ambrose's *Ike's Spies*, 175.

45 His wife, Clover: Grose, 496.

45 Eisenhower spoke briefly: Eisenhower, "Remarks at the Cornerstone-Laying Ceremony for the Central Intelligence Agency Building, Langley, Virginia" [American Presidency Project].

46 "What's in it?": *New York Times*, November 4, 1959; see also "CIA Observes 50th Anniversary of Original Headquarters Building Cornerstone Laying," accessed via cia.gov/news.

4: *"Program of Covert Action"*

47 "originated the plan": Vandenbroucke, "Anatomy of a Failure."

47 At the same time: For State Dept. vs. CIA, see Secretary of State Herter's memorandum in FRUS VI, p. 656, doc. 387; Pfeiffer, 27–28 [Official History]; Welch, 106; *Current Intelligence Weekly Review*, December 10, 1959 [CIA/FOIA].

48 Just one day later . . . J. C. King: Pfeiffer, 29–30 [Official History]; Bissell, 83; Smith, 331.

48 Allen Dulles penciled out: See footnote in Pfeiffer, 29–30 [Official History].

49 "beginning of the serious anti-Castro programs": Pfeiffer, 31 [Official History].

49 Late that Friday morning: Pfeiffer, 32 [Official History].

49 "one of the most secret": *FRUS X*, doc. 169.

49 "covert contingency planning": Grose, 494.

50 Eisenhower's tendencies: Gleijeses, 4, quoting letter from Gordon Gray, December 3, 1974.

50 "At the conclusion": Ibid. Gray gives no date for the meeting but places it in early January. The first NSC meeting that month with Dulles and Eisenhower in attendance was January 11.

50 Nixon opined: *FRUS VI*, doc. 410.

51 Nixon also began a dialogue: Beschloss, 136; see also Brodie, 399.

51 Nixon knew at once: Ambrose's *Nixon*, 545.

51 "the stepped-up campaign": *FRUS VI*, docs. 427, 436.

52 Castro had begun to look like a "madman": *FRUS VI*, doc. 436.

52 Anastas Mikoyan arrived: See Fursenko and Naftali, 36–39.

52 The Soviets were no more sure: See Brodie, 394.

53 "Mikoyan's visit marks": Briefing notes, "Director's Copy," dated February 17, 1960 [CIA/FOIA].

53 *La Coubre*: This incident was covered extensively in the press and is described in many histories; see Quirk; also Szulc's *Fidel*.

53 "positive and aggressive": Gleijeses, 4, quoting letter from Gordon Gray, December 3, 1974.

53 "What We Are Doing in Cuba": Pfeiffer, 245–46 [Official History].

54 inspired by James Bond: Dulles wrote of his affection for Bond and Ian Fleming in "Our Spy-Boss Who Loved Bond," *Life*, August 28, 1964 [Dulles Papers].

54 "Here is a book": Grose, 491.
54 Ian Fleming happened to visit: This tale is related in Thomas, 207 (and footnote on pp. 383–84), and Grose, 495.
55 At a meeting of the Special Group: Pfeiffer, 66–67 [Official History].
55 The formal plan: Pfeiffer, 72–74 [Official History]; *FRUS VI*, doc. 486: "Memorandum of a Conference with the President, White House, Washington, March 17, 1960, 2:30 p.m."; see also the fully declassified text of the program in the September 2002 newsletter of SHAFR by David J. Ulbrich at www.shafr.org/newsletter/2002/sep/covert.htm.

5: *"A Question of Propriety"*

57 "deus ex machina": Blight and Kornbluh, 42.
58 young Bissell: Bissell, 1–14; Thomas, 88–93.
58 His sharpest rebuke: Ann Bissell, interview with author.
58 In college . . . nocturnal sport: Thomas, 92–93.
59 On one occasion: Bissell, 12–13.
59 "Dick was and is": Alsop, 58.
59 "if Dick has a fault": Bundy in "Memorandum for the President," February 25, 1961 [JFKL National Security Files Box 405].
60 "Some people argue": Bissell in *Washington Evening Star*, July 20, 1965 [Dulles Papers, Box 98, folder 8]; see also Bissell OH for Eisenhower Project at Columbia University.
60 the Georgetown Set: See Merry, 155.
61 "the domestic enemy": Burton Hersh, 326.
61 Bissell joined . . . but soon became restless: See Bissell, 74–78.
61 Bissell's first real taste: See Bissell, 80–87.
62 Along with the work, the society: Bissell, 79–80.
63 a letter to Allen Dulles: Bissell to Dulles, August 6, 1954 [Dulles Papers, box 8, folder 10].
63 Dulles responded: Dulles to Bissell, August 10, 1954 [Dulles Papers, ibid.].
63 This plane would come to be known: See Bissell, 95–140, for an extensive treatment of his work on the U-2. See also Ambrose's *Ike's Spies*, 269–75, for a description of the project and Bissell's "genius for administration."
64 The plane's first flight: Bissell, 112.
65 Many believed that next to President Eisenhower: For example, J. B. Smith, 323.
65 "It was a very gay time": Ann Bissell, interview with author.
66 In time, WH/4: Pfeiffer, 32; see also Kornbluh (containing the CIA inspector general's survey), 27.
66 "Guatemala scenario": Thomas, 204.
66 undated memorandum: Pfeiffer, 53.
66 Barnes was a world-class: Esterline, interview with Pfeiffer, 48.
67 "I know fair and neutral colleagues": Bissell, 179.
67 "Like those who no matter how great": Helms, 177.
67 "cool relationship": Bissell, 177.
67 Helms preferred: Powers, 103; Burton Hersh, 428.
67 He did not fit the usual profile: Bohning, 15; see also Blight and Kornbluh, 23.
68 "a very simple little kind": Esterline, interview with Pfeiffer, 3.
68 David Atlee Phillips: See Phillips's memoir, *The Night Watch*.
69 Droller was the same: See Phillips, 92.
69 "linguistic accomplishments": Kornbluh (containing the CIA inspector general's survey), 70.
69 E. Howard Hunt: Phillips, 91–92; Esterline, interview with Pfeiffer, 23; and Szulc's *Compulsive Spy*, 83–95.
69 "Listen to his music": Wyden, 32.

6: "The End Justified the Means"

70 The problem for the Americans: Bissell, 121–22; Ambrose's *Ike's Spies*, 281–89.
71 President Eisenhower considered: See Thomas, 216–18.
71 "great expositor": Bird, 195.
71 Bissell "argued for weeks": Weiner, 184.
71 Bissell himself admitted: Bissell, 125.
71 Bissell was really just confirming: Ambrose's *Ike's Spies*, 282.
73 "putting in the plumbing": Phillips, 91–92.
73 Each man found: Phillips, 92; see also Esterline, interview with Pfeiffer, 22.
74 Droller . . . "carried the counterrevolution": Burton Hersh, 429.
74 "Bender wants this done": Szulc and Meyer, 78.
74 "a powerful company": Johnson, 31.
74 the men of the brigade: Johnson, *Bay of Pigs*, 98–100; Triay, 7–36.
75 Starting in late May . . . recruits were whisked: The best description of the early training phase is in Johnson, 34–37. See also Wyden, 36.
76 He had been present: FRUS VI, doc. 486.
76 "emerged as the principal 'hawk' ": Pfeiffer, 90–92.
77 A July 15 memorandum: Memorandum for the Director, "Subject: The Cuban Pot Boils Over," July 15, 1960 [CIA/FOIA].
77 Congress was calling for action: Barrett, 433–35.
77 By May 1960: Mayer, quoting Gallup, 595.
77 50 percent of Americans: Gallup, July 1960; accessed via the Roper Center at roperweb.ropercenter.uconn.edu.
78 Khrushchev, in a hostile mood: See Quirk, 321; also Fursenko and Naftali, 52.
78 Allen Dulles . . . flew into Hyannis: Dulles's briefing of JFK is covered in Pfeiffer, 102–3, and Grose, 506–8.
79 "The United States is faced": *New York Times*, July 24, 1960.
79 "I just told Kennedy": Grose, 508.
80 "Are they falling dead": Wyden, 29; Brodie, 406. See also Srodes, 507.
80 "From the start of the 1960 campaign": Hinkle and Turner, 39.
80 "It is true, however": Bissell, 157; see also Thomas, 212–15 and 226–29.
81 Sometime in August: Hinkle and Turner, 33–34; see "Family Jewels . . . Subject: Johnny Rosselli" [CIA/FOIA] . See also "Interim Report: Alleged Assassination Plots Involving Foreign Leaders," 74–77.
81 "controlled all the ice-making machines": "Family Jewels."
82 "My philosophy during my last two or three years": Bissell, 157.
82 Among those who shared Bissell's view: Daughetry, 146–48.
83 "reasonable inference": "Interim Report: Alleged Assassination Plots Involving Foreign Leaders," 51. See also Ambrose's *Ike's Spies*, 301, and Weiner, 188.
83 "Eisenhower was a tough man": Bissell, 144.
83 "There's no question about it": Bohning, 27. See also Blight and Kornbluh, 85.
83 "I do remember my own feeling": Bissell, interview with Pfeiffer, 18.
84 an exodus: Draper, 61, 73.
85 "When I got there": Cruz, interview with author.
85 Conditions at the camp: Johnson, 43–45; Lynch, 19; Triay, 48–51.
85 The brigade honored his death: Johnson, 47–48.

7: "Shock Action"

86 Suddenly he was back: Much of this material is based on the coverage of the *New York Times*, September 19, 1960, through September 27, 1960.
87 By instruction of the State Department: *FRUS VI*, doc. 581.
87 "We are a mountain people": *New York Times*, September 20, 1960; see also Quirk, 336.

88 "a leader of the so-called Muslim movement": *New York Times*, September 20, 1960.
88 "He bent down": Szulc's *Fidel*, 525.
88 "Except for Negroes": Quirk, 338.
88 Raúl . . . threatened: *New York Times*, September 21, 1960.
89 "Ay! Don't worry": Quirk, 334.
89 He might not have been so insouciant: "Family Jewels"; Szulc's *Fidel*; Hinkle and Turner, 29–30.
89 "He is mistaken!": Fursenko and Naftali, 61.
89 "illiterate and ignorant millionaire": Quirk, 342.
90 "I don't know why we didn't embrace Castro": Beschloss, 101.
90 As Kennedy told his friend: Weisbrot, 34–35; see also Dallek, 288, re public opinion.
91 a ghoulish Nixon: Ambrose's *Nixon*, 570–71; T. H. White, 286–87.
91 "The threat of nuclear war": Fenton, *In Your Opinion*.
91 Theodore H. White dismissed: T. H. White, 291.
91 "the most difficult": Nixon, *Reader's Digest*, 286; see also Nixon's *Six Crises*, 351–57.
91 Nixon . . . urged: Ambrose's *Nixon*, 590–91.
92 KENNEDY ADVOCATES: Nixon's *Six Crises*, 353.
92 "Now the question was": Nixon, *Reader's Digest*, 286.
92 "For the first and only time": Nixon, *Six Crises*, 354.
93 "I had only one choice": Nixon, *Reader's Digest*, 288.
93 "The position was right": Nixon, *Reader's Digest*, 289; see also Brodie, 412–13.
94 "From this point on I had the wisdom": Seymour M. Hersh, 184.
94 "There has been, I believe": Dulles memo to John A. McCone [Dulles Papers, box 36, folder 1].
94 Seymour M. Hersh . . . insinuates: Seymour M. Hersh, 173–75.
95 Ted Lewis . . . made exactly this point: See *New York Daily News*, March 22, 1962 [Dulles Papers, box 36, folder 1].
95 Hersh trots out other likely suspects who might have revealed the invasion plan to Kennedy before the fourth debate. One of these, according to Hersh, 169–72, is Richard Bissell. There were several occasions when Bissell, who knew Kennedy through their mutual friend Joseph Alsop, might have secretly briefed Kennedy about the invasion before the election. Bissell himself acknowledged meeting Kennedy about a month before the election—early October—but wrote in his memoir that the meeting covered "general issues raised during the campaign" (Bissell, 159). Elsewhere, Bissell said that the meeting "had nothing to do with CIA business." Another possible leak to Kennedy (Hersh, 174–77) came from John M. Patterson, the governor of Alabama. Patterson, a Democrat and Kennedy supporter, would have known about the invasion plans because his state's Air National Guard had been approached by the CIA regarding the use of air guard pilots for the Cuba operation. Concerned by possible political implications for Kennedy, Patterson flew to New York sometime before the election and before the fourth Kennedy/Nixon debate and told the candidate what he knew. "He heard me out and thanked me."
95 "the Kennedy campaign had to find some way": Seymour M. Hersh, 174.
96 Castro put the Cuban military: Fursenko and Naftali, 67.
96 "The more we learned": Bissell, interview with Pfeiffer, 28.
96 And when brigade pilots: Taylor Report, "Narrative," 3.
97 The first delivery: Kornbluh (containing the CIA inspector general's survey), 75.
97 "would not produce": Gleijeses, 11.
97 "You're finally going after": Trest and Dodd, 17.
97 The object of the mission: Gleijeses, 10.

8: *"No Easy Matters"*

99 "strategy of reassurance": Schlesinger, *Thousand Days*, 125.
99 "Senator, I'm beyond retiring age": Grose, 511.
100 The CIA men arrived: *New York Times*, November 19, 1960.
100 "It was not the purpose of the briefing": Draft of "My Answer to the Bay of Pigs" [Dulles Papers].
100 "considerable influence": Bissell, 159–60.
100 "successful in sparking": "Briefing Papers Used by Mr. Dulles and Mr. Bissell—President-Elect Kennedy, 18 November 1960" [*FRUS SUP*, doc. 232].
100 It was expanding rapidly: Pfeiffer, 139.
101 some members of the Eisenhower administration: Ibid., 145–47.
101 The memo reads, in part: Drain's memo is quoted in Pfeiffer, 149.
101 Weiner interprets: Weiner, 191; see also Russo and Molton, 86–87.
102 "limited additional help": Pfeiffer, 155.
103 Tim Weiner again makes a case: Weiner, 192.
103 "Are we being sufficiently": *FRUS X*, doc. 613.
103 "The President made it clear": Pfeiffer, 166 [Official History].
103 "I will say this": Ibid.
103 "I want to call this": Robert Keith Gray, 329–30.
104 "a serious, earnest seeker": Ambrose's *Eisenhower: The President*, 607.
104 "No easy matters": Richard Reeves, 23.
105 January 3, the president held: *FRUS X*, docs. 2 and 3.
105 Eisenhower told his advisers: Ambrose's *Eisenhower: The President*, 609.
105 the CIA was not alone in its willingness: Bissell, 161.
105 Goodpaster . . . interjected: Strober, 322–23.
105 Colonel Jack Hawkins addressed: *FRUS X*, doc. 9.
107 disaster of another kind: *New York Times*, January 10, 1961. See also Salisbury, 145. Writing in a footnote that Paul Kennedy's erroneous article "fell so far below par as to raise questions of motivation," Salisbury seems to imply that Kennedy put out a CIA cover story knowingly.
107 In the official chronology: *FRUS X*, docs. 16–19; Wyden, 86–87.
108 "To hold a lodgment": *FRUS X*, doc. 19.
108 Kennedy and Eisenhower sat alone: Kennedy dictated a memo about this meeting to his secretary later the same day. Other records of this meeting include notes taken by adviser Clark Clifford and Secretary of Defense–designate Robert McNamara [all in JFKL, President's Office Files, box 29a]; see also Richard Reeves, 30, and Dallek, 304–5.

9: *"A Grenade"*

113 The inauguration of John F. Kennedy: Descriptions are based on extensive press coverage, January 19–21, 1961, in *New York Times*, *Washington Post*, and *Chicago Tribune*, as well as the "NBC News Time Capsule—The Kennedy Inauguration"; see also Thurston Clark's *Ask Not* for descriptions of the event and JFK's speech.
113 "Great floodlights": Schlesinger, *Thousand Days*, 1.
114 "A grenade": Bird, 199.
115 Wallace Carroll quoted Dickens: *New York Times*, January 21, 1961.
116 "I have never heard a better speech": Burke OH for JFKL.
116 "We have no resentment": *New York Times*, January 21, 1961; see also Higgins, 79.
116 "golden interlude": Schlesinger, *Thousand Days*, 207.
116 Allen Dulles . . . briefed the group: *FRUS X*, docs. 30 and 31.
117 "the present plan": *FRUS X*, doc. 27.

117 Not until the moment he became president: Schlesinger, *Thousand Days,* 233.
117 "Have the Joint Chiefs": Bissell OH for JFKL.
118 When the five Pentagon men: Wyden, 88.
118 "Military Evaluation": *FRUS X,* doc. 35.
118 "a peculiar and ambiguous document": Schlesinger, *Thousand Days,* 238.
119 The use of that innocuous word: Wyden, 89.
119 It nearly collapsed: Johnson, 60–61.
120 A typical experience: Penabaz's diary entry appeared in the *New York Herald Tribune,* May 4, 1961. See also Triay, 12–13.
120 Grayston Lynch entered the picture: Lynch, 48–51.
121 "How much four-engine time": Persons, 5–8.

10: *"A Stone Falling in Water"*

122 Allen Dulles hosted: Armory OH for JFKL. See also Thomas, 237.
122 "the alchemical magic": Goodwin, 170.
123 "By gosh, I don't care": Armory OH for JFKL.
123 "Have we determined": JFK note to Bundy, February 6, 1961. JFKL, NSA files, box 35a.
124 "Defense and CIA now feel": *FRUS X,* doc. 39.
124 Having a man like Mac Bundy: See profile of Bundy, January 1, 1961; see also portraits of Bundy in Bird and Goldstein.
124 The *Harvard Lampoon* . . . pithy verse: Quoted in *Time,* November 15, 1961.
125 "so small you almost needed": Lincoln, 249.
125 "He was the brightest": Halberstam, *Best and Brightest,* 44.
125 The White House meeting: *FRUS X,* doc. 40.
126 More surprising to Bissell: Bissell, 166–68.
127 "Allen and Dick didn't just": Szulc and Meyer, 103.
127 "Obviously, you present a plan": Dulles OH for JFKL.
127 "There is always going to be": From Bissell's interview on "The Science of Spying," an NBC special, May 4, 1965 [Dulles Papers, box 8, folder 10].
127 "Could not such a force": *FRUS X,* doc. 40.
128 "with the women": Richard Reeves, 82.
129 "As you know, there is great pressure": *FRUS X,* doc. 43.
129 "I'm a team man": Mann OH for Eisenhower Project at Columbia.
130 "Since I think you lean": *FRUS X,* doc. 47.
130 Bissell's paper: *FRUS X,* doc. 46.
130 Thomas Mann's paper: *FRUS X,* doc. 45.
130 "stone falling in water": Gleijeses, 28.
131 "We might be confronted": Schoultz, 153.
131 "If he hadn't gone ahead": RFK quoted in Gleijeses, 25.
131 "this antsy-pantsy bunch of liberals": Bundy quoted in Gleijeses, 26.
132 "You can't mañana this thing": Armory OH for JFKL.
132 "That's understandable, Mr. President": Goodwin, 172.
132 "In a sense, there never is": See Dulles's draft of "My Answer to the Bay of Pigs" [Dulles Papers, box 62, folder 16].
132 By the end of April . . . the Cubans: Fursenko and Naftali, 99n.
132 Thomas Mann later recalled: Mann OH for JFKL.

11: "*Too Spectacular*"

134 Arthur Schlesinger sank: Schlesinger, *Thousand Days,* 240.
134 Working off a written report: *FRUS X,* doc. 58; see also Bissell, 168–70.
135 "swift and penetrating": Schlesinger, *Thousand Days,* 241.
135 "None of us looked": Srodes, 525; see also Barrett, 441–43, for evidence that

the CIA did not peddle its plan quite as hard as some critics would later assert. Briefing a House Armed Services subcommittee on March 10 about the invasion plan, Allen Dulles acknowledged that Castro "had developed a very large militia" and that his troops had "pretty good fighting qualities." Rather than give false assurances that Cubans would jump to the aid of the brigade, Dulles told the subcommittee that most Cubans seemed to *like* Castro.

135 The best evidence of this: *FRUS SUP*, docs. 244 and 247.
136 the newest, just-completed evaluation: *FRUS X*, doc. 56.
137 "a demoralizing shock": *FRUS X*, doc. 58.
137 "Castro remains firmly in control": Sherman Kent, Memorandum for the Director. "Is Time on Our Side in Cuba?" March 10, 1961 [CIA/FOIA].
138 "We were led to believe": McNamara OH for JFKL.
138 "Too spectacular": Richard Reeves, 70–71.
138 "It is hard to believe": Bissell, 169.
138 Starting work that same Saturday: *FRUS X*, doc. 68.
139 Tracy Barnes . . . had come to prefer: *FRUS SUP*, doc. 248.
139 Jack Hawkins shared: Bissell, 171.
139 they considered the new site: *FRUS X*, doc. 62.
139 "How can we have a victorious landing": Phillips, 102.
139 "They have done a remarkable job": *FRUS X*, doc. 64.
140 "The President did not like": *FRUS X*, doc. 65.
140 Bissell returned yet again: *FRUS X*, doc. 66.
140 "he wouldn't take yes": Bissell, 170.
141 "It must be admitted": Bissell, 172.
141 This is not to say that the Mafia: CIA "Family Jewels . . . ," 13–14.
142 "I don't know how they got": Quoted in Bissell, 157.
143 Maheu handed the pills: Hinkle and Turner, 72–75; "Interim Report: Alleged Assassination Plots Involving Foreign Leaders," 80–82.
143 "a scoundrel, a cheat": Esterline, interview with Pfeiffer, 68.
143 Johnny Rosselli later testified: "Interim Report: Alleged Assassination Plots Involving Foreign Leaders," 81.
143 "Did you see the paper?": Ibid., 82.
143 Smathers . . . recalled a conversation: Beschloss, 13.
144 "We've only got a week": Wyden, 116.
144 "If you don't come out of this": Ibid.
145 The new council: Szulc and Meyer, 107; see also Schlesinger, *Thousand Days*, 244.
145 "Definitely no!": *New York Times*, March 23, 1961.

12: "*Albatross*"

146 "What do you think of this damned invasion?": Schlesinger, *Thousand Days*, 246.
146 "the worst one we've got": Dallek, 354.
146 his "albatross": Ibid., 356.
147 "Do you know anything": Richard Reeves, 76–77; Acheson OH for JFKL.
147 Chester Bowles attended: Bowles, 326–29.
147 "You can't have him": Bowles OH for JFKL. "So poor Dick might have been spared this Bay of Pigs horror," Bowles reflected. "He could have gotten out in January, three months before it happened."
148 Bissell began with a discussion: *FRUS X*, doc. 74.
148 McGeorge Bundy supported [footnote]: Bundy in "Memorandum for the President," February 25, 1961, JFKL, National Security Files, box 405.
148 "I have the impression": Schlesinger, *Journals*, 149.
148 "On Tuesday, April 4th": Mann's memo is in *FRUS X*, doc. 75.

149 "long answers to short questions": Halberstam, *The Best and the Brightest*, 17.
150 "I think you can kill this thing": Bowles OH for JFKL, 1970.
150 In the corner, in tiny letters: Ibid.
150 Fulbright was aware: See Johnson and Gwertzman's *Fulbright*, 173–77; see also Fulbright OH for JFKL and Schlesinger's *Thousand Days*, 251.
152 *Air Force One* landed at 11:20 A.M.: For times on March 30, 1961, and other days, see the President's Appointments, which can be viewed in PDF at jfklibrary.org.
152 the list spelled out chores: *FRUS X*, doc. 72.
153 Dennison had been briefed: Pfeiffer, 125.
153 "I will be prepared": *FRUS X*, doc. 73.
153 "You mean . . . I'm to go down there": Wyden, 125.
154 journal a young enlisted man named Don Roberts: Don Roberts's journal, March–April 1961; Roberts's interview with author; see also "Noblesville Man Recalls Bay of Pigs Invasion," *Noblesville Daily Times*, April 15, 2008.
155 The printed schedules: The President's Appointments, March 31–April 4, 1961; see also Quirk, 364–65.
155 The Secret Service had picked up rumors: Quirk, 364.
155 Some of the president's advisers: Beschloss, 107–8; see also Thomas, 251.
156 "I'm having a meeting": Johnson and Gwertzman, 175.
156 president's counselors had arrived: The April 4 meeting is covered in Richard Reeves, 79–81; Wyden, 146–50; and *FRUS X*, doc. 80.
156 "God, it was tense": Johnson and Gwertzman, 176.
157 "Suppose they can't establish": Goodwin, 175.
157 In his own memoir: Bissell, 174.
158 "a brave, old-fashioned": Schlesinger, *Thousand Days*, 252.
158 "In my mind, our moral right": Nitze, 184.
158 "I took the opportunity": Quoted in Bissell, 175.
158 "Damn it to hell": Quoted in Wyden, 149.
159 "This is not the right way": Ibid.
159 "I'd say, let 'er rip!": Richard Reeves, 81.
159 "I don't know what his feelings were": Mann OH for JFKL.
160 "With large numbers of people": Rusk, 210.
160 One joke making the rounds: Rusk, 197.
160 "I served President Kennedy": Rusk, 195–96.
161 "among the worst fiascoes": Janis, 14; see Janis 14–47 for chapter on Bay of Pigs.
161 "I liked all the young men": Clifford OH for JFKL.
162 "The President again indicated": *FRUS X*, doc. 80.
162 "We better sleep on it": Richard Reeves, 82.
162 "It is one thing": Schlesinger, *Thousand Days*, 255–56.
163 Kennedy called him over: Ibid., 252.
163 No need, Rusk responded: Wyden, 150–51.

13: *"Infinite Trouble"*

164 "When you asked me": *FRUS X*, doc. 81; see also Schlesinger, *Thousand Days*, 252–53.
165 "You know, I've reserved the right": Schlesinger, *Thousand Days*, 256.
165 "We seem now destined": Schlesinger, *Journals*, 109.
165 "It is apparent": Ibid., 109–10.
166 TAD SZULC, 74, DIES: *New York Times*, May 22, 2001.
166 "a passion for meeting odd strangers": Salisbury, 148.
167 Szulc asked Wilson: Wyden, 144.

167 "totally taken aback": Don Wilson, interview with author.
167 "Get me Allen Dulles": Sperber, 623.
168 "It was a remarkable meeting": Don Wilson, interview with author.
168 "stupid, stupid idea": Persico, 475.
168 According to several accounts: Descriptions of this episode are included in Beschloss, 109; Catledge, 259–65; Richard Reeves, 83–84; Salisbury, 148–56; Talese, 5, 7; and Wyden, 143–46.
168 "I was worried not so much": Catledge, 261.
169 "a careful, accurate, and devastating": Schlesinger, *Thousand Days*, 261.
169 "I think he would withdraw": Schlesinger, "Memorandum for the President," April 6, 1961 [JFKL].
169 "Gil Harrison came through": Schlesinger memorandum written later on April 6, 1961 [JFKL].
170 "Kennedy, after all": Halberstam, *Powers That Be*, 375.
170 "I can't believe what I'm reading!": Beschloss, 109.
170 "cable of this Russian diplomat": Esterline, interview with Pfeiffer.
171 KGB made of this intelligence: Fursenko and Naftali, 90–91.
171 Nearly every day: Szulc, *Castro*, 542.
171 "Really, rather than Central Intelligence": Castro speech, April 8, accessed via Castro Speech Database.
171 First thing that morning: Schlesinger, *Journals*, 110; see also Schlesinger's *Thousand Days*, 257.
172 "The integrity and credibility": Schlesinger, *Thousand Days*, 271.
172 Tracy Barnes handled: The Stevenson briefing is covered in Martin, 622–24; Thomas, 255; and Wyden, 156–58.
172 "guardedly indicated": Walter Johnson (ed.), *The Papers of Adlai E. Stevenson*, 53.
172 "We told him about the exile group": Martin, 624.
173 the landing . . . had been scheduled: *FRUS X*, doc. 85.
173 "Tracy was one of the sweetest guys": Esterline, interview with Pfeiffer, 47–48.
173 "Knowing Tracy": Thomas, 393n.
173 "Look, I don't like this": Martin, 624.
173 "wholly disapproves of the project": Schlesinger, *Journals*, 110.
173 At the door: Bohning, 32–34; Thomas, 252; Wyden, 159–60.
174 "Things were going on": Ann Bissell, interview with author.
174 "I just remember": Ibid.
174 Under him in WH/4: Kornbluh (containing the CIA inspector general's survey), 27.
175 they had come to tell him: Bohning, 32–34.
176 "The atmosphere was calm, serious": Ibid.
176 "Usually such a remark": Bissell, 182–83.
177 "Usually when we went": Houston, interview with author.
177 "When I saw the coast": Padgett, interview with author.
177 "We were instructed today": Roberts's journal entry.
177 "Everybody knows something big": Ibid.
177 "a very unusual thing": King, interview with author.
178 "You tell people": Ibid.
178 revised Rules of Engagement: *FRUS X*, doc. 87.
178 Arthur Schlesinger wrote one last: *FRUS X*, doc. 86.
179 The party . . . was "messy, disordered": Schlesinger, *Journals*, 110.
179 "I hear you don't think": Schlesinger, *Thousand Days*, 259.

14: *"A Fanatical Urge to Begin"*

180 By 10:00 A.M., the president: Richard Reeves, 85.
180 ninth press conference: Full transcript at American Presidency Project.

181 The last meeting: *FRUS X*, doc. 92.
181 His briefing notes: *FRUS X*, doc. 93.
182 In the car: Wyden, 162–63.
182 Gray also took Bissell aside: Bissell, 175–76.
183 The present concept: *FRUS X*, doc. 93.
183 "I know everybody is grabbing": Beschloss, 114.
183 The air base at Happy Valley: Persons, 74–77; Ferrer, 137.
184 an "emergency" cable from CIA: *FRUS X*, doc. 98; see also Bohning, 39.
184 Hawkins promptly cabled: Ibid.
185 Guevara informed the Soviet: "Record of Conversation," from S. M. Kudryavtsev's diary, April 14, 1961 (accessed via the National Security Archive website www.gwu.edu/~nsarchiv/).
185 "As far as I know": Bissell, 183.

15: *"This Is the Aggression"*

190 Based on U-2: CIA, Report 3034, April 13, 1961 [CIA/CREST]; see also Kornbluh (containing "Analysis" by Richard Bissell), 168.
190 a ninth Invader taxied: Ferrer, 140–41.
190 Gus Ponzoa was still: For descriptions of Ponzoa's flight, see Ferrer, 147–51; Persons, 80; and Wyden, 176–79.
191 the CIA had removed the tail gun turrets: Higgins, 134.
192 At about the same time . . . the three planes of Linda: For description of Linda and Puma flights, see Ferrer, 147–58.
193 he glanced up: Rodríguez, 132.
193 "What are these planes?": Wyden, 180; see also Rodríguez, 133, and Szulc's *Fidel*, 546.
193 "This is the aggression": Johnson, 90.
194 Captain Mario Zuniga had flown: Ferrer, 140; Trest and Dodd, 63–66; Wyden, 174–76.
194 "I am one of the twelve": *Miami Herald*, April 16, 1961, and *Washington Post*, April 16, 1961.
195 Cuban and American pilots . . . gathered: Persons, 79; Ferrer, 160–61.
196 If these initial estimates: Hawkins, *Record of Paramilitary Action Against the Castro Government of Cuba*; Taylor Report, "Narrative," 15; Kornbluh, 168.
196 In Washington, the exhausted men: Hunt, 191.
197 "with the help of God": Martin, 594.
197 "It won't work": Ibid., 605.
197 "Stevenson was miscast": McKeever, 491–92; for more on Stevenson's relationship with JFK, see Beschloss, 46–48.
198 Just two days earlier: *Washington Evening Star*, April 14, 1961.
198 No sooner did Frederick H. Boland: United Nations, General Assembly, Official Records.
199 President Kennedy's public schedule: The President's Appointments, April 15, 1961.
200 "We are also a revolutionary country": *New York Times*, April 16, 1961.
200 He named Philip Bonsal: *Washington Evening Star*, April 16, 1961.
200 "Mr. President," Bundy said: Schlesinger, *Journals*, 111.
200 "bound to be all right": Goldstein, 43.
201 a "salvation" for Jacqueline: Anthony, 162–63; see also Richard Reeves, 89.
201 "Can you imagine me": Beschloss, 116.
201 "That was an interesting race": *New York Times*, April 16, 1961.
201 A photograph taken of him: *Washington Evening Star*, April 16, 1961.
202 press was asking questions: Schlesinger, *Thousand Days*, 272; *New York Times*, April 16, 1961.

202 "If any of our planes": *Washington Post*, April 16, 1961.
202 Pieces of made-in-U.S.A. shells: Ibid.
203 "We are naturally interested": *New York Times*, April 16, 1961.
203 They contacted the State Department's: Cleveland OH for JFKL; Martin, 626; Wyden, 186–87.
203 "I thought I was giving Stevenson": Wyden, 187, fn.
203 Raúl Roa was the first to speak: United Nations, First Committee, 1,149th Meeting, Saturday, April 15, 1961, at 3:00 P.M.; see also *New York Times*, April 16, 1961.
205 Among those watching: Phillips, 106.
205 The two other ships: Hinkle and Turner, 61.
206 Aboard the freighters: Johnson, 94; Lynch, 69; Triay, 90.
206 "The death was very difficult": Silveira, interview with author.

16: *"The Air Will Be Yours"*

207 National Photographic Interpretation Center: Bissell, 104; Dobbs, 137.
207 The damage to Castro's air force: Hawkins, 32; Wyden, 193–94.
208 "definitely destroyed": Taylor Report, "Narrative," 15.
208 At least seven: Taylor Report, "Memorandum for the Record," April 25, 1961, 2.
208 Castro had apparently left them: Ibid., 9.
208 Castro claimed [footnote]: Rodríguez, 133.
208 At 9:00 A.M., the nation's top military brass: *FRUS X*, doc. 107.
209 "growing evidence of consternation": Persons, 81.
210 "I had been assured": Ferrer, 164.
210 "We're gonna have": Ibid., 145.
210 "not in our wildest imagination": Persons, 81.
210 "You could catch a fish": Cruz, interview with author; see also Johnson, 94.
210 An empty stomach: Silveira, interview with author.
211 "sudden sinking sensation": Lynch, 70.
211 "Until April 1961": Ibid.
212 His stomach was bothering him: Dallek, 367.
212 Such afflictions were nothing new: Dallek, 398–99; see also Dallek's "The Medical Ordeals of JFK," *Atlantic*, December 2002. For more on JFK's health, see Gilbert, *The Mortal Presidency*, and an interview with Dr. Jeffrey Kelman—who examined JFK's medical records with Robert Dallek—that appeared on PBS's *Newshour* on November 18, 2002.
213 Kennedy did not leave the house: The President's Appointments, April 16, 1961.
213 As if to remind Kennedy: *Chicago Daily Tribune*, April 17, 1961.
214 Fidel Castro was concluding: *Miami Herald*, April 17, 1961; Szulc, *Castro*, 547; Quirk, 369.
214 "Sunday went by": Castro and Fernández, 191.
214 "a reign of terror": *Time*, April 28, 1961.
214 "If not, then the world": Szulc and Meyer, 124.
215 "expedition days": Ann Bissell, interview with author.
216 "I was prepared to run it": Thomas, 247.
216 "Go ahead": Wyden, 195.
216 "puzzling circumstances": *New York Times*, April 16, 1961.
216 Pedersen had spent the morning: Wyden, 189.
216 "deliberately tricked": Beschloss, 115.
216 "I've got to resign": Walter Johnson (ed.), *The Papers of Adlai Stevenson*, 54.
217 In the minds of some: See chapter 9 of Jeff Broadwater's *Adlai Stevenson and American Politics*. See also, for example, Charles Murphy's "The Record Set

Straight," in *Fortune*, September 1961, or Stewart Alsop's "The Lessons of the Cuban Disaster," in the *Saturday Evening Post*, June 24, 1961. Nearly every account of the Bay of Pigs has featured Stevenson's phone call to Rusk as pivotal.

217 "this chance decision": Hunt, 195.
217 Cabell had been a highly decorated: See Cabell's memoir, *A Man of Intelligence*.
218 "Do we have approval": Wyden, 195–96.
218 "Fuck Cabell!": Thomas, 259.
218 Greatly disturbed: *FRUS X*, doc. 105.
219 men came together to sing: Johnson, 100; Lynch, 72; Triay, 72.
220 "Don't let them do anything": Wyden, 195.
221 Kennedy was in the master bedroom: Beschloss, 116.
221 "suddenly found out": Rusk's testimony to Taylor Committee, tenth meeting, May 4, 1961, 10.
221 "I'm not signed on to this": Schlesinger, *Thousand Days*, 273.
222 "Redhead, do you know": Fay, 185.
222 "There is going to be": Hugh Sidey in *Time*, April 16, 2001.
222 The phone rang: The tale of the cancellation of air strikes is related in *FRUS X*, doc. 108; see also *FRUS SUP*, doc. 261; Taylor Narrative, 17; and Hawkins, *Record of Paramilitary Action*, 33–34.
222 "The President has directed": Cabell, 366; *FRUS X*, doc. 231; *FRUS SUP*, doc. 261.
222 "to hold the hand": Ibid.
223 "I, of all people": Ibid.
223 "The Secretary informed us": *FRUS X*, doc. 108.
223 "I offered the prediction": Hawkins, "Record of Paramilitary Action," 34.
224 "I don't think there's any point": Bissell, 174.
224 Five thousand yards: Hawkins, "Record of Paramilitary Action," 27; Lynch, 73; Wyden, 216–17; and "Sequence of Events," prepared by CIA for the Taylor Committee and included as an annex to the committee's report.
225 "There's been a little change": Phillips, 107.
225 "Probably out of cowardice": Bissell, 185.
225 "Goddamn it, this is criminal": Bohning, 48.
225 "I know that some of you": Bissell, 185.
225 "I almost went to jail": Esterline, in Blight and Kornbluh, 46.
226 "The Cuban Brigade was doomed": Ibid., 237.

17: *"There Goes the War"*

227 Operation Zapata started: *FRUS X*, docs. 9, 27, 109; Lynch, 41–43; Hawkins, *Record of Paramilitary Action*.
229 Richard Bissell had no clear picture: Bissell, 194–95; also Bissell's interview with Pfeiffer, 33.
230 The first brigademen: *FRUS X*, doc. 109; Johnson, 103–5; Lynch, 83–85; Wyden, 217–21.
231 "lit up like Coney Island": Lynch, 83.
232 "Castro still has operational aircraft": Lynch, 88.
233 The time was just after 1:00 A.M.: Wyden, 221. (Hawkins's *Record* has this as 1:49.)
233 "All of us had to live": Cabell, 377.
233 "foot-dragging": Ibid., 375.
233 "I'm not asleep": Hunt, 202–3.
234 "Success was no longer relevant": Cabell, 370.
234 "I want you to think up things": Wyden, 204.
234 "Surely Cabell realizes": Kirkpatrick OH for JFKL, 11.

234 When Shoup picked up the receiver: Shoup OH for JFKL, 16; Jablon, 80.
235 "How did things go?": Wyden, 205. Lemnitzer gave a different version; he claimed he was not contacted by Gray until about 7:00 A.M. Gray insisted he would not have waited five more hours to alert Lemnitzer. See Binder, 267.
235 Gar Thorsrud was in: Wyden, 201–2.
235 "Complete plan amended": *FRUS SUP*, doc. 261.
235 "There goes the whole": Ferrer, 162.
236 the pilots were staggered: Haas, 157.
236 "The Commander in Chief is calling": Wyden, 248–49; Szulc, *Castro*, 549–50.
237 "What are you doing?": Castro and Fernández, 107.
237 Lynch recommended scrapping: Lynch, 88.
237 San Román also consented: Johnson, 108; Wyden, 221.
238 frustrations at Red Beach: *FRUS X*, doc. 109; Lynch, 91–94.
238 "You could hear": Silveira, interview with author.
238 When the landing craft hit: Johnson, 106, 108.
239 At about 3:30 A.M.: Rodríguez, 134; see also Wyden, 250–51. Szulc's *Castro*, 551, has the time of Castro's call as 4:30 A.M.
239 Castro seemed to understand instantly: Szulc, *Castro*, 551.
239 "Take up strategic positions": Kornbluh, chronology of events, 309.
239 Since the previous evening: Quirk, 372.
240 For all the criticism: Cabell, 376–77; *FRUS SUP*, doc. 261.
240 Just minutes before: *FRUS X*, doc. 111.
241 Cabell did not decline this time: Cabell, 377.
241 "No," said the president: Richard Reeves, 91.
242 Richard Bissell put in a call: *FRUS SUP*, doc. 261; *FRUS X*, doc. 111.
242 Edward Ferrer had flown in near silence: Ferrer, 171–77; Wyden, 232–33.
243 he looked down and realized: Wyden, 233.
243 "Look, mister": Lynch, 95.
244 And when it opened fire: Johnson, 112; see also *FRUS X*, doc. 109.
244 "I was holding a coffee pot": *Life*, May 10, 1963.
244 "Everybody fire": Johnson, 112.
244 "Yes, I know": McKeever, 488.
245 "I told him all about it": Martin, 628.
245 "you just cut the throats": Coffey, 355.
245 Burke was "horrified": Wyden, 206.
246 Many decades later . . . Marquet: Marquet, interview with author; see also Triay, 104.
247 Over at Blue Beach: Hawkins, *Record*, 35.
248 brigade gunners . . . found it nearly: Lynch, 108.
248 It was just before 9:30 . . . Carreras returned: Wyden, 229–30.
248 The first three overshot: Lynch, 113.
249 "What the hell": Lynch, 114.
249 The Young Presidents: Brochure from Young Presidents [Dulles Papers, box 87, folder 6].
249 "the notorious American": Beschloss, 116.
249 "Revolutions are in progress": *Summary of Remarks by Allen W. Dulles to the American University of Presidents' Young Presidents' Organization* [Dulles Papers, box 87, folder 6].
250 President Kennedy was touching down: The President's Appointments, April 17, 1961.
250 "I don't think it's going": Reeves, 92.
250 The ground war began: Hawkins, *Record*, 36; Johnson, 122–23.
250 the command of Máximo Cruz: Johnson, 122–23; see also Cruz, interview with author.

251 "This seemed the only logical": Lynch, 114; see also *FRUS X*, doc. 109.
251 "Don't desert us": Wyden, 231.
251 "We are under air attack": Lynch, 116.
252 the two cargo ships . . . had separated: Lynch, 117.
252 "I must announce": *New York Times*, April 18, 1961; U.N. General Assembly, First Committee, 1,150th Meeting, Monday, April 17, 1961, at 11:00 A.M.
253 "I was shocked": Walter Johnson (ed.), *The Papers of Adlai E. Stevenson*, 54.
253 "By sea and air": Castro and Fernández, 71; Quirk, 371.
253 At 3:15 P.M. he arrived at the town: Szulc, *Castro*, 552; Wyden, 257.
254 "There were not a hundred": Cruz, interview with author.
254 "Maybe there will be a miracle": *Life*, May 10, 1963.
254 The advancing troops: Castro and Fernández, 105, 108.
255 "They had no idea": Cruz, interview with author; see also Johnson, 123.
255 One of the best gunners: *Life*, May 10, 1963.
255 five two-plane sorties: Ferrer, 173–204.
256 "It was awful": *Life*, May 10, 1963.
256 the redheaded buzzards: Ibid.
256 "I've got a T-33 on my tail": Johnson, 125.
256 José Crespo barreled: Ferrer, 197–200; Wyden, 241.
256 The American pilots were prohibited: *FRUS X*, doc. 115.
257 Later that evening: Ferrer, 200.
257 Lem Jones distributed: Johnson, 129; Szulc and Meyer, 131–32.
257 "I am very happy": Johnson, 128.
258 About two thousand shells: Ibid., 134.
258 "Whenever we heard": *Life*, May 10, 1963.
258 Allen Dulles landed: *FRUS SUP*, doc. 259; Grose, 257; Wyden, 265–66.

18: *"Sour Like You Wouldn't Believe"*

260 Castro's troops were on the move: Descriptions of the Battle of the Rotunda are included in Johnson, 134–39; Rodríguez, 183–86; and Wyden, 272–73.
260 Millions of . . . crabs: *Life*, May 10, 1963.
260 Máximo Cruz was among: Cruz, interview with author.
261 "It was scary as shit": Triay, 101.
261 "prehistoric monsters": *Life*, May 10, 1963.
261 "just like hell": Johnson, 135.
261 One of the bravest: *Life*, May 10, 1963.
262 Máximo Cruz was badly injured: Cruz, interview with author; Johnson, 136–37.
262 "Are you the commander": Johnson, 137.
262 The Cuban government reported [footnote]: See, for example, Castro and Ramonet, 258.
263 *"Lieutenant, don't leave me"*: Triay, 101–2.
263 He gave orders: *FRUS X*, doc. 109; Johnson, 137.
263 For several hours: *FRUS X*, doc. 109; Lynch, 120–21.
263 Aboard the *Blagar*: Lynch, 121; Wyden, 275.
264 A squadron of six: Beerli, "Narrative of Air Activity," April 26, 1961; see also Johnson, 140.
264 "Of course we did not ask": Cabell, 379.
264 Radio Swan encouraged: Kornbluh, 315; Quirk, 372.
265 "horrible morning": Bissell, 188.
265 "Here they were telling": Rostow, 209.
265 "Mac, if you and the President": Wyden, 266.
265 "It was terrible": Bissell, 188.
266 "I'd rather be called an aggressor": Thomas, 262.

266 News agencies were reporting: Beschloss, 120; Szulc and Meyer, 133.
266 "Mr. President, I send you": Full text of this letter is in *FRUS X*, doc. 117; see also Beschloss, 120, and the *Washington Evening Star*, June 18, 1961.
267 Kennedy's breakfast: Beschloss, 120–21; Szulc and Meyer, 135.
267 "It's a serious situation": *New York Times*, April 19, 1961.
267 Oliva conferred: Johnson, 141.
268 "It's better than to be killed": Wyden, 274.
268 "I was sure they were coming": Johnson, 142.
268 "Where have you been": Ibid., 143.
268 He liked better: Lynch, 123.
268 "Now we will hit them!": Johnson, 144.
268 Oliva felt ashamed: Ibid.
269 "I think you will find": *FRUS X*, doc. 119.
269 In late morning: *FRUS X*, doc. 121.
269 "because it cannot easily be": *FRUS X*, doc. 119.
269 at least one witness: Jones, 116 (quoting Wheeler's OH for JFKL).
270 "a public line they were to take": Dutton OH for JFKL.
270 "Well, don't you think": Harlan Cleveland OH for JFKL, 27–28.
270 "Nobody knew what to do": *FRUS X*, doc. 121.
270 "a military operation which was": Burke OH for Eisenhower/Columbia, 219.
270 "He wouldn't have": Burke OH for JFKL, 19.
271 "It is late!": *FRUS X*, doc. 121.
271 increasingly urgent requests: *FRUS X*, doc. 125.
272 "kept shaking his head": Giglio, 60.
272 Five minutes later: Schlesinger, *Thousand Days*, 275–76.
272 Reston asked the president: Beschloss, 122.
273 "We are under attack": Richard Reeves, 93.
274 The *Atlántico* and the *Caribe*: *FRUS X*, doc. 116; Lynch, 120, 122; Wyden, 275–76.
274 "Prepare unmarked Navy planes": *FRUS X*, doc. 123.
274 Burke contacted Dennison: *FRUS X*, doc. 124.
275 "Watch for them": *Life*, May 10, 1963.
275 "They were beautiful": Johnson, 148.
276 "It is very questionable": "Briefing of Secretary of State Designate Rusk," *FRUS SUP*, doc. 236.
276 American contract crews can be used: *FRUS X*, doc. 120.
276 Each of the planes: Ferrer, 207.
276 At 4:20 P.M., Admiral Clark: *FRUS X*, doc. 125.
276 When Castro's militia first saw: Ferrer, 207–8; Lynch, 128; Rodríguez, 195.
277 "It was a long and grim day": Schlesinger, *Thousand Days*, 277.
277 At 4:00 P.M. he sat down: The President's Appointments, April 18, 1961; Schlesinger, *Thousand Days*, 276–77; *Washington Post*, April 20, 1961.
278 Cleveland was impressed: Cleveland OH for JFKL.
278 the State Department contacted: *FRUS X*, doc. 130.
278 "to understand the importance": Ibid.
279 Máximo Cruz . . . was seen: Johnson, 149.
279 "I was not going to leave my men": Cruz, interview with author.
279 Admiral Burke . . . sent a cable: *FRUS X*, doc. 132.
279 "Anything you can do": *FRUS X*, doc. 133.
279 I was asked once again: *FRUS X*, doc. 134.
280 He remained there: The President's Appointments, April 18, 1961.
280 "radiant . . . in a gown of pink": *Washington Post*, April 20, 1961.
280 This was the first gala: Sanford Fox files, "Social Events," January 20–April 19, 1961, JFKL.

280 "What we need now": *Washington Post*, April 20, 1961.
281 "The shit has hit the fan": Thomas, 262–63.
281 Walt Rostow skipped: Rostow, 209; Thomas, 263; Wyden, 269–70.
282 Do you people realize: *FRUS X*, doc. 135.
282 "Let me take two jets": Beschloss, 122; Richard Reeves, 93.

19: *"The Loneliest Man"*

283 "Admiral," President Kennedy repeated: Freedman, 144; also Wyden, 270–71, and Richard Reeves, 94.
283 At one point, Kennedy's secretary: Lincoln, 254.
284 "For had the U.S. Navy and Air Force": Sorensen, 297.
284 "The limits and dilemmas of power": Rostow, 210.
284 The Cuban Revolutionary Council had been sequestered: Johnson, 156–57.
285 "Where is Berle?": Richard Reeves, 94.
285 "I am in the President's office": Schlesinger, *Journals*, 113; see also Schlesinger's *Thousand Days*, 277–79, for his description of the Oval Office meeting.
286 "That's a deeper commitment": Richard Reeves, 94.
286 "The President shouldn't appear": Beschloss, 123.
286 "Keep your chin up": Wyden, 271; Bissell, 189.
286 "I can think of happier": Schlesinger, *Journals*, 114; see also Blight and Kornbluh, 97–98.
286 "Somehow . . . it was difficult": Rostow, 210.
287 "He must be the loneliest man": O'Donnell, 272.
287 The cable from CIA headquarters: *FRUS X*, docs. 136 and 150; *FRUS SUP*, doc. 256.
287 "Now we'll smash them!": Ferrer, 213–14.
287 "We did it for the Cubans": Trest and Dodd, 82–83.
288 the Alabama pilots: Persons, 8–14; Trest and Dodd, 30, 87.
288 Pete Ray: Gup, 108–120; Wise and Ross, 76–83.
288 "We were sitting": Janet Ray, interview with author.
289 Telegram JCS 994369: *FRUS X*, doc. 140.
289 At 2:01 A.M. . . . Dennison had written: *FRUS X*, doc. 138; Wyden, 243.
289 At 3:41 A.M.: *FRUS X*, doc. 141.
290 According to Grayston Lynch: Lynch, 127.
290 "If jet cover": Ibid.
290 John Kennedy was still: O'Donnell, 272; and *Washington Post* for weather.
291 "We were ordered to fly": Clark testimony, Taylor Committee, seventh meeting, May 1, 1961.
292 "The mistake, made in Washington": Lynch, 129.
292 More recently . . . Howard Jones: Jones, 120.
292 Somehow this telegram: *FRUS SUP*, doc. 256.
293 Although some reliable sources: Ferrer, 213.
293 Notably, author Peter Wyden: Wyden, 239.
293 another possibility: Wyden, 242.
293 "Will devote my entire": *FRUS X*, 140.
293 ordered to burn: Jones, 120; Wyden, 299.
294 "I'm hit": Ferrer, 214; Wyden, 237.
294 Meanwhile, Pete Ray's B-26: See Gup, 118–19; Persons, 1–3; Trest and Dodd, 85–86; Wyden, 240.
294 By 7:50 A.M., the war room: *FRUS X*, 142.
294 There were valiant efforts: Johnson, 159–63.
295 "Regardless of whether": *FRUS X*, 142.
295 "mile after mile": Schlesinger, *Journals*, 114. For descriptions of the meeting at Opa Locka, see also Schlesinger's *Thousand Days*, 279–83, and Wyden, 207–8.

295 "as unhappy as men": Berle OH for JFKL.
296 "It is this which I request": Schlesinger, *Thousand Days*, 280.
296 "It seemed to me": Berle OH for JFKL.
296 He had slept little: Richard Reeves, 95, 677.
296 Arthur Schlesinger's call: Richard Reeves, 96.
297 San Blas fell: Johnson, 158.
297 "Blue Beach is under attack": Ibid., 160.
297 "It don't look good": Don Roberts's journal, April 18–19, 1961.
297 "like a kamikaze": Houston, interview with author.
298 "a full battle meal": Padgett, interview with author.
298 Rear Admiral Clark reported: *FRUS X*, doc. 144.
298 "We are out of ammo": Ibid., doc. 145.
298 "Out of ammunition": Ibid., doc. 146.
298 "Final instructions": Ibid., doc. 145.
298 Atmosphere in U.N.: Ibid., doc. 148.
299 "Believe evacuation impossible": Ibid., doc. 149.
299 Direct DD to take personnel: Ibid., doc. 151.
300 "The trees were good cover": *Life*, May 10, 1963.
300 "Danteesque": Johnson, 164.
300 The Last Stand: Johnson, 163–66; Rodríguez, 201–5; Wyden, 281–82.
301 Playa Girón was under: Castro and Fernández, 120, 122.
301 Castro's planes: Manuel Penabaz's diary in *New York Herald Tribune*, May 7, 1961.
301 "Hold on," Lynch urged: Johnson, 168.
301 "Am destroying all equipment": Kornbluh, 319; Wyden, 285.
301 Before fleeing: Johnson, 168–70.
302 Men were running: Manuel Penabaz's diary in *New York Herald Tribune*, May 7, 1961.
302 Oliva asked somebody: Johnson, 171.
302 "Here are the Americans!": Ibid.
302 "Seeing them come": Castro and Fernández, 124–26.
302 "They weren't hitting": Padgett, interview with author.
303 Captain Crutchfield later stated: Wyden, 282–83.
303 the destroyers turned around: *FRUS X*, doc. 155.
303 "We turned our tails": Padgett, interview with author.
303 John Kennedy spent much: For Kennedy's mood and behavior that afternoon, see Beschloss, 123; Rose Kennedy, 400; Thomas Reeves, 272; Wyden, 292; and Marguerite Higgins in the *Washington Evening Star*, July 21, 1965.
304 "We've got to do something": Richard Reeves, 95.
304 "I told him": Rostow, 210–11.
304 "The present situation": *FRUS X*, doc. 157.
305 The flight back: Schlesinger, *Thousand Days*, 283.
305 "Our visitors": Schlesinger, "Memorandum for the President," April 19, 1961, President's Office Files, box 65, JFKL.
306 "I know something": Richard Reeves, 97.
306 the men of the CIA's WH/4 task force: For the CIA's mood and behavior, see Hunt, 209; Bohning, 50; Thomas, 264; Phillips, 109; and Wyden, 293.
307 "The minute I saw him": Nixon, *Reader's Digest*, November 1964.
307 "I was sick of lying": Hunt, 210.
308 "We should pick ourselves up": Beschloss, 124–25.
308 Most of these were broad musings: Benson, 25; see also Beschloss, 127–28.
309 Sorensen stepped into the corridor: Beschloss, 128.

20: *"The Way Things Are Going"*

313 Newspapers across the country: Quotes are from the April 20, 1961, editions.
314 General Lauris Norstad: Beschloss, 129.
314 "Now Kennedy is revealed": Schlesinger, *Journals*, 120.
314 "How could I have been": Sorensen, 309.
314 "For the first time": *New York Times*, April 23, 1961.
314 "Reactions around the table": *FRUS X*, doc. 158. See also Bowles's *Promises to Keep*, 330, and his 1970 OH for JFKL.
315 "Bobby's harsh polemic": Goodwin, 187.
315 "rather a weeper": Dallek, 369.
315 "When I took exception": *FRUS X*, doc. 158.
316 "But let the record show": The full transcript of Kennedy's speech is in Benson's *Writing JFK*. See also Schlesinger, *Thousand Days*, 287–88; and Johnson, 174.
316 The first of these instructed: *FRUS X*, doc. 159.
317 Presidential Task Force on Vietnam: *FRUS I*, docs. 31–32; see also Freedman, 310.
317 "I want to be fair": *Washington Post*, April 21, 1961.
317 "President Kennedy has tried": Nixon, *Reader's Digest*, November 1964.
317 more effusive version: Hinkle and Turner, 96.
317 Nixon slipped in: *Chicago Tribune* and *Washington Post*, April 21, 1961; see also Ambrose, *Nixon*, 632.

21: *"Defeat Is an Orphan"*

319 "In the first place": *New York Times*, April 21, 1961.
319 "There is only one": Schlesinger, *Thousand Days*, 289.
320 "The question naturally": *New York Times*, April 21, 1961.
320 "The President said that he could not understand": Schlesinger, *Thousand Days*, 290.
320 "Allen Dulles and Dick Bissell": Ibid., 120.
320 "Many key pieces": *Washington Post*, April 22, 1961.
320 "on the sideline": Jeffreys-Jones, 123.
321 That Friday, Kennedy appointed: *New York Times*, April 22–25, 1961.
321 "There were the same": Wyden, 306.
321 Since Wednesday afternoon: Regarding the travails of the fleeing brigade, see Johnson, 181–91; Lynch, 133–43; Triay, 114–26; and Wyden, 296–98.
322 One of the injured, Máximo Cruz: Cruz, interview with author.
322 President Kennedy had authorized: *FRUS X*, doc. 161.
322 "We could only take": Houston, interview with author.
323 Fidel Castro spent: Szulc, *Fidel*, 554; Triay, 97.
323 These were very good days: Szulc and Meyer, 144–45.
324 "Sir, we can't put": Johnson, 188–89.
324 "I hope you keep": Cruz, interview with author.
324 "At one point": Silveira, interview with author.
324 "I saw me go outside": Gonzáles, interview with author.

22: *"No One Knows How Tough"*

326 "My God, the bunch": Beschloss, 130.
326 "No one knows": Dialogue comes from Ambrose, *Eisenhower: The President*, 638–39; see also *FRUS SUP*, doc. 258, for "Notes by General Eisenhower on Luncheon Meeting," and Eisenhower, *Diaries*, 387–89.
327 "I say I am all in favor": *Los Angeles Times*, April 23, 1961.

328 "a very dreary account": Eisenhower, *Diaries*, 390.
328 "could not have happened": Ambrose, *Eisenhower: The President*, 639.
328 "Would you like to see": Ibid., 640.
329 "We were screwed": Bohning, 50.
329 "I guess that kind of put an end": Esterline, interview with Pfeiffer, 7.
329 Tracy Barnes . . . was never quite the same: Thomas, 267.
329 that first Sunday: Thomas, 266–67.
330 "You know, don't you": Bird, 198.
330 "If this were": Bissell, 191.
330 "Dick Bissell presents": Schlesinger, "Memorandum to the President," President's Office Files, box 72.
330 "Bissell gap": *New York Times*, April 30, 1961.
330 "I voted for this": Bissell, 191.
330 "The risks are very high": Ibid.
331 The *New York Times* opined: *New York Times*, April 26, 1961.
331 On April 27, Grayston Lynch: Lynch, 146–50.
332 "You know, we'd been through": Thomas Reeves, 272.
332 "All during the weekend": Pitts, 215.
332 "By God, if they think": Fay, 186.
332 "the fellow who knew little": Quoted in Lilienthal, June 15, 1961; Acheson OH for JFKL.
332 "The worse I do": Schlesinger, *Journals*, 120–21.

23: *"Success Is What Succeeds"*

333 "When the crunch came": Russo and Molton, 125.
333 "the lesson was burned": Goldstein, 44.
334 "no one can doubt": Schlesinger, *Thousand Days*, 297.
334 "You know I wish": Goldstein, 41.
334 "get your ass": Bohn, 25.
334 "The President's advisers must": Goldstein, 41–42; Kornbluh, 19.
335 "I hope you'll be": Bundy, "Memorandum to the President," National Security Files, box 405, JFKL, May 16, 1961.
335 The Situation Room: See Bohn, *Nerve Center*, 1–3, and Richard Reeves, 114.
336 memo to Vice President Johnson: Kennedy's "Memorandum for Vice President," April 20, 1961, and Johnson's response, April 28, 1961, are available online at jfklibrary.org.
337 On April 27, the Presidential Task Force: *FRUS I*, docs. 35–36; Freedman, 310–11; see also W. Bundy OH for JFKL, 1972, regarding the atmosphere in the White House on April 20 that precipitated action on Vietnam.
337 Kennedy committed: Bird, 202.
337 "There is building up": *FRUS X*, doc. 172.
338 Vice President Johnson: Ibid., 119; Halberstam, *Best and Brightest*, 134–35.
338 "Don't worry, Lyndon": Mann, 324.
339 "if this kind of an operation": Shoup testimony, Taylor Committee, twelfth meeting, May 8, 1961.
339 "didn't come up": Burke OH for JFKL.
339 a 1973 interview: Burke OH for Eisenhower/Columbia.
340 Some . . . later charged: Lynch, 149–50.
340 "The proximate cause": Taylor Committee, Memorandum No. 2: "Immediate Causes of the Failure of the Operation Zapata," June 13, 1961.
341 "leaders of the operation": Ibid., Memorandum No. 3: "Conclusions of the Cuba Study Group," June 13, 1961.
342 "All hands are strongly reminded": USS *Murray*, "Plan of the Day for Friday 28

April 1961," signed by Robert L. McElroy Jr., executive officer. A copy of the plan was included in a PowerPoint presentation by Bruce King and shared with the author.

342 "I am not that kind of man": Johnson, 211.
342 "I was discouraged": Ibid., 211, 213.
343 He first floated: Johnson, 229; Milton Eisenhower, 272.
343 a tree-planting ceremony: Beschloss, 163.
343 "I put those men in there": Goodwin, 186.
344 "I want to ask you": Milton Eisenhower, 274–75. See also Johnson, 227–43, for a full treatment of the Tractors for Freedom episode.
344 He initially grew uneasy: Milton Eisenhower, 276.
344 Barry Goldwater and William Fulbright: Ibid., 281.
345 A Gallup poll: Mayer, 604.
345 "When Nikita remarked": Milton Eisenhower, 283.
345 "last chance" cable: Milton Eisenhower, 292.

24: *"It Will Be a Cold Winter"*

346 Kennedy considered: Fursenko and Naftali, 105–6.
346 "as a cripple": Beschloss, 186, 193.
347 "Can six million people": Beschloss, 200.
347 "He treated me": Richard Reeves, 166.
347 "If the U.S. wants": Ibid., 169–71.
347 "Roughest thing": Ibid., 172.
348 "There are limits": Ibid., 176.
348 "the United States should risk": Ibid., 180.
348 "a time of sustained": Beschloss, 308.
348 Samuel Lubell found: "The People Speak," released July 5, 1961, in JFKL, National Security Files, box 302A.
348 "I hope the President": Weisbrot, 61.
349 "Had I been wiser": Goodwin, 197. His meeting with Guevara is covered in Goodwin, 197–207. See also Mark White, *The Kennedys and Cuba: The Declassified Documentary History*, 63–65, for the text of Goodwin's "Memorandum for the President," August 22, 1961.
350 "We were both trapped": Goodwin, 207.
351 Harvey was a different story: See Stockton's *Flawed Patriot* for a biography of Harvey.
351 "you're our James Bond?": Russo and Molton, 106.
352 "You know, Dick, it's impossible": Goodwin, 188.
352 Operation Mongoose: See Bohning, 76; Freedman, 153.
352 "Everyone involved": Srodes, 545.
352 "chewed out": Bissell, 201.
353 170-page internal report: The Kirkpatrick Report is in Kornbluh's *Bay of Pigs Declassified.*
353 "hatchet job": Kirkpatrick OH for JFKL.
353 "I think he never forgave": Halpern OH in Weber's *Spymaster*, 123.
354 "I talked to him a great deal": Dulles OH for JFKL.
354 "Your successes are unheralded": Srodes, 549.
354 "Allen Dulles has left": Moscow News Service [Dulles Papers, box 112, folder 21].
355 farewell dinner: Powers, 118.
355 Dulles wrote to Bissell: Correspondence [Dulles Papers, box 8, folder 10].
355 "I think that whole period": Ann Bissell, interview with author.
355 "Your father is truly": Ibid.

25: *"A Man Who Knows"*

356 Living conditions: Numerous details of the brigade's imprisonment are taken from Johnson, 105–45; also from Triay, 130–55.
357 "Request permission": Triay, 135.
358 "What you need": Johnson, 303.
358 "He is a cigarette smoker": *New York Times*, September 19, 1962; see also Wise and Ross, 278–79.
359 Robert Kennedy bluntly warned: Pérez-Cisneros, Donovan, and Koenreich, 71.
359 "a private humanitarian effort": *New York Times*, September 5, 1962.
360 possible "decoy" of anti-Castro forces: Pérez-Cisneros, Donovan, and Koenreich, 83.
360 "elimination by illumination": Powers, 141.
360 "Private citizen—sincere": Pérez-Cisneros, Donovan, and Koenreich, 86.
361 "I am aware": Ibid., 88.
361 "He's the greatest": Johnson, 314.
361 "Remember, don't say anything good": Ibid.; Pérez-Cisneros, Donovan, and Koenreich, 97.

26: *"Abyss of Destruction"*

363 a U-2 passing 70,000 feet: Fursenko and Naftali, 221–22; Richard Reeves, 368.
363 "We have some big trouble": Richard Reeves, 368.
363 Thus began: The account of the Cuban Missile Crisis is drawn primarily from Michael Dobbs's *One Minute to Midnight*, Robert Kennedy's *Thirteen Days*, and Richard Reeves's *President Kennedy*, 370–425.
364 When the Joint Chiefs: Robert Kennedy, 126.
364 "It was clear to me": Quoted in Weisbrot, 72; see also Fursenko and Naftali, 182–283.
365 Donovan first learned: Pérez-Cisneros, Donovan, and Koenreich, 142–43.
365 "The purpose of these": Kennedy's televised address, October 22, 1962, accessed at the American Presidency Project.
365 "Do you, Ambassador Zorin": Dialogue is from Dobbs, 131–32.
366 On Saturday, November 24, Kennedy met: Johnson, 321.
367 "We will": Mahoney, 217.

27: *"There Are No Obstacles"*

368 the attorney general called together: The final phase of the prisoner release is covered extensively in Johnson, 321–46; Wise and Ross, 282–89; and Pérez-Cisneros, Donovan, and Koenreich, 148–87; this chapter also draws on oral histories of participants conducted by the JFKL "Cuban Prisoners Release Project" in 1964, as well as press coverage.
369 "It wasn't a question": Nolan OH for JFKL, 1967.
369 "This was the sort of thing": Nolan, interview with author.
370 "our kind of guy": Dolan OH for JFKL "Cuban Prisoners Release Project."
370 Just before the president was due: R. Rasenberger, interview with author.
371 "My brother made a mistake": *New York Times*, December 26, 1962.
371 Armed with a whopping copy: Nolan, R. Rasenberger, interviews with author.
372 "Some of the CEOs": R. Rasenberger, interview with author.
372 "We were taking everything": Nolan, interview with author.
372 Many companies: Pérez-Cisneros, Donovan, and Koenreich, 203–8.
372 A large chart on the wall: *New York Times*, December 26, 1962.

372 Before the merchandise drive: *New York Times*, December 31, 1962.
373 He regularly called: Oberdorfer, "Log on Special Project," December 3–January 14, 1963, from the Personal Papers of Louis F. Oberdorfer, JFKL.
374 There was no telling: Nolan, interview with author.
375 "We thought we'd go back": Ibid.
376 "The plate of slop": *Newsweek*, January 7, 1963.
376 "Fidel is coming": Nolan OH for JFKL .
376 "My God": *Newsweek*, January 7, 1963; see also Johnson, 338; Wise and Ross, 284; and Triay, 144.
377 "John, what are you going to do now?": Nolan OH for JFKL.
378 "Bob, they are all in": Dolan OH for JFKL "Cuban Prisoners Release Project."
378 Late on Christmas Eve: Nolan, interview with author.
379 "My brother told me": Ibid.
379 "Most of us": Jones for JFKL "Cuban Prisoners Release Project."
379 "wholly extraordinary": *New York Times*, December 26, 1962.
379 "It was very uncomfortable": R. Rasenberger, interview with author.
379 Kennedy delivered: *New York Times*, December 31, 1962; see also Russo and Molton, 231.
380 "a group of the bravest men": Johnson, 346.
380 "The great forces": *New York Times*, December 31, 1962.

Epilogue: *"It Could Have Been Worse"*

381 "the most momentous figure": Nixon, *Reader's Digest*, November 1964.
382 Harder to dismiss is the theory: See, for example, Russo and Molton.
382 "Kennedy was trying": Weiner, 271.
382 Howard Hunt wrote: Hunt, 15.
383 "I was a boy": Don Roberts, interview with author.
383 The "Gentlemen's Agreement": Halberstam, *Powers That Be*, 447–48.
383 "demented patriotism": Victor Bernstein and Jesse Gordon, "The Press and the Bay of Pigs," *Columbia University Forum*, Fall 1967.
384 "Maybe if you had printed": Catledge, 264.
384 "That era was beginning to end": Halberstam, *Powers That Be*, 447–48.
384 "could see what was really going on": Ibid., 449.
385 "season of memoirs": Marguerite Higgins, *Washington Evening Star*, July 21, 1965.
385 "This isn't the time": Sorensen, *Look*, August 10, 1965.
385 "There is certainly nothing to suggest": Schlesinger, *Thousand Days*, 294.
386 IKE SPEAKS OUT: *Newsday*, September 10, 1965.
386 Richard Bissell was interviewed: *Washington Evening Star*, July 20, 1965.
387 "My ten years": Bissell, 239–40.
387 "I think anyone": *Washington Evening Star*, July 20, 1965.
387 He had never made: Srodes, 551.
388 "This story is being written": This quote and other references to Dulles's work on "My Answer to the Bay of Pigs" are taken from the Dulles Papers, box 62, multiple files.
389 Dulles abruptly withdrew it: Allen Dulles, letter to John "Jack" Fischer, October 12, 1965.
390 "rising tide of dark suspicion": *New York Times*, April 25, 1966.
391 "Kennedy wanted the facts": Goodwin, 40.
391 "[I]f he was not looking": Richard Reeves, 72.
391 Castro later claimed: Rodríguez, 133.
392 "In any large": Bissell, "An Analysis of the Cuban Operation," January 18, 1962, in Kornbluh, 133–34.

392 "a rallying point": *FRUS SUP*, doc. 236: "Briefing of Secretary of State Designate Rusk," January 1961.
392 Both Dulles and Bissell: See, for example, Bissell in Kornbluh, 173.
393 "With hindsight": Gleijeses, 37.
393 "There will be no employment": *FRUS X*, doc. 95.
394 "I'll go back to": W. Bundy OH for JFKL.
395 "house to house in Havana": Quoted in Goldstein, 37.
395 "An invasion force": Draper, 102.
398 Nixon wanted to halt: Nixon's attempt to use the CIA in Watergate is recounted in Powers, 259–64.
398 When you get in: Quoted in Powers, 260–61.
398 "Tell them that if it gets out": Powers, 261.
399 "a most unwelcome": Bissell, 242.
399 "would remain silent": Talbot, 49.
400 "I feel an obligation": Bissell, 243.
400 a joint interview with Peter Kornbluh: Kornbluh, 258–66.
400 "Had I known": Hawkins quoted in Bohning, 39–40.
400 "I was really disgusted": Hawkins to Bohning, *Miami Herald*, January 5, 1997.
401 "And he knew why": Blight and Kornbluh, 46.
401 "It is clear in retrospect": Ibid., 65.
401 "the deus ex machina": Ibid., 42.
402 "ruined his life": Wyden, 331.
402 Janet Ray: Ray, interview with author.

BIBLIOGRAPHY

Published Materials

Alsop, Joseph W. *I've Seen the Best of It*. New York: W. W. Norton, 1992.

Ambrose, Stephen E. *Eisenhower: Soldier and President*. New York: Simon & Schuster, 1990.

———. *Eisenhower: The President*. New York: Simon & Schuster, 1983–84.

———. *Ike's Spies: Eisenhower and the Espionage Establishment*. Jackson: University Press of Mississippi, 1981. Reprint, 1999.

———. *Nixon: The Education of a Politician, 1913–1962*. New York: Simon & Schuster, 1987.

Anthony, Carl Sferrazza. *The Kennedy White House: Family Life and Pictures, 1961–1963*. New York: Touchstone, 2001.

Barrett, David M. *The CIA & Congress: The Untold Story from Truman to Kennedy*. Lawrence: University Press of Kansas, 2005.

Benson, Thomas W. *Writing JFK: Presidential Rhetoric and the Press in the Bay of Pigs Crisis*. College Station: Texas A&M University Press, 2004.

Beschloss, Michael R. *The Crisis Years: Kennedy and Khrushchev, 1960–1963*. New York: Edward Burlingame, 1991.

Binder, L. James. *Lemnitzer: A Soldier for His Time*. Dulles, Va.: Brassey's, 1997.

Bird, Kai. *The Color of Truth: McGeorge Bundy and William Bundy: Brothers in Arms*. New York: Simon & Schuster, 1998.

Bishop, Jim. *A Day in the Life of President Kennedy*. New York: Random House, 1964.

Bissell, Richard M., Jr., with Jonathan E. Lewis and Frances T. Pudlo. *Reflections of a Cold Warrior: From Yalta to the Bay of Pigs*. New Haven, Conn.: Yale University Press, 1996.

Blight, James G., and Peter Kornbluh, eds. *Politics of Illusion: The Bay of Pigs Invasion Reexamined*. Boulder, Colo.: Lynne Rienner Publishers, 1998.

Blum, William. *Killing Hope: U.S. Military and CIA Interventions Since World War II*. Monroe, Maine: Common Courage Press, 2004.

Bohn, Michael K. *Nerve Center: Inside the White House Situation Room*. Dulles, Va.: Brassey's, 2003.

Bohning, Don. *The Castro Obsession: U.S. Covert Operations Against Cuba, 1959–1965*. Dulles, Va.: Potomac, 2006.

Bonsal, Philip W. *Cuba, Castro, and the United States*. Pittsburgh, Pa.: University of Pittsburgh Press, 1971.

Bowles, Chester. *Promises to Keep: My Years in Public Life, 1941–1969*. New York: Harper & Row, 1971.

Bradlee, Benjamin C. *Conversations with Kennedy*. New York: W. W. Norton, 1975.

Brashler, William. *The Don: The Life and Death of Sam Giancana.* New York: Harper & Row, 1977.
Broadwater, Jeff. *Adlai Stevenson and American Politics: The Odyssey of a Cold War Liberal.* Farmington Hills, Mich.: Twayne, 1994.
Brodie, Fawn N. *Richard Nixon: The Shaping of His Character.* New York: W. W. Norton, 1981.
Brown, Eugene. *J. William Fulbright: Advice and Dissent.* Iowa City: University of Iowa Press, 1985.
Cabell, Charles P. *A Man of Intelligence: Memoirs of War, Peace, and the CIA.* Colorado Springs: Impavide Publications, 1997.
Castro, Fidel, and Ignacio Ramonet. *Fidel Castro: My Life.* New York: Scribner, 2008.
Castro, Fidel, and José Ramón Fernández. *Playa Girón: Bay of Pigs: Washington's First Military Defeat in the Americas.* College Park, Ga.: Pathfinder, 2001.
Catledge, Turner. *My Life and* The Times. New York: Harper & Row, 1971.
Clarke, Thurston. *Ask Not: The Inauguration of John F. Kennedy and the Speech That Changed America.* New York: Holt, 2004.
Coffey, Thomas M. *Iron Eagle: The Turbulent Life of General Curtis LeMay.* New York: Crown, 1986.
Coltman, Leycester. *The Real Fidel Castro.* New Haven, Conn.: Yale University Press, 2003.
Cuordileone, K. A. "Politics in an Age of Anxiety: Cold War Political Culture and the Crisis in American Masculinity, 1949–1960," *Journal of American History* 87, no. 2 (September 2000).
Dallek, Robert. *An Unfinished Life: John F. Kennedy, 1917–1963.* Boston: Little Brown, Back Bay, 2003.
Daugherty, William J. *Executive Secrets: Covert Action and the Presidency.* Lexington: University Press of Kentucky, 2004.
Dobbs, Michael. *One Minute to Midnight: Kennedy, Khrushchev, and Castro on the Brink of Nuclear War.* New York: Alfred A. Knopf, 2008.
Draper, Theodore. *Castro's Revolution: Myths and Realities.* New York: Praeger, 1962.
Edwards, Bob, and Kenneth Dunne. *A Study of a Master Spy: Allen Dulles.* London: Housmans, 1961.
Eisenhower, Dwight D. *The Eisenhower Diaries.* Edited by Robert H. Ferrell. New York: W. W. Norton, 1981.
———. *Waging Peace: The White House Years, 1956–1961.* Garden City, N.Y.: Doubleday, 1965.
Eisenhower, Milton S. *The Wine Is Bitter: The United States and Latin America.* Garden City, N.Y.: Doubleday, 1963.
English, T. J. *Havana Nocturne: How the Mob Owned Cuba . . . and Then Lost It to the Revolution.* New York: William Morrow, 2008.
Farber, David. *The Age of Great Dreams: America in the 1960's.* New York: Hill & Wang, 1994.
Fay, Paul B., Jr. *The Pleasure of His Company.* New York: Harper & Row, 1966.
Fenton, John M. *In Your Opinion: The Managing Editor of the Gallup Poll Looks at Polls, Politics, and the People from 1945 to 1960.* Boston: Little, Brown, 1960.
Ferrer, Edward B. *Operation Puma: The Air Battle of the Bay of Pigs.* Miami: International Aviation Consultants, 1982.
Franqui, Carlos. *Family Portrait with Fidel: A Memoir.* Translated by Alfred MacAdam. New York: Random House, 1984.
Freedman, Lawrence. *Kennedy's Wars: Berlin, Cuba, Laos, and Vietnam.* New York: Oxford University Press, 2000.
Fursenko, Aleksandr, and Timothy Naftali. *One Hell of a Gamble: The Secret History of the Cuban Missile Crisis: Khrushchev, Castro, and Kennedy, 1958–1964.* New York: W. W. Norton, 1997.

Giglio, James N. *The Presidency of John F. Kennedy*. 1991. Reprint, Lawrence: University Press of Kansas, 2006.
Gilbert, Robert E. *The Mortal Presidency: Illness and Anguish in the White House*. New York: Basic Books, 1992.
Giniger, K. S. "Chief Spy: The Story of Allen Dulles." *Washington Post*, July 3, 1960.
Gjelten, Tom. *Bacardi and the Long Fight for Cuba: The Biography of a Cause*. New York: Viking, 2008.
Gleijeses, Piero. "Ships in the Night: The CIA, the White House, and the Bay of Pigs." *Journal of Latin American Studies* (February 1995).
Goldstein, Gordon M. *Lessons in Disaster: McGeorge Bundy and the Path to War in Vietnam*. New York: Henry Holt, 2008.
Goodwin, Richard N. *Remembering America: A Voice from the Sixties*. Boston: Little, Brown, 1988.
Gray, Robert Keith. *Eighteen Acres Under Glass*. New York: Macmillan, 1962.
Greenberg, David. *Nixon's Shadow: The History of an Image*. New York: W. W. Norton, 2003.
Grose, Peter. *Gentleman Spy: The Life of Allen Dulles*. Boston: Houghton Mifflin, 1994.
Grossman, Richard L., ed. *Let Us Begin: The First 100 Days of the Kennedy Administration*. New York: Simon & Schuster, 1961.
Gup, Ted. *The Book of Honor: The Secret Lives and Deaths of CIA Operatives*. New York: Random House, Anchor Books, 2001.
Haas, Michael E. *Apollo's Warriors: U.S. Air Force Special Operations During the Cold War*. Maxwell AFB, Ala.: Air University Press, 1997.
Halberstam, David. *The Best and the Brightest*. 1969. Reprint, New York: Random House, 1992.
———. *The Powers That Be*. New York: Alfred A. Knopf, 1979.
Hawkins, Jack. "Classified Disaster." *National Review*, December 31, 1996.
Helms, Richard. *A Look Over My Shoulder: A Life in the Central Intelligence Agency*. New York: Random House, 2003.
Hersh, Burton. *The Old Boys: The American Elite and the Origins of the CIA*. New York: Scribner, 1992.
Hersh, Seymour M. *The Dark Side of Camelot*. Boston: Little, Brown, Back Bay, 1997.
Higgins, Trumbull. *The Perfect Failure: Kennedy, Eisenhower, and the CIA at the Bay of Pigs*. New York: W. W. Norton, 1987.
Hine, Thomas. *Populuxe: From Tailfins and TV Dinners to Barbie Dolls and Fallout Shelters: The Look and Life of Midcentury America*. Woodstock, N.Y.: Overlook Press, 2007.
Hinkle, Warren, and William W. Turner. *The Fish Is Red: The Story of the Secret War Against Castro*. New York: Harper & Row, 1981.
History of an Aggression: Testimony and Documents from the Trial of the Mercenary Brigade Organized by the U.S. Imperialists That Invaded Cuba on April 17, 1961. 1964.
Hunt, E. Howard. *Give Us This Day*. New Rochelle, N.Y.: Arlington House, 1973.
Jablon, Howard. *David M. Shoup: A Warrior Against War*. Lanham, Md.: Rowman & Littlefield, 2005.
Janis, Irving L. *Groupthink: Psychological Studies of Policy Decisions and Fiascoes*. 1972. Reprint, Boston: Houghton Mifflin, 1983.
Jeffreys-Jones, Rhodri. *The CIA and American Democracy*. New Haven, Conn.: Yale University Press, 1989.
Johnson, Haynes. *The Bay of Pigs: The Leaders' Story of Brigade 2506*. New York: W. W. Norton, 1964.
Johnson, Haynes, and Bernard M. Gwertzman. *Fulbright: The Dissenter*. Garden City, N.Y.: Doubleday, 1968.
Johnson, Walter, ed. *The Papers of Adlai E. Stevenson*. Vol. VIII, *Ambassador to the United Nations, 1961–1965*. Boston: Little, Brown, 1972.

Jones, Howard. *The Bay of Pigs*. New York: Oxford University Press, 2008.
Kaiser, David. *American Tragedy: Kennedy, Johnson, and the Origins of the Vietnam War.* Cambridge, Mass.: Harvard University Press, Belknap Press, 2000.
Kennedy, Robert F. *Thirteen Days: A Memoir of the Cuban Missile Crisis*. 1968. Reprint, New York: W. W. Norton, 1971.
Kennedy, Rose Fitzgerald. *Times to Remember.* Garden City, N.Y.: Doubleday, 1974.
Kenney, Charles. *John F. Kennedy: The Presidential Portfolio: History as Told Through the Collection of the John F. Kennedy Library and Museum*. New York: Public Affairs, 2000.
Kirkpatrick, Lyman B., Jr. *The Real CIA*. New York: Macmillan, 1968.
Korda, Michael. *Ike: An American Hero*. New York: HarperCollins, Perennial, 2007.
Kornbluh, Peter, ed. *Bay of Pigs Declassified: The Secret CIA Report on the Invasion of Cuba*. New York: New Press, 1998.
Light, Robert E., and Carl Marzani. *Cuba Versus CIA*. New York: Marzani and Munsell, 1961.
Lilienthal, David E. *The Journals of David E. Lilienthal: The Harvest Years, 1959–1963.* New York: HarperCollins, 1971.
Lincoln, Evelyn. *My Twelve Years with John F. Kennedy*. New York: D. McKay, 1965.
López-Fresquet, Rufo. *My Fourteen Months with Castro*. Cleveland: World, 1966.
Lynch, Grayston L. *Decision for Disaster: Betrayal at the Bay of Pigs*. Dulles, Va.: Brassey's, 1998.
Mahoney, Richard D. *Sons and Brothers: The Days of Jack and Bobby Kennedy*. New York: Arcade, 1999.
Mann, Robert. *A Grand Delusion: America's Descent into Vietnam*. New York: Basic Books, 2001.
Martin, John Bartlow. *Adlai Stevenson and the World: The Life of Adlai E. Stevenson*. Garden City, N.Y.: Doubleday, 1977.
Matthews, Christopher. *Kennedy and Nixon: The Rivalry That Shaped Postwar America.* New York: Simon & Schuster, 1996.
Mayer, William G. "American Attitudes Toward Cuba." *Public Opinion Quarterly* 65: 585–606.
McKeever, Porter. *Adlai Stevenson: His Life and Legacy*. New York: William Morrow, 1989.
McNamara, Robert. *Blundering into Disaster: Surviving the First Century of the Nuclear Age*. New York: Pantheon, 1986.
Merry, Robert W. *Taking On the World: Joseph and Stewart Alsop, Guardians of the American Century*. New York: Viking, 1996.
Monahan, James, and Kenneth O. Gilmore. *The Great Deception: The Inside Story of How the Kremlin Took Over Cuba*. New York: Farrar, Straus & Cudahy, 1963.
Morris, John G. *Get the Picture: A Personal History of Photojournalism*. New York: Random House, 1998.
Nitze, Paul H., with Ann M. Smith and Steven L. Rearden. *From Hiroshima to Glasnost: At the Center of Decision: A Memoir.* New York: Grove Weidenfeld,1989.
Nixon, Richard M. "Cuba, Castro, and John F. Kennedy: Some Recollections on United States Foreign Policy." *Reader's Digest*, November 1964.
———. *Six Crises*. Garden City, N.Y.: Doubleday, 1962.
O'Donnell, Kenneth P., and David F. Powers, with Joe McCarthy. *Johnny, We Hardly Knew Ye: Memories of John Fitzgerald Kennedy*. 1970. Reprint, Boston: Little, Brown, 1972.
Pérez-Cisneros, Pablo, John B. Donovan, and Jeff Koenreich. *After the Bay of Pigs: Lives and Liberty on the Line*. Self-published, Miami, 2007.
Perlstein, Rick. *Nixonland: The Rise of a President and the Fracturing of America*. New York: Scribner, 2008.
Persico, Joseph E. *Edward R. Murrow: An American Original*. New York: McGraw-Hill, 1988.

Persons, Albert C. *Bay of Pigs: A Firsthand Account of the Mission by a U.S. Pilot in Support of the Cuban Invasion Force in 1961*. Jefferson, N.C.: McFarland, 1990.
Phillips, David Atlee. *The Night Watch*. New York: Atheneum, 1977.
Pitts, David. *Jack and Lem: John F. Kennedy and Lem Billings: The Untold Story of an Extraordinary Friendship*. New York: Carroll & Graf, 2007.
Powers, Thomas. *The Man Who Kept Secrets: Richard Helms and the CIA*. New York: Alfred A. Knopf, 1979.
Quirk, Robert E. *Fidel Castro*. New York: W. W. Norton, 1993.
Rabe, Stephen G. *Eisenhower and Latin America: The Foreign Policy of Anticommunism*. Chapel Hill: University of North Carolina Press, 1988.
Reeves, Richard. *President Kennedy: Profile of Power*. 1993. Reprint, New York: Touchstone, 1994.
Reeves, Thomas C. *A Question of Character: A Life of John F. Kennedy*. New York: Free Press, 1991.
Reporting on Cuba. Havana: Cuban Book Institute, 1967.
Rodríguez, Juan Carlos. *The Bay of Pigs and the CIA*. Translated by Mary Todd. New York: Ocean Press, 1999.
Rogers, William C., Barbara Stuhler, and Donald Koenig. "A Comparison of Informed and General Public Opinion on U.S. Foreign Policy." *Public Opinion Quarterly* 31, no. 2 (Summer 1967).
Rostow, W. W. *The Diffusion of Power: An Essay in Recent History*. New York: Macmillan, 1972.
Rusk, Dean, as told to Richard Rusk. *As I Saw It*. New York: W. W. Norton, 1990.
Russo, Gus. *Live By the Sword: The Secret War Against Castro and the Death of JFK*. Baltimore: Bancroft Press, 1998.
Russo, Gus, and Stephen Molton. *Brothers in Arms: The Kennedys, the Castros, and the Politics of Murder*. New York: Bloomsbury, 2008.
Safford, Jeffrey J. "The Nixon-Castro Meeting of 19 April 1959." *Diplomatic History* 4, no. 4 (Autumn 1980).
Salisbury, Harrison E. *Without Fear or Favor: An Uncompromising Look at the* New York Times. New York: Ballantine Books, 1980.
Schlesinger, Arthur M., Jr. *Journals, 1952–2000*. New York: Penguin, 2007.
———. *A Thousand Days: John F. Kennedy in the White House*. 1965. Reprint, Boston: Houghton Mifflin, Mariner Books, 2002.
Schoultz, Lars. *That Infernal Little Cuban Republic*. Chapel Hill: University of North Carolina Press, 2009.
Senate Select Committee to Study Governmental Operations with Respect to Intelligence Activities. *Alleged Assassination Plots Involving Foreign Leaders*. Washington, D.C.: Government Printing Office, 1975.
Skierka, Volker. *Fidel Castro: A Biography*. Translated by Patrick Camiller. Cambridge, U.K.: Polity Press, 2004.
Smith, Joseph Burkholder. *Portrait of a Cold Warrior*. New York: G. P. Putnam's Sons, 1976.
Sorensen, Theodore C. *Kennedy*. New York: Harper & Row, 1965.
Sperber, A. M. *Murrow: His Life and Times*. New York: Freundlich Books, 1986.
Srodes, James. *Allen Dulles: Master of Spies*. Washington, D.C.: Regnery, 1999.
Stockton, Brayard. *Flawed Patriot: The Rise and Fall of CIA Legend Bill Harvey*. Dulles, Va.: Potomac Books, 2006.
Strober, Gerald S., and Deborah H. Strober. *"Let Us Begin Anew": An Oral History of the Kennedy Presidency*. New York: HarperCollins, 1993.
Sullivan, Michael J., III. *American Adventurism Abroad: Invasions, Interventions, and Regime Changes Since World War II*. Malden, Mass.: Blackwell, 2008.
Szulc, Tad. *Compulsive Spy: The Strange Career of E. Howard Hunt*. New York: Viking, 1974.

———. *Fidel: A Critical Portrait.* New York: HarperCollins, 1986.

Szulc, Tad, and Karl E. Meyer. *The Cuban Invasion: The Chronicle of a Disaster.* New York: Ballantine Books, 1962.

Talbot, David. *Brothers: The Hidden History of the Kennedy Years.* New York: Free Press, 2007.

Taubman, William. *Khrushchev: The Man and His Era.* New York: W. W. Norton, 2003.

Thomas, Evan. *The Very Best Men: The Daring Early Years of the CIA.* 1995. Reprint, New York: Simon & Schuster, 2006.

Trest, Warren, and Donald Dodd. *Wings of Denial: The Alabama Air National Guard's Covert Role at the Bay of Pigs.* Montgomery, Ala.: NewSouth Books, 2001.

Triay, Victor Andres. *Bay of Pigs: An Oral History of Brigade 2506.* Gainesville: University Press of Florida, 2001.

Tully, Andrew. *CIA: The Inside Story.* New York: William Morrow, 1962.

United Nations General Assembly. *Official Records.* 984th Plenary Meeting, Saturday, April 15, 1961, at 10:30 A.M.

———. First Committee, 1,149th Meeting, Saturday, April 15, 1961, at 3:00 P.M.

———. First Committee, 1,150th Meeting, Monday, April 17, 1961, at 11:00 A.M.

U.S. Department of State. *Foreign Relations of the United States, 1958–1960,* Vol. VI, *Cuba* (*FRUS VI*). Washington, D.C.: Government Printing Office, 1991.

———. *Foreign Relations of the United States, 1961–1963,* Vol. I, *Vietnam, 1961* (*FRUS I*). Washington, D.C.: Government Printing Office, 1988.

———. *Foreign Relations of the United States, 1961–1963,* Vol. X, *Cuba, 1961–1962* (*FRUS X*). Washington, D.C.: Government Printing Office, 1997.

———. *Foreign Relations of the United States, 1961–1963,* Vols. X–XII, microfiche supplement (*FRUS SUP*). Washington, D.C.: Government Printing Office, 1998.

Vandenbroucke, Lucien S. "Anatomy of a Failure: The Decision to Land at the Bay of Pigs." *Political Science Quarterly* (Autumn 1984).

———. "The Confessions of Allen Dulles: New Evidence on the Bay of Pigs." *Diplomatic History* 8, no. 4 (Autumn 1984).

Weber, Ralph E., ed. *Spymasters: Ten CIA Officers in Their Own Words.* Wilmington, Del.: SR Books, 1999.

Weiner, Tim. *Legacy of Ashes: The History of the CIA.* 2007. Reprint, New York: Random House, Anchor Books, 2008.

Weisbrot, Robert. *Maximum Danger: Kennedy, the Missiles, and the Crisis of American Confidence.* Chicago: Ivan R. Dee, 2001.

Welch, Richard E., Jr. *Response to Revolution: The United States and the Cuban Revolution, 1959–1961.* Chapel Hill: University of North Carolina Press, 1985.

Wenger, Andreas. *Living with Peril: Eisenhower, Kennedy, and Nuclear Weapons.* Lanham, Md.: Rowman & Littlefield, 1997.

White, Mark J., ed. *The Kennedys and Cuba: The Declassified Documentary History.* Chicago: Ivan R. Dee, 1999.

White, Theodore H. *The Making of the President, 1960.* New York: Atheneum, 1961.

Wise, David, and Thomas B. Ross. *The Invisible Government.* New York: Random House, 1964.

Wyden, Peter. *The Bay of Pigs: The Untold Story.* New York: Touchstone, 1979.

Yoder, Edwin M., Jr. *Joe Alsop's Cold War: A Study of Journalistic Influence and Intrigue.* Chapel Hill: University of North Carolina Press, 1995.

Unpublished Sources (Archives and Databases)

Allen W. Dulles Papers, Department of Rare Books and Special Collections, Princeton University Library

Cavalier Magazine. Profile of Dulles, April 1954.

Columbia University Forum. "The Press and the Bay of Pigs."

Dulles, Allen. *My Answer to the Bay of Pigs*. Unpublished manuscript and notes for *Harper's Magazine* article, Summer–Fall 1965. File also includes letters from Willie Morris and Jack Fischer of *Harper's*, a letter from Dulles as to why he will not publish, and a note from Mrs. Dulles regarding the manuscript.

———. *Summary of Remarks by Allen W. Dulles to the American University of Presidents' Young Presidents' Organization*, San Juan, April 17, 1961.

"Invocation Offered by the Rev. Dr. Frederick Brown Harris . . . November 3, 1959."

Letter: Bissell to Dulles, August 6, 1954.

Letter: Dulles to Bissell, August 10, 1954.

Letter: Bissell to Dulles, February 27, 1962.

Letter: Dulles to Bissell, March 6, 1962.

Life. "Our Spy-Boss Who Loved Bond," August 28, 1964.

Moscow News Service. Re retirement of Dulles, September 28, 1961.

Newsday. "Ike Speaks Out: Bay of Pigs Was All JFK's," September 10, 1965.

New York Daily News article by Ted Lewis, March 22, 1962.

Parade Magazine. Profile of Dulles by Ronald W. May, January 8, 1961.

"The Science of Spying," NBC News (Bissell quoted on transcript).

Washington Star, March 21, 1962.

Washington Star article by Marguerite Higgins, July 21, 1965.

The American Presidency Project (speeches and press conferences by Dwight Eisenhower and John Kennedy, accessed via www.presidency.ucsb.edu)

Castro Speech Database (speeches and other public utterances by Fidel Castro, based on records of the Foreign Broadcast Information Service and made available by the University of Texas, at www1.lanic.utexas.edu/la/cb/cuba/castro.html)

CIA/CREST (Digitized CIA documents accessed at the National Archives, College Park, Md.)

Correspondence: John A. McCone to Richard M. Bissell, March 7, 1962, accepting Bissell's resignation.

Interview with Allen W. Dulles. Television transcript from *Ladies of the Press*, WOR-TV, January 19, 1963.

Memorandum for the Director, April 14, 1961 (regarding Dulles's speech to the Young Presidents).

CIA/FOIA (Declassified CIA documents made available at foia.cia.gov)

Beerli, Stanley W. "Chronological Sequence of Events," April 26, 1961.

Current Intelligence Digest. "Czech Arms Photographed in Cuba," August 29, 1960.

Current Intelligence Weekly Review, December 10, 1959.

———, February 11, 1960.

Hawkins, Jack. *Record of Paramilitary Action Against the Castro Government of Cuba, 17 March 1960–May 1961*. Prepared May 5, 1961.

Kent, Sherman. *Memorandum for the Director (Subject: "The Cuban Pot Boils Over")*, July 15, 1960.

———. *Memorandum for the Director (Subject: "Probable International Reactions to Certain Possible U.S. Courses of Action Against the Castro Regime")*, January 27, 1961.

"The Military Build-Up in Cuba." *A Report Prepared by an Ad Hoc Committee of the United States Intelligence Board*, February 9, 1961.

John F. Kennedy Memorial Library, Boston, Mass.

National Security Files.

President's Office Files.

Papers of Richard N. Goodwin.
Papers of Arthur M. Schlesinger Jr.
Papers of Louis Oberdorfer.
President's Appointment Books (accessed via jfklibrary.org).
White House Central Files.
White House Staff Files.

Lawrenceville School
"Castro Stresses Importance of Youth . . ." Article in Lawrenceville student newspaper by Miner H. Warner.
"Fidel Castro Speech." Transcript of Castro's speech at Lawrenceville School, April 21, 1959.

Miscellaneous
King, Bruce. PowerPoint Presentation on Bay of Pigs. Made available to author by Mr. King.
"NBC News Time Capsule—the Kennedy Inauguration." NBC's television coverage of JFK's inauguration, with commentary by Chet Huntley and David Brinkley. Accessed via Hulu.com.
Pfeiffer, Jack B. *Official History of the Bay of Pigs Operation*, Vol. III. Internal 1979 CIA history, in National Archives in College Park, Md., and made available by Professor David M. Barrett of Villanova University in PDF format at: www14.homepage.villanova.edu/david.barrett/bop.html.
Roberts, Don E. Private journal, 1961. Made available to author by Mr. Roberts.
Taylor Report. The complete report by General Maxwell Taylor's Cuba Study Group is available in PDF files from the Paperless Archives. Sections of the report also appear in FRUS X and in *Operation Zapata: The "Ultrasensitive" Report and Testimony of the Board of Inquiry on the Bay of Pigs* by Luis Aguilar.

The National Security Archive at George Washington University (holds numerous declassified Bay of Pigs documents, including transcripts of oral histories by CIA historian Jack Pfeiffer of Richard Bissell and Jacob Esterline, available online at www.gwu.edu/~nsarchiv/bayofpigs)

Oral Histories and Interviews

These originate from at least one of the following: The Oral History Collection at the John F. Kennedy Library (JFKL); the Eisenhower Administration Project at Columbia University (Eisenhower/Columbia); interviews conducted by CIA historian Jack B. Pfeiffer (Pfeiffer); or those conducted by the author (author). In some cases, multiple interviews have been consulted.

Acheson, Dean G. (JFKL, 1964).
Alsop, Joseph W. (JFKL, 1964).
Armory, Robert (JFKL, 1966).
Berle, Adolph A. (JFKL, 1967).
Bissell, Ann (author, 2009).
Bissell, Richard (JFKL, 1967; Eisenhower/Columbia, 1973; Pfeiffer, 1975).
Bovo, Esteban (author, 2009).
Bowles, Chester (JFKL, 1965, 1970).

Bundy, McGeorge (JFKL, 1964).
Bundy, William P. (JFKL, 1964, 1972).
Burke, Arleigh A. (JFKL, 1967; Eisenhower/Columbia, 1972).
Cleveland, Harlan (JFKL, 1978).
Clifford, Clark (JFKL, 1974).
Cuban Prisoners Release Project; group interview with Louis F. Oberdorfer, John B. Jones, and Mitchell Rogovin (JFKL "Cuban Prisoners Release Project," 1964).
Cutler, Lloyd N. (JFKL "Cuban Prisoners Release Project," 1964).
Dolan, Joseph F. (JFKL "Cuban Prisoners Release Project," 1964).
Dulles, Allen (JFKL, 1964).
Dutton, Frederick G. (JFKL, 1965).
Eisenhower, Milton S. (Eisenhower/Columbia, 1967).
Esterline, Jacob D. (Pfeiffer, 1975).
Fulbright, William J. (JFKL, 1964).
Gonzáles, Juan Jesús (author, 2009).
Gonzáles, Máximo Cruz (author, 2009).
Gray, Gordon (Eisenhower/Columbia, 1966).
Gutiérrez, Armando (author, 2009).
Houston, Billy (author, 2009).
Izaguirre, Jorge Gutiérrez (author, 2009).
King, Bruce (author, 2009).
Kirkpatrick, Lyman (JFKL, 1967).
Mann, Thomas C. ((JFKL, 1968).
Marquet, Jorge (author, 2009).
Martínez, Raúl V. (author, 2009).
McNamara, Robert (JFKL, 1964).
Nolan, John (author, 2009; JFKL, 1967).
Padgett, Jim (author, 2009).
Prettyman, Barrett Jr. (JFKL, 1969).
Rasenberger, Raymond J. (author, 2009).
Ray, Janet (author, 2009).
Roberts, Don E. (author, 2009).
Rostow, Walter (JFKL, 1964).
Rubino, Mike (author, 2010).
Rusk, Dean (JFKL, 1969).
Shoup, David M. (JFKL, 1967).
Silveira, Jorge (author, 2009).
Sorensen, Theodore C. (JFKL, 1964; OH for Eisenhower/Columbia, 1977).
Wheeler, Earle (JFKL, 1964).
Wilson, Don (author, 2009; JFKL, 1970).
Ziegman, Bob (author, 2009).

INDEX